AN INTRODUCTION

TO

THE HISTORY

OF THE

LAW OF REAL PROPERTY

WITH ORIGINAL AUTHORITIES

BY

KENELM EDWARD DIGBY, M.A.

Permanent Under Secretary of State for the Home Department
Late Vinerian Reader in English Law, and formerly Fellow of Corpus Christi College
in the University of Oxford

ASSISTED BY

WILLIAM MONTAGU HARRISON, M.A.

Of Lincoln's Inn, Barrister-at-Law; Vinerian Scholar, and
Fellow of All Souls College, Oxford

FIFTH EDITION

THE LAWBOOK EXCHANGE, LTD.
Clark, New Jersey

ISBN 978-1-58477-495-2

Lawbook Exchange edition 2005, 2015

The quality of this reprint is equivalent to the quality of the original work.

The Lawbook Exchange, Ltd.
33 Terminal Avenue
Clark, New Jersey 07066-1321

Please see our website for a selection of our other publications and fine facsimile reprints of classic works of legal history:
www.lawbookexchange.com

Library of Congress Cataloging-in-Publication Data

Digby, Kenelm Edward, Sir, 1836-1916.
An introduction to the history of the law of real property : with original authorities / by Kenelm Edward Digby ; assisted by William Montagu Harrison -- 5th ed.
p. cm.
Originally published: Oxford : Clarendon Press, 1897.
Includes bibliographical references and index.
ISBN 1-58477-495-9 (cloth : alk. paper)
1. Real property -- England -- History--To 1500. 2. Real property--England--History--16th century. I. Harrison, William Monatgu. II. Title.

KD829.D54 2005
346.1204'3--dc22 2004053813

Printed in the United States of America on acid-free paper

AN INTRODUCTION

TO

THE HISTORY

OF THE

LAW OF REAL PROPERTY

WITH ORIGINAL AUTHORITIES

BY

KENELM EDWARD DIGBY, M.A.

Permanent Under Secretary of State for the Home Department
Late Vinerian Reader in English Law, and formerly Fellow of Corpus Christi College in the University of Oxford

ASSISTED BY

WILLIAM MONTAGU HARRISON, M.A.

Of Lincoln's Inn, Barrister-at-Law; Vinerian Scholar, and Fellow of All Souls College, Oxford

FIFTH EDITION

Oxford
AT THE CLARENDON PRESS
LONDON: HENRY FROWDE, M.A.
OXFORD UNIVERSITY PRESS WAREHOUSE, AMEN CORNER, E.C.
AND
STEVENS & SONS, LIMITED, 119 & 120 CHANCERY LANE

M DCCC XCVII

Oxford

PRINTED AT THE CLARENDON PRESS

BY HORACE HART, M.A.

PRINTER TO THE UNIVERSITY

PREFACE TO THE FIRST EDITION

My object in undertaking this work was to attempt in some degree to supply a want which at present greatly impedes the study of English law at the Universities. There is no really elementary work on the English law of real property adapted for the use of students who have not and may never have any practical experience in the working of the law. Almost all elementary books have been written from the professional rather than from the educational point of view; excellent as many of them are as introductions to a practical knowledge of law, they are scarcely available for purposes of legal education at an University. Blackstone's treatise stands almost alone in adequately satisfying both demands. It has been the fashion of late to dwell on the defects rather than on the merits of that great work, and there are obvious reasons why it fails to satisfy the requirements of the present time. Nevertheless Blackstone still remains unrivalled as an expositor of the law of his day. Throughout the following pages his work is referred to as at once the most available, and the most trustworthy authority of the law of the eighteenth century.

In considering the mode in which the elementary principles of the important branch of English law, which is the subject of this treatise, can best be dealt with, there can be little question that it is necessary to begin by sketching the history and development of rights over land. Hardly one of the main classifications of these rights which is recognised at the present day—the distinction, for instance, between the legal and the equitable interest, the notion of an *estate* in lands with its consequences, as distinct from *property* in things personal, the distinction between freehold, leasehold, and copyhold tenure—can be explained without tracing if possible the origin, at all events the development, of the conceptions on which it is based. It seems therefore necessary to start from the earliest elements of English law, and to trace the development by the action of the tribunals and of legislation of the germs which are found in our earliest authorities, till we are at last enabled to give something like a systematic classification of the congeries of ancient custom and mediaeval and modern innovation called the law of real property. It seems best, in the first instance, to trace the growth of the law chronologically till the period is reached at which the structure has attained its permanent features, when an attempt may be made to arrange its various branches systematically; it being always borne in mind that the nature and attributes of the various classes of rights are to be accounted for by reference rather to their history than to any principles of jurisprudence. This stage in the history of English law appears to me to have been reached before the reign of Henry VIII. I have attempted in the Appendix to Part I, Tables I, II, and III, to arrange systematically the main branches of the law of land as it stood at the commencement of this reign. It will be seen that much of this classification is taken from Blackstone, who followed one of the greatest of English lawyers, Sir Matthew Hale.

In the arrangement summarised in Table I, as will be seen, I am largely indebted to Mr. John Austin's Lectures on Jurisprudence. The remarkable analysis of juristic conceptions which he instituted, but unfortunately left incomplete, is, as it seems to me, a κτῆμα ἐς ἀεί; it is, in great part, work done which must enter largely into the basis of any attempt to recast English law on true principles of systematic arrangement.

Part II of this work treats mainly of the growth of the two branches of the law of real property which are of the greatest importance in modern law, the history and development of Uses and Trusts, and of Wills of land. The former is perhaps the most curious and important chapter in the history of the law of land. The extreme technicality of our modern law, the mysteries of conveyancing, and the anomalous opposition of Equity and Law, are mainly due to the unhappy piece of legislative reform called the Statute of Uses. It is this Statute, with the marvellous interpretations to which its provisions have been subjected, which renders any real simplification of the law of real property impossible, without a more thorough rebuilding of the whole structure from its foundations, and substitution of a systematic or scientific for a historical classification, than is at all likely to be undertaken at present. Here, therefore, it is necessary to pursue the same method as in Part I, and to attempt first to trace the development of the law, and then to summarise and arrange it under the principal classes which are due to the historical causes whose action has been discussed. This I have attempted to do in the last chapter on 'Titles.'

My object throughout has been to attempt to explain the leading principles of the law as it exists at present by reference to its history. For antiquarian research I am painfully conscious that I have neither sufficient knowledge nor leisure. I have endeavoured to state with accuracy such matters connected with the antiquities of our law as are necessary to explain its later developments, or as seemed to possess an intrinsic interest so great that the omission of them from an outline of the history of the law of land would not be justified. I have endeavoured on the same principle to select the original authorities which form the backbone of this treatise. Experience abundantly proves that no account can give so vivid and trustworthy a picture of the history of law as the original authorities themselves. For the purposes of legal education they are of the utmost value. But so little attention has been paid to the abundant materials we possess, they still exist for the most part in so inaccessible a form, that they can hardly be said to be available to the student. The principal statutes bearing on real property are sufficiently conspicuous. In the selection of extracts from text-writers and reported cases there was more difficulty. The extracts from Bracton occupy a large space. This is, I hope, justified by their intrinsic interest, and by the historical importance of the work of that great lawyer, the merits of which have, I think, been somewhat underrated.

The difficulty which perpetually encounters those who have to give instruction in law to University students is this—where is the line to be drawn between principle and detail? what is the point to which the teacher can usefully go without burdening the student with minor rules which, however important as pieces of professional knowledge, are useless for educational purposes? This is a question which every one who has to encounter the difficulty in practice must solve for himself. In the present work I have endeavoured to draw the line at the point to which, as it seems to me, University students, even if they enter upon the study not as preparatory to the practice of the profession, but as forming part of a liberal education, might properly be brought.

The proofs of the first chapter were already revised before the appearance of the first volume of Mr. Stubbs' excellent and learned Constitutional History. I was, however, enabled to insert several references to his work, and in one or two cases to introduce some modification into the text. I have also to thank him and other friends for some valuable suggestions and criticisms on the first chapter.

I have refrained from over-burdening the notes with references to authorities. It will be seen that I throughout refer to Blackstone as the great authority on the earlier law, and to the admirable work of Mr. Joshua Williams as the most available treatise on the law of the present day. I have only inserted such references to other works, as appeared to me to be proper in order to introduce students to the leading authorities to be found in any fairly furnished law library.

1 PAPER BUILDINGS, TEMPLE.
January 15th, 1875.

PREFACE TO THE FOURTH EDITION

THE principal changes in the present edition consist of the addition of translations of the extracts from Glanvill and Bracton, which I hope may be of use.

An important reaction has recently taken place in opposition to the view that the source of the law and custom which developed into the manorial system is to be found in the Teutonic village community. Mr. Seebohm in this country and M. Fustel de Coulanges in France have contended with great force, in opposition to the view taken by most of the recent English and German writers, that the origin of the feudal law and custom of the Middle Ages is to be found in the Roman *latifundium*, rather than in the Teutonic village community, the very existence of which is questioned by Fustel de Coulanges. An admirable account of the history and present position of this controversy will be found in the Introduction to Professor Paul Vinogradoff's recent work on 'Villainage in England' (Oxford, 1892). Notwithstanding the powerful criticism with which the views previously accepted have been assailed by the writers referred to, it still seems to me that the evidence derived from the records of manorial courts, the history and character of rights of common, the phenomena of the 'common fields,' and the authority of the earliest of English legal text-writers lead to the inference that in England at all events the free Teutonic village community was not a fiction but a fact, and that the manor was probably developed out of the community, and not the community out of the manor. The mass of evidence collected by Professor Vinogradoff in the remarkable work above referred to, appears to me strongly to confirm this view. I have seen therefore no reason to modify in any material particular the account, avowedly more or less conjectural, which, following the authors referred to in the notes, was given in previous editions of the probable origin and growth of manors, and of the relation of the lord of the manor to the freeholders and copyholders within its ambit.

June, 1892.

PREFACE TO THE FIFTH EDITION

SINCE the last edition of this book much additional light has been thrown on the early history of English law by the appearance of the elaborate and (so far as our present knowledge goes) exhaustive work of Sir F. Pollock and Mr. F. Maitland, *History of English Law before the time of Edward I.* It will be seen that some alterations and additions in the earlier chapters are due to their investigations and criticisms. Mr. Maitland's later work, *Doomsday and Beyond*, was not published until the proof-sheets of the earlier chapters had been revised.

Being unable, owing to the pressure of official work, to devote much time to the preparation of this edition, I have been fortunate enough to be able to avail myself of the aid of Mr. W. M. Harrison, of All Souls College, to whom I am indebted for a careful revision of the text and notes, especially of the earlier chapters, by reference to the latest authorities.

May, 1897. KENELM E. DIGBY.

CONTENTS

PART I.

THE COMMON AND EARLY STATUTE LAW RELATING TO LAND.

CHAPTER I.

CHAPTER II.

CHAPTER III.

CHAPTER IV.

CHAPTER V.

APPENDIX TO PART I.

PART II.

THE MODERN LAW OF REAL PROPERTY.

CHAPTER VI.

CHAPTER VII.

CHAPTER VIII.

CHAPTER IX.

CHAPTER X.

PART I

THE COMMON AND EARLY STATUTE LAW RELATING TO LAND

THE HISTORY OF THE LAW OF REAL PROPERTY

CHAPTER I.

INTRODUCTORY. ELEMENTS OF THE LAW OF LAND BEFORE THE REIGN OF HENRY II.

THE English law of land is of a mixed origin. The customs of the early Teutonic invaders, the effect of conquest and settlement of the land on a large scale, the gradual and what may be called the natural growth of feudal ideas, the effect of the Norman Conquest in developing these ideas into a system of law and in importing doctrines unknown before, the subsequent influence of the Roman and Canon law, all these are elements of which account must be taken in attempting to trace the growth of the law of land. CHAP. I. SECT. I. § 1.

By the time of the reign of Henry II a definite system of law may be said to have arisen. This will be the subject of the next chapter. In the present an attempt will be made to take some account of the elements out of which the system of the law of land ultimately grew.

SECTION I.

ANGLO-SAXON CUSTOMARY LAW.

§ 1. *Effect of the Teutonic Settlement.*

The earliest element in the English law of land is in all probability the Teutonic. Whatever traces may have existed

CHAP. I. SECT. I. § 1.

of the laws of Rome at the time of the earliest Teutonic invasion, no vestige of them is to be found in the evidence we possess of the Anglo-Saxon customary law [1]. The conquerors, unlike the tribes which overran Italy, Gaul, and Spain, retained the customs, the religion, and the language which they brought with them uninfluenced by the people whom they dispossessed. Moreover, these customs were of pure home-growth, without any admixture of the element of Roman law or civilization. 'Our forefathers,' says Mr. Freeman, 'came from lands where the Roman eagle had never been seen, or had been seen only during the momentary incursions of Drusus and Germanicus [2].'

The mode in which Teutonic settlement was effected is matter of conjecture only. There is however no doubt that it was the work of successive bodies of invaders during parts of the fifth and sixth centuries. But the process was not merely that of invasion by bodies of armed men, it was the migration of whole communities bringing with them the organization and the customs which had regulated their life at home [3].

[1] Mr. Seebohm, in his English Village Community, chaps. VIII–XI, and Professor Ashley in his preface to the translation of Fustel de Coulanges, Origin of Property in Land, favour the view that the basis of the English Manorial System was laid during the Roman occupation of Britain, and that its main features are to be traced in the later developments of Roman law. Whether or not M. Fustel de Coulanges has made good the similar proposition with regard to feudalism in Gaul, there seems to be no sufficient evidence to justify its application to the early history of land-tenure in England. It appears to be opposed to the view of the best authorities on early English History. Probably some few doctrines and practices of Roman law were introduced by the clergy after the adoption of Christianity, especially that of disposition by will (compare Tacitus, Germania, c. 20, 'nullum testamentum'), but the large infusion of Roman law which exists in our own was mainly of much later introduction. See Stubbs, Constitutional History, i. p. 62. (The references are to the 1st edition.) Pollock and Maitland, Hist. of Eng. Law, i. Introd. p. xxxi.

[2] Freeman, Norman Conquest, i. p. 20; and compare Stubbs, Const. Hist. i. p. 11, Green, Making of England, p. 140.

[3] 'The invaders come in families, and kindreds, and in the full organization of their tribes: the three ranks of men, the noble, the freeman, and the læt: even the slaves are not left behind.' Stubbs, Const. Hist. i. p. 64. See Green, Making of England, p. 154.

It is probable that when the invaders had dispossessed the natives of a large tract of land the allotment of the territory was effected in a regular mode, so as to reproduce the main features of land-tenure with which they had been familiar in their Continental homes. The Britons seem to have been so completely exterminated or driven westward, or those that remained reduced to so abject a state of servitude, that no appreciable influence was exercised by the native element upon Teutonic customs.

There is no direct evidence as to the mode in which the conquered portions of the territory were colonized by invaders. Materials for conjectures more or less probable are afforded by the records of similar proceedings in the case of other Teutonic and Scandinavian conquests[1], and by the nomenclature and legal and other phenomena which are found existing in later times. It must be borne in mind that the invaders, though still retaining many habits derived from ancient Teutonic customs, had attained to a certain degree of political organization at the time of the invasion. The body of invaders is a regular army led by a chief, and divided into 'hundreds' of warriors, who are united by a bond of real or supposed kinship, and probably come from neighbouring homes[2].

There can be little doubt that regard was paid to this division of the host into hundreds in the distribution of the conquered territory. It is impossible to trace the exact links of connexion between the hundreds of warriors who constituted the sub-divisions of the Teutonic army and the territorial hundred of later times; there can however be no question that the two are connected, and the most plausible conjecture

[1] Stubbs, Const. Hist. i. p. 72.

[2] 'Centeni ex singulis pagis sunt, idque ipsum inter suos vocantur, et quod primo numerus fuit, jam nomen et honor est.' Tacitus, Germania, c. 6. This too was the number of the assessors of the princeps for judicial purposes. 'Eliguntur in iisdem conciliis et principes qui jura per pagos vicosque reddunt. Centeni singulis ex plebe comites consilium simul et auctoritas adsunt.' Ib. c. 12.

CHAP. I. SECT. I. § 1.

seems to be that a definite area of territory, though probably not of uniform size, was in the original process of colonization assigned to each hundred, that the name then gradually ceased to have a personal, and began to acquire a territorial signification, that it was adopted as the most important division for fiscal and judicial purposes, and that, as the whole country became colonized and brought under a uniform system of organization, the boundaries of isolated hundreds would be extended till they touched each other, and thus the present division of the county into hundreds, or districts of the same kind but bearing different names, was effected [1].

But though the settlement of the hundred bore an important part, as will be seen later, in the development of one element of the manorial system, there are other features of the Teutonic settlement which appear to have a still more important bearing on the history of the law of land.

The inquiry is here complicated by the necessity of giving some answer, without sufficient materials, to the questions—What were the main features of primitive land-tenure amongst the forefathers of the English? How and in what forms had these features developed at the time of the migration? and how far did they survive, and in what ways were they affected by, the process of conquest and colonization?

The earliest form of systematic land-tenure, the settlement of the 'village community,' has of late received so much learned investigation that its main features may probably be regarded as having been recovered [2]. When the Teutonic

[1] See Stubbs, Const. Hist. i. pp. 96, 97.

[2] I refer especially to the writings of Von Maurer, and to Professor Nasse's short treatise On the Agricultural Community of the Middle Ages, translated by Col. Ouvry (Macmillan, 1871), p. 28. See also Sir H. Maine, Village Communities, Lects. iii and v; and Mr. Morier's essay in the volume on Land Tenure published by the Cobden Club (Macmillan, 1870); and compare the description of the 'Mark System' in Stubbs, Const. Hist. i. pp. 49–52; and Green, Making of England, pp. 180–187. On the other hand, the name and the very existence of the 'mark' has been powerfully questioned by Fustel de Coulanges in his works L'Alleu et le Domaine Rural (Paris, 1889), and Les Origines du Système Féodal,

nations ceased to be purely nomad, a state from which some tribes appear to have been only just emerging in Caesar's time [1], the first definite settlement or appropriation of land would be by a group of households forming a family, or a small cluster of families, the bond of union being real or supposed kinship, and occupying a definite area of land.

The characteristics of this settlement appear to have been as follows. Each community occupied a territory, which was divided into three, or rather four, portions. There was, first, the township in which the houses and their surroundings are appropriated and held by the heads of families in individual proprietorship. Here probably we have the earliest instance of separate or individual property. As a whole the district would probably not be regarded as individual property at all. The notion that the ownership of the soil of the whole district is vested in the king or some great lord is in all probability of later growth. But from the earliest times of permanent settlements the house which the freeman had built and the curtilage which he had enclosed must have been regarded as his own property [2], held in dependence on no other man or body of men. We shall find that in later times house property in towns is regarded as having a more absolute and independent character than property in agricultural or common land [3].

Secondly, there was the arable portion, or the district of cultivated land, in which separate plots were held, for a time at all events, in severalty, by individual members of the community, subject to certain customary regulations as to common

(Paris, 1890), both of which were published after his death. M. Fustel de Coulanges, however, does not deal with the English evidence available as throwing light on the existence and character of the village community. The main features of the village community have been reproduced with great clearness by Mr. Seebohm in his work on The English Village Community, whether or not we accept his view of the historical relation of the village community to the manor.

[1] Caesar, de Bell. Gall. vi. 22.

[2] 'Suam quisque domum spatio circumdat.' Tacitus, Germania, c. 16.

[3] As to tenure in burgage, see below, p. 48.

CHAP. I. SECT. I. § 1. cultivation and enjoyment. The most usual of these were that the arable land should be divided into three fields (*campi*), one of which should lie fallow every third year, and that the whole community should have rights of common pasturage on the fallow portion, and on the stubbles of the cropped fields at certain periods between harvest and seed-time. It appears probable that these three fields were not always on the same spot; fresh land would be broken up, and land which had been cultivated would go out of cultivation and be used only for pasturage [1]. It would necessarily follow that the portions of land allotted to individuals were not held by them as permanent or separate property; they were beneficially enjoyed for a time and then returned to the common stock, the proprietor receiving other allotments in their place.

The meadow-land was dealt with in a similar way. It was open for common pasturage during the interval between hay-harvest and the new growth of the grass. It was then fenced off in separate parcels, which were for the time appropriated to the various heads of families.

Lastly, there was the common land or wastes not appropriated to individuals at all, on which the whole community had rights of pasturage, wood-cutting, or the like. The various rights over the common territory were regulated by the village assembly, consisting of all the freemen.

Traces of this mark system [2] became indelibly fixed in our law. The house with its surroundings was regarded as the absolute property of the possessor. Hence probably in towns and larger villages arose the conception of tenure in burgage, the form of tenure which in feudal times came the nearest to absolute property in land. The practice of re-allotting from time to time portions of the arable or meadow land is occa-

[1] Nasse, p. 10; and see Tacitus, Germania, c. 26, and Stubbs, Const. Hist. i. p. 19.

[2] I preserve this expression which has become common, though Fustel de Coulanges has thrown considerable doubt upon the accuracy of the use of the term 'mark' otherwise than in the sense of 'boundary.' See Pollock, Land Laws, Note C.

sionally noticed in later times[1]. The right of pasturage on the arable land or 'common field,' the right that is which each cultivator had at a particular time of year to put his cattle on the plots of his neighbours as well as his own, and for that purpose to have the fences removed, appears in our law under the name of common of shack[2]. The right of common pasturage during some months of the year on meadow-lands, which for the greater part of the spring and summer are appropriated for hay to individuals, is still more common. Lands subject to these rights are often known as Lammas lands, Lammas-day (August 13, O. S.) being the time at which the common rights begin[3]. Lastly, the rights of common enjoyment over the waste become curtailed, and transformed into rights which at some forgotten period the lord of the manor is supposed to have granted to his tenants or to neighbouring freeholders.

On the whole, we may fairly conjecture that the hundreds of warriors did, when they had subdued a portion of territory, divide it among families who formed villages or townships, bearing strong traces of the Teutonic 'mark system.' Probably to each of these townships a definite district would be allotted, consisting of land already occupied by or adapted for dwelling-houses and their appendages, of arable land, of pasture land, and of wastes, marshes, and woods. The share

[1] See Coke upon Littleton, 4 a. Pratt *v.* Graeme, 15 East's Reports, 235.

[2] See Corbet's case, Coke's Reports, part vii. 5 a. 'In the county of Norfolk there is a special manner of common called "shack," which is to be taken in arable land, after harvest until the land be sowed again, &c.; and it began in ancient time in this manner: the fields of arable land in this country consist of the lands of many and divers several persons, lying intermixed in many and several small parcels, so that it is not possible that any, without trespass to the others, can feed their cattle in their own land, and therefore every one doth put in their cattle to feed *promiscue* in the open field.' Often the right is of a more extensive character than is here described, and is in practice enjoyed, though as will appear hereafter often without legal justification, by the neighbouring inhabitants.

[3] The name is also sometimes applied to arable land over which rights of common exist, such as are mentioned in the last note.

CHAP. I. SECT. I. § 1.

which was allotted to each member (whether uniform in size or not is doubtful) was called by various names, all bearing the common interpretation of land sufficient for the support of a family[1]. There can be little question that the main features of the mark system were reproduced, so far as regards mode of enjoyment of the arable, pasture, and waste land within the district.

From the first the township or village community must have been regarded as forming a part of the larger aggregate, the hundred. Perhaps there was a village assembly which regulated the affairs of the village, but had not any judicial functions. It was probably concerned mainly with matters relating to the common cultivation of the arable land, the mode of using the pasture, meadow, and waste land, the admission of new settlers in the district, the raising contributions for common purposes, and such matters, exclusively relating to the interest of the township. These functions devolved in later times partly on the manorial court, partly on the vestry of the parish; the former being the assembly of landholding inhabitants considered as tenants of a lord, the latter of landholding inhabitants considered as members of a parish, the township being considered as an ecclesiastical division[2]. Each township contributed a certain number of

[1] Hide, terra familiae, familia, mansa, mansus, cassata, &c. See Stubbs, Const. Hist. i. p. 21.

[2] Even up to the date of the transfer of the powers of the vestry to the parish council by the Local Government Act of 1894 (57 & 58 Vict. c. 73) the functions of the manorial courts and of the vestry were not always kept distinct. It was very common to find that an idea still prevailed that the parishioners assembled in vestry had the power of regulating rights over the waste lands within the parish. Acts of control were frequently exercised over such lands by parish officers. As will be pointed out later, there was, except under special circumstances, no legal justification for this notion; it doubtless descended from a time before the lawyers had precisely defined the relative rights of the lord of the manor and of commoners having common appendant, appurtenant, or in gross. See the observations of Lord Chancellor Hatherley in Warrick *v.* Queen's College, Oxford; Law Reports, 6 Chancery Appeals, p. 723; and see below, Ch. III. § 18.

representatives to the court of the hundred, which probably, amongst its other functions, exercised civil and criminal jurisdiction in the district[1].

It may well have been the case that, besides the bodies of invading warriors, there were numerous isolated migrations of small bodies, who, without attempting conquest on a large scale, settled down on vacant lands, and reproduced the features of the village communities of their former homes. Such small communities, if they existed, must in process of time have become merged in the larger aggregates as the country became more extensively settled, or have fallen under the power of some great lord, the territory occupied by them becoming part of his domain.

One of the most interesting questions, if there were materials for anything more than conjectures more or less plausible, is, how far were districts of conquered land at or soon after the primitive settlement assigned to the king or chief or his principal followers to be held by them in severalty, and, if such assignments were made, what was the relation of the allottees of such districts to the dwellers on them?

In primitive times, when a body of invaders has succeeded in conquering a portion of territory and settles down upon the land which it has won, that territory is looked upon as the property of the community at large, rather than of the individual chief, king, or leader. At the same time the presence of the chief—the leader whose personal or hereditary eminence inspires his followers with the belief in his kinship with the gods—is a necessary element in the process of conquest and settlement. But he is not at first regarded as owner of the land. No doubt the chief would as part of his functions regulate the original distribution of the land[2]; but this he would do as head or leader of the community, not as having appropriated the soil to himself and granted it out

[1] Stubbs, Const. Hist. i. p. 102.

[2] Id. i. p. 71.

CHAP. I. SECT. I. § 1. to his followers. What the community had won would be regarded as belonging to the community at large.

Still it seems probable that a large district of land was from the first allotted to the successful leader of the conquering host, who seems to have at once been recognized as king [1]. But it must be borne in mind that the title and office of king did not at first involve any necessary relation to the land.

The idea of separate or individual property in land had, as above seen, been developed before the migration, to what extent it is difficult to say; but it is not improbable that the conception of separate ownership, which was probably at first confined to the house and its enclosure, had before the Teutonic conquest attached to the larger domains allotted to or appropriated by the leader of a body of victorious colonists. It seems therefore probable that, as happened in other cases about the same period [2], from the first settlement a large domain would be reserved for or allotted to the king. Whether or not that domain would include lands occupied by townships, so that the townships would be regarded as existing on the land of the king, and under a peculiar obligation to render to him dues in rent, in money, or kind, is doubtful. It would seem more probable that the allotment should in the first instance have been from land not appropriated to or occupied by townships, but comprising a large district inhabited only by scattered settlers or the natives who remained. Thus probably originated the notion of the royal domain; the lands would be tilled for the king's benefit by Teutonic or native slaves, some of the more distant portions might be loaned or lent by him to tenants.

It is impossible to say whether in the original allotment similar districts were assigned to the immediate followers of the king, the leaders of the second rank, or whether by the various means which will be mentioned later they acquired the ownership of such districts at periods subsequent to the

[1] Stubbs, Const. Hist. i. p. 66.

[2] Compare Gibbon, iv. 187 (Milman's ed.).

Teutonic conquest. The large amount of land available for division, the probability that the ownership of a domain by a great man was not altogether unfamiliar to the Teutonic settlers from the date of the earliest migration, seem to give ground for a conjecture that in many cases such districts were allotted to the king's immediate followers at the time of the original partition of the soil. If this were the case, the nature of their ownership and their relation to the dwellers on the soil would present the same features as characterized the district allotted to the king.

On the whole, therefore, we may conjecture that as a general rule the different bodies of settlers divided the land into townships or districts bearing the main features of the Teutonic community, that probably a large district was allotted to the leader as his domain, and perhaps smaller districts to the king's immediate followers.

Over and above the land thus settled would be a large amount of surplus land, increased perpetually, as the boundaries of the occupied territory are enlarged, by further conquests and dispossession of the native inhabitants.

§ 2. *Bookland and Folkland.*

From very early times it was common to make grants of land to religious bodies or to individuals. The grants were effected by the king as the chief of the community, with the consent of the great men, who in conjunction with the great ecclesiastics, after the introduction of Christianity, formed the Witenagemot, or Assembly of the Wise. The grant was made by means of a 'book' or charter[1]. Land thus granted

[1] Whether the land was actually considered as transferred by the book, as by a modern deed under 8 and 9 Vict. c. 106, or whether any additional ceremony resembling livery of seisin was requisite (see below, chap. III. § 13 (2)), is a point on which I have not been able to find authority. The analogy of the practice of other nations would seem to show that something like delivery of a piece of turf, a bough, &c., would be considered essential. Kemble, Cod. Dipl. i. v, seems to think that this was so in early times, that the practice then went out, and the book and taking possession under it was sufficient, till the practice was revived by the

CHAP. I. SECT. I. § 2.

was said to be 'booked' to the grantee, and was called bocland or bookland. Thus bookland comes to mean land held under a written instrument by private persons or churches; who or whose predecessors are, or at least are supposed to have been, grantees of the community. The practice seems, after the introduction of Christianity, to have prevailed chiefly in favour of religious houses, and in this way the great ecclesiastical corporations acquired their property. Frequent gifts were also made to individuals, chiefly the king's thegns or *ministri*[1].

In process of time the conception of bookland seems to be coextensive with that of alodial land[2]. The term 'alodial' originally had no necessary reference to the mode in which the ownership of land had been conferred; it simply meant land held in absolute ownership, not in dependence upon any other body or person in whom the proprietary rights were supposed to reside, or to whom the possessor of the land was bound to render service[3]. It would thus properly apply to the land which in the original settlement had been allotted to individuals, while bookland was primarily applicable to land the title to which rested on a formal grant. Before long, however, the words appear to have been used synonymously to express land held in absolute ownership, the subject of free disposition *inter vivos* or by will[4]. Later, when the conception of 'tenure' had become more general, the meaning of 'alodium' seems to be land which would descend to the heir[5].

Normans under the form of livery of seisin. See too Palgrave, Rise and Progress of the English Commonwealth, ii. ccxxvii; and Essays in Anglo-Saxon Law (Boston, 1876), p. 110; Pollock, Land Laws, chap. I. p. 199; Fustel de Coulanges, L'Alleu, p. 131. Pollock and Maitland, Hist. of Eng. Law, ii. p. 86.

[1] And hence the expression tain- or thegn-land. This seems to mean not a particular species of tenure, but land which was as a fact held or owned by a king's thegn.

[2] Pollock and Maitland, Hist. of Eng. Law, i. p. 37.

[3] See Freeman, Norman Conquest, i. p. 84 (2nd ed.).

[4] See Stubbs, Const. Hist. i. p. 76, n. 3.

[5] See below, p. 26.

As a general rule, when such a grant was made to an individual, it is expressed in the charter itself that he is to hold the land free from all burdens, that he is to be under no obligation to render anything in the shape of money payment or services of any kind to the grantor of the land, with the exception of the threefold service, the *trinoda necessitas*, to which all lands were subject. This consisted of the duty of rendering military service (*expeditio*), and of repairing bridges and fortresses (*pontis arcisve constructio*). These were duties imposed on all landholders, distinct from the feudal services of later times, but tending more and more to become duties attaching to the possession of the land owed to and capable of being enforced by the king or the great man of the district[1].

It is also generally expressed in the charter that the grantee[2] of the land is to be entitled to grant the land away to whomsoever he pleases in his lifetime, or to leave it by his last will, and that, if not disposed of, it is to descend to his representatives[3]. These powers however seem to have depended upon the form of the gift as expressed in the charter; the power of alienation might be restricted so that the land could not be granted away from the kindred[4], or the descent of the land might be confined to lineal descendants, or to heirs male or female. In these respects it was a principle of Anglo-Saxon customary law that the nature

[1] See Kemble, Cod. Dipl. i. lii, and Stubbs, Const. Hist. i. pp. 76, 190.

[2] Or person to whom the land is granted. This termination is always used in a passive sense.

[3] The capacity of selling the land is often mentioned in Domesday as a characteristic of absolute ownership. See Freeman, iv. p. 732; and Allen on the Royal Prerogative, p. 145.

[4] 'The man who has bookland, and which his kindred left him, then ordain we that he must not give it from his "mægburg" [kindred], if there be writing or witness that it was forbidden by those men who at first acquired it, and by those who gave it to him, that he should do so; and then let that be declared in the presence of the king and of the bishop before his kinsmen.'—Laws of Alfred, cap. 41; Stubbs, Select Charters, p. 63, 4th ed.

CHAP. I. SECT. I. § 2.

and extent of the rights of the grantee depended upon the form of the gift[1].

The king himself might be the grantee under one of these grants[2]. In that case he held the land thus granted like any other private individual; it was his private property which he could dispose of as he pleased.

In the later grants it is very common to find words expressing that rights of jurisdiction are conveyed together with the land[3]. These rights were extremely profitable, and became an important source of revenue to the great lords of districts. The rights were regarded as taken away from the hundred court and vested in the grantee as the owner of a franchise or liberty or district exempt from the jurisdiction of the hundred. The machinery of the hundred court would however be preserved, except that the territorial court would be presided over by the great man or his representative. To this court all the dwellers within the district would have recourse and become suitors. Thus the great man of the district acquired the headship or presidency of the courts held within the district, and by a gradual change the village assembly passes into the court of the tenants of the lord, called in later times the court baron or customary court; while the court leet of later times probably represents the

[1] See Kemble, Saxons in England, i. p. 308; Codex Diplomaticus, i. Introduction, pp. xxxii–xxxvi.

[2] See a grant by Æthelwulf to himself, A.D. 847, Cod. Dipl. cclx.

[3] This is commonly expressed by the words 'sac' and 'soc,' a jingle to which it is difficult to attach a precise meaning. It imports 'jurisdiction,' 'the franchise of holding a court.' See Stubbs, Const. Hist. i. p. 184, note 2, and Pollock and Maitland, Hist. of Eng. Law, i. pp. 20, 563. These words appear not to be found in charters before the reign of Edward the Confessor (Kemble, Cod. Dipl. i. xlvi). Kemble has collected seven instances of a grant of the right of jurisdiction over a thief caught within the granted district (infangethef, furis comprehensio) in charters between A.D. 823 and 1018. Some of these however appear to be of questionable authority. And see Laws of Edward the Confessor, xxii, Stubbs, Select Charters, p. 78.

jurisdiction of which the hundred court was deprived by express grant[1].

In all discussions on Anglo-Saxon law bookland is contrasted with 'folkland.' The most recent and probably the most correct view is that folkland simply means land subject to customary law, as opposed to land which was held under the terms of a charter. It would seem that the view that folkland means public land or land of the people, though till recently generally accepted, must be abandoned as resting on insufficient evidence[2]. It appears that folkland might either be land occupied by individuals or families or communities, or it might be waste or unoccupied land. The only characteristic which can be universally ascribed to it is, that it is not bookland. It has never been the subject of a grant by the king and the Witan. The king and the Witan have power, which is frequently exercised, to make grants of it, subject where the land is actually held by individuals or communities to their possessory rights. It then ceases to be folkland and becomes bookland. It seems moreover that it was not unusual for a relation resembling what would in later times be called a tenure to exist between the community or its chief and the person who was in possession of folkland. There is evidence that in some cases various rents, dues, or services in money or kind had to be rendered for the enjoyment of rights over the folkland[3]. On the whole we possess but little information as to the relations of the possessor of folkland to the king or the community, or as to the duties and services under which it was held. That rights over folkland were sometimes made the subject of disposition by its individual possessors, but that this could only be carried out by the assistance of the king as the head of the

[1] See Stubbs, Const. Hist. i. pp. 106, 184.

[2] See Pollock and Maitland, Hist. of Eng. Law, i. p. 39, Pollock, Land Laws, 3rd ed. p. 20.

[3] See Kemble's Saxons in England, i. 294–298; Allen's Royal Prerogative, p. 134; Stubbs' Const. Hist. i. p. 76.

CHAP. I. SECT. I. § 2.

community, appears from a curious document of the date A.D. 871–889[1], purporting to be a will of a certain Ælfred, in which, after disposing of his bookland, he requests the king to allow his son to succeed to the folkland which he himself holds, and if not, he leaves his son instead an equivalent out of his booklands. This shows that, in all probability, no individual rights enjoyed over folkland could be permanently alienated either *inter vivos* or by will without the consent of the community or its chief.

Any person who had proprietary rights over land, might in his turn permit another to have the beneficial enjoyment of the land on such terms as might be agreed on between them. Land thus dealt with was called laenland. This practice was especially common on ecclesiastical lands. We find instances of lands leased for two or three lives[2], or for other periods, with rents reserved in money, in kind, or in labour[3]. The conception of the legal effects of 'loans' of lands would be that the property or dominion remained in the lessor or lender, the person having the 'laen' possessing only the usufructuary enjoyment to a greater or less extent according to the terms of the loan[4]. Thus if the latter incurred forfeiture for treason the rights of the lessor would not be affected[5].

[1] Cod. Dipl. cccxvii. Kemble (Saxons in England, i. p. 181, note 1) has collected several curious instances of requests by testators to the king that their wills might be allowed to stand. These wills must, one would think, in most cases relate to interests over the folkland. Bookland was generally or universally the subject of free disposition by will. The idea however that the power of disposition possessed by the grantee depended upon the form of the gift may perhaps account for these expressions.

[2] See specimen below, p. 57. Very commonly, however, the land was leased or lent for the life of the lessee. See specimens of these 'conventiones' in the Domesday of St. Paul's. See below, p. 49.

[3] See as to laenland, Kemble, Saxons in England, i. p. 310.

[4] Cod. Dipl. i. lxii.

[5] See the case of Helmstan, Kemble, Saxons in England, i. p. 311. It seems that the laen was in this country rather the precursor of the lease or leasehold than of the *feudum* or *beneficium*. In Germany, however, *lehn* = *feudum*, *lehnrecht* = feudalism, feudal system.

CHAP. I. SECT. I. § 2.

Besides the land dealt with by grant and thus turned into bookland, and the land which was enjoyed by individuals otherwise than under a charter, there remained a very large proportion of the land of the country lying waste and uncultivated, and used only for pasture of sheep and cattle, for feeding swine on the acorns and beechmast, or for supplying wood for building, repairs, and fuel. What proprietary rights were recognized over land of this character?

It was primarily regarded as the common stock from which grants might be made. Bede in the eighth century speaks of it as land which ought to be granted to ecclesiastics or to warriors, but instead of this proper use, 'persons who have not the least claim to the monastic character have got so many of these spots into their power under the name of monasteries, that there is really now no place at all where the sons of nobles or veteran warriors can receive a grant[1].' When the country was brought under the government of a single king, this land seems to have been regarded as in an especial manner the property of the king, and is frequently spoken of as the king's folkland[2]. Besides the grants of whole districts of this land to be held as bookland, we frequently find that rights of pasturage and other beneficial rights over it are granted away to individuals by the king in the usual form[3]. There can be but little doubt that this unoccupied land came to be more and more regarded as the land of the king—*terra regis*[4]. And hence grew in later times the conception that all the land was originally vested

[1] Epistola ad Ecgbirhtum Archiepiscopum, quoted in Kemble, Saxons in England, i. p. 290.

[2] See Nasse, 'On the Agricultural Community of the Middle Ages,' p. 28.

[3] Thus Offa of Mercia in 772 grants to Æthelnoth, Abbot of SS. Peter and Paul, lands 'cum campis et silvis vel omnibus ad se pertinentibus bonis et ad pascendum porcos et pecora et jumenta in silva regali aeternaliter perdono, et unius capreae licentiam in silva quae vocatur Sænling ubi meae vadunt.' Cod. Dipl. cxix.

[4] See Stubbs, Const. Hist. i. 193.

CHAP. I. SECT. I. § 2.

in the crown[1], that the king is prima facie the owner of all unoccupied land, even of the shore of the sea below high-water mark. Sometimes the king would have exclusive rights over this unoccupied land, more commonly his rights would exist side by side with those of the inhabitants of the neighbouring villages[2]. In early times these rights were probably regarded as rights which the king would share in common with others. Later the property was looked on as vested in the king, the commoners having rights *in alieno solo.*

As the smaller kingdoms become subject to or are merged in the greater, and the king becomes the king of the whole nation, the notion that the unoccupied land is the royal domain appears to be more strongly developed. The actual ownership of this land and a sort of suzerainty over the rest of the land of the country comes to be vested in the king. It is common to find such expressions as *terra juris mei, pars telluris meae.* And throughout the country the claim of the king to certain dues, services, and proprietary rights, varying in different localities, is recognized[3].

What has been said of the king applies also, though in a less degree, to the great men of the nation, the king's thegns and the great ecclesiastical persons and bodies. Whether or not any districts were assigned to powerful individuals at the time of the original allotment of the territory, there can

[1] 'Tout fuit in luy et vient de luy al commencement.' (Year Book, 24 Edw. III, 65, quoted in Blackstone, ii. p. 51, note.)

[2] See Cod. Dipl. cclxxvi, where there is a grant of a villa 'et communionem marisci quae ad illam villam antiquitus cum recto pertinebat;' and cclxxxviii; and see Kemble, Introduction to Cod. Dipl. i. p. xl.

[3] We hear frequently of royal rights of pasturage, of rights of free quarter for royal messengers, of having the royal huntsmen, horses, dogs, and hawks kept. (See Cod. Dipl. i. liv; Kemble, Saxons in England, i. 293.) Compare Cnut's law, lxx: 'I command all my reeves that they justly provide for me out of my own property, and maintain me therewith, and that no man need give me anything as farm aid (feorme-fultume), unless he himself be willing.' (Thorpe, Ancient Laws and Institutes, p. 413, ed. 1840.) It appears from this passage that the king had certain rights in the various villae which were looked after by reeves or bailiffs.

be no doubt that large districts soon become the property or domains of great men. This may have been due partly to conquest and colonization by small detached bodies under a leader; or in particular communities leading men may in some cases have acquired by gift or purchase such domains. But after the new communities had attained to complete organization, the principal mode of creating such properties was doubtless the grant of portions of the folkland by the process above described. Thus there arose a class of territorial magnates, partly the successors of the princes whose petty lordships or principalities came to be held in subordination to and dependence on the king of the whole country, partly bishops, churches, or great men who had acquired, by grant or otherwise, large tracts of land. These territorial magnates are supreme over the land, both occupied and unoccupied within their districts. But they are also subordinate to the king of the nation; when therefore grants are made by such persons, it is worthy of observation that they are almost always expressed to be with the assent of the king. Thus the king is acknowledged as a sort of over-lord, whose consent is necessary to enable the inferior magnate to dispose of the unoccupied land within his district [1].

§ 3. *Relation of Lord and Man.*

Such were the fundamental notions of proprietary rights over land which prevailed amongst our Teutonic forefathers. But there is another element in Teutonic custom, at first wholly unconnected with the holding or ownership of land, which came in process of time to form an important element in the complex structure called the law of real property. This is the relation of lord and man, which gradually developed into the relation of lord and tenant [2]. The primitive form of this relation is found in the description of the mutual

[1] See the grant of Oswald Bishop of Worcester, given below, p. 57.

[2] See Stubbs, Const. Hist. i. p. 153, note.

CHAP. I. SECT. I. § 3.

connexion of *princeps* and *comes* described by Tacitus [1]. It was in its earliest form the association of a chief and his chosen

[1] Tacitus, De Situ, Moribus, et Populis Germaniae, cc. 13, 14: 'Insignis nobilitas, aut magna patrum merita, principis dignationem etiam adolescentulis adsignant: ceteris robustioribus ac jam pridem probatis adgregantur: nec rubor inter comites adspici. Gradus quinetiam et ipse comitatus habet, judicio ejus, quem sectantur: magnaque et comitum aemulatio, quibus primus apud principem suum locus; et principum, cui plurimi et acerrimi comites. Haec dignitas, hae vires, magno semper electorum juvenum globo circumdari, in pace decus, in bello praesidium. Nec solum in sua gente cuique, sed apud finitimas quoque civitates id nomen, ea gloria est, si numero ac virtute comitatus emineat: expetuntur enim legationibus, et muneribus ornantur, et ipsa plerumque fama bella profligant. Quum ventum in aciem, turpe principi, virtute vinci; turpe comitatui, virtutem principis non adaequare. Jam vero infame in omnem vitam ac probrosum, superstitem principi suo ex acie recessisse. Illum defendere, tueri, sua quoque fortia facta gloriae ejus adsignare, praecipuum sacramentum est. Principes pro victoria pugnant; comites pro principe. Si civitas in qua orti sunt longa pace et otio torpeat, plerique nobilium adolescentium petunt ultro eas nationes, quae tum bellum aliquod gerunt; quia et ingrata genti quies, et facilius inter ancipitia clarescunt, magnumque comitatum non nisi vi belloque tueare: exigunt enim principis sui liberalitate illum bellatorem equum, illam cruentam victricemque frameam. Nam epulae et convictus, quamquam incompti, largi tamen adparatus, pro stipendio cedunt. Materia munificentiae per bella et raptus.'

TRANSLATION.

'Lofty descent or the great exploits of his ancestors may stamp a mere youth with the dignity of a chief; or else men gather round the more stalwart warriors, whose worth has stood the test of time; and it is no disgrace to be found amongst the ranks of the followers. Moreover the band of followers itself comprises different grades, ranged according to the judgment of the chief, and great is the rivalry amongst the followers who should stand first in the estimation of his chief; and amongst the chiefs, who should have the most numerous, and most enthusiastic band of followers. It is the basis of the rank and of the power of a chief to have around him at all times a band of picked youths; they are his glory in time of peace, his bodyguard in time of war. And it is not only amongst his own people that pre-eminence in the number and valour of his followers brings to the chief renown and fame. Neighbouring tribes recognize it likewise, for such men are most acceptable on embassies, and are graced with gifts, and generally their renown is enough to turn the scale in war. In the day of battle it is shameful for a chief to be surpassed in valour, it is shameful for followers to fall behind their chief in valour. It is an abiding and life-long disgrace to have returned alive from a field where the chief has fallen. To guard and protect the chief—to make even their own deeds of daring redound to his glory, is their most sacred duty.

band of followers in warfare. This was characterized by the most absolute devotion of the *comes* to the *princeps*. The chief was regarded as the fountain of honour and the giver of gifts to those who were bound by oath to follow him. In our own early records this relation of *princeps* and *comes* has developed into the relation of lord and man. It has become a tie of mutual service, responsibility, and protection in every relation of life, and is regarded as one of the principal bases of social order[1]. So far was this idea carried, that the fact of rendering even menial service to a person of exalted rank was thought to reflect nobility on the person rendering it[2]. But this relation is not at first necessarily connected with the holding of land; the relation is that of *princeps* and *comes*, of king and his thegns, of lord and man, not of lord and tenant.

When however a territory was occupied by a conquering tribe, probably, as has been said above, the most fertile parts

The chief fights for victory, the followers for the chief. If their own community has slept for long in peace and quiet, most of the noble youths seek of their own accord those nations which may at the time be more or less engaged in warfare, not only because rest is naturally distasteful to them, but also because renown is more easily won in the midst of danger. Nor can the chief keep a great band of followers together without recourse to war and fighting, for it is their habit to demand of the bounty of the chief now a war-horse, now a shield stained with blood, and the badge of victory. Moreover feasts and banquets, rude, indeed, yet plentiful, serve instead of pay. The materials of munificence are supplied by warfare and rapine.' See Fustel de Coulanges, Origines du système féodal, Chap. II.

[1] 'And we have ordained, respecting these lordless men of whom no law can be got, that the kindred be commanded that they domicile him to folk-right, and find him a lord in the folk-mote; and if they then will not or cannot produce him at the term, then be he thenceforth a "flyma" [runaway], and let him slay him for a thief who can come at him; and whoever after that shall harbour him, let him pay according to his "wer," or by it clear himself.'—Laws of Athelstan, Stubbs, Select Charters, p. 66; and see Freeman, Norman Conquest, i. p. 96.

[2] See the chapter in Kemble, Saxons in England, i, on 'the Noble by Service.' The thegn grows out of the *comes*; he is a servant, but a servant ennobled by the dignity of him whose attendant he is. Freeman, i. p. 85.

CHAP. I. SECT. I. § 3.

of the land would be appropriated by the chief and his followers. The principal share would fall to the chief, who, as the head of the community, would regulate the management and distribution of the whole. The lands occupied by the *comites* would not probably in any other sense have been considered to have been granted to them by the chief. No relation or duty, as between the chief and the *comites*, would arise from the fact of the grant of the lands. That relation already existed independently of the grant of the lands. No doubt the *comites* occupying the lands would be in a sense bound to military service, not in the first instance as landholders, but by reason of their personal relation to the chief. When the idea of a nation as an organized political community has been developed, it is probable that the obligation of military service for the defence of the community attaches in every case to the holding of land by the freeman. This seems to have been universal from the time of the earliest charters. There was no escape for the landholder from the *trinoda necessitas*. This, it must be observed, is different from tenure by knight service, though it must be taken into account amongst the causes which led to the growth of military tenures.

In the records of the Anglo-Saxon period it seems that a gradual development can be traced, marking the stages in the progress of the relation of *princeps* and *comes* towards that of lord and tenant. At first we have the purely Teutonic institution of the *comitatus*. The king has around him *comites* or *gesiths*, who form his counsellors, his body-guard, and personal attendants. The abundance of unoccupied land enables him from time to time to make grants of portions of territory to them. Gradually the *gesith* or companion ceases to be heard of, and the *thegn* or *minister* takes his place. It seems to be difficult at first to distinguish between the two. The duties of the thegn seem to be more distinctly warlike than those of the *gesith*, and the position of the thegn seems to have come more and more to imply possession of a large district of land. Thus in the relation of the thegn to the king we see the germs of the later relation of the king to the tenant *in capite* holding of him by military service [1]. CHAP. I. SECT. I. § 3.

The relation of the king to the thegn is reproduced on a smaller scale by the relation between the great men and their dependants. A great thegn might have lesser thegns standing in a relation to him closely analogous to that in which he stood to the king [2].

Thus from the earliest times there would exist in the various bodies of original settlers a *princeps* or lord, supposed to be sprung from a lineage higher than that of common humanity. In many cases there arose in this way a sort of hereditary chieftainship. Amongst his other functions, the chief, prince, or king is supreme over the land. He has himself the most extensive rights of enjoyment over it, and he has the power of granting similar rights to others. Thus he passes into the lord of the district—of the land itself, as well as of the men who dwell thereon. When his district or petty kingdom becomes merged in and subject to a larger kingdom, he in his turn becomes subordinate to the superior prince. There is not yet any formal surrender and regrant of the land; but the supremacy of the superior prince is acknowledged, as in other matters, so in making grants of portions of the district of which the inferior is lord. There is as yet no distinct conception of the relation of superior lord, mesne lord, and tenant; but there is a relation which by an easy transition may assume those feudal characteristics.

The development of these lords of districts no doubt was brought about in other ways than that above indicated. The grants of enormous tracts of land by the king and his witan must frequently have comprised whole village communities, and had the effect of imposing a lord or superior landowner upon the district, whose yoke would in all probability be harder

[1] Stubbs, Const. Hist. i. pp. 152-157.

[2] Id. i. p. 158.

CHAP. I. SECT. I. § 3. than the more distant suzerainty of the king[1]. And no doubt in communities consisting of free and equal cultivators of the soil, sometimes in troublous times a chief arose who became their leader in war and their first magistrate in peace[2]. This appearance of a chief in a small community may also have been aided by the tendency which has been observed in these small communities, for particular families to possess or acquire an ascendency[3]. The chief was often a member of a family enjoying a species of hereditary pre-eminence. These chiefs doubtless became in process of time lords of districts of land.

Thus there can be no question that towards the end of the Anglo-Saxon period it became common for large districts of land to be held by lords or great men, king's thegns or others; and, as has been seen, extensive tracts were also held by religious corporations.

Of such districts a large portion was retained by the lord in his own hands. This portion was called *terra dominica, terrae dominicales*, or domain lands. On this portion stood the principal house, the *mansio* or manor-house as it was called in later times. The lands were cultivated for the benefit of the lord by serfs, or perhaps often by freemen bound to render agricultural services[4]. On the remainder of the

[1] When the land granted was already occupied by possessors having a durable interest which the customary law would protect, the grant must have been of the nature of a grant of a lordship or of seignorial rights. Compare the grant of Leofric (Earl of Mercia, eleventh century), Cod. Dipl. dccccxxxix, where half the town of Coventry and many villages are granted to the Church of the Blessed Virgin at Coventry, 'cum saca et socna et teloneo et themo et omnibus consuetudinibus sicut eas a rege Eadwardo melius unquam tenui.' The right of jurisdiction and the profits arising from the district courts were the most important of these seignorial rights. See Stubbs, Const. Hist. i. pp. 183–187, and above, p. 14, note 3.

[2] See Sir H. Maine's account (Village Communities, p. 143) of the probable mode in which the manor grew out of the mark.

[3] See Freeman, Norman Conquest, i. p. 82; Sir H. Maine, Village Communities, p. 145.

[4] See Hale, Introduction to the Domesday of St. Paul's, p. xxx

occupied lands the rights of the lord were rather in the nature of a seignory or lordship. He had no right to the actual possession or enjoyment of the land itself, but only to the rents or dues to be paid or rendered by the persons in occupation of the soil. His rights over the waste or unoccupied land have already been spoken of. CHAP. I. SECT. I. § 3.

The principal of these territorial magnates was the king. Besides his position as supreme lord of all the land in the kingdom, he was also the largest landowner. He filled the former position as chief of the nation, the latter as having acquired by the ordinary modes of acquisition a larger area of land than any other great man in the kingdom. It cannot however be supposed that these two capacities were kept entirely distinct. Traces can be discovered of a growing tendency before the Conquest for the unoccupied land to become regarded as the *terra regis*. After the Conquest the process is complete, and the king becomes the supreme landowner, the lord paramount of all the land, whose rights differ from those of any other lord not so much in kind as in degree [1].

(Publications of Camden Society). And see the document entitled Rectitudines Singularum Personarum in the Ancient Laws and Institutes, p. 432. In the Domesday of St. Paul's we find that praedial services were due from three classes of persons, called villani, cotarii, bordarii. In the Rectitudines (placed by Thorpe next after the laws of Cnut) we find praedial services due from villani, cotsetle, geburi. The villani are serfs attached to the hides or land on which they live; the cotarii and bordarii are identical with the cotsetle and geburi, and are cottagers with still smaller holdings than the villani, and bound to lighter services. See Nasse, pp. 36–42. Opposed to these classes bound to praedial service we find in the Rectitudines the 'Taini lex,' 'Thegn law,' thus described—'Taini lex est ut sit dignus rectitudine testamenti sui et ut ita faciat pro terra sua scilicet expeditionem, buhrbotam et brigbotam.' The whole document is interesting, as an indication of a stage in the history of tenure by knight-service, tenure in socage, and copyholds.

[1] See Freeman, Norman Conquest, i. p. 94; ii. pp. 52, 53; iv. p. 24; Allen on the Royal Prerogative, p. 150; Stubbs, Const. Hist. i. p. 143.

CHAP. I. SECT. I. § 4.

§ 4. *Summary of Anglo-Saxon Customary Law.*

Thus in the period preceding the Norman Conquest the growth of various conceptions can be traced in the customary [1] law of land out of which the remarkable structure called the Law of Real Property was ultimately developed. There are present the elements of the idea of tenure, or of the rights and duties which constitute the relation of a landholder to his lord. This is found in the relation of lord and man which in some cases has developed into the relation of lord and tenant. But the creation of a tenure is not as yet regarded as the universal consequence of a grant of land. It is however probable that even the free alodial landowners in many cases became the vassals or tenants of the king or great lord, by 'commending' themselves to him, acknowledging him as their lord, and receiving in return his protection [2]. One evidence of the growth of the conception of tenure is to be found in the changed sense of the word '*alodium*' as used in Domesday. It is sometimes there applied to hereditary and alienable land, which nevertheless is held of a superior lord [3]. Other expressions in Domesday seem to indicate a transitional period between absolute independence and feudal tenancy. Thus it is common to say of the holder of land *cum ea ire potuit quo voluit*; that is, that he was at liberty to commend himself or become the man, vassal, or tenant of any lord he pleased [4]. On the whole, the evidence seems to point to the conclusion that

[1] On the difference between customary law and positive law properly so called, see below, Chap. II. Though there is apparently a large mass of written Anglo-Saxon law, it will be found to throw but little light on the law of land. Where it deals with this subject, it refers to and presupposes the existence of customary law. See on the character of this written law, Stubbs, Select Charters, p. 60.

[2] 'Liberi homines commendati' is a very common expression in Domesday. See Sir H. Ellis, General Introduction to Domesday, i. p. 64.

[3] Thus it is common in Domesday Book to meet with such expressions as 'ipse tenuit in alodio de Rege Edwardo.' See Allen on the Royal Prerogative, p. 196; Freeman, Norman Conquest, iv. p. 38, notes; Sir H. Ellis, General Introduction to Domesday, i. p. 55.

[4] Hallam, Middle Ages, ii. p. 86 (eighth edition).

the early relation of *princeps* and *comes* had tended more and more to be connected with the holding of land; that the king was regarded by his thegns as the lord from whom they might look for grants of land, sometimes in the shape of large districts booked to them, to be held alodially; sometimes in the shape of beneficial possessory rights over the public land, for which dues and services would be payable, and which could not be permanently alienated without the king's consent [1]. Whether the land was free or burdened, every free landowner was subject to the burden of military service; which was deemed not an incident of tenure, but a duty to the State.

The relation subsisting between the king and his thegns was reproduced on a smaller scale in the case of the great lords who had acquired or inherited districts of land. The dwellers within the district were tending to become their tenants. This was the case especially with the classes of serfs and freemen bound to agricultural service. Tenure by knight-service is unknown till after the Norman Conquest; tenure by suit of court, rent, or agricultural services—what in later times would be called tenure in socage or in villenage—certainly in substance existed before. Doubtless too the lord before the Conquest had in many cases acquired what in later times was the great characteristic of a manor. The free assembly of the village had become the lord's court [2]. To this court was usually attached, either by virtue of the express grant under which the lands were held, or by long usage, the jurisdiction which in the Anglo-Saxon system properly be-

[1] See especially the instances given by Kemble of the consent of the king being required for testamentary alienation; above, p. 16, note 1. Sometimes we find instances of a person simply being allowed, in the first instance, beneficial or possessory rights over the land, which afterwards becomes his independent alodial property. Thus land held, in the first instance, as laenland, is found in some cases to be converted into absolute property, the lord, to use the language of the later law, releasing his reversion to the tenant. 'Now there are three hides of this land which Archbishop Oswald booketh to Eadric his thane, even as he before held them as laenland.'—Kemble, Saxons, p. 313.

[2] See above, p. 8.

CHAP. I. SECT. I. § 4.

longed to the court of the hundred. And just as the unoccupied land of the community had come to be regarded, first as the king's folkland, and secondly as the *terra regis*, so had the waste, unoccupied, or common land of the village community come to be regarded as the lord's waste, over which the dwellers within the district exercised certain customary rights.

Besides the elements of the conception of tenure, Anglo-Saxon customary law contributed certain other principles of permanent influence, modified more or less by the changes consequent upon the Conquest, to the conception of the rights of private property in land.

Of these the principal are (1) the conception of the duration of an interest in lands. The Anglo-Saxons conceived the idea of an estate of inheritance in lands, an interest which would descend to successors *in infinitum*. They also had the idea of inheritances limited to particular descendants, as for instance to the males of the family. Such peculiar characteristics could be impressed upon the interest in lands by the form of the original gift. Estates for life were also known; these seem to have been especially common in the *conventiones* or leases under which lands were held by *firmarii* upon ecclesiastical property[1].

(2) Another important point is the freedom of alienation both *inter vivos* and by will, which was characteristic of bookland. Probably where there was no express charter the right of alienation was ordinarily limited by the claims of the family[2]. The history of the right of alienation *inter vivos* will be traced later: the right of alienation by will ceases altogether with the introduction of Norman law, except in

[1] See many specimens of these leases for lives in the Domesday of St. Paul's, p. 123, &c. It was very common for ecclesiastical bodies to lease their territory to firmarii, the lessee standing in the place and having all the rights of the lord, rendering to the lessors fixed rents in kind or money. Leases of particular portions of land within the district were also (probably) common.

[2] See Pollock and Maitland, Hist. of Eng. Law, ii. p. 316.

some particular localities and boroughs, and is not revived till a new class of proprietary rights arises, which supersedes, in great measure, the old law.

(3) Upon the death of the landowner, his land, as a rule, subject to many important modifications by local custom, descended to all the sons equally, as contrasted with the rule of primogeniture, which was of Norman introduction. The history of the law on this point will be noticed in reference to a passage in Glanvill [1].

SECTION II.

Effects of the Norman Conquest.

Such are the main outlines of the customary law of land prevailing among the Anglo-Saxons. It was of home-growth, and but little influenced by the legal ideas which had developed on the Continent since the decline of the Roman Empire. No doubt, in its framework and language, an Anglo-Saxon charter resembled those in use elsewhere; but this arises not so much from the identity of legal conceptions as from the fact that these instruments were everywhere drawn up by the clergy, who shared in the common training, ideas, and phraseology of the Universal Church [2].

We have seen that the early Teutonic customs had by the time of the Conquest developed into what may be called, for want of a better name, a kind of feudalism. There were, at all events, two of the principal elements of feudalism—the relation of king and thegn, of lord and man, and the development of great territorial lordships, of which by far the most numerous were those enjoyed by the king. We cannot doubt that these two elements of feudalism were becoming blended;

[1] Below, Chap. II. § 6.

[2] See Sir F. Palgrave, Rise and Progress of the English Commonwealth, ii. p. cciv.

CHAP. I. SECT. II.

that the thegn was gradually passing into the tenant *in capite*[1], the man of the lord of a district into his tenant. But these names, together with the whole apparatus of modern legal terminology, had not yet arisen.

Another type of feudalism had by the time of the Conquest been developed on the Continent. On the Continent the primitive Teutonic customs had been affected, not only, as in England, by the natural consequences of conquest and settlement of fresh lands, but by the fact that the inhabitants of the lands thus conquered were living in a state of culture and civilization far superior to that of their conquerors. Hence it was that the barbarian tribes which overran Italy, Gaul, and Spain, adopted the religion and laws of the conquered nations, modified to some extent by old barbarian usages. For the present purpose it is only important to notice the effect of this medley of barbarian usage and Roman law[2] upon the attributes of property in land.

What the elements of Roman law and custom were which contributed to the growth of feudalism on the Continent has been a question much discussed, on which views widely differing are entertained. The latest investigator has rejected the theory that feudal tenure had any connexion with the practice which prevailed under the Empire of making grants of lands to veterans. According to Fustel de Coulanges[3] the germs of feudal tenures are to be found in the Roman practice which there seems reason to believe was very ancient, of creating a precarious tenure by the granting of the request of a poor man to a great landowner to be permitted to enjoy the produce of a piece of land during his life. What the usual *quid pro quo* for the concession was is not clear. Probably the transaction gave rise to a relation of personal dependence

[1] A tenant-in-chief, that is, a tenant holding immediately of the king.

[2] See Maine, Ancient Law, p. 364, and for an elaborate account of the causes which led to feudal tenure, Palgrave, Rise and Progress of the English Commonwealth, i. p. 495, &c., and ii. p. cciv.

[3] Les Origines du système féodal. Paris, 1890.

between the small usufructuary and the powerful owner. The practice may be traced with various developments tending to define the nature of the relation created by the beneficial concession throughout the period of the Empire. It survived the barbarian invasions of Gaul, and prevailed largely during the Merovingian period. In time the land beneficially granted becomes itself called a *beneficium*. By steps which it seems impossible exactly to trace the personal relation which seems always to have existed between the benefactor and the benefited person takes the form of the tie of military service, and binds together the lord paramount, the mesne lord, and the tenant, till the whole body politic becomes organized on this basis.

These *beneficia* in process of time receive the name of *feuda*[1], which in its earliest acceptation means land which has been granted to be held of the donor, as opposed to alodial land.

The principal agents by which alodial owners of land were turned into feudal tenants were probably *conquest*, and *need of protection*. The lot of the conquered is always hard, and doubtless the alodial holder of land was glad to retain the enjoyment of a portion of his property on such terms as the

[1] The word *feudum* is not found earlier than the close of the ninth century. Stubbs, Const. Hist. i. p. 251, note 1. Its etymology has given rise to much controversy. Blackstone (ii. p. 45) thinks that it comes from two words in 'the Northern languages, *fee*, signifying conditional stipend or reward, and *odh*, *proprietas*.' Sir. F. Palgrave believes it to be simply a colloquial abbreviation of *emphyteusis* (Rise of English Commonwealth, ii. p. ccvii). Diez, however (Etymologisches Wörterbuch der Romanischen Sprachen), *sub voce* FIO, shows that *feudum* is a Latin recoinage of a word sprung from an old Teutonic root—Lombardian *fiu*, Old High German *fehu* (*vieh*), Gothic *faihu*, signifying cattle, or, generally, property; cattle being probably amongst the earliest subjects of property (see *sub voce* FEOH in Bosworth, Anglo-Saxon Dictionary, and compare *pecus*, *pecunia*). Hence *feudum*, the *d* being added for euphony (compare *feuum* in Domesday). Hence *fief*, *fee*, *feoffment*, &c.; and see Littré, Dictionnaire de la Langue Française, *sub voce* FIEF. Sir H. Maine (Early History of Institutions, p. 157, &c.) describes the creation amongst the ancient Irish of a relation analogous to that of lord and vassal by the gift of stock by the chief, and its voluntary or forced acceptance by the tribesman.

CHAP. I. SECT. II. conqueror chose to impose. The usual conditions were that the old free proprietor should become the 'man' of the conqueror, and should be bound to military service. Moreover, in those troubled times it often became a necessity for the poor alodial holder to enter into the train of retainers of a powerful lord in order to obtain protection: hence the practice of 'commendation,' of becoming the man or vassal of the lord, receiving in return the protection without which the preservation of life and property was impossible. An element in this process was the surrendering of the alodial lands, to be received back under the condition of rendering military or other service.

Such is in outline the probable account of the origin of the great characteristic of feudalism—military tenure of lands; known in our law by the name of tenure in knight-service, or in chivalry.

It was created by the tie of homage, the solemn act by which the tenant acknowledged his lord as him of whom he held his land, and to whom he was bound to render service; and from which, on the other hand, arose the duty on the part of the lord of protecting his tenant. The lord himself (where the lord was other than the highest) was in the same way the vassal or tenant of some other over-lord. But between the superior or chief lord and the tenant who held his lands of the vassal of the superior lord there was no immediate relation of service and protection or otherwise.

The system of military tenure of lands prevailed in Normandy before the Conquest of England, and it seems probable that the customary law of that country had elaborated with some minuteness and technicality the various rights and duties of lord and tenant by military service[1]. They were his tenants bound to render to him military service whom William summoned when the news of the death of Edward was brought to him. The fact that by the terms of their tenure they were not bound to service beyond the sea caused

[1] See Stubbs, Const. Hist. i. p. 249.

him some difficulty [1]. The rapid introduction in the century succeeding the Conquest of a strict definition of the mutual duties of lord and tenant, and of a highly technical legal phraseology, leads to the conclusion that these must have been to some extent imported at the Conquest; and that amongst the Normans must have been found, what the Anglo-Saxons certainly did not possess, a class, if not of trained lawyers, at all events of men habituated to abstract reflection on the prevailing customs, able to express them in legal phraseology, and to draw conclusions from the established principles of customary law.

From the mixture of Anglo-Saxon customary law with the Norman, the blending process beginning under the influence of the strong rule of the Conqueror, and forced on with rapid strides by the vast territorial confiscations which followed the Conquest, arose the Common Law relating to land. It must not be supposed that a new system of rules of law was consciously introduced and forced upon the conquered race [2]; the new structure was the result of the political and social changes wrought by the great Conquest; of the process of settlement and reorganization under a powerful ruler, who would brook no *imperium in imperio*; and of the convergence of two distinct streams of customary law.

The effect of the Norman Conquest upon the land law of England is best dealt with by considering the change wrought, first, in the relation of the king to all the land in the country; secondly, in the development of the idea of tenure, or the rights and duties constituting the relation of lord and tenant; and thirdly, in the growth of the manorial system.

[1] See Palgrave, Normandy and England, iii. p. 300.

[2] Blackstone and other writers regard the 'feudal system' as a set of rules consciously devised to serve certain purposes, and voluntarily or compulsorily adopted by the various communities in which they prevailed. See Blackstone, book ii. ch. 4, 'Of the Feodal System.' But laws, especially in early times, 'are not made, but grow.'

CHAP. I. SECT. II. § 1.

§ 1. *Relation of the King to the Land.*

By the conquest or acquisition of England William succeeded to all the rights of the Anglo-Saxon kings. The rights over the land which they had became his. The great possessions held by them in their private capacity devolved upon William, and no distinction any longer existed between the king's ownership of land in his private capacity and his suzerainty over the unoccupied land as chief of the nation[1]. All alike became *terra regis*. Besides the land to which he thus became entitled as the legitimate successor of the Anglo-Saxon kings, all the land held by those who had resisted him was, by the customary law of both England and Normandy, forfeited to the king.

The enormous amount of land thus forfeited, the vast grants made to William's Norman followers, the practice of making grants of land to the same person in different parts of the country so as to prevent the creation of a too powerful territorial aristocracy, are matters dwelt on in all histories of the period. Besides the actual dispossession, a vast quantity of the land of the kingdom was deemed to have been forfeited or surrendered to the king, and regranted by him[2].

That the powerful followers of the Conqueror to whom he granted districts of land should become his tenants, bound to render military service to him, was in accordance with Norman customs, and also necessary for the consolidation of the Conqueror's power. It seems probable that in every case these grants were made in return for the tenant doing homage to William, and binding himself to military service. The free landowners who received back their lands as tenants of the

[1] See above, p. 25.

[2] As to the repurchasing of the conquered land by the English, see Freeman, iv. p. 25; v. pp. 20, 26; and Stubbs, Const. Hist. i. p. 259. According to Mr. Freeman, v. pp. 24, 787–798, it was necessary at the time of Domesday to a good title to any land except that held by ecclesiastical bodies that the tenant should be able to adduce evidence of a grant, regrant, or confirmation by William.

king would also be bound to service, military or other. The military service would probably at first be measured by the existing custom of the equipment of one fully-armed man for every five hides of land[1]. In the course of the century succeeding the Conquest some lands become exempt from, others subject to, military service. The landowner bound to military service becomes the tenant in chivalry (*per militiam*); the *miles* becomes the *knight*; and where land is held by military service every portion amounting to twenty pounds in annual value constitutes a '*knight's fee*,' for which the service of a knight fully armed and equipped must be rendered[2].

Thus the notion of military tenure, at all events as between the king and the great barons, rapidly took root after the Conquest. But there is another element in the conception of the relation of the king to the land of the country which must not be lost sight of. It has been seen that before the Conquest the whole land was subject to the burden of the *trinoda necessitas*. There can be little doubt that after the Conquest this burden came to be regarded as a service due to the king quite irrespective of the fact whether the landholder bound to render it was the king's tenant or not. This probably is the explanation of the famous oath taken by 'all landholders' at the council of Sarum in 1086[3]. And the

[1] 'Si rex mittebat alicubi exercitum, de quinque hidis tantum unus miles ibat, et ad ejus victum vel stipendium de unaquaque hida dabantur ei iiii. solidi ad duos menses. Hos vero denarios regi non mittebantur sed militibus dabantur. Si quis in expeditionem summonitus non ibat, totam terram suam erga regem forisfaciebat. Quod si quis remanendi habens alium pro se mittere promitteret, et tamen qui mittendus erat remaneret, pro l. solidis quietus erat dominus ejus.'—Domesday, Customs of Berkshire, Stubbs, Select Charters, p. 87.

[2] Stubbs, Const. Hist. i. p. 264.

[3] 'There came to him his witan and the landholders that were throughout England, and they became his men, and all submitted themselves to him and were his men, and swore fealty to him, and that they would defend him against all other men.' Saxon Chronicle, A. D. 1086; Stubbs, p. 81; quoted in Blackstone, ii. p. 49. Compare Laws of William I, cap. 2; 'Statuimus etiam ut omnis liber homo foedere et sacramento affirmet, quod infra et extra Angliam Willelmo regi fideles esse volunt, terras et honorem illius omni fidelitate cum eo servare, et ante eum contra inimicos

CHAP. I. SECT. II. § 1. form of homage which was adopted after the Conquest to create the feudal tie between a mesne lord and his tenant always contained a saving of the allegiance due to the king[1]. A powerful ruler like William, who had had abundant experience of the tendency of continental feudalism to make the vassal a formidable rival to the king, was not likely to throw away the advantage of the existence of a principle forming so important an aid to the central authority as the Anglo-Saxon *trinoda necessitas.* No doubt, in times when the central authority was weakened, the barons succeeded for a time, especially during the reign of Stephen, in shaking off their allegiance to the crown and summoning their tenants to serve them in their private wars. In the long run, however, the strong and vigorous centralization effected by William, and organized by Henry II, resulted in firmly establishing the principle, that where the land was held of a mesne lord by military service, *propter patriae tuitionem*, the service was regarded as due not to the mesne lord, but to the king. This is the distinguishing characteristic between English and Continental feudalism[2], and was fraught with consequences of the

defendere.' (Select Charters, p. 83.) See Freeman, Norman Conq. v. p. 64, 366, 382.

[1] See the form of homage given below, Chap. II. § 3.

[2] The following passage from the Ordonnances of St. Lewis, c. 49, A. D. 1270, gives a graphic picture of the relation of king or supreme lord, mesne lord and tenant, under the French feudalism. The text modernized is as follows:—Si un seigneur dit à son homme lige : 'venez avec moi ; car je veux faire la guerre à mon seigneur, qui m'a refusé justice en sa cour,' le vassal doit lui répondre : 'Sire, j'irai vers mon seigneur m'informer s'il est ainsi que vous dites.' Alors il viendra trouver le chef seigneur, et lui dira : 'Sire, mon seigneur m'a dit que vous lui avez refusé justice en votre cour ; je me présente devant vous pour savoir la vérité, car je suis sommé de l'accompagner pour vous faire la guerre.' Et si le chef seigneur répond que son intention n'est pas de lui faire justice en sa cour, le vassal se joindra à son seigneur, qui sera tenu de l'équiper à ses dépens. Mais s'il refusait de marcher avec lui, il en perdrait de droit son fief. Si, au contraire, le chef seigneur lui répond : 'Je rendrai volontiers justice à votre seigneur en ma cour,' le vassal doit venir trouver son seigneur, et lui dire: 'Sire, mon chef seigneur m'a dit, qu'il vous rendra volontiers justice en sa cour.' S'il lui répond qu'il ne veut plus se soumettre à son jugement et qu'il lui enjoigne de se rendre à la sommation qu'il lui a faite, alors le

most vital import to the growth of the English constitution. The only exception to this principle seems to have been when the lord himself personally attended the king. In that case he might summon his military tenants to attend with him, or exact a pecuniary equivalent in lieu of service, called scutage or escuage[1].

§ 2. *Development of the idea of Tenure.*

A principal result of the Norman Conquest upon the customary law of land seems to have been the development of the idea of tenure, the more precise definition of the mutual rights and duties of lord and tenant, and, as a necessary consequence, the introduction of a technical phraseology. This result was not brought about by any positive enactment. It was due to the introduction of Norman customs and ideas, and their combination with Anglo-Saxon customs and ideas.

Thus was produced what is called the feudal system, or the feudal mode of holding lands. We find that wherever there is a duty imposed on the possessor of land, whether of a military or other character, the tendency after the Conquest was to regard the duty as the *service* by which the land was *held* of the king or lord. Thus the Anglo-Saxon custom that every five hides should furnish a fully-armed man would be transformed into a tenure of so much land by the duty or service of providing a *miles*. The duty of attendance on the lord's court became the tenure by suit and service, and the duty of performing agricultural service on the lord's domain became the service by which the land of the poor freeholder or villein was held.

Domesday bears abundant traces of the growth of the idea of tenure, though we still hear of the men (*homines*) of a lord rather than of his tenants. The land is everywhere spoken of as having been *held* of King Edward or some other lord.

vassal pourra le refuser, de droit, sans craindre de perdre son fief, ni autre chose. (Isambert, Rec. d'Anc. Lois, ii. p. 416.) See below, Chap. III. § 11.

[1] As to scutage, see below, Chap. III. § 5.

CHAP. I. SECT. II. § 2. The word *feudum* or *feuum* is used to designate the land which is held as a benefice and not alodially[1]. The personal relation of lord and man is closely connected with, and generally, though not always, merged in the relation of lord and tenant[2]. The various modes in which land was held by different classes of persons before the Conquest were now tending to become different species of tenure, and gradually acquiring definite technical names. Thus land held by religious houses, which before the Conquest was always free from all temporal service except the *trinoda necessitas*, is now said to be held by the tenure called *libera eleemosyna* (free alms or frankalmoign[3]). It is however still regarded as free from all temporal dues, and the religious corporation is only bound to spiritual service. The services due to the king, which if rendered to one of less exalted rank would have been considered degrading to a freeman, were still in the time of Domesday rendered by the *taini regis*[4], but were no doubt becoming connected with the holding of the land, and passing into the exalted tenure of *magnum servitium*, or grand serjeanty[5]. Hence it was that lands held by this tenure can

[1] See above, p. 31, and the Index to Domesday.

[2] Compare the following passages:—'Non fuit de feudo sed tantum fuit homo suus.' (Kelham, Domesday Illustrated, p. 212.) 'Homo (effectus est) antecessoris sed terram suam sibi non dedit.' (Ib. 233.) 'Milites habebant sub se quatuor ita liberi ut ipsi erant.' (Ib. 272.)

[3] See Ellis, General Introduction to Domesday, i. p. 258. The word is however used in Domesday in a more general sense, and is sometimes applied to the case of restoration of lands to a layman which had been held by his father or himself. See Freeman, Norman Conq. v. pp. 31, 804–806. See further as to frankalmoign, Pollock, Land Laws, p. 36, and Challis, Real Property (2nd ed.), p. 11.

[4] Ellis, General Introduction to Domesday, i. p. 45.

[5] This name does not appear in Domesday. No doubt at that time the accurate distinction between different species of tenure had not arisen. Probably these distinctions were not accurately drawn till the great impulse given to the development of the Common Law by the action of the tribunals organized by Henry the Second. The following may serve as an instance of grand serjeanty:—By an inquisition taken 31 Edw. I, one Soloman de Champs is said to hold certain lands called Coperland and Atterton near Dover of the king *in capite* 'by the sergeantry and service of holding the king's head between Dover and Whitsan whenever he

only be held of the king. But most important of all is tenure *per militiam*, in chivalry or by knight-service. Here again the evidence afforded by Domesday seems to show that this species of tenure had not yet definitely taken its place in the legal classification of rights of property, but was gradually becoming recognized [1]. No doubt military tenure first prevailed between the king and his immediate tenants—those who had actually received new grants of land, or their old lands regranted to them. By the Anglo-Saxon law the public duty was imposed on such tenants of rendering military service for the defence of the country. Continental feudal notions would transform this public duty into the obligation of rendering military service to the king as lord of the tenants' land. But his position as king as well as lord was never wholly lost sight of. If a mesne lord, that is a lord who was himself a tenant of the king or of some superior lord, made a grant of land to be held of himself by military services, though the land was of course held of the mesne lord, the military service, as has been seen, was regarded as due not to the immediate lord but to the king [2]. There is much that is obscure in the history of the growth of military tenure. There are some recorded instances soon after the Conquest of exemptions from the general obligation of military service being obtained in favour of some lands in consideration of other lands being bound by an obligation to furnish a certain number of *milites*. It seems probable that the general extension of the practice of exempting some lands from military

crossed the sea between those ports, and there should be occasion for it.' Hasted, Kent, iv. p. 39; Camden, Britannia, ed. 1610, p. 348.

[1] We find however in two passages the expression (i. 10 b, and i. 32) 'servitium unius militis' applied to a new tenure; this became the regular technical term for the military service due for a knight's fee. 'T.R.E. (tempore regis Edwardi) valebat XL sol. et post L sol. modo IIII lib. et servitium unius militis.' (Ellis, General Introduction, i. 262.) Tenants holding of the king are sometimes spoken of as 'barones regis.' According to Sir H. Ellis, i. p. 58, 'miles' has not acquired the technical sense of 'knight.'

[2] See Bracton, fol. 35, given in Chap. III. § 11.

CHAP. I. SECT. II. § 2. service and burdening others led to the distinction between military and non-military tenures[1] which exists in its complete form by the beginning of the reign of Henry II[2].

Besides the duty of military service which constituted the essential characteristic of tenure in chivalry, various incidental rights and duties came to be attached to the relation of lord and tenant *per militiam,* some of which became the most important attributes of that relation[3]. The first in order of time was that of relief, or the dues which the heir of the tenant was bound to render to his lord on being admitted tenant and rendering homage. This was confounded with the custom of rendering heriots on the death of the man or vassal which prevailed before the Conquest[4]. The origin however of the practice of rendering heriots and of paying reliefs was different. The heriot probably originated in the practice of returning to the *princeps* the horse or the armour with which he had furnished the *comes*[5]; it was of purely Teutonic origin[6]. The relief originated with the practice of regarding lands as benefices to be held of the grantor. The admission of the heir as tenant in his ancestor's place was by the feudal theory a favour to be bought with a price, but which could not, if the

[1] See Stubbs, Const. Hist. i. 264.

[2] In the first half of the twelfth century socagers are found serving in the army. Pollock and Maitland, Hist. of Eng. Law, i. p. 275.

[3] Mr. Freeman attributes the development and organization of the system of feudal burdens to the 'malignant genius' of Randolf Flambard, minister of William Rufus. Norman Conq. v. 377, &c.

[4] See the Laws of Cnut (71, 72) as to the amount of heriots due upon the death of an eorl, a king's thegn, &c.; Stubbs, Select Charters, p. 74. From this law was borrowed the provision of William I as to reliefs:—'De relief a cunte ki al rei afert—viii cheuals enfrenez e enscelez (les iiii) e iiii haubercs e iiii haumes e iiii escuz e iiii lances e iiii espees. Les autres ii chaceurs et ii palefreis a freins et a cheuestres.' (Thorpe, Ancient Laws and Institutes, p. 474.) Similar provisions follow as to the relief to be paid by barons, vavassors, and villeins. It is probably from the existence of Cnut's law that the idea has arisen that heriots are exclusively of Danish origin.

[5] See the passage in Tacitus given above, p. 20, note 1; 'exigunt enim principis sui liberalitate illum bellatorem equum, illam cruentam victricemque frameam.'

[6] See Kemble, Saxons in England, i. p. 178.

proper steps were taken, be withheld by the lord. It was thus entirely a result of the conception of tenure [1].

The aid for marrying the eldest daughter of the lord is recorded as having been taken for the daughter of Henry I on her marriage with the Emperor. It appears however to have been levied as a tax on all land, not exclusively from the tenants in chivalry [2]. These *auxilia* or aids were apparently not at first strictly defined, limits were probably imposed on them by customs which were observed or exceeded according to the rapacity or power of the lord. Finally, they were restricted to a reasonable aid for ransoming the lord if he were taken captive, for making the eldest son a knight, and for marrying once the eldest daughter [3].

The incidents of the greatest importance are those of wardship and marriage. These became rights of the greatest value to the lord, and most burdensome to the tenant. They are frequently spoken of as if they constituted the essence of tenure. Pure feudalism had but a short life in England. These incidents of tenure, the only justification of which was to be found in their aiding towards the completeness of the military tie between lord and tenant, soon lost every rational basis. It appears from the charter of Henry I, that the widow or some other near relation was to be allowed by their lord to be the guardian of the children [4]. It will be seen that by the time of Glanvill the lord had acquired the right of assuming the guardianship of the person of the minor and of his lands,

[1] See further as to reliefs, below, Ch. II. § 4 (1).

[2] 'Anno igitur sequenti data est filia regis imperatori, ut breviter dicam, sicut decuit; Rex itaque cepit de unaquaque hida Angliae tres solidos.'—Henr. Huntingd., Hist. lib. vii; Stubbs, Select Charters, p. 98.

[3] See Magna Carta (John), cc. 12 and 15; below, Ch. II. § 4 (1), and III. § 5; Blackstone, ii. p. 64; and the Statute 'Confirmatio Cartarum,' 25 Edw. I.

[4] 'Si vero uxor cum liberis remanserit, dotem quidem et maritationem habebit, dum corpus suum legitime servaverit, et eam non dabo nisi secundum velle suum. Et terrae et liberorum custos erit sive uxor sive alius propinquorum qui justius esse debeat. Et praecipio quod barones mei similiter se contineant erga filios et filias vel uxores hominum suorum.'—Charter of Henry I, c. 4; Stubbs, Select Charters, p. 101.

CHAP. I. SECT. II. § 2. restoring them to him on his coming of age without accounting for the mesne profits [1]. Further, the heir on coming of age was obliged to purchase the delivery of the lands (called livery or *ousterlemain*) by payment of a fine of half a year's profits of the land.

Some traces of the right of the lord to consent to the marriage of the daughter or sister of a tenant appear in the time of Domesday [2]. In the time of Henry I, the lord simply has the right to prevent the daughter of his tenant being given in marriage to his enemy [3]. The absolute right of the lord to the disposal of the daughter of his tenant in marriage is recognized by Glanvill in the strongest terms, but it was not till nearly the end of the twelfth century that the claim of the lords to control the marriage of the sons of the tenant as well was definitively established [4]. This extension of the practice was without any shadow of justification on feudal grounds; originating simply with the grasping and illegal avarice of the great lords, it passed into a firmly established right of property.

[1] See below, Chap. II. § 3 (2).

[2] See Freeman, Norman Conq. v. p. 374, and compare the following entry: 'Hanc terram tenuit Sirof de episcopo tempore Regis Edwardi, quo mortuo dedit episcopus filiam ejus cum hac terra cuidam suo militi, qui et matrem pasceret, et episcopo inde serviret.' i. fol. 173; and see below, Chap. II. § 4 (4); Chap. III. § 3.

[3] 'Si quis baronum vel aliorum hominum meorum filiam suam nuptum tradere voluerit sive sororem sive neptim sive cognatam, mecum inde loquatur; sed neque ego aliquid de suo pro hac licentia accipiam, neque defendam ei quin eam det, excepto si eam vellet jungere inimico meo. Et si mortuo barone sive alio homine meo filia haeres remanserit, illam dabo consilio baronum meorum cum terra sua. Et si mortuo viro uxor ejus remanserit et sine liberis fuerit, dotem suam et maritationem habebit, et eam non dabo marito nisi secundum velle suum.'—Charter of Liberties of Henry I, c. 3; Stubbs, Select Charters, p. 100. By the Ordonnances of St. Lewis (ch. 63, Isambert, ii. p. 433) it appears that the right of the lord to a veto on marriage only existed in the case of the daughter of a tenant after the death of the father.

[4] According to Blackstone (ii. p. 71) the extension of the right of marriage to males was the result of a strained construction of a clause in Magna Charta (see below, Chap. III. § 3), but there is evidence of the right being exercised as early as, if not earlier than, the year 1193. See Pollock and Maitland, Hist. of Eng. Law, i. pp. 305, 306.

One of the most valuable of the lord's rights was that of escheat, or the right of having the lands of the tenant on failure of his heirs. This right arises directly from the relation of lord and tenant. The tenant is conceived as having only an *estate* in the lands—an interest which though it may be capable of descending to heirs, *in infinitum*, was something short of absolute ownership. The lord has a possibility of the lands reverting to him, which the tenant cannot defeat.

Such are the main characteristics of the relation of lord and tenant in chivalry. It does not appear that in early times there was any difference, except in the leading feature of military service, between the rights of the king and of any mesne lord. The law as to aids, reliefs, marriage, and wardship was the same in both cases [1].

§ 3. *Development of the Manorial System.*

It has been said that before the Conquest large districts of land were held by persons or corporations, the dwellers upon which, holding beneficially plots of land, usually of small size, were bound to render services, either in money, kind, or labour, to the lord or supreme landowner of the district. The probable connexion of these districts with the Teutonic mark has already been alluded to [2]. It is probable that the Conquest wrought but little immediate change in the relation of such persons to their lord. A Norman lord might be substituted for a Saxon, but the dues and services would substantially continue the same. We now find that these districts receive the name *maneria*, or manors [3]. In Domesday the words *mansio*, *villa*, *manerium* [4] are synonymous. After the Conquest England is

[1] It appears that in later times special rights were claimed by the king, which were not claimable by mesne lords. Of these the principal were primer seisins and fines on alienation. Blackstone, ii. 66, 71.

[2] See Freeman, Norman Conq. v. p. 460, &c.

[3] The earliest appearance of the word is in the reign of Edward the Confessor, who was fond of introducing Norman language and customs. See Ellis, General Introduction to Domesday, p. 225.

[4] Fleta (temp. Edward I), lib. vi. cap. 51, carefully distinguishes between *mansio*, *villa*, and *manerium*. *Mansio* consists of a single house or habitation

CHAP. I. SECT. II. § 3.

parcelled out into manors varying greatly in size; having as a rule fixed boundaries, often coinciding, as is still the case at the present day, with the boundaries of the parish. In some cases manors were diminished or added to, and new manors created [1]. Probably however there was no great addition after the Conquest to the number of manors [2].

It has already been seen that, although the word 'manor' is of Norman introduction, substantially the relation of lord of a manor and his tenants existed before the Conquest. It is probable however that the idea of the legal relation between the lord and the smaller holders of land within the manor received more exact definition at the hands of Norman lawyers and justices [3]. The lord is regarded in his relation to those below him as lord of the soil; in relation to the king or superior lord he is regarded as tenant. He stands in the same relation to the land of the district as the king fills in relation to the land of the whole country. *Prima facie* all rights over the land within the district which are not claimed by any individual are regarded as vested in the lord. The free holders of land become his tenants; he is not only lord of his men, but lord of the land, he is entitled to escheat on failure of the

(*nulli vicina*). *Villa* implies the existence of several habitations near each other. Each of these includes the tenements appertaining to or usually held with them. A *manerium* may consist of several *villae*, or of a single *villa*. But a *villa* cannot be more extensive than a manor, though it may comprise many *parochiae*. The word '*villa*' was always used in writs to express the district where the lands in question in the action lay. See specimen below, Chap. II. § 2; Glanvill, lib. i. c. 6.

[1] See Sir H. Ellis, General Introduction, p. 234, &c.

[2] This is probably to be accounted for by the history of manors. A manor court owed its existence to long-established custom, the creation of a new court was probably regarded as beyond the power even of the crown. See Coke, Copyholder, xxxi: 'Hence it is that the king himself cannot create a perfect manor at the present day, for such things as receive their perfection by the continuance of time come not within the compass of the king's prerogative.' As to the effect of the statute Quia Emptores (18 Edw. I) see below, Chap. IV. § 5.

[3] It is significant that the word 'barones' in Domesday means not so much great territorial lords, as the justices of the king. The title was perpetuated in the Barons of the Exchequer until abolished for the future by the Judicature Act 1873. See Ellis, General Introduction, i. p. 44.

tenants' heirs, the rights of pasturage on the unoccupied lands enjoyed by the inhabitants of the district come to be regarded as *jura in alieno solo*—rights exercised over the land the ownership of which is vested in the lord. It must be remembered that the king is not only the supreme but the largest landowner in the country. He is lord of many manors in various districts. What is said therefore of the relation of tenants to their lords must be understood to apply also to the king when he is lord of the manor.

The holders of land within the manor may, for the purposes of legal history, be conveniently divided into the following classes. First, the tenants in knight-service or in chivalry, whose tenure must, if the views above stated be correct, have originated since the Conquest by grant, or commendation involving a regrant. The characteristics of this tenure have already been sufficiently detailed. Secondly, there are the freemen, bound to render service, other than military service, in money, produce, attendance at the lord's court, or labour; or rather, as they would be called after the Conquest, free tenants holding by such services. In Domesday we find these tenants spoken of as *sochemanni*, *socmanni*, or *liberi socmanni*[1]. The services to which they were bound seem to have been usually fixed or certain, and not capable of being exacted arbitrarily by the lord, such as the rendering of a certain

[1] The derivation of the word has given rise to much controversy. The generally accepted derivation is from 'soc,' an old word meaning a ploughshare, the socage tenant being bound to agricultural service. But this was far from being universally the case; probably in early times it was the exception rather than the rule. There can be little question that the word is connected with *soca*, *socn*, 'jurisdiction,' from the Anglo-Saxon *secan*, 'to seek.' The free landholders had probably by the time of the Conquest been brought nearly universally into the condition of persons owing suit or attendance at the court of some great man. Thus the *sochemanni* are probably the free suitors or attendants (*secta*, *sequor*) of the lord's court, who came in process of time to be regarded as tenants holding in *socage*, by the tenure of such suit or service. These tenants were usually brought under the obligation of rendering some fixed rent or service, and hence the later conception of the essential characteristic of socage tenure. See Stubbs, Const. Hist. i. p. 273. See further as to the position of these socmen Vinogradoff, Villainage in England, pp. 196–203.

amount of agricultural service, or paying a fixed rent in money or produce. Sometimes a free tenant would only be bound by the oath of fealty. It seems that in fact the line between the services rendered by free tenants and by the non-free was in many cases not clearly marked [1]. They were doubtless regulated by local customs, and in some cases free men would be bound to render base services. The important thing was the status of the person rendering the services, not the service rendered. In process of time the nature of the services rendered, especially the characteristic of fixity or certainty, came to be regarded as the mark of a distinct species of freehold tenure called free socage.

Socage tenure is thus described by Littleton, who wrote in the reign of Edward IV [2]:—'Tenure in socage is where the tenant holdeth of his lord the tenancy by certain service for all manner of services, so that the service be not knight's service. As where a man holdeth his land of his lord by fealty and certain rent for all manner of services; or else where a man holdeth his land by homage, fealty and certain rent for all manner of services; or where a man holdeth his land by homage and fealty for all manner of services; for homage by itself maketh not knight's service.'

It seems that the changes in the direction of feudalism wrought by the Conquest affected the small free proprietors far less than the lords of great districts. Such of them as had not already become 'men' of some lord no doubt speedily entered into the condition of tenants; but they retained to a great extent, and in some localities almost entirely, their ancient customs.

[1] No doubt there was often a tendency to depress the free *socmannus* to a condition of serfdom; or at all events to require from him services unworthy of a free man. Instances of the oppression of free socmen are given by Vinogradoff, Villainage in England, p. 204. We find a distinction between free socage and villein socage; the latter being the tenure where the services, though certain, are such as are unworthy of a free man. A tenant holding by such services would in the time of Bracton (see below, Chap. III. § 13) not lose his status as a free man, but would hold by base tenure.

[2] Littleton, Tenures, sect. 117. Sir E. Coke's translation.

The chief characteristics of socage tenure were, (1) on the death of tenant in socage the land, if '*antiquitus divisum*,' descends to all the sons. This was the case in Glanvill's time [1], but under the influence of Norman lawyers the rule of primogeniture had become general in the next century, except in the case of the Kentish tenure of gavelkind [2]; and in other localities where special customs retained their hold.

(2) The socage tenant is free from the obligation to military service by reason of tenure, nor is he always bound to render homage to his lord. The oath of fealty is universal, and sometimes constitutes his sole service. Whatever additional service may be due from him must be fixed and certain; the most usual was a fixed payment of rent.

(3) Some of the 'incidents' of tenure by knight-service had their counterpart in tenure in socage. The socage tenant was liable to aids and relief. The latter usually took the form of double rent for the first year after the tenant's death [3]. Tenant in socage was however free from the oppressive incidents of feudal wardship and marriage; the guardian in socage was the next of kin who could not inherit, and was accountable at the termination of the wardship for the profits of the lands [4].

An important class of socage tenants were those who held

[1] See below, Chap. II. § 6.

[2] Before the Conquest, gafolcund or gavelkind lands meant simply 'rent-paying' lands. Kemble, Introd. to Cod. Dipl. i. lxi. Gavelkind retained the characteristics of Anglo-Saxon law in a more perfect form than any other species of property in land. See Blackstone, ii. p. 84. Gavelkind lands (1) descended to all the sons equally, (2) were usually devisable by will, (3) did not escheat in case of attainder and execution for felony, (4) could be aliened by the tenant at the age of fifteen. The first and last of these characteristics still distinguish gavelkind lands from other freeholds. How it was that these customs survived is a question of great difficulty; possibly the very fact that the hand of the Conqueror fell so heavily and at so early a date on the great men of the county operated to preserve the old customs amongst the poorer freeholders, whose insignificance was their best protection. (See Freeman, iv. p. 34.)

[3] See the Statute 28 Edw. I stat. 1.

[4] According to Littleton, sec. 118, 'Every tenure which is not tenure in chivalry is a tenure in socage.' Bracton, on the other hand, distinguishes socage tenure from tenure by uncertain but non-military services. See lib. ii. cap. 16; below, Chap. III. § 11.

CHAP. I. SECT. II. § 3.

lands of lords by this tenure in towns. By the time of Glanvill this class of tenants had obtained the distinctive name of burgage tenants [1]. Besides the above-mentioned characteristics of socage tenure these burgage tenants retained in many cases local customs, especially as to the descent of lands, and as to devising them by will. One of the most remarkable of these is styled borough English, which is thus described by Littleton: 'Some boroughs have such a custom that if a man have issue many sons and dieth, the youngest son shall inherit all the tenements which were his father's within the same borough as heir unto his father by force of the custom the which is called borough English [2].' By the statute 12 Car. II. c. 24, tenures in chivalry, with all their peculiar incidents, were abolished and turned into 'free and common socage [3].'

When land was held of the king not by military service, but under the obligation to render some small thing 'belonging to war,' as, for instance, to 'yield to him yearly a bow, or a sword, or a dagger, or a knife, or a pair of gilt spurs, or an arrow or divers arrows,' this was called tenure by petit serjeanty [4].

Tenants of land holding by any one of the above-mentioned tenures—*libera eleemosyna* or frankalmoign, grand serjeanty, knight-service, socage, burgage, and petit serjeanty—were regarded as free holders having an estate or interest in lands worthy of a freeman, and involving no service derogatory to the status of freedom. Some time before the reign of Henry II, but apparently not so early as Domesday [5], the expression

[1] See Glanvill, lib. xii. cap. 3; below, Chap. II. § 2.

[2] Littleton, sec. 165. For the history of this term, and an account of the extent and probable origin of this and similar customs of descent, see Elton, Origins of English History, chap. viii. p. 183, &c., and Pollock and Maitland, Hist. of Eng. Law, ii. p. 277.

[3] See Chap. IX.

[4] Littleton, sec. 159. For the origin of the distinction into grand and petit serjeanty, see Pollock and Maitland, Hist. of Eng. Law, i. p. 304.

[5] It is characteristic of the history of the growth of tenure that in Domesday (if the index is correct) we hear of different classes of tenants, but not of different species of tenure; of *liberi homines*, but not of *liberum*

liberum tenementum was introduced to designate land held by a freeman by a free tenure. Thus freehold tenure is the sum of the rights and duties which constitute the relation of a free tenant to his lord. The mode of granting or conveying *liberum tenementum* was by the process called a feoffment (*feoffari, feoffamentum*). The grantor is called the feoffor, the grantee the feoffee. Whether or not any formal mode of giving possession of the land granted by the delivery of a clod or some other similar act thereupon had been common among the Anglo-Saxons, is doubtful; but by the time of Henry II we find the two essential elements of a conveyance of a freehold interest in lands were (1) formal delivery of possession (technically called livery of seisin [1]); (2) words accompanying, indicating the nature and extent of the grantee's interest and the services to be rendered for it [2].

Besides the lands of the manor held by free or freehold tenants, the lord retained in his own hands the domain—*terrae dominicales*—portions of which were sometimes let to farmers, and portions cultivated by persons bound to render agricultural services for the benefit of the lord [3]. The Domesday of St. Paul's leaves little doubt that there were frequently, especially upon ecclesiastical lands, *farmers* holding land under conventions or covenants, and rendering for it rent in kind or money. These would probably differ from the tenants in socage, for they would not be bound to the lord by homage or fealty; they would simply hold under the covenant or lease. Specimens of these leases are given in the Domesday of St. Paul's; they are usually for the life of the tenant. The convention was merely binding as between the tenant and

tenementum; of *milites*, but not of tenure *per militiam*; of *socmanni*, but not of *socagium*; of *villani*, but not of *villenagium*.

[1] The proper meaning of the word 'seisin' is possession as of freehold; i.e. the possession which a freeholder has.

[2] See the specimen of a charter of feoffment of the time of Henry II given below, p. 61.

[3] If the lord retained no lands in his own hands, but all the lands within the manor were held by free tenants, he was said to have a seignory, or a seignory in gross.

CHAP. I. SECT. II. § 3. the lord, it created no estate as between the tenant and third persons. In later times a lease of land for life becomes a freehold interest held by socage or other tenure; a lease for years becomes a new species of rights over land, called leasehold interests or chattels real.

Besides these, there are the non-free inhabitants, a large and important class, by whose forced service the domain of the lord, that is, the land not held of him by freemen rendering free services, or by farmers, was mainly cultivated. We find a variety of names applied in Domesday to this servile peasantry (e.g. *villani*[1], *nativi, custumarii, servi, cotarii bordarii*). These names appear to fall into four classes, pointing respectively to social standing, economic condition, difference of services, and differences of holding. Thus *villanus* frequently, and *nativus* always, points to the status of servitude, *cotarius* or *bordarius*[2] to the fact of the tenant's holding being only a croft without any share in the common fields, *custumarius* to the certainty of the services. But in course of time, under the influence of legal theory, all these different classes are reduced to one level, the terms *villanus, nativus, servus,* being applied indifferently to any person belonging to the non-free classes, and the term *bordarius* passing almost altogether out of use[3]. These non-free inhabitants were *adscripti glebae,* tied to the land; they could not remove from one manor to another. They seem to have held plots of land of considerable extent, and the very fact of their not being removable, of son succeeding father in the occupation of his plot, and in the obligation to render services, no doubt gave rise to various customs, or helped to preserve customs already in existence, such as allowing the tenant's

[1] See the title of the Ely Domesday (Stubbs, Select Charters, p. 86), where it is provided that the inquiry should be based on the oaths of (amongst others) six villani from every villa. The villeins on the manors in the king's hands at the time of the Survey appear to have usually enjoyed or acquired some peculiar privileges. In later times the copyhold tenants on these manors were called tenants in ancient demesne. See Blackstone, ii. p. 99.

[2] See above, p. 24, note 4.

[3] See Vinogradoff, Villeinage in England, pp. 44–48, and 140-150.

eldest or youngest son, or all his sons in equal shares, to succeed to the father's beneficial interests (usually on making some payment to the lord), recognizing estates of inheritance, for life, or years, allowing the tenant to feed his cattle on the waste, and the like. These customs virtually gave the non-free tenant rights and duties in relation to his lord, and, as will be seen, grew into local laws. If the tenant could not depart from the land, no more could the lord remove him so long as he rendered the service due to the lord[1]. There would be little distinction between the lowest class of freemen and the highest class of the non-free: the one would gradually pass into the other. Freemen sometimes held lands by villein services[2]. This relation of the non-free inhabitants to the land gradually passes into an interest recognized by custom under the name of *villenagium*, and finally into a tenure protected by law under the name of copyhold or customary tenure[3].

Such were the various phases of the relation of lord and tenant which took root in the interval between the Conquest and the reign of Henry II. It remains to notice what has from the date of the complete constitution of manors been

[1] 'Cil qui custiuent la terre ne deit lum trauailer se de leur droite cense, noun le leist a seignurage de partir les cultiueurs de lur terre pur tant cum il pussent le dreit servise faire.' 'Those who cultivate the land ought not to be harassed beyond their proper fixed amount; nor is it lawful for the lords to remove the cultivators from the land so long as they are able to render the due service.'—Laws of William the Conqueror, xxix; Thorpe, Ancient Laws and Institutes, p. 480. See also laws xxx, xxxi.

[2] A distinction is found in later law books between villeins regardant and villeins in gross. Though much importance is attached to this distinction by text-writers (see Coke Lit. 123 b, and Blackstone, ii. p. 93), Vinogradoff (Villeinage in England, pp. 48-55) appears to have established that there was no real distinction between the status of the villein regardant and of the villein in gross. Sometimes, no doubt, the lord would lay claim or prove his title to the villein by reference to the fact of his being attached to a particular manor, in which case he would be spoken of as a villein regardant, but there would be nothing to prevent the lord from claiming or dealing with the same villein apart from the manor, in which case he would be spoken of as a villein in gross.

[3] As to the condition of the non-free classes after the Conquest, see Stubbs, Const. Hist. i. pp. 426-431.

CHAP. I. SECT. II. § 3.

their most important characteristic—the manorial courts. When a large district comprising several manors was held by a single lord in whom was vested by grant or long usage the complete jurisdiction of the hundred, the district was called a *liberty* or *honour*[1]. In such a case there might be, and usually was, only one court held for the whole; but that court was regarded as the court of each several manor[2]. The honour is merely the aggregate of several manors, it has no distinct or separate organization[3]. It is therefore only necessary to inquire into the constitution and nature of the manor courts.

The principal manorial court is the Court Baron, or the assembly of the freehold tenants of the lord. Besides the Court Baron, in many manors there is also a Court Leet, which is sometimes held with the Court Baron; and wherever, as is usually the case at the present day, there are copyholders[4] within the manor, there is also a third court, called the Customary Court. This court too is often held with a Court Baron. It is, however, probable that this classification is due to the lawyers of the thirteenth or fourteenth century, and that in early times no distinction between the different courts was recognized[5].

'A court baron,' says Sir Edward Coke, 'is the chief prop and pillar of a manor, which no sooner faileth, but the manor falleth to the ground[6].' The same passage gives Coke's view of the history of these courts: 'For when the ancient kings of this realm, who had all the lands of England in demesne, did confer great quantities of land upon some great personages, with liberty to parcel the land out to other inferior tenants, reserving such duties and services as they thought convenient,

[1] See Assize of Clarendon, c. 9, Stubbs, Select Charters, 143; Magna Carta, c. 43; ib. p. 302.

[2] Scriven on Copyholds, i. p. 5.

[3] Stubbs, Const. Hist. i. p. 400.

[4] See Chap. V. § 6.

[5] See Maitland, Introduction to 'Select Pleas in Manorial Courts' Selden Society), Vol. II. p. xvi and Note A.

[6] Coke, Copyholder, xxxi.

and to keep courts where they might redress misdemeanours within their precincts, punish offences committed by their tenants, and decide and debate controversies arising within their jurisdiction; these courts were termed court barons.'

Thus, according to the older explanation, the manor courts, like the manor itself, resulted originally from a grant by the crown. Probably, however, though a grant may in fact in many cases have added to the powers and jurisdiction of the manorial courts, the court baron is primarily the successor of the ancient assembly of the village or township. When the district in which the township is situated comes under the power of a great man by express grant or otherwise, the court of the township becomes the court of the great man. It has been seen that it was common to acquire exemptions for particular districts from the court of the hundred, and this must have become almost universal, except in cases where, as seems to have sometimes happened, the hundred court itself came to be amalgamated with the court of some great lord [1]. Thus either by the creation of a franchise exempt from the jurisdiction of the hundred court, or by the amalgamation of the hundred with the manorial courts, the jurisdiction civil and criminal exercised by the court of the hundred comes to be exercised in the manorial courts. The court baron exercised civil jurisdiction especially in matters relating to the freehold lands within the manor [2]. Criminal jurisdiction was amongst the functions of the court leet, and depended on a real or supposed grant from the crown. It has already been seen that the later Anglo-Saxon grants usually contained words expressly granting the right of jurisdiction [3], probably referring to the criminal jurisdiction exercised by the court leet.

The manor courts therefore may be regarded as representing one side of the old assembly of the township, in which the jurisdiction properly belonging to the hundred court has come to be vested. The constitution of the court baron is con-

[1] Stubbs, Const. Hist. i. p. 400.

[2] See below, Chap. II. § 2.

[3] See above, p. 14.

CHAP. I. SECT. II. § 3.

sistent with this view. The freemen, or rather, as they have now come to be, the freehold tenants of the manor, are the judges of the court; the lord or his steward is simply the president. Thus the continuance of a sufficient number of freehold tenants within the manor is essential to the maintenance of the court baron, and so to the continuance of the manor itself. The functions of this court were partly administrative, partly judicial. The business relating to the interests of the various dwellers within the manor was here transacted; probably in some manors the customs of the manor would from time to time be declared in this court, grants of the waste sanctioned, rights of common regulated. The judicial functions of this court varied in different manors. The court leet held either separately or in conjunction with the court baron had jurisdiction over crimes committed within the manor, and the court baron over civil suits arising within the same limits, especially over all matters relating to the freehold. This jurisdiction however was gradually curtailed and overridden by the judicial organization carried into effect by Henry II.

In some respects the characteristics of the leet, even more than those of the court baron, seem to carry us back to the earliest form of political organization [1]. The leet is the assembly of the whole community, and seems to date from a time when that community was small, and could gather under a tree, on the side of a hill, or upon a village green [2], and transact business affecting the interests of all its members. The principal matters dealt with in the leet were the view of frank-pledge [3], the presentment and punishment of offences

[1] 'The leet is the most ancient court in the land.' Year Book, 7 Hen. VI, 12 b.

[2] Ritson on Courts Leet, p. ix.

[3] The style of the court in later times is the 'view of frank-pledge.' This was the production of the pledges or persons responsible for each other keeping the peace. Frank-pledge (A.S. frið-borh) ought properly to have been rendered 'pledges of peace.' The Normans however seem to have mistaken *frið*, 'peace,' for *fri*, 'free,' and hence the erroneous translation.

and nuisances, the regulation of the quality and prices of provisions, particularly of bread and ale. The leet is said to be derived out of the Sheriff's 'tourn.' The conception of the lawyers is that the organization of the counties and hundreds having been arranged by king Alfred, a portion of the jurisdiction of the courts of the county and hundred was at some time or other granted by the crown to the various lords of manors. As has been seen above, it is probably more correct to describe all the species of manorial courts as the successors of the old Teutonic moots or assemblies, which have by grant or usurpation obtained for their suitors immunity from the regular jurisdictions, and by acquiring in process of time different functions have come to be regarded as different courts. In some respects the court leet retained in the most marked form the traces of its origin. It has always been regarded as the court of the residents within the district, not of the tenants of the manor [1], and the matters of which it takes cognizance are for the most part not connected with tenure [2].

The customary court does not come to be of importance till copyhold or customary tenure has become established, and the notice of it may therefore be deferred [3].

Thus the great features of the period extending from the Conquest to the beginning of the reign of Henry II are the establishment of the notion of tenure and the development of the manorial system. Every free tenant (and none other is regarded as having a legal interest in the land at all) holds of and in relation to a lord. The lord who is not in actual possession has a seignory, which he in his turn holds of a superior, till the head of the system—the king—is reached.

[1] So far is this carried that a stranger passing by may be compelled to serve on the leet jury. The fact of his being found within the district is deemed sufficient residence. Ritson, p. 56.

[2] The jurisdiction of the leet was probably cut down by the 42nd chapter of Magna Carta (ed. 1217, Stubbs, p. 346), by which it is provided that the sheriff is to make his tourn in the hundred twice only in the year, and that the view of frank-pledge is to take place only at Michaelmas.

[3] See Chap. V. § 6.

CHAP. I. SECT. III. § 1.

The gradual definition of the respective interests of lord and tenant, the development of the various kinds of interests in lands, their distinction in point of duration, joint ownership, and so forth, belongs to the period when the constitution was so far organized as to admit of the action of regular tribunals having regard to precedent and authority. The reign of Henry II is the period to which the origin of the English law of land in its modern form must be referred. It will be seen in the next chapter how great an advance had been made before the end of that reign in the direction of the separation of law and custom, and of establishing fundamental legal principles on a firm basis.

SECTION III.

Original Documents.

§ 1. *Anglo-Saxon Grants of Bookland.*

The following three charters are taken from Kemble's Codex Diplomaticus Ævi Saxonici, as specimens illustrating the main characteristics of Anglo-Saxon customary law above referred to.

Gift of Lands to a Church by Uuihtræd of Kent.

A.D. 700 or 715.

In nomine Domini Dei nostri Jesu Christi[1]. Ego Uuihtredus rex Cantuariorum prouidens mihi[2] in futuro, decreui dare[3] aliquid

[1] 'A Saxon charter properly so called, and distinguished from a will or the record of a synodal decree, consists of all or some of the following portions: i. the invocation, ii. the proem, iii. the grant, iv. the sanction, v. the date, vi. the teste.' Kemble, Introd. to Cod. Dipl. i. p. ix. Charters frequently begin with 'In nomine Domini,' 'In nomine Domini nostri Jhesu Christi,' &c.

[2] The charter then usually goes on to state some religious ground for the gift. 'As a general rule it may be observed that before the tenth century the proem is comparatively simple, that about that time the influence of the Byzantine court began to be felt, and that from the latter half of that century pedantry and absurdity struggle for the mastery.'—Kemble, Introd. to Cod. Dipl. i. p. x.

[3] No formal words of grant appear to have been required; the usual expressions are, dono, trado, dabo et concedo. 'The granting words are

omnia mihi donanti, et, consilio accepto, bonum uisum est conferre basilicae beatae Mariae genetricis Dei, quae sita est in loco qui dicitur Limingae, terram IIII aratorum quae dicitur Pleghelmestun, cum omnibus ad eandem terram pertinentibus, juxta notissimos terminos etc. . . . . terrulae quoque partem ejusdem Dei genetrici beatae Mariae similiter in perpetuum possidendum perdono, cujus uocabulum est Rumininingseta, ad pastum uidelicet ouium trecentorum, ad australem quippe fluminis quae appellatur Liminaea, terminos uero huius terrulae ideo non ponimus quoniam ab accolis undique certi sunt. Quam donationem meam uolo firmam esse in perpetuum, ut nec ego seu haeredes mei aliquid imminuere praesumant. Quod si aliter temptatum fuerit a qualibet persona sub anathematis interdictione sciat se praeuaricari [1], ad cuius confirmationem pro ignorantia litterarum signum sanctae crucis expressi, et testes idoneos ut subscriberent rogavi, id est Berhtuualdum archiepiscopum uirum uenerabilem.

✠ Ego Berhtuualdus episcopus rogatus consensi et subscripsi.

✠ Signum [2] manus Uuihtredi regis.

✠ Signum manus Æthilburgae reginae.

(Other signatures follow in the same form.—Codex Diplomaticus, i. p. 54, no. xlvii.)

Gift by Oswald, Bishop of Worcester. A.D. 963.

✠ Ego Oswold ergo Christi crismate praesul iudicatus, dominicae incarnationis anno DCCCCLXIII, annuente regi Anglorum

numerous and manifold, and, though part of the formulary, do not appear to be introduced according to any settled and invariable rule. It may be observed of them in general that they are much simpler than the corresponding forms of the Continent, and especially that they show no such strict and formal combinations as those met with in Roman documents. Do, dono, concedo, trado, are the most in use, sometimes singly, sometimes combined; and one noticeable peculiarity is that in place of the present tense do, we usually have the future dabo.'—Kemble, ib. p. xxviii.

[1] A clause threatening terrible consequences, generally excommunication and eternal punishment, to any who do not respect the grant, is the fourth characteristic feature in Anglo-Saxon charters. Kemble observes (Cod. Dipl. i. p. lxv) that 'the exclusively clerical nature of the sanction in Anglo-Saxon charters (even where these are grants by private individuals) is evidence of our being indebted for the forms of these instruments to Roman clergymen.' In the later charters this clause often presents the extreme of extravagance and pedantry in its language.

[2] The charters of the Anglo-Saxons were *signed*, not *sealed*. The use of the seal was introduced by the Normans. See Kemble, Cod. Dipl. i. ci.

CHAP. I. SECT. III. § 1.

Eadgaro Ælfereque Merciorum comite[1], necnon et familiae Wiogornensis aecclesiae, quandam ruris particulam unam uidelicet mansam[2], in loco qui celebri a soliculis nuncupatur æt Heortford uocabulo, cuidam ministro meo nomine Æþelnoð perpetua largitus haereditate, et post vitae suae terminum duobus tantum haeredibus[3] immunem derelinquat, quibus defunctis ecclesiae Dei in Weogorna ceastre restituatur.

(Then follow the boundaries.)

Scripta est haec cartula his testibus consentientibus quorum inferius notantur nomina.

(Then follow the names. — Codex Diplomaticus, ii. p. 399, no. dix.)

CHARTER OF CNUT. A. D. 1033.

☧ REGNANTE imperpetuum Deo et Domino nostro Jhesu Christo, cum cujus imperio hic labentis saeculi prosperitas in adversis successibus sedulo permixta et conturbata cernitur, et omnia uisibilia et desiderabilia ornamenta hujus mundi ab ipsis amatoribus cotidie transeunt, ideo beati quique ac sapientes cum

[1] This grant is made with the assent of the king and of the earl. This seems to have been usual in the grants of bookland by great men. See above, p. 19, and compare the grant by Wulfric, A. D. 947, Cod. Dipl. vol. ii. p. 273.

[2] According to Kemble (Saxons in England, i. p. 92) *mansa*=*familia* as applied to land, an expression for the hide which was enough for the support of a single family, and which varied in different localities: and see Spelman, sub voc., and above, p. 8, note 1.

[3] Kemble has collected (Cod. Dipl. i. p. xxx seq.) various other instances of grants of interests in lands short of absolute and unqualified inheritances. Two of the most remarkable are the following :—'In jus possessionemque sempiternam sibimet ad habendum quamdiu vivat, suoque relinquendum fratre germano diutius superstes si fuerit . . . . et sic semper in illa consanguinitate paternae generationis, sexuque virili, perpetualiter consistat adscripta.' 'Rus etiam hoc modo donatum est, ut suum (? semen) masculum possideat et non femininum : et post obitum prosapiae illius, data sit tam villa quam universa terra, quae in sua potestate est, ad religiosam ecclesiam, quae nuncupatur Eofeshâm.' The case in the text of a grant for life with a further interest to one or two other persons for life, with ultimate reversion to the grantor, is by no means uncommon, especially in leases of church lands. 'An early Anglo-Saxon council had indeed prohibited such grants of a longer term than the life of the grantee, but this, which had probably never been well observed, had fallen into utter desuetude in the tenth century.'—Kemble, Cod. Dipl. i. p. xxxiv. The absence of technical language which prevailed to so great an extent after the Conquest is very remarkable in these grants of limited interests.

his fugitivis saeculi divitiis aeterna et jugiter permansura gaudia caelestis patriae magnopere adipisci properant, iccirco ego Cnut rex Anglorum caeterarumque gentium in circuitu persistentium gubernator et rector, quandam mei proprii juris portionem[1], VII terrae mansas, illo in loco ubi jamdudum solicolae illius regionis nomen imposuerunt Hortun, meo fideli ministro quem noti atque affines Boui appellare solent confirmo haereditatem[2], quatinus ille bene perfruatur ac perpetualiter possideat, quamdiu Deus per suam mirabilem misericordiam uitam illi et uitalem spiritum concedere uoluerit, deinde namque sibi succedenti cuicumque libuerit cleronomi jure haereditario derelinquat, ceu supradiximus, in aeternam haereditatem. Maneat igitur hoc nostrum immobile donum aeterna libertate jocundum cum universis quae rite ad eundem locum pertinere dinoscuntur, tam in magnis quam in modicis rebus, in campis, pascuis, pratis, siluis, riuulis, aquarumque cursibus, excepto quod communi labore quod omnibus liquide patet, uidelicet expeditione, pontis constructione, arcisve munitione[3]. Si autem tempore contigerit aliquo quempiam hominum aliquem antiquiorem librum contra istius libri libertatem producere pro nichilo computetur. Si quis autem tetri daemonis instinctu hoc nostrum decretum infringere uoluerit, sit ipse a sanctae Dei aecclesiae consortio separatus, et infernalibus aeternaliter flammis cum Juda Christi proditore cruciandus, nisi hic prius digna satisfactione poenituerit quod contra nostrum deliquit decretum. Acta vero est praesens pargameni scedula anno dominicae incarnationis millesimo XXXIII, indictione uero prima[4]. Istis terminis supradicta terra circumgirata est.

(The boundaries follow in Anglo-Saxon.)

Ista cartula illorum testium testimonio est corroborata quorum hic uocabula litteris uidentur caraxata. ✠ Ego Cnut gubernator sceptri huius insulae hanc nostri decreti breuiunculam almae crucis notamine muniens roboraui. ✠ Ego Æðelnoð Dorouernensis archiepiscopus consensi et subscripsi. ✠ Ego Ælfric archiepiscopus corroboraui. ✠ Ego Brihtwold episcopus confirmaui. ✠ Ego Ælfwine episcopus, etc.—(Codex Diplomaticus, vi. p. 180, no. MCCCXVIII.)

[1] See above, p. 17.

[2] It should be observed that even in this more elaborate form of charter there is no technical form of words used to express the nature of the estate which the grantee is to take or the manner in which it is to be held.

[3] See above, p. 13.

[4] As to the indictions or cycles of fifteen years, see Kemble, Cod. Dipl. i. p. lxxvii.

§ 2. *A Feoffment in Fee of the time of Henry II.*

A comparison of the following document with the Anglo-Saxon grants above given will illustrate the main features of the change which took place in the law of land after the Conquest. It should be especially observed that the charter purports only to be evidence of a grant which had already taken place. The grant of the freehold is effected by actual delivery of the possession, the words written or spoken point out the nature and extent of the interest taken. Then follow the words *sibi et haeredibus suis*, which have now a technical signification, and denote that the interest to be taken by the grantee is a fee[1], or an estate of inheritance; in other words, an estate descendible to the heirs of the grantee so long as any are in existence, as opposed to an estate given to last only during the grantee's own life. Then follow the words which form the great characteristic of grants of land for the period extending from the reign of Henry II to the eighteenth year of Edward I, '*tenendum de me et haeredibus meis.*' There is no longer the conception that property in land is absolute, the property is divided between the tenant in actual possession and his lord, or if there be more than one superior lord, between the tenant, the mesne lord, and the king, each 'holding of' the other. If any subordinate interest, say for instance that of the tenant in possession, is eliminated, the whole of such interest at once devolves upon his immediate superior. So if the heirs of the tenant fail, the land 'escheats' to the immediately superior lord. Thus in consequence of this relation between tenant and lord, the tenant's interest is regarded as something less than the whole property—as an *estate* of greater or less extent *in point of duration*, for instance as lasting only for his life, or till all his legitimate

[1] Fee has now two senses: (1) it means land holden of a lord, as opposed to land owned alodially = fief; (2) an estate of inheritance, as opposed to an estate for life—*feodum* as opposed to *liberum tenementum*, also used in a secondary sense for an estate for life. *Feodum* or fee usually bears the second of the above senses.

heirs have failed. Henceforth therefore the law speaks of *estates*, and not of property or ownership in land. The notion of tenure also involves the notion of correlative rights and duties existing between the lord and his tenant, of which the service reserved in the grant is the principal. The service mentioned in the following grant is that which is regularly due for a single knight's fee [1]. The latter part of the charter follows the character of the forms in use before the Conquest.

FEOFFMENT IN FEE.

RICARDUS de Luci omnibus hominibus suis atque amicis Francis et Anglis tam praesentibus quam futuris totius Angliae salutem. Sciatis me dedisse et concessisse Radulfo Britono Terram Chiggewillae cum omnibus pertinentibus eidem terrae sibi et haeredibus suis [2] ad tenendum de me et de haeredibus meis in feodo et haereditate per servicium unius militis [3]. Quare volo et firmiter praecipio quod idem Radulfus et haeredes sui terram illam teneant in bene et in pace et libere et quiete et honorifice, in bosco et plano in pratis et pasturis in aquis in viis et semitis et in omnibus aliis rebus quae terrae illi pertinent. Testibus, etc.— Madox, Formulare Anglicanum, no. cclxxxviii.)

[1] See more on this point, below, Chap. III. § 11.

[2] For the effect of these words see below, Chap. III. § 15.

[3] That is, the service of a single knight or fully-armed horseman to serve at his own expense for forty days in the year (Stubbs, Const. Hist. i. p. 432). This is the usual form for expressing that the lands are to be held by actual military service. The minimum of land constituting a knight's fee seems by this time to have been fixed at the area which was worth twenty pounds annual value. See Stubbs, Const. Hist. i. p. 264. For an account of the probable history of the gradual introduction of knights' fees, see Stubbs, ib. p. 262, and above, pp. 34, 39.

CHAPTER II

STATE OF THE LAW RELATING TO LAND IN THE REIGN OF HENRY II

CHAP. II. IN the preceding chapter an attempt has been made to trace the working of the various elements of which the common law relating to land is composed. It has been seen that the convergence of distinct streams of customary law, aided by the process of conquest and settlement of the land and the growth of political organization under a powerful ruler, had resulted in the establishment of a general body of law prevailing throughout the country, with some variations in particular localities.

This body of law may properly be called customary law. It rests for the most part not on any distinct enactment of a legislator or body of legislators, nor does it appeal for its authority to recorded judicial decisions. At the same time it fixes the rights and duties of the inhabitants of the country, it is recognized and enforced by the authority of the assemblies and tribunals. In this early stage of legal history law and custom cannot be distinguished. That a practice is customary is all the justification which would be required if its legality were called in question[1]. In

[1] See Maine, Village Communities, p. 68.

a maturer state of society the distinction between law and custom comes to be clearly marked, though the unhappy phraseology of our legal text-books has tended to obscure the matter by identifying custom with the common law [1]. CHAP. II.

According to the analysis of Mr. Austin [2], which however is applicable only to a civilized community after it has attained to regular legislative and judicial institutions, positive law properly so called may be referred to two sources—direct legislation, and the action of the tribunals. In other words, laws are made either directly in the shape of general rules imposed by or under the authority of the supreme power in the community, or they are made indirectly by the tribunals in deciding upon particular cases.

The latter class of laws are sometimes called judge-made, or judiciary laws. If Mr. Austin's view that judicial decisions are properly ranked as one of the sources or efficient causes of positive law be accepted, the following may suffice as an account of the mode in which they produce their effect. Inasmuch as the decision of a particular case in a civilized community depends upon some general rule, that is, rests on the assumption that a righteous judge would always give the same decision under the same circumstances, every decision either consists in the application of an actually pre-existing rule of law, or proceeds as if there had been such a rule, when in fact there was none. In the latter case the tribunal in effect makes a law for itself *ex post facto*. Add to this the tendency in every civilized community that one decision should become the precedent for another, in other words, that a rule once applied by a tribunal of competent authority should be acted upon by other tribunals in similar

[1] See Blackstone, i. p. 68. On the distinction between custom and law, and the inaccuracy involved in speaking of custom as a source of law, see Austin, Jurisprudence (Campbell's edition), pp. 553–560. Mr. Austin's analysis should however be taken with the qualification suggested by Sir H. Maine (Village Communities, pp. 66–68), that it is applicable only to a mature system of jurisprudence, and not to law in its earlier stages.

[2] See Lectures xxviii, xxix, xxxvii.

 circumstances, and we have the account of what is called judicial legislation [1]. Suppose, for instance, that there is no fixed rule whether, on the decease of a tenant in fee simple, his grandson (son of a predeceased elder son) or his younger son succeeds to the lands. The question arises for judicial decision. The tribunal decides (no matter on what ground, whether adopting a custom, or following some rule of some other system of law, or on considerations of general expediency) that the grandson is entitled in preference to his uncle. This solemn decision by a competent tribunal is recorded, and becomes a precedent for other similar decisions. Thus a rule of law is created. It is impossible to say precisely at what point a rule thus acted upon by a tribunal becomes a rule of law. Sometimes a single decision is sufficient, sometimes it requires a series of similar decisions before it can be asserted that the principle forming the ground of the decision has been erected into a rule of law. The simplicity or complexity of the proposition, the weight and eminence of the tribunal, the circumstances attending the decision, all influence the conditions requisite for the establishment of the proposition as a rule of law. When however it is for all practical purposes certain that a definite rule, having been the ground of judicial decision on one or more occasions, will be again acted upon by the tribunals whenever occasion arises, the rule may be said to have become a rule of law. It may have existed previously as a rule of custom, or a rule of a foreign system of law, but its adoption by the tribunals gives it a new and different character, and causes it to take its place amongst the laws of the land.

[1] Judicial decisions are usually spoken of in the text-books (see the chapter in Blackstone, vol. i. Of the Laws of England) not as the source of laws, but as evidence of a preexisting law. The examination of this view, which would at the present day have few theoretical supporters, though its practical influence is still considerable, would occupy too much space. The reader is therefore referred to the lectures of Mr. Austin mentioned above.

It is not necessary here to inquire whether this analysis of judiciary law is applicable in equal degree to all systems of law. It appears at all events to afford a sufficiently accurate description of the main process by which in our own country law customary has been transmuted into law positive. The early date at which this process began, and the rapid and effective mode in which the concentrated action of the courts was brought to bear so as to create a uniform body of law, may be traced in the extracts from Glanvill and Bracton given in this and the next chapter.

As has been said above, positive law properly so called does not arise until a community has progressed sufficiently to have attained to settled legislative and judicial institutions. Accordingly in our own country we find the first existence of a body of law properly so called, as opposed to a floating mass of custom, contemporaneous with the completion of the political organization. The reign of Henry II is the starting-point of the history of modern English law, as well as of the modern English constitution.

Of the two sources of law above noticed, direct or proper legislation, and indirect or judicial legislation, the field of direct legislation, or of Statute Law, is as yet very limited. There are however various important legislative acts during this reign. But with the exception of the great changes made in the procedure of the tribunals, especially in the institution of the grand assize and recognitions [1], they have little bearing on the law relating to land.

It is to the organization of the judicial institutions of the country that the rapid development of the Common Law [2]

[1] See extracts from Glanvill, below, §§ 2 and 9.

[2] The expression Common Law will henceforward be frequently employed. It must be borne in mind that the expression is used (1) in opposition to Statute Law, (2) in opposition to Equity, (3) in opposition to Civil or Roman Law. The Common Law is (1) that portion of the present or former law of the land which does not rest on Statute; the judicial decisions of the Courts of Common Law, the King's Bench, Common Pleas, Exchequer, as they existed up to November 1, 1875, when the new

CHAP. II. relating to land which took place in the interval between the beginning of the reign of Henry II and the end of that of Henry III is owing. It has been seen, in the preceding chapter, that in the various manors the manor court had jurisdiction over questions arising within the manor. But supreme over all was the King's Court (Curia Regis), which partook of the character of the supreme Court Baron, and was also the chief national legislative and judicial institution of the country [1]. The king, in his combined capacity of sovereign of the nation and lord paramount of all the land, asserted his right to adjudicate by himself or his representatives [2] upon all questions relating to the freehold, and to control the local jurisdictions of the lords of the manors. The jurisdiction of the royal or central court was exercised partly at Westminster or elsewhere, where the king's court happened to be in attendance upon the king's person, partly by the organization of *itinera* or progresses by members of the Curia Regis for judicial and other purposes throughout the country [3].

Thus there came into existence regular judicial institutions with all their concomitants. The practice of recording decisions [4] given by men who became in fact professional judges,

arrangement and consolidation of the Courts by the Judicature Acts 1873 and 1875 took effect, are according to Blackstone the evidence, according to Austin the source, of the Common Law. (2) In its second sense, Common Law is that portion of the law which was administered in the former Common Law tribunals, and thus is opposed to Equity, or the law administered by the Court of Chancery before Nov. 1, 1875, and to the law administered in the Ecclesiastical tribunals and their successors (the Courts of Probate and Divorce), and the Court of Admiralty, which also on Nov. 1, 1875, ceased to have a separate existence, and were succeeded by the Probate Division of the High Court of Justice. (3) When opposed to Civil or Roman Law, Common Law includes Equity.

[1] As to the Curia Regis, its composition and relation to the Council, see Stubbs, Select Charters, p. 22; and for the formation of a regular Supreme Court of Justice by Henry II, see the extract from Benedictus Abbas (i. 207) in Stubbs, ib. p. 131, and see Const. Hist. i. pp. 598–604.

[2] See the form of writ given below, § 2.

[3] See, for an account of the history of these circuits, Stubbs, Select Charters, p. 141, and Const. Hist. i. p. 604.

[4] The Rotuli Curiae Regis, the earliest law reports at present printed, begin in the sixth year of the reign of Richard I.

the discussion and sifting of points of law, the desire to attain to uniformity of legal rules throughout the country, are all characteristic of the time of Henry II. CHAP. II.

Amongst the causes of the rapid development of the Common Law as a system should be taken into account the powerful effect upon men's imagination of the Roman Law[1]. There can be little question that acquaintance with a mature system of foreign law must have greatly accelerated the process of simplifying and systematizing floating custom, and of bringing the body of native customary law into some resemblance to a regular *corpus juris*. The direct effect of the Roman Law upon the law of England is not however very conspicuous till the reign of Henry III, when its influence appears in almost every line of Bracton's great treatise.

The connexion of the growth of the Common Law with the development of judicial institutions is strikingly exemplified in the treatise which goes by the name of Glanvill, who was Chief Justiciar for the last nine years of this reign. The object of this work is the exposition of the practice of the King's Court. It deals principally with procedure or the mode of enforcing legal rights, but incidentally also with the rights themselves. In the county courts held before the sheriff, and in the courts of the lords of the manors, so great was the variety of the customs which were observed and enforced, that Glanvill declines to attempt any statement of them[2]. But in the reign of Henry II the principle had become firmly established that the king or his justices had cognizance of every suit relating to land. No plea relating to the freehold could be held unless the proceeding was commenced by writ or precept issuing from the king under the

[1] In this country the growth of the study of the Roman Law is marked by the lectures of Vacarius in Oxford, A. D. 1149. From this time forward the study of the Civil and Canon Law progressed rapidly, without at first coming into collision, as was afterwards the case, with the Common Law. It has, however, been lately doubted whether Vacarius did in fact teach in Oxford. See Pollock and Maitland, Hist. of Eng. Law, i. p. 98.

[2] See Glanvill, lib. xii. cap. 6, and lib. xiv. cap. 8.

CHAP. II. great seal. Directly or indirectly, means were provided for bringing the suit before the representatives of the king [1], and thus the authority of the royal court was felt throughout the length and breadth of the land; the rules which the Curia Regis observed became the general law of the land. In some localities customs still prevailed which were sufficiently strong to be adopted as local laws. Thus in Kent, in many boroughs, notably in London and York, local customs obtained the force of laws which differed in some respects, especially as to the mode of devolution of lands *ab intestato* and power of disposition by will, from the general law of the land. The tendency however of the action of the Curia Regis, subject to these and other important exceptions, was to establish a uniform system of law and to override local custom.

The treatise of Glanvill being principally upon procedure, the rights recognized and enforced by the Curia Regis are only incidentally noticed. The following extracts will however be found to throw light on some of the most important points in the early law of land.

Extracts from Glanvill.

§ 1. *Customary and Positive Law.*

The following extract from Glanvill's preface illustrates the transition above indicated from customary law to positive law properly so called, and the introduction of the allusion to Roman Law seems to show how powerful an influence the conception of a systematic body of written law had upon the writer's mind.

Glanvill. *De Legibus et Consuetudinibus Regni Angliae.*

Regiam potestatem non solum armis contra rebelles et gentes sibi regnoque insurgentes oportet esse decoratam, sed et legibus ad subditos et populos pacifice regendos decet esse ornatam. . . . Cum tantae aequitatis sit suae celsitudinis curia, ut in ea nullus judicum tam attritae frontis, tam temerariae sit praesumptionis, qui a justitiae tramite aliquatenus audeat declinare, aut veritati

[1] See below, § 2.

ullatenus praesumat contraire. Ibi enim pauperem non opprimit adversarii potentia, nec a limitibus judiciorum propellit quemquam amicorum favor aut gratia. Legibus namque regni et consuetudinibus de ratione introductis et diu obtentis, et, quod laudabilius est, talium virorum, licet subditorum, Rex noster non dedignatur consilio, quos morum gravitate, peritia juris et Regni consuetudinibus, suae sapientiae et eloquentiae praerogativa, aliis novit praecellere, et ad causas mediante justitia decidendas, et lites dirimendas, nunc severius nunc mitius agendo, prout viderint expedire, ipsis rerum argumentis comperit cum ratione promptissimos. Leges namque Anglicanas, licet non scriptas, leges appellari non videtur absurdum, cum hoc ipsum lex sit quod principi placet et legis habet vigorem [1], eas scilicet quas super dubiis in consilio definiendis procerum quidem consilio, et principis accedente auctoritate, constat esse promulgatas. Si enim ob scripturae solummodo defectum leges minime censerentur, majoris procul dubio auctoritatis robur ipsis legibus videretur accommodare scriptura, quam vel decernentis aequitas, vel ratio statuentis. Leges autem et jura regni scripto universaliter concludi nostris temporibus omnino quidem impossibile est, cum propter scribentium ignorantiam, tum propter earum multitudinem confusam; verum sunt quaedam in curia generalia et frequentius usitata, quae scripto commendare non mihi videtur praesumptuosum, sed et plerisque perutile, et ad adjuvandam memoriam admodum necessarium. Horum itaque particulam quandam in scripta redigere decrevi, stilo vulgari, et verbis curialibus utens ex industria, ad notitiam comparandam eis qui hujusmodi vulgaritate minus sint exercitati.

Translation.

It is right and fitting that the authority of the king should not only be garnished with arms to oppose rebels and foreigners when they attack him and his kingdom, but should also be graced with laws, for the peaceful government of all people beneath his sway. . . . For such is the equity which marks the court of his Highness, that in that court no judge can wear a brow so brazen, or be so rash and presumptuous in his conduct as to venture

[1] See Just. Inst. i. 2. 6. Glanvill is here defending the application of the term 'law' to the body of customs which prevailed in England. He contends that at any rate that portion of the customs prevailing throughout England, which have been recognized and acted upon by the king and his council, may legitimately be called 'laws,' and for this position the authority of the Institutes is referred to. As to the apparent reluctance to use the term 'law,' see Stubbs, Const. Hist. i. p. 574, note 1.

CHAP. II. § 1. to swerve in the slightest degree from the path of justice, or in any way to act contrary to the truth. For there the poor man is not weighed down by the power of his adversary, nor is any one shut out from access to the judgment-seat by partiality or favour of private friends. For regard is paid to the laws of the kingdom and the customs which have their origin in reason, and have long prevailed, and, what is still more worthy of praise, our King disdains not the advice of such men, subjects though they be, whom he knows to stand pre-eminent in character and in knowledge of the law and of the customs of the kingdom, and of the first rank in wisdom and eloquence; whom also he finds to be most ready with the help of reason to decide suits, and to put an end to strifes by the arm of justice, acting sometimes with strictness, sometimes with leniency, as they see to be expedient, according to the very truth of the matter before them. For though the laws of England are unwritten, it seems not unfitting to give them the name of laws, since law is nothing else than the pleasure of the chief of the state which has the force of a law. Such for instance are those laws which are recognized as established, when doubtful points are resolved in council, by the advice of the great men with the sanction of the king's authority. For if merely for want of writing these resolutions were determined to be no laws, it would necessarily follow that the laws would owe their force and authority to writing rather than to the justice and reason of the authority by which they are laid down. Moreover it is altogether impossible that all the laws and customs of the kingdom should in our time be embodied in writing, partly because of the ignorance of scribes, partly because of the intricacy and number of the laws themselves; but there are certain general matters in common use which, as it seems to me, it would not only not be presumptuous to set down in writing, but rather very useful to many persons, and indeed necessary in order to aid the remembrance of them. I have therefore determined to set down some portion of these in writing, purposely using an ordinary style, and the language of every-day life; in order to bring these matters to the knowledge of those who have but little experience of ordinary legal affairs.

§ 2. *Supremacy of Curia Regis in matters relating to the Freehold.*

The following passages illustrate what has been said above as to the concentration of jurisdiction relating to the freehold in the hands of the Curia Regis, and the consequent establishment of a uniform system of law.

The fundamental rule, now completely recognized, which produced this result was that no one was bound to answer in the court of his lord concerning his freehold without the king's writ [1].

The writs given below (lib. i. cap. 6, lib. xii. cap. 3) constitute the appropriate mode of commencing that form of real [2] action called a writ of right. The object of this proceeding is to determine a disputed right of property in the land, the question to be decided being—which of the two litigants has the greater right (*majus jus habet*) to the land in question. Opposed to the writ of right is, as will be seen later, the mode of remedy which only goes to decide which of the two has the right to the *possession* of the land. A writ of right might before Magna Carta either be brought directly in the Curia Regis, in which case the writ is addressed to the sheriff, and is similar in form to other actions; or it might be commenced in the territorial court by writ from the king; thence, if the court should be proved to have failed in doing right, the suit might be removed into the county court by precept of the sheriff, and from thence again by writ from the king into the Curia Regis. By an important provision of Magna Carta the right

[1] See Maitland, Introduction to 'Select Pleas,' Selden Soc. vol. ii. liv.

[2] The distinction between real and personal actions is given by Bracton (102; see Reeves, vol. i. 336). Real actions had for their object the assertion of the claimant's right to the possession or property of a freehold interest in land, and resulted in the recovery of the right. Personal actions usually had for their object the assertion of the right to damages for injuries to persons or to property, or for breaches of contract. Like many other distinctions in our law, this phraseology was borrowed from the Roman Law, and is derived from the distinction between *actiones in rem* and *actiones in personam.* The Roman *actio in rem* had for its object the assertion of the right of property in anything which was the subject of property, whether movable or immovable. *Actiones in personam* had for their object the assertion of an obligation incumbent on a particular person to do or render something to the plaintiff. The prominence of freehold interests in lands, as the subject-matter of rights, accounts for the narrower scope of 'real actions' in English Law. See further as to real actions below, § 9.

CHAP II. § 2. to issue the writ so as in the first instance to bring the suit in the king's court was abandoned [1]. After this enactment proceedings were instituted in the first instance in the branch of the Curia Regis called after Magna Carta the Court of Common Pleas[2] only when the lord gave, or was supposed to have given, licence to the tenant to bring his action in that court [3], or when the lord held no court, or when the tenant held directly of the king [4].

Lib. xii. c. 25. Praeterea sciendum quod secundum consuetudines regni nemo tenetur respondere in curia domini sui de aliquo libero tenemento [5] suo sine praecepto [6] domini regis vel ejus capitalis justiciae [7].

Lib. i. c. 5. Cum clamat quis domino regi aut ejus justiciis [8] de feodo [9] aut de libero tenemento suo, si fuerit querela talis, quod

[1] Magna Carta (John) c. 34:—'Breve quod vocatur "praecipe" de cetero non fiat alicui de aliquo tenemento unde liber homo amittere possit curiam suam.'

[2] 'Communia placita (suits between subject and subject) non sequantur curiam nostram, sed teneantur in aliquo loco certo.' (c. 17.) From this time forward the Court of Common Pleas had exclusive jurisdiction in the case of all real actions.

[3] This was expressed by the addition at the end of the writ of the words 'Quia dominus remisit curiam suam.' This became in process of time a mere form. See Blackstone, iii. Appendix 1, § 4.

[4] See Blackstone, iii. p. 195; Fitzherbert, Natura Brevium, i. pp. 1–5.

[5] The word 'tenements' now becomes the technical expression for freehold interests in things immovable, considered as subjects of property, they being not 'owned,' but 'holden.' This word is however not confined to this class of interests, but is also applied to the class of rights called incorporeal hereditaments; see below, Appendix to Part I, § 1 (7), (11). For the technical meaning of 'lands,' 'tenements,' and 'hereditaments,' see Blackstone, ii. chap. 2.

[6] The writ or precept addressed by the king to the sheriff or chief lord as the case might be. This was the regular mode of commencing an action at law.

[7] As to the office and functions of the chief justiciar, see Stubbs, Select Charters, pp. 16, 17, and Const. Hist. i. p. 346.

[8] As to the justices, see Stubbs, Select Charters, p. 17.

[9] The word 'feodum' has now lost its original sense of land granted to be held as a benefice opposed to land granted to be held alodially; see above, p. 31. No alodial land remained in England. Feodum or fee is now always used in its secondary sense of 'an estate of inheritance' (see p 60), i.e. an interest in land descendible to heirs. (As to who 'heirs' are, see below, § 6.)

debeat vel quod dominus rex velit eam in curia sua deduci tunc is qui queritur tale breve de summonitione habebit:— CHAP. II. § 2.

c. 6. Rex Vicecomiti[1] salutem. Praecipe A. quod sine dilatione reddat B. unam hidam[2] terrae in villa[3] illa unde idem B. queritur quod praedictus A. ei deforceat: et nisi fecerit, summone eum per bonos summonitores quod sit ibi coram me vel justiciariis meis in crastino post octabas clausi Paschae[4] apud locum illum, ostensurus quare non fecerit. Et habeas ibi summonitores et hoc breve. Teste Ranulpho de Glanvilla apud Clarendon[5].

Lib. xii. c. 1. Praedicta quidem placita de recto[6] directe et ab initio veniunt in curia domini regis, et ibi, ut dictum est, deducuntur et terminantur. Quandoque etiam licet ab initio non veniant in curia domini regis quaedam placita de recto, veniunt tamen per translationem, ubi curiae diversorum dominorum probantur de recto defecisse: tunc enim mediante comitatu[7] possunt a comitatu, ex diversis causis quae superius expositae sunt, ad capitalem curiam domini regis transferri[8].

[1] As to the office of the sheriff, see Stubbs, Select Charters, pp. 9, 14, 22, and for the history of the term *vicecomes* see Const. Hist. i. 269, note 1.

[2] As to the hide, see above, p. 8, note 1.

[3] The writ specifies the district in which the lands are situate. As to the villa, see above, p. 43, note 4.

[4] See Spelman, Glossary, s. v. Clausum.

[5] The mode of trial of a writ of right forms the subject of the remainder of the first and second book of Glanvill. His account, though very curious in reference to the history of the law of procedure, has no bearing on that of the law of land. The cause, when ripe for trial, was decided either by the duel, or, under the great improvement of the law effected by an ordinance of Henry II, of which we only hear in Glanvill, by the grand assize; that is, by the verdict of twelve milites of the neighbourhood, chosen by four other milites summoned by the sheriff for the purpose.

[6] Placita de recto, 'suits concerning the (freehold) right to lands'; 'writs of right.'

[7] For county courts held before the sheriff, see Stubbs, Const. Hist. i. pp. 114, 393, &c.

[8] The writ by which the cause was removed into the county court was called the writ of *tolt*—that by which it was removed from the county court into the curia regis, the writ of *pone*; see specimens in Blackstone, iii. App. 1. Bracton, foll. 329–333, gives an elaborate account of the grounds and mode of transfer of the writ of right from the court baron to the county court, and from the county court to the curia regis. This transfer must have been very common from the earliest times, and it became in process of time a matter of course, the grounds alleged in the writs of *tolt* and *pone* being merely fictitious.

CHAP. II. § 2.

c. 2. Cum quis itaque clamet aliquod liberum tenementum vel servitium tenendum de alio per liberum servitium, non poterit inde trahere tenentem in placitum sine brevi domini regis vel ejus justiciarum; habebit ergo ad dominum suum, de quo idem clamat tenere, breve de recto. Quod, si placitum fuerit de terra, tale erit:—

c. 3. Rex Comiti W. salutem. Praecipio tibi quod sine dilatione teneas plenum rectum N. de decem carucatis terrae in Middleton, quas clamat tenere de te per liberum servitium feodi unius militis [1] pro omni servitio, vel per liberum servitium centum solidorum per annum pro omni servitio [2], vel per liberum servitium unde duodecim carucatae terrae faciunt feodum unius militis pro omni servitio [3], vel quas clamat pertinere ad liberum tenementum suum quod de te tenet in eadem villa, vel in Mortune, per liberum servitium, etc. vel per servitium, etc. vel quas clamat tenere de te de libero maritagio [4] M. matris suae, vel in liberum burgagium [5], vel in liberam eleemosynam [6], vel per liberum servitium eundi tecum in exercitum domini regis cum duobus equis ad custum suum pro omni servitio, vel per liberum servitium inveniendi tibi unum arbelastarium in exercitum domini regis per quadraginta dies pro omni servitio, quas R. filius W. ei deforciat. Et nisi feceris, Vicecomes de Northamptone faciat, ne amplius inde clamorem audiam pro defectu justiciae.

c. 6. Solent autem placita ista in curiis dominorum, vel eorum qui loco dominorum habentur, deduci, secundum rationabiles consuetudines ipsarum curiarum; quae tot et tam variae sunt, ut in scriptum de facili reduci non possunt.

[1] See above, p. 61, note 3.

[2] It became at this time very common to commute services due for the land for a money payment. This would not affect the tenure of the lands. Whether the tenure was by knight-service or in socage would still depend on the nature of the services in respect of which the commutation was paid.

[3] The language here, which is the common form, seems to point to the process of composition for the general burden of military service by burdening some lands specially with the service to the freedom of the others, and thus constituting knights' fees. See above, p. 39.

[4] As to 'frank marriage,' see below, p. 101, note 2.

[5] As to burgage tenure, see above, p. 48, and Littleton, lib. ii. c. 10. §§ 162–171.

[6] As to libera eleemosyna, see above, p. 38, and Littleton, lib. ii. c. 6. §§ 133–142.

TRANSLATION.

Book xii. chap. 25. Further it is to be observed that according to the customs of the kingdom no one is bound to answer in the court of his lord concerning any free tenement of his without the writ of our lord the king or his chief justiciar.

Book i. chap. 5. When any one complains to the king or his justices concerning a fee or any freehold tenement of his, if the complaint be of such a character as that it ought to be brought, or if our lord the king desires that it should be brought in his own court, then the complainant shall have a writ of summons as follows:—

Chap. 6. The king to the sheriff greeting. Command A. that without delay he restore to B. one hide of land in such a township from which the said B. complains that the aforesaid A. is keeping him out by force, and if he doth it not, summon him by good summoners to be in such a place before me or my justices on the morrow after the octave of Easter to show cause wherefore he hath not done it. And have there the summoners and this writ. Witness Ranulph de Glanville at Clarendon.

Book xii. chap. 1. The above-mentioned writs of right are brought directly and in the first instance in the court of our lord the king, and there, as has been said, they are proceeded with and determined. Sometimes also, although certain pleas of right are not in the first instance brought in the court of our lord the king, they come thither by transfer, when the courts of the different lords are proved to have failed in doing justice; for then through the medium of the county court they may be removed from the county court into the chief court of our lord the king on the various grounds which have been explained above.

Chap. 2. When therefore any one claims to hold of another by free service any freehold tenement, or claims any service, he cannot force the tenant into suit concerning such a matter without the writ of our lord the king or his justices, he shall have therefore a writ of right directed to the lord of whom he claims to hold. If the suit be concerning land the writ will be in the following terms:—

Chap. 3. The king to Earl W. greeting. I command thee that without delay thou shouldest do full right to N. concerning ten plough-lands in Middleton, which he claims to hold of thee by the free service of one knight's fee in lieu of all other service, or by the free service of 100 shillings by the year in lieu of all other service, or by the free service of the union of twelve plough-lands

CHAP. II. § 2. to constitute one knight's fee in lieu of all other service, or which he claims to belong to his free tenement which he holds of thee in the same township, or in Mortune by the free service, &c. or by the service, &c. or which he claims to hold of thee as part of the land given in frank-marriage on the marriage of M. his mother, or in free burgage, or in free alms, or by the free service of going with thee to the army of our lord the king with two horses at his own cost in lieu of all service, or by the free service of finding for thee one cross-bowman for the army of our lord the king for forty days for all service, from which lands R. the son of W. is keeping him out by force. And if thou dost it not, let the sheriff of Northampton do it, that I may hear no more complaint concerning that matter of failure of justice.

Chap. 6. Further these suits are conducted in the courts of the lords or of their substitutes according to the reasonable customs of the various courts, which are so numerous and so different that they cannot easily be described in writing.

§ 3. *Relation of Lord and Free Tenant.*

The following passages state the substance of the law as to the relation between the lord and his freehold tenant and their mutual rights and duties. This branch of the law is treated more elaborately by Bracton, but the outline here traced by Glanvill remains substantially unaltered.

The tie which created the relation of lord and tenant, at all events tenant by military service, was homage. Bracton [1], borrowing from the definition of *obligatio* by the Roman lawyers [2], defines homage as '*juris vinculum quo quis astringitur ad warrantizandum, defendendum, et acquietandum tenentem suum in seisina versus omnes per certum servitium in donatione nominatum et expressum ; et etiam vice versa quo tenens re obligatur et astringitur ad fidem domino suo servandam et servitium debitum faciendum.*' In the same passage Bracton gives a more detailed statement of the consequences of homage, the obligation it imposes on lord and tenant, and the modes by which the tie may be dissolved [3]. This however belongs so entirely

[1] Fol. 78 b. [2] See Institutes of Justinian, iii. 13.
[3] See Reeves, i. pp. 310–312.

to the obsolete portion of our law that it is needless to pursue the subject into further detail. If by any means, such as escheat for felony, or failure of heirs [1], or repudiation of his duties as lord, the tie was dissolved as between the tenant and his immediate lord, the intermediate seignory was as it were taken away, and the relation of lord and tenant arose between the tenant and the superior lord of whom the intermediate lord himself had held. The superior lord could not in this case refuse to accept the homage of the tenant, who, as Bracton more than once says, had all along been '*tenens suus, quamvis per medium.*' In the same way, if the tenant alienated the whole of his land the alienee would be tenant of the lord of whom the land had been held, and he would be compelled to receive the homage of the alienee.

Lib. ix. c. 1. Praedictis restat continuandum de homagiis faciendis et releviis recipiendis. Mortuo siquidem patre vel alio quocunque alicujus antecessore, tenetur dominus feodi ab initio recipere homagium recti haeredis, sive fuerit infra aetatem haeres ipse, sive plenam habuerit aetatem, dummodo masculus sit. Feminae enim nullum homagium facere possunt de jure [2], licet plerumque fidelitatem [3] dominis suis praestare soleant. Veruntamen si fuerint maritatae, mariti earum homagium dominis suis de feodo illarum facere debent. Ita dico si feoda illa homagium debeant. Sin autem haeres masculus fuerit et minor, nullam de jure vel de ipso haerede vel de tenemento suo habere debet custodiam dominus feodi, donec ipsius haeredis receperit homagium; quia generaliter verum est quod nullum servitium sive relevium sive aliud potest quis ab haerede, sive fuerit major sive minor, exigere, donec ipsius

[1] See below, § 4.

[2] This seems to have been changed in later times. Littleton speaks of a woman doing homage; lib. ii. c. 1. § 87.

[3] 'Fealty is the same that *fidelitas* is in Latin. And when a freeholder doth fealty to his lord he shall hold his right hand upon a book and shall say thus: Know ye this, my lord, that I shall be faithful and true unto you, and faith to you shall bear for the lands which I claim to hold of you, and that I shall lawfully do to you the customs and services which I ought to do, at the terms assigned, so help me God and his Saints. And he shall kiss the book. But he shall not kneel when he maketh his fealty, nor make such humble reverence as is aforesaid in homage.'—Littleton, Coke's translation, lib. ii. c. 2. § 91.

CHAP. II. haeredis receperit homagium de tenemento unde servitium habere
§ 3. clamat. Potest autem quis plura homagia diversis dominis facere de feodis diversis diversorum dominorum. Sed unum eorum oportet esse precipuum, et cum ligeancia factum; illi scilicet domino faciendum, a quo tenet suum capitale tenementum is qui homagium facere debet. Fieri autem debet homagium sub hac forma, scilicet ut is qui homagium facere debet, ita fiat homo domini sui, quod fidem illi portet de illo tenemento unde homagium suum praestat, et quod ejus in omnibus terrenum honorem servet, salva fide debita domino regi et haeredibus suis[1]. Ex hoc liquet quod vassallus non potest dominum suum infestire, salva fide homagii sui, nisi forte se defendendo, vel nisi ex praecepto principis cum eo iverit contra dominum suum in exercitum[2]. Et generaliter nihil de jure facere potest quis salva fide homagii quod vertat ad exhaeredationem domini sui vel ad dedecus corporis sui. Si quis ergo plura homagia pro diversis feodis suis fecerit diversis dominis qui se invicem infestent; si capitalis dominus ejus ei praeceperit quod secum in propria persona sua eat contra alium dominum suum, oportet eum ejus praecepto in hoc obtemperare, salvo tamen servitio alterius domini de feodo quod de eo tenet. Patet itaque ex praedictis, quod si quis aliquid ad exhaeredationem domini sui fecerit, et super hoc convictus fuerit, feodum quod de eo tenet de jure amittet et haeredes ejus. Idem quoque erit si manus violentas quis in dominum suum injecerit eum laedendo vel atroci injuria afficiendo, et hoc fuerit in curia versus eum legitime comprobatum. Sed utrum in curia domini sui teneatur quis se defendere versus dominum suum de talibus objectis, quaero; et utrum dominus suus possit eum ad id faciendum distringere per considerationem curiae suae[3] sine praecepto domini regis vel ejus justiciarum, vel sine brevi domini regis vel ejus capitalis justiciae. Et quidem de jure poterit quis hominem suum per judicium curiae suae deducere et distringere ad curiam suam venire.

* * * * * *

Sin autem non poterit quis tenentes suos justiciare, tunc demum ad curiae refugium erit necessarium decurrere. Potest autem homo liber masculus homagium facere, tam is qui aetatem habet, quam is qui infra aetatem est, tam clericus quam laicus. Episcopi

1 Compare the form of homage given in Littleton, lib. ii. c. i. § 85. The ceremony was public, in the court of the county or hundred or in the court baron, so that the lord might have witnesses of the fact.

2 See above, p. 36.

3 The technical expression for the judgment of a court, which begins 'Therefore it is considered,' &c.

vero consecrati homagium facere non solent domino regi etiam de baroniis suis. Sed fidelitatem cum juramentis interpositis ipsi praestare solent. Electi vero in episcopos ante consecrationem suam homagia sua facere solent. CHAP. II. § 3.

TRANSLATION.

It remains to add to what has been said above something concerning the doing of homage and the taking of reliefs. So soon as the father or other ancestor is dead, the lord of the fee is bound in the first instance to receive the homage of the lawful heir, whether the heir be under age or whether he have attained full age, provided he be a male. For no woman can by law do any homage, although generally they are accustomed to render fealty to their lords. But if they are married their husbands ought to do homage to their lord for the fees of their wives. I mean if homage is due in respect of those fees. But if the heir be a male and under age, no wardship either of the person or of the lands of the heir is due to the lord until he has received the homage of the heir; because it is true as a general rule that no one can claim from the heir, whether he be of full age or under age, any service or relief or anything else until he has received the homage of the heir for the tenement in respect of which he claims the service. Further a tenant may do several homages to different lords for their different tenements respectively. But one of those homages ought to be the principal, and accompanied by allegiance. This should be rendered to that lord of whom the tenant holds his principal tenement. Now homage ought to be rendered in this form, that he from whom homage is due will become the man of his lord, so that he will govern himself faithfully as regards that tenement in respect of which he is rendering homage, and that in all respects he will preserve the honour of his lands, always excepting the faith due to our lord the king and his heirs. From this it is clear that the vassal cannot wage war on his lord without violating his homage, except perhaps in self-defence, or except where at the command of the king he goes with him as a member of his army against his lord. And in general no one can lawfully or without violating his homage do anything which may tend to the disherison of his lord or the dishonouring of his person. If therefore any one has rendered several homages in respect of different tenements of his to different lords who are hostile to each other, if his chief lord has commanded him to attend him in his own person in fighting against some other lord of his, he must obey his lord's command in this matter, without prejudice to the services due to the other lord

CHAP. II. § 3. for the fee which he holds of him. It is manifest therefore from what has been said that if any one has done anything tending towards the disherison of his lord, and is convicted of so doing, he and his heirs will according to law lose the tenement which he holds of that lord. The same will also be the case if a tenant lays violent hands on his lord, doing him hurt or grievous injury, and this be proved against him in court according to law. But whether a tenant is bound to defend himself in the court of his lord against accusations of this kind I doubt; also whether his lord can distrain him so to do by the judgment of his court without the writ of our lord the king or his chief justice. And indeed by law a lord may by the judgment of his court compel his man to appear and distrain him to come to his court.

* * * * * *

But if a lord may not administer justice to his own tenants, it will be necessary to have recourse to the protection of the royal court.

Moreover every free male tenant can do homage as well he who is under age as he who is of full age, whether he be in orders or a layman. Bishops however after consecration do not do homage to our lord the king even in respect of their baronies. But it is usual for them to take the oaths of fealty. However it is usual for bishops-elect, before their consecration, to render homage.

§ 4. *Feudal Incidents.*

The following extracts detail the various incidental rights and duties appertaining to the relation of lord and tenant as they existed in Glanvill's time.

(1) Reliefs, Aids.

Lib. ix. c. 4. Mutua quidem debet esse dominii et homagii fidelitatis connexio, ita quod quantum homo debet domino ex homagio, tantum illi debet dominus ex dominio praeter solam reverentiam. Unde si aliquis alicui donaverit aliquod tenementum pro servitio et homagio suo, quod postea alius versus eum diracionaverit, tenebitur quidem dominus tenementum id ei warrantizare[1] vel competens escambium ei reddere. Secus est tamen

[1] The doctrine of warranty was based upon one of the most primitive of the rules of early Teutonic law. (Warranty = the Anglo-Saxon 'Teám.') When a person had been wrongfully deprived of a portion of his property —a slave, a horse, or an ox—and found it in the possession of another, the true owner could of course claim that which was his own. If the person

de eo qui de alio tenet feodum suum sicut haereditatem suam, et unde fecerit homagium; quia licet is terram illam amittat, non tenebitur ei dominus ad escambium. Mortuo vero patre vel antecessore alicujus ut praedictum est, et haerede relicto qui infra aetatem sit, nullum jus habet dominus feodi in custodia haeredis vel haereditatis, nisi prius recepto homagio haeredis. Recepto vero homagio, in custodia ipsius domini remanebit haeres ipse cum haereditate sua sub forma praedicta, donec plenam habuerit aetatem. Tandem vero eodem ad aetatem perveniente et facta ei haereditatis restitutione, quietus erit a relevio[1] ratione custodiae. Mulier vero haeres alicujus relicta, sive plenam habuerit aetatem, sive infra aetatem fuerit, in custodia domini sui remanebit, donec de consilio domini sui maritetur[2]. Verum si infra aetatem fuerit, quando dominus suus in custodiam illam receperit, tunc, ipsa

having the thing in his possession had bought it from a third person, he could vouch the third person to warranty, that is, call upon him to defend the title to the chattel, and, if the superior title were established, to make recompense to the evicted possessor. If the warranty was not accepted, the person vouching to warranty must establish that he purchased from the person vouched (and for this purpose the Anglo-Saxon laws contain elaborate provisions as to the necessity of a purchaser providing witnesses of the purchase), and the identity of the thing purchased with that claimed. (See Laws of Hlothaere and Edric, 7, 16, Thorpe, Ancient Laws and Institutes, fol. ed., pp. 13, 14; Laws of Ine, 75, Thorpe, p. 65.) The person vouched to warranty might in his turn vouch a second person, and the second vouchee a third, but no further vouching was permitted. (See Leg. Long. lib. 2. tit. 28. l. 5, Canciani, i. p. 232; Laws of Ethelred, 8, 9, Thorpe, p. 123.) Upon the acceptance of the warrantor the suit as to the title to the chattel proceeded between the claimant and the warrantor, and if the claimant was successful he recovered the chattel, and the warrantor was bound to recompense his vendee. If at the time of the claim the vouchee were dead, the possessor of the thing claimed could 'vouch the tomb' of the vendor, and follow his property wherever it were for the purpose of obtaining a recompense. (Laws of Ine, 53, Thorpe, 59; and see Alfred and Guthrum's Peace, art. 4, ib. p. 67; Laws of King Edward, ib. p. 68; and see the form of oath to be taken by the claimant and the innocent purchaser, ib. p. 76.) In the development of the English law of land the doctrine of warranty was applied mainly to the obligation on the part of the donor of land and his heirs to defend the estate of the donee and his heirs. The primitive rules of law formed the basis of doctrines of the greatest complication and technicality, which, as will be seen later, received a most important practical application in affording facilities for the conversion of an estate 'tail' into an estate in fee simple. See below, Chap. V. § 2.

[1] As to relief, see above, p. 40.

[2] As to the right of marriage, see above, p. 42.

CHAP. II. § 4 (1). maritata, quieta erit haereditas illa a relevio, quantum ad se et quantum ad virum suum. Sin autem habuerit aetatem eo tempore, licet aliquamdiu in custodia domini sui remaneat antequam maritetur, relevium tamen dabit maritus suus qui illam in uxorem duxerit. Semel autem praestitum relevium a marito alicujus mulieris, utrumque, scilicet tam maritum quam uxorem, tota vita sua de relevio ipsius haereditatis acquietabit. Quia nec mulier ipsa nec secundus maritus suus, si secundo nupserit praemortuo viro suo, nec primus maritus suus praemortua uxore sua, terram illam iterum relevabit. Cum autem haeres masculus et notus haeres aetatem habens relinquatur, in sua haereditate se tenebit, ut supra dictum est, etiam invito domino; dum tamen domino suo, sicut tenetur, suum offerat homagium coram probis hominibus, et suum rationabile relevium. Dicitur autem rationabile relevium alicujus, juxta consuetudinem regni de feodo unius militis, centum solidi; de socagio vero quantum valet census illius socagii per unum annum; de baroniis vero nihil certum statutum est, quia juxta voluntatem et misericordiam domini regis solent baroniae capitales de releviis suis domino regi satisfacere[1]. Idem est de serjanteriis. Si vero dominus ipse nec homagium, nec rationabile relevium ipsius haeredis velit recipere, tunc relevium ipsum salvo custodiat, et per probos homines id saepius domino suo offerat. Qui si nullatenus id recipere voluerit, tunc haeres ipse de domino suo domino regi vel ejus justiciis conqueratur, et tale breve inde habebit:—

c. 5. Rex vicecomiti salutem. Praecipe N. quod juste et sine dilatione recipiat homagium et rationabile relevium R. de libero tenemento quod tenet in illa villa, et quod de eo tenere clamat; et nisi fecerit, summone eum per bonos summonitores quod sit coram me vel justiciis meis eo die ostensurus quare non fecerit.

c. 8. Postquam vero convenerit inter dominum et haeredem tenentis sui de rationabili relevio dando et recipiendo, poterit idem haeres rationabilia auxilia[2] de hominibus suis inde exigere, ita tamen moderate secundum quantitatem feodorum suorum et

[1] Compare the charter of Henry I, c. 3, Stubbs, Select Charters, p. 100. 'Si quis baronum, comitum meorum sive aliorum qui de me tenent, mortuus fuerit, haeres suus non redimet terram suam sicut faciebat tempore fratris mei, sed justa et legitima relevatione relevabit eam. Similiter et homines baronum meorum justa et legitima relevatione relevabunt terras suas de dominis suis.' The amount of relief payable by a baron was fixed by Magna Carta, c. 2. See Chapter III. § 1.

[2] As to aids, see above, p. 41.

secundum facultates, ne nimis gravari inde videantur, vel suum contenementum amittere. Nihil autem certum[1] statutum est de hujusmodi auxiliis dandis vel exigendis, nisi ut praedicta forma inviolabiliter observetur. Sunt praeterea alii casus in quibus licet dominis auxilia similia, sed sub forma praescripta, exigere ab hominibus suis: veluti si filius et haeres suus miles fiat, vel si primogenitam filiam suam maritaverit. Utrum vero ad guerram suam manutenendam possint domini hujusmodi auxilia exigere, quaero[2]. Obtinet autem quod non possunt ad id tenentes distringere de jure, nisi quatenus facere velint. Possunt autem domini tenentes suos ad hujusmodi rationabilia auxilia reddenda etiam suo jure, sine praecepto domini regis vel ejus capitalis justiciae, per judicium curiae suae distringere per catalla quae in ipsis feodis invenerint, vel per ipsa feoda si opus fuerit; ita tamen quod ipsi tenentes inde deducantur juste secundum considerationem curiae suae et consuetudinem rationabilem. Si ergo ad hujusmodi auxilia rationabilia reddenda posset aliquis dominus tenentes suos ita distringere, multo fortius districtionem eo modo licite poterit facere pro ipso relevio suo, vel pro necessario servitio suo de feodo suo sibi debito. Verum si dominus potens non fuerit tenentem suum pro servitiis suis vel consuetudinibus justiciare; tunc decurrendum erit ei ad auxilium regis vel capitalis justiciae, et tale breve inde habebit:—

c. 9. Rex Vicecomiti salutem. Praecipio tibi quod justicies[3] N. quod juste et sine dilatione faciat R. consuetudines et recta servitia quae ei facere debet de tenemento suo quod de eo tenet in illa villa, sicut rationabiliter monstrare poterit eum sibi deberi, ne oporteat eum amplius inde conqueri pro defectu recti.

TRANSLATION.

Book ix. c. 4. The tie of fealty between lord and vassal ought to be mutual so that the obligation of the vassal towards the lord by reason of homage should correspond with the obligations of the lord towards the vassal by reason of his lordship— except only as regards personal reverence. Hence if one has made a grant to a person of a tenement in return for his service and homage, to which tenement a third person has subsequently established an adverse right, the lord will be bound to warrant that tenement to

[1] See Magna Carta (John), c. 12; below, Chap. III. § 5.

[2] See above, p. 35, and below, Chap. III. § 11.

[3] A writ of justicies was in the nature of a special commission to the sheriff, giving him authority to adjudicate in the particular case in the county court.

CHAP. II. § 4 (1). his grantee, or to provide him with an equivalent recompense. It is otherwise in the case of a person who has inherited the fee which he holds of another, and for which he has done homage; because although he lose that land, his lord will not be bound to provide him with a recompense. Now in the case before mentioned, after the death of the father or ancestor of any one, where there is an heir surviving who is under age, the lord of the fee has no right to the custody of the person or land of the heir unless he has first received the homage of the heir. But after he has received the homage, the heir himself and the inheritance will remain in the wardship of the lord in the manner above-mentioned until the heir attains full age. When however he has attained full age and has obtained restitution of the inheritance he will be free from relief by reason of the wardship. A female however, who is left an heiress, whether she be of full age or whether she be under age, will remain in wardship to her lord until she marries by her lord's advice. But if she be under age when her lord obtains the wardship, then when she is married that inheritance shall be free from relief, as far as relates to the woman and her husband. But if at the commencement of the wardship she be of full age, although she may remain for some length of time under the guardianship of her lord before she is married, nevertheless her husband on his marriage shall give a relief. But a relief once paid by the husband of any woman shall for the whole of their lives free them both from any further relief. Neither the woman herself nor her second husband, if her first husband should die and she should marry again, nor her first husband if she should die before him, shall pay a relief for that land a second time. But when a male and acknowledged heir of full age survives, he shall abide in his inheritance as has been said above even against his lord's will, provided that he offers to his lord, as he is bound, his homage and his reasonable relief in the presence of respectable witnesses. A reasonable relief according to the custom of the kingdom is said to be for a knight's fee 100 shillings; but for socage land the value of one year's rent of the socage land. For baronies no fixed amount of relief is established, because the amount of the relief to be paid to our lord the king by baronies held in chief is according to his pleasure and clemency. The same is the case as regards lands held by serjeanty. But if the lord refuses to receive the homage and reasonable relief of the heir, then let the heir keep the relief in his own hands and make repeated tender of it to his lord by respectable men. If the lord will by no means be willing to receive it the heir may prefer a complaint concerning his lord to the king, or his justices, and he shall have the following writ in the matter:—

Chap. 5. The king to the sheriff greeting. Command N. that he do lawfully without delay receive the homage and the reasonable relief of R. for the free tenement which he holds in that township in which he claims to hold of him, and if he doth it not, summon him by good summoners to appear before me on such a day to show wherefore he hath not done it.

Chap. 8. Now after an agreement has been made between the lord and the heir of his tenant as to giving and accepting a reasonable relief, the heir may require from his own tenants reasonable aids for the purpose. He must however do this reasonably, in proportion to the size of their fees and their means, so that they may not seem to be too heavily burdened on that account, or be made to forfeit their tenements. Now there is no fixed limit ordained as to the amount of aids of this kind which may be given or required, except that the rule above-mentioned is to be kept inviolate. There are besides other cases in which it is lawful for a lord to require similar aids from his tenants subject to the above-mentioned rule, for instance upon the occasion of his son and heir being made a knight, or upon the marriage of his eldest daughter. But whether lords can require aids of this kind from their tenants for the maintenance of their private wars I doubt. It is settled however that they cannot lawfully distrain their tenants for that purpose, contrary to their wills. But the lords may distrain their tenants to render reasonable aids of the kind above-mentioned even in their own right, without the writ of our lord the king or his chief justiciar, by the judgment of their own courts executed upon the chattels which they may find upon the land, or upon the land itself if necessary, provided that recourse is had against the tenants according to law, in pursuance of the judgment of their court and according to a reasonable custom. If therefore a lord may in this manner distrain his tenants to render reasonable aids of this kind, much rather is it in his power to make a distraint in that manner for his reliefs, or for the necessary service due to him from his fee. But if the lord be not powerful enough to do justice on his tenant for his services or customary rights he must then have recourse to the aid of the king or his chief justice, and he shall have the following writ in the matter:—

Chap. 9. The king to the sheriff greeting. I command thee that thou shouldest do justice on N. to the end that he justly and without

CHAP. II. § 4 (2). delay perform for R. the customs and proper services which he ought to render to him for that fee which he holds of him in that township, according as they may reasonably be proved to be due to him, that I may not hear him any longer complain of a failure of justice.

(2) Guardianship in Chivalry or Knight Service.

Lib. vii. c. 9. Sunt enim quidam haeredes, de quibus constat eos esse majores, alii unde constat esse minores, alii de quibus dubium est utrum sint majores an minores. Haeredes vero majores statim post decessum antecessorum suorum possunt se tenere in haereditate sua, licet domini possint feodum suum cum haerede in manus suas capere[1]; ita tamen moderate id fieri debet, ne aliquam disseisinam haeredibus faciant: possunt enim haeredes, si opus fuerit, violentiae dominorum resistere, dum tamen parati sunt relevium et alia recta servitia eis inde facere. Si vero constet eos esse minores, tunc ipsi haeredes tenentur esse sub custodia dominorum suorum donec plenam habuerint aetatem (si fuerint haeredes de feodo militari), quod sit post vicesimum et unum annum completum, si fuerit haeres et filius militis vel per feodum militare tenentis. Si vero haeres et filius sokemanni fuerit, aetatem habere intelligitur tunc cum quindecim compleverit annum[2]. Si vero fuerit filius burgensis, aetatem habere tunc intelligitur, cum discrete sciverit denarios numerare et pannos ulnare, et alia paterna negotia similiter exercere. Plenam itaque custodiam habent domini filiorum et haeredum hominum suorum et feodorum suorum, ita quod plenam inde habent dispositionem, ut in ecclesiis, in custodiis ipsis constitutis, concedendis, et in mulieribus (si quae in eorum custodiam exciderint) maritandis, et in aliis negotiis disponendis, secundum quod propria negotia sua disponere solent; nihil tamen de haereditate de jure alienare possunt ad remanentiam[3]. Ita tamen quod haeredes ipsos honorifice pro quantitate

[1] See above, p. 42. There was a distinction between wardship of the lands and wardship of the body. The lord was entitled to both except when the infant's father was still alive. In that case the father was entitled as against the lord to the wardship of the body. This carried with it the right to the marriage of the infant. See Littleton, lib. ii. c. 4. § 114. Statute of Marlebridge, c. 16, Coke's 2nd Institute 133.

[2] In Bracton's time (fol. 86) the tenant in socage has no guardian after fifteen, but is still in many respects a minor, but in the time of Littleton the period of full age was finally fixed at fourteen; lib. ii. c. 5. § 123. As to tenants in socage, see above, p. 45, &c.

[3] 'In perpetuity.' The word is sometimes used by Glanvill to express 'estate of inheritance.'

haereditatis interim habeant, et debita etiam defuncti pro quantitate haereditatis et temporis quo illis custodia deputatur acquietent; unde et de debitis antecessorum de jure respondere tenentur. Negotia quoque ipsorum haeredum agere possunt, et placita[1] de jure eis acquirendo movere et prosequi, si emissa fuerit de aetate contra minorem exceptio. Respondere autem non tenentur pro illis nec de recto nec de disseisina nisi in unico casu[2] . . . . . .

Restituere autem tenentur custodes haereditates ipsis haeredibus instauratas et debitis acquietatas, juxta exigentiam temporis custodiae et quantitatis haereditatis[3]. Si vero dubium fuerit utrum fuerint haeredes majores an minores, tunc procul dubio domini tam haeredes quam haereditates in custodia habebunt, donec aetas rationabiliter probetur per legales homines de vicineto et per eorum sacramentum.

c. 10. Si vero plures habuerint dominos ipsi haeredes sub custodia constituti, capitales eorum domini, id est, illi quibus ligeantiam debent, sicut de primis eorum feodis, eorum habebunt custodiam; ita quod de caeteris feodis relevia et alia recta servitia dominis ipsorum feodorum facere tenentur. Et sic custodia eis per totum sub forma praescripta remanebit. Notandum tamen quod si quis in capite de domino rege tenere debet, tunc ejus custodia ad dominum regem plene pertinet, sive alios dominos habere debeat ipse haeres sive non; quia dominus rex nullum habere potest parem multo minus superiorem[4]. Veruntamen ratione burgagii tantum non praefertur dominus rex aliis in custodiis. Si vero dominus rex aliquam custodiam alicui commiserit[5], tunc distinguitur utrum ei custodiam pleno jure commiserit, ita quod nullum eum inde reddere compotum oporteat ad scaccarium, aut aliter. Si vero ita plene ei custodiam commiserit, tunc poterit ecclesias vacantes donare, et alia negotia sicut sua recte exercere[6].

[1] Pleas, suits: *placita coronae* or *criminalia* are criminal suits as opposed to *placita civilia* or civil suits; *communia placita*, suits between subject and subject. Hence the Court of Common Pleas. See Magna Carta (John), c. 17; Stubbs, Select Charters, p. 299.

[2] Glanvill proceeds to mention the case referred to.

[3] But the guardian in chivalry was not obliged to account for the mesne profits.

[4] See Magna Carta, c. 37; below, Chap. III. § 2.

[5] See as to the grant or sale of wardship by the king, the provisions of Magna Carta (John), c. 4; below, Chap. III. § 2; and see Littleton, lib. ii. c. 4. § 116.

[6] See further as to guardianship in chivalry, below, Chap. III. § 2.

CHAP. II.
§ 4 (2).

TRANSLATION.

Book vii. chap. 9. Some heirs are notoriously of full age, some are notoriously under age. In other cases it is a matter of doubt whether the heir is or is not of age. Heirs of full age may enter upon their inheritance immediately after the death of their ancestor, although the lords may take into their own hands the land together with the heir in possession; this ought however to be done in a peaceable manner, so as not to cause any disseisin to the heirs. For the heirs, if there be occasion, may resist the violence of the lords, provided that they are prepared to render the relief and perform the other services which are justly due. If however it is ascertained that the heirs are under age, then the persons of the heirs are held to be in the custody of the lords until they have obtained full age, and this is after the attainment of the twenty-first year, if the tenant be the son and heir of a knight, or of one holding a knight's fee. If he be the son and heir of a socman, he is held to be of age when he has completed his fifteenth year. But if he be the son of a burgage tenant he is held to be of full age as soon as he can keep correct accounts, measure cloth, and in similar matters transact his father's business. And thus the lord has the complete custody both of the persons of the sons and heirs of their tenants and also of their estates, so as to have complete power of disposing of both. As for instance, when heirs are in wardship, the lord is entitled to make grants of ecclesiastical benefices, and to have the marriage of any female wards, who may have come under wardship, and to manage their affairs generally, in the same way as he is accustomed to manage his own. The lords cannot however by law alienate any part of the inheritance in perpetuity. Nevertheless the lord must in the mean time maintain the heir with due honour, having regard to the value of the inheritance, and must even discharge the debts of the deceased tenant so far as the amount of the inheritance and the duration of the wardship will permit, and to this extent the lord is bound by law to answer for the debts of the predecessors in title. Moreover the lord may transact business on behalf of the heir, and institute and prosecute suits to protect his rights, if the adversary sets up the nonage of the heir as a defence. A lord however is not bound to make himself a defendant in the place of the heir either in a writ of right or in case of a disseisin except in a single instance. . . . .

Further the guardians are bound to restore to the heirs their inheritances in good condition and freed from debts, this obligation being measured by the duration of the wardship and the amount of the inheritance. If however it be doubtful whether the heir be of full age or not, then without question the lord shall have both the person and lands of the heir in his wardship until reasonable proof of his age be given by the oaths of competent men of the neighbourhood.

Chap. 10. If however the heirs in wardship have more lords than one, their chief lords, that is to say, those to whom the heirs owe allegiance, in respect of their first fiefs, will have their wardship. They are however bound, in respect of their other fiefs, to render reliefs and other fitting services to the lords of those fiefs. And thus the chief lord will retain the wardship over the whole under the rule above-mentioned. It is however to be observed that if any one should hold in chief of our lord the king, in that case the wardship of such a one belongs entirely to our lord the king, whether the heir should have other lords or not, because our lord the king can have no competitor, much less any superior. Nevertheless in the solitary case of burgage tenure our lord the king is not preferred to others in wardship. If however our lord the king commits to another the wardship of the heir, a distinction is to be observed between an unconditional grant of the wardship, so that the guardian is not bound to render any account concerning it to the Exchequer, and a restricted grant. If indeed the grant is unconditional, then the guardian will be able to present to vacant benefices, and to manage, in a lawful manner, the affairs of the estate as if it were his own.

(3) Guardianship in Socage.

Lib. vii. c. 11. Haeredes vero sokemannorum, mortuis antecessoribus suis, in custodia consanguineorum suorum propinquiorum erunt; ita tamen quod si haereditas ipsa ex parte patris descenderit, ad consanguineos ex parte matris descendentes custodia ipsa referatur. Sin autem ex parte matris haereditas ipsa descenderit, tunc ad consanguineos paternos custodia pertinet. Nunquam enim custodia alicujus de jure alicui remanet, de quo habeatur suspicio quod possit vel velit aliquod jus in ipsa haereditate clamare [1].

[1] See as to the rights and duties of guardian in socage, Littleton, lib. ii. c. 5. § 123. When the heir arrives at the age of fourteen he may oust the guardian, and call upon him to render an account of the issues and profits of the land. If the guardian has provided the heir with a marriage, he is bound to account for the value of the marriage. Guardianship in socage exists at the present day, but a new power of appointing a guardian by the will of the father was given by 12 Car. II, c. 24. s. 8, and has been extended to the mother by the Guardianship of Infants Act 1886 (49 and 50 Vict. c. 27). See below, Chap. IX.

CHAP. II. § 4 (3).

TRANSLATION.

Book vii. chap. 11. The heirs of socage tenants shall on the death of their ancestor be under the guardianship of their nearest relations, provided however that if the inheritance has descended from the father's side, the wardship belongs to relations on the mother's side, but if the inheritance has descended from the mother's side, then it belongs to the relations of the father. For the wardship is never by law placed in the hands of any one of whom any suspicion can be entertained that he may or will claim any right to the inheritance.

(4) MARRIAGE OF FEMALE TENANTS.

Lib. vii. c. 12. Mulier vero vel mulieres, si haeredes alicujus remanserint, in custodia dominorum suorum remanent. Quae, si infra aetatem fuerint, in custodia erunt, donec plenariam habent aetatem [1]: et cum habuerint aetatem, tenetur dominus earum eas maritare, singulas cum suis rationabilibus portionibus. Si vero majores fuerint, tunc quoque in custodia dominorum suorum remanebunt, donec per consilium et dispositionem dominorum maritentur. Quia sine dominorum dispositione vel assensu nulla mulier, haeres terrae, maritari potest de jure et consuetudine regni. Unde si quis filiam vel filias tantum habens haeredem illam vel illas in vita sua sine assensu domini sui maritaverit, inde juste secundum jus et consuetudinem regni perpetuo exhaeredatur, ita quod inde de caetero nihil recuperare poterit nisi per solam misericordiam; et hoc ea ratione, quia cum maritus ipsius mulieris haeredis alicujus homagium de tenemento illo facere tenetur ipsi domino, requirenda est ipsius domini ad id faciendum voluntas et assensus; ne de inimico suo, vel alio modo minus idonea persona, homagium de feodo suo cogatur recipere [2]. Verum si quis licentiam quaerit a domino suo filiam suam et haeredem alicui maritandi, tenetur dominus aut consentire, aut justam causam ostendere quare consentire non debeat; aliter enim etiam contra ipsius voluntatem poterit mulier ipsa de consilio patris sui et pro voluntate libere maritari. . . . . . .

Si semel legitime nuptae fuerint, tunc, si viduae factae fuerint, postmodum non tenebuntur iterum sub custodia dominorum esse;

[1] This was fourteen, extended, so far as relates to the right of the lord to hinder a marriage, by the Statute of West. I, c. 22, to sixteen. Littleton, lib. ii. c. 4. § 103. See above, p. 42.

[2] In Bracton's time this strictness was somewhat relaxed (fol. 88), and by the Statute of Merton, 20 Hen. III, cc. 6, 7 (below, Chap. III. § 3), a definite penalty was imposed.

licet teneantur assensum eorum requirere in se maritandis praedicta ratione[1]. CHAP. II. § 4 (4).

TRANSLATION.

Book vii. chap. 12. If the surviving heirs are females they will remain under the wardship of their lords. If they are under age they will be in wardship until they have attained full age, and when they are of age, the lord is bound to provide them with a marriage, providing each with her reasonable share of the inheritance. If however they are of full age, in that case too they will remain in the wardship of their lord until they are married by the advice and disposal of their lord. For by the law and custom of the realm no woman, being an heiress of land, can be married without the disposal and assent of her lord. Hence if any one having only a daughter or daughters has during his lifetime given the heiress or heiresses in marriage without the assent of his lord, according to the law and custom of the realm he is by right for ever deprived of the inheritance, so that thereafter he can recover no part of it except by mere grace. And the reason is, because the husband of the woman who is the heiress of any one is bound to do homage for that tenement to her lord, therefore the free will and consent of the lord is necessary for the doing of homage, lest he should be compelled to receive homage for his fee from his enemy, or from a person on some other grounds unsuitable. But if any one seeks license from his lord to marry to any one his daughter and heiress, the lord is bound either to assent or to show good reason why he should not assent, for otherwise the woman shall be at liberty to marry by the advice of her father and her own free will contrary to the will of the lord. . . . .

If a woman has once been lawfully married, and becomes a widow, she will not afterwards again come under the wardship of the lord, although she is bound to apply for the assent of the lord to her marriage for the reason above given.

§ 5. *Escheat and Forfeiture.*

The law of escheat for failure of heirs remains in substance at the present day as it is stated in the following passage, the practical difference being that, as it is but comparatively

[1] See Magna Carta, 1217, c. 8; below, Chap. III. § 4; and for more on the subject of 'marriage,' below, Chap. III. § 3.

CHAP. II. § 5. seldom the case at the present day that freehold lands are held of any known mesne lord, escheat on failure of heirs of a freeholder usually is to the Crown as lord paramount.

Escheat was formerly divided under the heads of escheat *propter defectum sanguinis* (failure of heirs), and escheat *propter delictum tenentis* (for the felony of the tenant)[1]; the latter kind of escheat however has, together with forfeiture for the same causes, been abolished by 33 and 34 Vict. c. 23.

Lib. vii. c. 17. Ultimi haeredes aliquorum sunt eorum domini[2]. Cum quis ergo sine certo haerede moritur, quemadmodum sine filio, vel filia, vel sine tali haerede de quo dubium non[3] sit ipsum esse propinquiorem haeredem et rectum, possunt et solent domini feodorum feoda illa tanquam escaetas in manus suas capere et retinere; quicunque sint domini, sive rex, sive alius. Praeterea vero si quis veniens dicat se inde haeredem rectum, si per misericordiam domini sui, vel per praeceptum domini regis, hoc impetrare poterit, inde placitabit, et sic, si quod jus inde habuerit, diracionare poterit; ita tamen quod interim terra illa in manu domini feodi remaneat: quia quotienscunque dubitaverit aliquis dominus de haerede tenentis sui, utrum sit rectus haeres an non, terram illam tenere poterit, donec hoc ei legitime constiterit. Idem quoque dictum est supra de haerede ubi dubium sit an sit major an minor: in hoc tamen est differentia, quod in uno casu intelligitur interim haereditas illa quasi escaeta ipsius domini; in alio vero casu, non intelligitur esse sua, nisi de custodia. Sin autem nullus appareat qui haereditatem ipsam tanquam haeres requirat, tunc ipsi domino remanet haereditas ipsa escaeta ad remanentiam; ita quod de illa disponere potest, sicut de sua propria, ad libitum suum. Praeterea si quae mulier ut haeres alicujus in custodiam domini sui devenerit, si de corpore suo forisfecerit, haereditas sua domino suo pro delicto ipsius remanet escaeta. Praeterea si quis de felonia convictus fuerit, vel confessus in curia, eo per jus regni exhaeredato, terra sua domino suo remanet escaeta. Notandum quod si quis in capite de domino rege tenuerit, tunc tam terra quam omnes res mobiles suae, et catalla penes quemcunque inveniantur, ad opus domini regis

[1] See Blackstone, ii. chap. 15.

[2] As to whether title by escheat can properly be considered as falling under descent, see Blackstone, ii. p. 245.

[3] 'Non' is omitted in the printed texts, but is sanctioned by the MSS. and is necessary to the sense.

capientur sine omni recuperatione alicujus haeredis. Sin autem de alio quam de rege tenuerit is qui utlagatus est[1], vel de felonia convictus, tunc quoque omnes res suae mobiles regis erunt. Terra quoque per unum annum remanebit in manu domini regis, elapso autem anno, terra eadem ad rectum dominum, scilicet ad ipsum de cujus feodo est, revertetur, veruntamen cum domorum subversione et arborum extirpatione. Et generaliter quotiescunque aliquis aliquid fecerit vel dixerit in curia, propter quod per judicium curiae exhaeredatus fuerit, haereditas ejus ad dominum feodi de quo illa tenetur tanquam escaeta solet reverti. Forisfactura autem filii et haeredis alicujus patrem non exhaeredat neque fratrem, neque alium quam seipsum. Praeterea si de furto fuerit aliquis condemnatus, res ejus mobiles et omnia catalla sua vicecomiti provinciae remanere solent, terram autem, si qua fuerit, dominus feodi recuperabit statim, non expectato anno. Cum quis vero per legem terrae fuerit utlagatus, et postmodum beneficio principis paci restitutus, non poterit ea ratione haereditatem, si quam habuerit ille vel haeredes sui, versus dominum suum (nisi ex misericordia ipsius domini et beneficio) recuperare; forisfacturam autem et utlagariam solet dominus rex damnatis remittere, nec tamen aliena jura ideo quaerit infringere.

TRANSLATION.

Book vii. chap. 17. The ultimate heir of a freeholder is his lord. When therefore any one dies without an ascertained heir, as for instance without a son or a daughter or without any person who is unquestionably the next and rightful heir, the lord may and usually does take into his hands that fee as an escheat and retain it, whether the lord be the king or another.

And further if any person comes and says that he is the rightful heir of that fee, if by the grace of the lord or the writ of our lord the king he is able so far to prevail, he shall be admitted to suit, and thus, if he has any right to the inheritance, he will be able to establish it. Nevertheless in the mean time that land shall remain in the hands of the lord, because whenever the lord has a doubt concerning the heir of his tenant, whether or not he be the rightful heir, he may hold the land until the matter be established according to law. The same thing too has been said above when it is doubtful whether the heir is of full age or a minor. There is however

[1] The law of forfeiture in the case of outlawry is not affected by the Statute 33 and 34 Vict. c. 23. See for process of outlawry, Blackstone, iii. 283.

CHAP. II. § 5. this difference, that in the former case the inheritance is in the mean time regarded as an escheat belonging to the lord himself, in the latter it is not regarded as the property of the lord except by way of wardship. But if no one comes forward to claim the inheritance as heir, then the inheritance itself remains in the hands of the lord permanently as an escheat, so that he can dispose of it as his own at his pleasure. Further if any woman, when she has as heir of any person become subject to the wardship of the lord, loses her chastity, her inheritance remains in the lord's hands as an escheat for her default. Furthermore if any one be convicted of felony, or have confessed to felony in open court, he becomes disinherited by the law of the land, and all his land passes to his lord as an escheat. It is to be observed that if any such person holds in chief from our lord the king, then not only his land but also all his moveable goods and chattels, in whosesoever hands they may be found, shall be seized for the benefit of our lord the king, and the heir of such person shall not be entitled to recover any of them. But if a person, holding of any one other than the king, is outlawed or is convicted of felony, then too all his movable property shall belong to the king. His land too shall remain for one year in the hands of our lord the king, but after the lapse of a year the same land shall revert to the rightful lord, that is to say to him whose fee it is, nevertheless with buildings thrown down and trees rooted up. And speaking generally so often as any one has done anything or made any confession in court by reason of which he has by the judgment of the Court been disinherited, his inheritance reverts as an escheat to the lord of the fee of whom it is held. But the forfeiture of a son and heir of any one works no disherison of his father or brother or of any other person than himself. Further if any one be convicted of theft, his moveable goods and all his chattels pass to the sheriff of the county, if however he have any land the lord of the fee shall recover it at once without waiting the year. But if any one has been outlawed by the law of the land, and afterwards by the royal clemency been reinstated, he cannot on that account recover against his lord any inheritance which may have belonged to himself and his heirs, unless by an act of grace and favour on the part of the lord; for though our lord the king often remits forfeiture and outlawry incurred by conviction, he does not in so doing attempt to derogate from the rights of other persons.

§ 6. *Descent of an Estate of Inheritance.*

The great characteristic of a *feodum* in the second sense of the term as an estate of inheritance[1] is its capacity of descending to heirs, whether lineal descendants or collaterals. We have not as yet arrived at the distinction between different estates of inheritance, between estates in fee simple and estates in fee tail. The following passage contains in outline a statement of the law of descent which prevailed till it was recast by the Inheritance Act of 1833 (3 and 4 Will. IV, c. 106). The law as to the descent of socage estates, as stated in this passage, though still traceable in Bracton[2], before long became obsolete, and the same rules as to descent prevailed in lands held in socage and by knight-service. The equal division of lands amongst all the sons only continued as a local custom in certain boroughs, and in the county of Kent, where it is still the rule. The point as to the respective rights of the younger son and a grandson (child of a predeceased elder son) was by Bracton's time settled by the adoption of the general principle that the issue represents the ancestor *in infinitum*[3].

Lib. vii. c. 3. Haeredum autem alii sunt proximi, alii sunt remotiores; proximi haeredes alicujus sunt quos ex suo corpore procreaverit, ut filius vel filia. Quibus deficientibus vocantur[4] haeredes remotiores, scilicet nepos vel neptis ex filio vel filia recta linea descendens, in infinitum. Item frater et soror, et ex illis ex transverso descendentes. Item avunculus, tam ex parte patris quam ex parte matris, et matertera similiter, et ex illis descendentes. Cum quis ergo haereditatem habens moriatur, si unicum filium haeredem habuerit, indistincte verum est quod filius ille patri suo succedit in toto. Si plures reliquerit filios, tunc distinguitur utrum ille fuerit miles, sive per feodum militare tenens, aut liber sokemannus. Quia si miles fuerit, vel per militiam

[1] See above, p. 60.

[2] See Bracton, 76 a. Pollock and Maitland, Hist. of Eng. Law, ii. p. 267.

[3] See Bracton, 64 b.

[4] Notice the influence of the phraseology of Roman Law. This expression was properly applied to the action of the praetor. See Just. Inst. iii. 5.

CHAP. II. § 6. tenens, tunc secundum jus regni Angliae primogenitus filius patri succedit in totum; ita quod nullus fratrum suorum partem inde de jure petere potest. Si vero fuerit liber sokemannus, tunc quidem dividetur haereditas inter omnes filios, quotquot sunt, per partes aequales, si fuerit socagium illud antiquitus divisum, salvo tamen capitali mesuagio primogenito filio pro dignitate aesneciae suae; ita tamen quod in aliis rebus satisfaciet aliis ad valentiam. Si vero non fuerit antiquitus divisum, tunc primogenitus secundum quorundam consuetudinem totam haereditatem obtinebit, secundum autem quorundam consuetudinem postnatus filius haeres est[1]. Item si filiam tantum unam reliquerit quis haeredem, tunc id obtinet indistincte quod de filio dictum est. Sin autem plures filias, tunc quidem indistincte inter ipsas dividetur haereditas, sive fuerit miles, sive sokemannus pater earum; salvo tamen primogenitae filiae capitali mesuagio sub forma praescripta. Notandum autem quod si quis fratrum vel sororum, inter quos dividitur haereditas, sine haerede de corpore suo moriatur, tunc illa portio, quae defuncti erat, inter caeteros superstites dividetur. Maritus autem primogenitae filiae homagium faciat capitali domino de toto feodo. Tenentur autem postnatae filiae, vel earum mariti, servitium suum de suo tenemento capitali domino facere per manum primogenitae vel ejus mariti. Nullum tamen homagium vel etiam fidelitatem aliquam tenentur mariti postnatarum filiarum marito primogenitae filiae inde facere in vita sua, nec earum haeredes primi vel secundi: tertii vero haeredes ex postnatis filiabus exeuntes, secundum jus regni homagium tenentur facere de suo tenemento haeredi filiae primogenitae et rationabile relevium. Praeterea sciendum est quod mariti mulierum quarumcunque, nihil de haereditate uxorum suarum donare possunt sine consensu haeredum suorum, vel de jure ipsorum haeredum aliquid remittere possunt nisi in vita sua[2]. Si vero filium habuerit quis haeredem, et praeterea filiam habuerit vel filias, filius ipse succedit in totum: unde contingit quod si quis plures habuerit uxores, et ex qualibet

[1] As to borough English, see Blackstone, ii. 83; above, p. 48.

[2] Before the Married Women's Property Act 1882 (45 and 46 Vict. c. 75), the husband by the marriage acquired an estate in his wife's lands during the joint lives of himself and his wife. This estate in certain events (death of wife having had issue born alive and capable of inheriting) was enlarged into an estate by the 'curtesy' of England (per legem Angliae), i. e. an estate for the husband's own life. See below, Chap. III. § 16. It has recently been decided that the husband's estate by the curtesy is not affected by the above statute. See Hope v. Hope; Law Reports (1892) 2 Chancery, p. 336.

filiam vel filias, extremo autem ex postrema unicum filium, ille filius solus obtinet haereditatem patris; quia generaliter verum est quod mulier nunquam cum masculo partem capit in haereditate aliqua; nisi forte aliud speciale fiat in aliqua civitate, et hoc per longam consuetudinem ejusdem civitatis. Si vero habuerit quis plures uxores, et ex qualibet earum filiam vel filias, omnes filiae erunt pares ad haereditatem patris, eodem modo ac si omnes essent ex eadem matre[1]. Cum quis autem moriatur sine haerede filio vel filia, si habuerit nepotes vel neptes ex filio vel filia, tunc quidem indubitanter succedent ipsi eodem modo quo predeterminatum est supra de filio vel filiabus, et sub eadem distinctione. Illi enim qui recta linea descendunt, semper illis preferuntur qui ex transverso veniunt. Cum quis autem moriatur habens filium postnatum, et ex primogenito filio praemortuo nepotem, magna quidem juris dubitatio solet esse, uter illorum preferendus sit alii in illa successione, scilicet utrum filius an nepos. Quidam enim dicere volebant filium postnatum rectiorem esse haeredem quam nepotem talem, ea videlicet ratione, quia filius primogenitus cum mortem patris non expectaret, nec expectavit quousque haeres ejus esset, et ita cum postnatus filius superviveret tam fratrem quam patrem, recte ut dicunt patri succedit. Aliis vero visum est nepotem talem de jure avunculo suo esse praeferendum. Cum enim nepos ille ex filio primogenito exierit, et de corpore suo exstiterit haeres, in totum jus quod pater suus, si adhuc viveret, haberet, ipse patri suo succedere debet. Ita dico si pater suus non fuerit ab avo suo forisfamiliatus[2], etc.

c. 4. Deficientibus autem hiis qui recta linea descendunt, tunc frater vel fratres succedent[3]: aut si non reperiantur fratres, vocandae sunt sorores; quibus praemortuis eorum liberi vocantur;

[1] As to co-parceners, see below, Chap. V. § 5.

[2] Glanvill proceeds to say that a son might be enfeoffed of a portion of his inheritance in his father's lifetime; by which proceeding the descendants would be barred, though not the son himself, from claiming the residue of the inheritance by descent. This practice however failed to obtain a permanent place in English law. The passage probably marks an attempt by the tribunals to give effect to a rule derived partly from the old practice of equal division, partly from the new doctrine of primogeniture, and partly from the civil law.

[3] The Inheritance Act, 1833 (3 and 4 Will. IV, c. 106), has introduced the important alteration in the law of descent that next after lineal descendants the inheritance shall go to the nearest lineal ancestor. This has based the succession of collaterals on a new principle. They now take, not as before directly from the person last seised, but as representing the common ancestor.

CHAP. II. § 6. post hos vero vocantur avunculi et eorum liberi; postremo materterae vel earum liberi; habita et observata distinctione superius praenotata, inter filios militis et filios sokemanni et nepotes similiter; habita quoque distinctione inter masculos et feminas.

c. 16. Quaeri potest de bastardo, qui nullum haeredem habere potest, nisi de corpore suo habuerit haeredem.

TRANSLATION.

Book vii. chap. 3. Of heirs some are next of blood, some are more remote. Heirs next of blood are those who are begotten of the body of the ancestor, as a son or a daughter. On failure of these the remoter heirs are called to the inheritance, for instance the grandson or grand-daughter descending in a direct line from a son or a daughter without limit. Next the brother and sister and their descendants. Next the uncle both on the father's and the mother's side, and the aunt in like manner and their descendants. When therefore any one who holds an inheritance dies, if he has an only son, it is without reserve true that that son is the successor of his father in the whole inheritance. If he has left more sons than one, then there is a distinction whether he was a knight, or a tenant of a knight's fee, or a free socman. Because if he were a knight or a tenant by knight service, then according to the law of England the first-born son succeeds his father in the whole inheritance, so that none of his brothers can demand of right any share therein. If however he be a free socage tenant, then the inheritance shall be divided between all the sons, however many they be, in equal shares, if that socage-land has been subject by ancient custom to division, saving however to the eldest son the chief messuage in consideration of the dignity due to his seniority. He must however make its value good to the others out of other property. But if there is no ancient custom of division, then the first-born son according to the custom of some places will get the whole inheritance, while according to the custom of other places the youngest son is the heir. Further if any one leaves an only daughter his heiress, then what has been said above as to an only son applies to the daughter without any distinction. But if he has left more daughters than one, then the inheritance shall be divided equally among them, whether their father was a knight or a socman, saving however to the eldest daughter the chief messuage according to the above-mentioned rule. And it should be observed that if any one of the brothers or sisters, amongst whom the inheritance is divided, dies without an heir of the body, then the share which belonged to the deceased shall be divided amongst the other survivors. Further the husband of the eldest daughter shall do homage to the chief lord for the whole fee. And the younger daughters or their husbands are bound to render to the chief lord their service for their tenement by the hand of the eldest daughter or her husband. Yet the husbands of the younger daughters are not bound to render any homage or even any fealty to the husband of the eldest daughter in respect of the land during their lives, neither are their heirs in the first or second generation bound to do so; but the heirs of the third generation, the issue of the younger daughters, are by the laws of the realm bound to render homage and reasonable relief to the heir of the eldest daughter. Further it is to be observed that the husband of any woman cannot make a gift of any portion of the inheritance of his wife without the consent of her heirs, nor can he release any portion belonging to the heirs except only for his own life. If moreover any one has a son and heir, and besides a daughter or daughters, the son succeeds to the whole; hence it follows that if any one has had more wives than one, and a daughter or daughters by each of them, and at last by the latest wife an only son, that son alone takes the inheritance of his father, because speaking generally it is true that a woman never shares with a man in any inheritance, unless there may be some special practice in a particular borough existing by virtue of long usage in that borough. If however any one has had several wives, and by each of them a daughter or daughters, all the daughters shall share equally in the father's inheritance, in the same way as if they had all been by the same mother. And when any one dies without a son or daughter as heir, if he has grandsons or grand-daughters, children of a son or a daughter, then there is no question but that the grandchildren succeed in the same way as has been before laid down concerning the succession of a son or daughter, and that the same rules apply. For lineal descendants are always preferred to collaterals. But when any one dies leaving a younger son and a grandson the son of a pre-deceased eldest son, there often arises a great question as to the law, which of the two should be preferred to the succession, that is to say whether the younger son or the grandson. For some used to be of opinion that the younger son was the rightful heir rather than the grandson, apparently on the ground that the first-born son, not having survived his father, never actually became his heir, and so the

CHAP. II. § 6.

CHAP. II § 6. younger son having survived both his father and his brother rightly in their view succeeds his father. Others however think that the grandson ought of right to be preferred to his uncle. For since the grandson is the issue of the eldest son, and is the heir of his body, he ought to succeed to all the rights which his father would have had if he had been still alive. This is my opinion, unless the father has been portioned by the grandfather, etc.

Chap. 4. On the failure of lineal descendants the brother or brothers will succeed, or, if there are no brothers, then the sisters come in; if these are pre-deceased, their children are next in order, and after these the uncles and their children, and in the last place aunts and their children, bearing in mind the distinction above explained between the sons of a knight and the sons of a socman, and the grandsons in like manner, observing also the distinction between males and females.

Chap. 16. A doubt may arise as to the case of a bastard, who cannot have any heir unless he have an heir of his body.

§ 7. *Alienation.*

The following passage shows that in Glanvill's time the conception that a tenant in fee simple might freely alienate his land had not been reached. He can only do so to a certain extent, and for certain purposes. But the restrictions upon alienation, with the exception of the prohibition of wills of land, were not of a feudal character; they are not, as was the case soon after the reign of Henry II, encroachments upon the freedom of the tenant devised by the selfishness and avarice of the lords [1]. They are the relics of primitive custom antecedent to the growth of feudal ideas.

We have seen that though in Anglo-Saxon times freedom of alienation in the case of bookland was the general rule, this freedom was deemed to depend on the power conferred on the grantee by the charter [2]; if there were no evidence of the grant of any such power, or if the land was hereditary land as opposed to bookland in the strict sense of the term, a distinc-

[1] See below, Chap. III. § 14. [2] See above, p. 13.

tion which is apparent in the following passage, the property of the family could not be wholly alienated[1]. This passage shows that traces of the old customary law prevailed in the time of Henry II. After this reign questions as to the right of alienation depend not on the duties of the freeholder towards his heir, but on his duties towards his lord. The distinction between the power of alienating the ancient inheritance of the family and the recent acquisition of the tenant is very characteristic of the history of alienation. It is very prominent in the customary law of France.

Liv. vii. c. 1. In alia enim acceptione accipitur dos secundum leges Romanas; secundum quas proprie appellatur dos, id quod cum muliere datur viro, quod vulgariter dicitur maritagium[2]. Potest itaque quilibet liber homo, terram habens, quandam partem terrae suae cum filia sua vel cum aliqua alia qualibet muliere, dare in maritagium, sive habuerit haeredem sive non; velit haeres,

[1] 'Si bocland autem habeat, quam ei parentes sui dederint, non mittat eam extra cognationem suam.' Leg. Hen. I, 70, § 21; Thorpe, Anc. Laws and Inst., fol. ed., p. 251. See Pollock and Maitland, Hist. of Eng. Law, ii, p. 307.

[2] The property which by Teutonic custom was given by the father of the bride to the husband on her marriage was called faderfioh or faderfeum (father's cattle; see above, p. 32, note). See Laws of Ethelbert, 81; Thorpe, fol. ed., p. 10. As to the distinction between this gift and dower, see below, Chap. III. § 4. As to maritagium, or frank-marriage, see Glanvill, lib. vii. c. 18. 'Liberum dicitur maritagium quando aliquis liber homo aliquam partem terrae suae dat cum aliqua muliere alicui in maritagium, ita quod ab omni servitio terra illa sit quieta, et a se et haeredibus suis versus capitalem dominum acquietanda. Et in hac quidem libertate ita stabit terra illa usque ad tertium haeredem, nec interim tenebuntur haeredes inde facere aliquod homagium: post tertium vero haeredem ad debitum servitium terra ipsa revertetur et homagium inde capietur.—Cum quis itaque terram aliquam cum uxore sua in maritagium ceperit, si ex eadem uxore sua haeredem habuerit filium vel filiam clamantem et auditum infra quatuor parietes, si idem vir uxorem suam supervixerit, sive vixerit haeres sive non, illi in vita sua remanet maritagium illud, post mortem vero ipsius ad donatorem vel ejus haeredes est reversurum. Sin autem ex uxore sua nunquam habuerit haeredem, tunc statim post mortem uxoris ad donatorem vel haeredes ejus revertetur maritagium.' In later times estates in frank-marriage came to be regarded as a particular kind of estates in special tail. See Coke upon Littleton, lib. i. c. 2. § 17. As to dower, see below, Chap. III. § 4; and as to the husband's life estate by the curtesy, ib. § 16, and above, p. 96, n. 2.

CHAP. II. § 7. si habuerit haeredem, sive non velit; immo etiam eo et contradicente et reclamante. Quilibet etiam, cuicunque voluerit, potest dare quandam partem sui liberi tenementi in remunerationem servitii sui vel loco religioso in eleemosynam, ita quod si donationem illam seisina fuerit secuta, perpetuo remanebit illi cui donata fuerit terra illa et haeredibus suis, si jure haereditario fuerit ei concessa. Si vero donationem talem nulla sequuta fuerit seisina, nihil post mortem donatoris ex tali donatione contra voluntatem haeredis efficaciter peti potest[1]; quia id intelligitur secundum consuetam regni interpretationem potius esse nuda promissio quam aliqua vera promissio vel donatio. Licet autem ita generaliter cuilibet de terra sua rationabilem partem pro sua voluntate, cuicunque voluerit, libere in vita sua donare; in extremis tamen agenti non est cuiquam hactenus permissum[2]; quia possit tunc immodica fieri haereditatis distributio, si fuisset hoc permissum illi qui fervore passionis instantis et memoriam et rationem amittit, quod non nunquam evenire solet; unde presumeretur quod si quis in infirmitate positus ad mortem, distribuere cepisset terram suam, quod in sanitate sua minime facere voluisset, quod potius proveniret illud ex furore animi quam ex mentis deliberatione. Posset tamen hujusmodi donatio in ultima voluntate alicui facta ita tenere, si cum consensu haeredis fieret et ex suo consensu confirmaretur. Cum quis autem de terra sua in maritagium vel alio modo donat, aut habet haereditatem tantum, aut questum tantum[3], aut haereditatem et questum. Si haereditatem tantum, poterit quidem ex eadem haereditate quandam partem donare, ut dictum est, cuilibet extraneo cuicunque voluerit. Si autem plures habuerit filios mulieratos, non poterit de facili praeter consensum haeredis sui[4] filio suo postnato de haereditate sua quantamlibet partem donare: quia si hoc esset permissum, accideret inde frequens prius natorum filiorum exhaeredatio, propter majorem patrum affectionem quam saepe erga postnatos filios suos habere solent. Sed numquid filio suo bastardo potest quis, filium et haeredem habens, de haereditate sua donare? Quod si verum est, tunc melioris conditionis est in hoc bastardus filius quam mulieratus postnatus; quod tamen verum est. Si vero questum tantum

[1] For without livery of seisin no estate would have passed.

[2] This restriction upon power of disposing of lands by will is a limitation of the usual freedom of alienation of privately-owned lands enjoyed before the Conquest.

[3] The contrast is here between hereditary land and land acquired by gift or purchase.

[4] See Pollock and Maitland, Hist. of Eng. Law, ii. p. 307.

habuerit is qui partem terrae suae donare voluerit, tunc quidem hoc ei licet, sed non totum questum, quia non potest filium suum haeredem exhaeredare. Veruntamen si nullum haeredem filium vel filiam ex corpore suo procreaverit, poterit quidem ex questu suo cuicunque voluerit quandam partem donare, sive totum questum haereditabiliter. Ita quod si inde seisitus fuerit is cui donatio illa facta fuerit in vita donatoris, non poterit aliquis haeres remotior donationem illam irritare. Potest itaque quilibet sic totum questum donare in vita sua, sed nullum haeredem inde facere potest, neque collegium[1], neque aliquem hominem; quia solus Deus haeredem facere potest non homo. Sin autem et haereditatem et questum habuerit; tunc indistincte verum est quod poterit de questu suo quantamlibet partem, sive totum, cuicunque voluerit donare, ad remanentiam, de haereditate vero sua nihilominus dare potest secundum quod praedictum est dum scilicet rationabiliter hoc fecerit. Sciendum autem quod si quis liberum habens socagium plures habuerit filios, qui omnes ad haereditatem aequaliter pro aequalibus proportionibus sunt admittendi, tunc indistincte verum est quod pater eorum nihil de haereditate vel de questu, si nullam habuerit haereditatem, alicui filiorum, quod excedat rationabilem partem suam quae ei contingat de tota haereditate paterna, donare poterit. Sed tantum donare poterit de haereditate sua pater cuilibet filiorum suorum de libero socagio in vita sua, quantum jure successionis post mortem patris idem consequuturus esset de eadem haereditate. Veruntamen occasione liberalitatis quod patres in filios vel etiam in alios exercere solent, juris quidem quaestiones in hujusmodi donationibus saepius emergunt[2].

TRANSLATION.

Book vii. chap. 1. The expression 'dower' is used in a different sense in the Roman Law, in which the term is properly applied to that which is given to the husband together with the wife, which we commonly call 'a marriage gift.' Thus every free man, being a tenant of land, may give with his daughter or any other woman a certain part of his land by way of marriage gift, whether he has

[1] 'Corporation.' For the precise meaning of a corporation, see note on the Statute 7 Ed. I, Chap. IV. § 2.

[2] Glanvill proceeds to put the case of a gift of land by a father to one of four or more sons and the death of the donee without issue. Who is to succeed? Not the father, for it is a maxim that 'nemo ejusdem tenementi simul potest esse haeres et dominus.' The same reasoning excludes the elder sons. On this point he says, 'Magna juris dubitatio et contentio in curia domini regis evenit vel evenire potest.'

CHAP. II. § 7. any heir or not, and whether the heir consent or not, nay even contrary to his express desire and protest. Any one also may give to whomsoever he pleases any part of his free tenement by way of remuneration for services, or in favour of a place of religion by way of free alms, with the consequence that, if the gift has been followed up by seisin, the land shall be held for ever by the donee and his heirs, if it was granted to him for an estate of inheritance. But, if the gift was not followed by livery of seisin, nothing can effectually be claimed by reason of such a gift after the death of the donor against the will of his heir, because such a transaction is regarded according to the established practice of the kingdom rather as a bare promise than as a valid promise or gift. And speaking generally any one may in his lifetime freely give to any one a reasonable part of his land at his pleasure. But a death-bed gift has never yet been sanctioned, and the reason is because at such a time there might well be an unreasonable dissipation of the inheritance, if persons should be allowed to dispose of their property when under the pressure of severe suffering both reason and memory fail them, as not seldom happens. The presumption therefore is that if any one brought by bodily ailment to death's door should have set about distributing his land in a manner which in health he would by no means have adopted, such conduct proceeded rather from derangement of mind than from deliberate choice. It may however be that a gift of this character made to any one in a last will may hold good, provided it be made with the consent of the heir, and be confirmed by him.

Now when any one makes a grant of land by way of marriage gift or in any other mode, either he possesses hereditary land only, or acquired land, or both hereditary land and acquired land.

If he has hereditary land only he may, as has been said above, give a certain part of that inheritance to any stranger he pleases. If however he have many sons born in lawful wedlock, he will not readily be able without the consent of his heir to grant to his younger son any part of his inheritance; because, if this were allowed, there would happen in consequence a disinherison of the elder son on account of the greater affection which fathers often feel towards their younger children. But it may be asked whether any one having a son and heir can make a gift of any part of his inheritance to his bastard son. If he may, it follows that the bastard son is in this respect in a better position than a younger legitimate son; which is nevertheless true. If however he who wishes to make a gift of a portion of his land have nothing but land which he has purchased, he may indeed do this, but not to the extent of the whole of the purchased land, because he may not disinherit the son who is his heir. However if there be no son or daughter begotten of his body, he may then give any part of his purchased land to any one he pleases, or the whole of it, for an estate of inheritance. So that if the donee shall be seised of that land in the lifetime of the donor no remoter heir shall be able to avoid the gift. And so in this manner any one may during his lifetime give away the whole of his purchased land, but he cannot make any person, whether a corporate body or an individual, heir thereof, because it is God alone and not man who can create an heir. But if he have both purchased and hereditary land, then it is true without distinction that he can give any part he pleases of his purchased land, or the whole of it, to any other person in perpetuity, and he can nevertheless give also part of his hereditary land according to what has been said above, provided he does it reasonably. It is further to be observed that if any one who holds land in free socage has more sons than one who ought all to be admitted to the inheritance in equal shares, then it is true without distinction that their father cannot make grants either of hereditary or purchased land (if he have no inherited land) to any one of his sons in excess of the reasonable share of the whole inheritance which belongs to such son. But the father may make a grant to any one of his sons of such portion of the inheritance of free socage lands as the donee would be entitled to receive after the death of his father by right of succession out of the same inheritance. However by reason of the liberality which fathers often practise towards their sons or even towards other persons, doubtful questions of law very often arise in gifts of this kind.

§ 8. *A Fine of Lands.*

The only direct way of conveying a freehold interest in lands in possession from one person to another was by feoffment accompanied by livery of seisin. But a practice prevailed as early as the reign of Henry II of conveying lands by means of a fictitious or collusive suit, commenced by arrangement by the intended alienee against the alienor, and then compromised with permission of the court by the defendant making his peace with the claimant and abandoning his defence. The whole transaction was then enrolled of record, and a document was drawn up, called in later times the foot, chirograph,

CHAP. II. § 8. or indenture of the fine, of which the following is a specimen. This operated as an assurance of lands binding upon all persons, whether parties or not, who did not within a given time, finally fixed (after having been extended indefinitely) at five years, put in their claim [1]. The doctrine of fines was formerly one of the most intricate branches of the law of real property. As however this mode of dealing with land was entirely abolished by the Act for the Abolition of Fines and Recoveries (3 and 4 Will. IV, c. 74), the subject belongs entirely to the antiquities of our law, and need not be discussed further.

Lib. viii. c. 1. Contingit autem multotiens loquelas motas in curia domini regis per amicabilem compositionem et finalem concordiam terminari, sed ex consensu et licentia domini regis, vel ejus justiciariorum, undecunque fuerit placitum, sive de terra sive de alia re. Solet autem plerumque concordia talis in communem scripturam redigi et per communem assensum partium; et per illam scripturam coram justiciis domini regis in banco residentibus [2] recitari, et coram eis utrique parti, sua scriptura per omnia alii concordans, liberari: et erit sub hac forma facta :—

c. 2. Haec est finalis concordia, facta in curia domini regis apud Westmonasterium in vigilia beati Petri Apostoli, anno regni Regis Henrici Secundi tricesimo tertio coram Ranulpho de Glanvilla justiciario domini regis, et coram H. R. W. et T. et aliis fidelibus domini regis qui ibi tunc aderant, inter Priorem et Fratres Hospitalis de Hierusalem, et W. T. filium Normanum et Alanum filium suum, quem ipse attornavit [3] in curia domini regis ad lucrandum et perdendum, de tota terra illa et de pertinentiis, excepta una bovata terrae et tribus toftis quas ipse W. tenuit: de qua terra tota (excepta praedicta bovata et tribus toftis) placitum fuit inter

[1] Blackstone, ii. 354.

[2] At this time the Curia Regis, sitting usually at Westminster, or where-ever the royal court happened to be. After Magna Carta (c. 17) the Court of Common Pleas was that in which fines were levied, and in which all other real actions were tried.

[3] An attorney, or as he is called in lib. x. c. 18, 'responsalis ad lucrandum vel perdendum,' was a person appointed by the suitor in open court to conduct the particular cause for him, upon which a writ issued to the sheriff commanding him to receive the person so appointed in the place of the principal.

eos in curia domini regis; scilicet quod praedictus W. et Alanus concedunt et testantur donationem quam Normanus pater ipsius W. ipsis inde fecit, et illam terram totam quietam clamavit de se et haeredibus suis domui Hospitalis et praefato Priori et Fratribus in perpetuum: excepta una bovata terrae praefata et exceptis tribus toftis quae remanent ipsi W. et Alano et haeredibus suis, tenenda de domo Hospitali et praedicto Priore et Fratribus in perpetuum, et per liberum servitium quatuor denariorum per annum pro omni servitio: et pro hac concessione et testificatione et quieta clamantia praefatus Prior et Fratres Hospitalis dederunt ipsi Wilhelmo et Alano centum solidos sterlingorum.

c. 3. . . . Et nota quod dicitur talis concordia finalis eo quod finem imponit negotio, adeo ut neuter litigantium ab ea de caetero poterit recedere. Alterutro enim non tenente vel non faciente quod convenit, et altera partium inde se conquerente, praecipietur vicecomiti quod ponat eum per salvos plegios quod sit coram justiciis domini regis inde responsurus quare finem illum non tenuerit.

Translation.

Book viii. chap. 1. Now it often happens that suits originated in the court of our lord the king are put an end to by a friendly agreement and final concord, provided the consent and licence of our lord the king or his justices is obtained, whatsoever be the subject-matter of the suit, whether land or anything else. In general a final concord of this character is reduced to writing between the parties and takes effect by their common consent, and the writing is read before the justices of our lord the king, and in their presence the document is delivered to both parties, one writing being an exact counterpart of the other; and it shall be drawn up in the following form:—

Chap. 2. This is a final concord, made in the court of our lord the king held at Westminster on the vigil of the blessed Apostle Peter in the thirty-third year of King Henry II before Ranulph de Glanvill the justiciar of our lord the king, and before H. R. W. and T. and other lieges of our lord the king who were then present, between the Prior and Brethren of the Hospital of Jerusalem and W. T. son of Norman and Alan son of W. T., whom he made his attorney in the court of our lord the king for gain and loss concerning all that land with the appurtenances, except one oxgang of land and three tofts, which the said W. held, concerning all which land (except the aforesaid oxgang and three

CHAP. II. tofts) there was a suit between them in the court of our lord the
§ 8. king, to wit that the aforesaid W. and Alan allow and bear witness to the gift which Norman the father of the aforesaid W. made thereof to the said Prior and Brethren and abandoned all claim to that land as regards himself and his heirs in favour of the House of the Hospital and the aforesaid Prior and Brethren for ever, except as to one oxgang of land and three tofts, which are retained by the said W. and Alan and their heirs to be held of the house of the Hospital and of the aforesaid Prior and Brethren for ever, by the free service of four pennies per annum in lieu of all other service; and for this grant, assurance and quit claim the aforesaid Prior and Brethren of the Hospital have given to the said W. and Alan one hundred shillings sterling.

Chap. 3. And observe that this is called a final concord because it puts an end to the transaction, so that neither of the litigants can thereafter go back from it. For if either of the parties do not abide by or act according to the agreement, and the other party complain thereof, the sheriff will be commanded to put that party under secure pledges to appear before the justices of our lord the king to answer wherefore he hath not abided by that fine.

§ 9. *Modes of recovering Seisin of Lands. Assizes of Mort d'Ancestor and of Novel Disseisin.*

A sketch of the history of the law of real property would not be complete without some notice of the remedies available for the ouster or dispossession of the freehold. The extracts given above (§ 2) are sufficient to show the nature of the supreme and final remedy by which a tenant in fee simple could assert his right, namely, by writ of right commenced either in the Curia Regis or the territorial court. The extreme complexity of the proceedings in the writ of right caused the adoption of other remedies, by which nothing was decided as to the question of the right of property, but merely that the one party had a right as against the other to the actual seisin or possession of the lands.

By seisin is meant, as has already been pointed out, possession as of freehold, that is the possession which a freeholder could assert and maintain by appeal to law. There was in fact no other kind of legal possession known at this early time. In later times the word seisin comes to be distinct from possession, the latter being applicable to the possession of a leaseholder or copyholder, the former being confined to the possession of a freeholder. It should however be observed that it was by no means necessary for a person to be seised as of right. There was a seisin as of right, and a seisin as of wrong. If the rightful freeholder was ousted and in fact lost his possession, he was disseised or put out of seisin, and the wrongdoer or disseisor was seised in his place, holding by wrong the estate from which he had ousted the rightful possessor. He had in fact a 'defeasible title[1],' and for many purposes acts done by him held good as if he had been rightfully seised. A person so seised by wrong was of course liable to be turned out by the rightful owner either by actual entry upon him, or by process of law. A complicated system of rules grew up as to the circumstances and conditions under which this right of actual entry existed, when it ceased, and when the only remedy was by calling in aid the action of the tribunals. The refinements arising on this part of the law it will not be necessary to discuss.

In the great majority of cases when litigation arose as to the right to land, it would be sufficient to decide which of the two litigants had the right of immediate actual possession; or rather, whether the plaintiff could make out a right to the possession as against the person actually in possession. It was comparatively seldom necessary to have recourse to the higher remedy of a writ of right in order to decide which of the two had the greater right to the land. These possessory actions, as the former class were called, must be brought within a fixed period, and different limits were from time to time assigned[2].

[1] Coke upon Littleton, 58 b.

[2] See as to different periods of limitation, Hale, History of the Common Law, p. 122.

CHAP. II. § 9.

The writ of Assize of mort d'ancestor was perhaps[1] instituted by the ordinance called the Assize of Northampton, A.D. 1176, and was applicable only to the particular case where, upon the death of the demandant's father or mother, brother or sister, uncle or aunt, nephew or niece, some person other than the lawful heir had entered upon the land. If the demandant could prove that the ancestor died seised 'in his demesne as of fee,' and that he (the demandant) was the right heir, the result of the decision of these points in his favour would be the establishment of the right of the demandant to the possession as against the tenant. Similar writs, varied in form to suit the circumstances, and called by different names, were used for the recovery of the possession by a person claiming as heir of a more distant relation. It will be seen from the form of the writ that this proceeding would not be applicable when lands had been devised by will, and therefore after the statutes conferring the power of devising lands by will this remedy was no longer available[2].

The Assize of novel disseisin[3] was applicable where the

[1] Cap. 4. 'Item si quis obierit francus-tenens, haeredes ipsius remaneant in tali saisina qualem pater suus habuit die qua fuit vivus et mortuus de feodo suo; et catalla sua habeant unde faciant devisam defuncti: et dominum suum postea requirant, et ei faciant de relevio et aliis quae ei facere debent de feodo suo. Et si haeres fuerit infra aetatem, dominus feodi recipiat homagium suum et habeat in custodia illum quamdiu debuerit. Alii domini, si plures fuerint, homagium ejus recipiant, et ipse faciat eis quod facere debuerit. Et uxor defuncti habeat dotem suam et partem de catallis ejus quae eam contingit. Et si dominus feodi negat haeredibus defuncti saisinam ejusdem defuncti quam exigunt, justitiae domini regis faciant inde fieri recognitionem per duodecim legales homines, qualem saisinam defunctus inde habuit die qua fuit vivus et mortuus; et sicut recognitum fuerit, ita haeredibus ejus restituant. Et si quis contra hoc fecerit et inde attaintus fuerit, remaneat in misericordia regis.' (Stubbs, Select Charters, p. 151.)

[2] See Blackstone, iii. p. 187.

[3] This is also referred to in the Assize of Northampton, cap. 5: 'Item justitiae domini regis faciant fieri recognitionem de dissaisinis factis super assisam, a tempore quo dominus rex venit in Angliam proximo post pacem factam inter ipsum et regem filium suum.' (Stubbs, Select Charters, p. 152.) The origin of the Assize of novel disseisin is ascribed by Pollock and Maitland (Hist. of Eng. Law, i. p. 124) to the Assize of Clarendon, 1166 A.D.; it certainly cannot be of later date than 1167 A.D.

demandant himself had been turned out of possession. The material points necessary for him to establish appear from the following writ[1]. If successful, the demandant would in this proceeding recover his possession, and also damages for the injury sustained.

This was the usual remedy for the recovery of the possession of lands. In certain cases which need not be here specified, it was necessary to resort to the writ of right. But as a rule all practical purposes were attained by means of one of the forms of action adapted to trying the right of possession.

The remedy by the Assizes of mort d'ancestor and novel disseisin was only applicable in particular cases. The remedy for the recovery of possession, applicable to all cases, whether falling under the two classes just mentioned or not, was the writ of entry. The law on this subject (now obsolete) is of far too intricate and complicated a character to be discussed here[2]. The remedy by assize was preferred when applicable, as being more expeditious[3]. In later times both the older proprietary and possessory remedies, or real actions as they were called, were superseded by the action of ejectment, the history of which is noticed below[4]. After having long fallen into disuse, these real actions were abolished by 3 and 4 Will. IV, c. 27, sec. 36.

Lib. xiii. c. 1. Generalia quae circa praemissa placita de recto frequentius in curia contingunt hactenus in parte sunt expedita. Nunc vero ea quae super seisinis solummodo usitata sunt restant prosequenda: quae quia ex beneficio constitutionis regni[5] quae

[1] See Blackstone's account of the Assize of Novel Disseisin, iii. p. 187.

[2] See Blackstone's sketch of the Writ of Entry, iii. p. 180, etc.

[3] 'Festinum remedium,' Stat. West. II, 13 Ed. I, c. 25.

[4] See Chap. V. § 1.

[5] This probably refers to the ordinance mentioned in Glanvill, ii. 7 (see above. § 2), which introduced the practice of referring the decision on a writ of right to the oaths of twelve men properly chosen, instead of deciding it by battle. This mode of trial *per recognitionem* (known as 'the grand assize') seems by the same ordinance to have been extended to questions of possession. From the practice of trial *per recognitionem* arose trial by jury in civil cases.

CHAP. II. § 9. Assisa nominatur in majori parte transigi solent per recognitionem, de diversis recognitionibus restat tractandum.

c. 2. Est autem quaedam recognitio quae vocatur de morte antecessoris. . . . . Cum quis itaque moritur seisitus de aliquo libero tenemento, ita quod inde fuerit seisitus in dominico suo sicut de feodo suo [1], haeres eandem seisinam antecessoris sui recte petere potest, et si major fuerit habebit tale breve :—

c. 3. Rex Vicecomiti salutem. Si G. filius T. fecerit te securum de clamore suo prosequendo, tunc summone per bonos summonitores duodecim liberos et legales homines de vicineto de illa villa, quod sint coram me vel justiciis meis ea die parati sacramento recognoscere [2], si T. pater praedicti G. fuit seisitus in dominico suo sicut de feodo suo de una virgata terrae in illa villa die qua obiit; si obiit post primam coronationem meam, et si ille G. propinquior haeres ejus est, et interim terram illam videant, et nomina eorum imbreviari facias, et summone per bonos summonitores R. qui terram illam tenet, quod tunc sit ibi auditurus illam recognitionem. Et habeas ibi summonitores, etc.

c. 32. Postremo de illa recognitione quae appellatur de nova disseisina restat dicendum. Cum quis itaque infra assisam domini regis, id est infra tempus a domino rege de consilio procerum ad hoc constitutum [3], quod quandoque majus quandoque minus censetur, alium injuste et sine judicio disseisiverit de libero tenemento suo, disseisito hujus constitutionis beneficio subvenitur, et tale breve habebit :—

c. 33. Rex Vicecomiti salutem. Questus est mihi N. quod R. injuste et sine judicio disseisivit eum de libero tenemento suo in illa villa, post ultimam transfretationem meam in Normaniam. Et ideo tibi praecipio quod si praefatus N. fecerit te securum de clamore suo prosequendo, tunc facias tenementum illud reseisiri de catallis quae in eo captae fuerunt, et ipsum cum catallis esse facias in pace usque ad clausum Paschae, et interim facias duodecim liberos et legales homines de vicineto videre terram illam et

[1] 'In his demesne as of fee'; the proper technical expression for an estate of fee simple in possession.

[2] The jury consist of neighbours who are assumed to know themselves or to have heard from others the true facts of the case and to be prepared to state them truly upon their oaths. The notion that the jury are to hear evidence and give the verdict in accordance with the evidence is of later growth.

[3] See above, p. 109.

nomina eorum imbreviari facias: et summone illos per bonos summonitores quod tunc sint coram me vel justiciis meis parati inde facere recognitionem. Et pone per vadium et salvos plegios praedictum R. vel ballivum suum, si ipse non fuerit inventus, quod tunc sit ibi auditurus illam recognitionem. CHAP. II. § 9.

c. 34. Brevia autem de nova disseisina diversis modis variantur secundum diversitatem tenementorum in quibus fuerint disseisinae. Si autem aut levetur fossatum aliquod aut prosternetur, aut si exaltetur stagnum alicujus molendini, infra assisam Domini Regis, ad nocumentum liberi tenementi alicujus, secundum haec brevia variantur in hunc modum.

c. 37. Praeterea si facta fuerit disseisina in communia pasturae[1] tunc breve tale erit. Rex Vicecomiti salutem: Questus est mihi N. quod R. injuste et sine judicio disseisivit eum de communi pastura sua in illa villa, quae pertinet ad liberum tenementum suum in eadem villa, vel in illa alia villa, post ultimam transfretationem meam in Normaniam. Et ideo tibi praecipio quod si praefatus N. fecerit te securum de clamore suo prosequendo tunc facias duodecim liberos, etc. videre pasturam illam et tenementum et nomina eorum, etc.

Translation.

Book xiii. chap. 1. The general matters which are of more frequent occurrence in the king's court in the prosecution of suits relating to the right to land have hitherto been in part discussed. It now remains to treat of the proceedings which are concerned with the seisin alone. These by the benefit of the ordinance of the kingdom which is called the Assize are for the most part prosecuted by the process of recognition. I must therefore treat of the different kinds of recognitions.

Chap. 2. Now there is one recognition which is called the recognition relating to the death of the ancestor. . . . Thus when any dies seised of any tenement, provided that he was seised in his demesne as of fee, the heir may demand the same seisin as his ancestor had, and if he be of age will be entitled to the following writ:—

The King to the Sheriff greeting. If G. son of T. shall give thee security for the prosecution of his claim, then summon by good summoners twelve free and competent men of the neighbourhood of that township, to be before me or my justices on such

[1] As to common of pasture, see below, Chap. III. § 18 (2).

CHAP. II. § 9. a day prepared to certify on oath whether T. the father of the aforesaid G. was seised in his demesne as of fee of one yard-land in such a township on the day on which he died, whether he died since my first coronation, and whether the said G. is his next heir, and in the meantime let them view that land, and cause their names to be enrolled, and summon by good summoners R. who holds that land, to be present to hear the verdict and have there the summoners, etc.

Chap. 32. In the last place it remains to treat of that recognition which is called the Assize of novel disseisin. Thus when any one within the Assize of our lord the king, that is, within the time appointed for this purpose by our lord the king upon the advice of his great men, which is fixed sometimes at a longer sometimes at a shorter limit, has disseised any one of his free tenement unjustly and without the judgment of a court, there is in aid of the disseisee the benefit of this ordinance, and he shall have the following writ:—

Chap. 33. The King to the Sheriff greeting. N. has complained to me that R. has illegally and without the judgment of a court disseised him of his free tenement in such a township, since the time of my last voyage to Normandy. And therefore I command thee that if the aforesaid N. gives thee security for the prosecution of his claim, thou shouldest cause the chattels which have been seised in that tenement to be restored thereto, and cause it with the chattels to be in peace up to the close of the octave of Easter, and in the mean time cause twelve free and competent men of the neighbourhood to view that land, and cause their names to be enrolled, and summon them by good summoners to be at that date before me or my justices prepared to deliver their verdict thereon. And bind the aforesaid R. or his bailiff by security and safe pledges to be present to hear that verdict.

Chap. 34. Moreover the writs of novel disseisin are varied in different ways according to the difference of the tenements in which the disseisins have taken place. Thus if a bank be levelled or thrown down, or if the water of any mill pool be raised so high as to injure any man's free tenement, and that act be done within the assize of our lord the king, the writs are varied to suit the circumstances in the following manner. . . .

Chap. 37. Moreover if a disseisin has been effected in the case of common of pasture there shall be the following writ. The

King to the Sheriff greeting. N. has complained to me that R. unjustly and without the judgment of a court has disseised him of his common of pasture in that township, which belongs to his free tenement in the same township, or in that other township, since I last crossed the sea to Normandy. And therefore I command thee if the aforesaid N. shall have given thee security for the prosecution of his claim, that thou shouldest thereupon cause twelve free, etc. to view that pasture and tenement, and cause their names, etc.

CHAP. II. § 9.

CHAPTER III

STATE OF THE LAW FROM THE END OF THE REIGN OF HENRY II TO THE END OF THE REIGN OF HENRY III.

CH. III.

In the period treated of in this Chapter we find the law of England falls into two great divisions, in respect of the modes in which it originates, namely, Statute Law, or law resting on express legislative enactment, and Common Law, or that portion of the law of the country which does not rest on express legislative enactment.

The Statute Book commences with Magna Carta, or rather with the third reissue in the ninth year of Henry III of the Charter granted by John. Although the later constitution of the legislature was not yet developed, Magna Carta and the other statutes of the reign of Henry III are of equal authority with any Act passed by Parliament after its full constitution was completed.

The field of Statute Law is at first confined and narrow. It chiefly consists in an authoritative declaration of rules which had previously existed as rules of law or custom, together with an amendment of them in some particulars. Of this character mainly are the enactments affecting private law[1] contained in Magna Carta.

[1] For the distinction between private and public law see Appendix to Part I, Table I.

With the rise of Statute Law the opposition between Common Law and Statute Law comes into prominence. We have not yet arrived at the time when the opposition between Common Law and Equity has begun. This double opposition has given an ambiguity to the expression 'Common Law.' As opposed to Statute Law, Common Law simply means law which is independent of legislative enactment: that is to say, a rule of Common Law is either a rule as it stood before some definite change was wrought in it by statute, or a rule of existing law recognised and acted upon by the courts but not resting on any statute[1]. It is plain that the great bulk of the rules of law prevailing at the period in question consisted of rules of Common Law. The sources of our knowledge of the Common Law from this time forward consist of (1) judicial records, including the forms of the writs by which actions were commenced, and reports of decisions; (2) authoritative text-books.

(1) *Judicial records*. Now that the jurisdiction of the royal Court in suits relating to the freehold was thoroughly established, and was exercised either by the Court fixed since Magna Carta[2] at Westminster, or by the itinerant judges sent to hold pleas throughout the country[3], a practice had arisen of keeping accessible records of the various cases brought before the superior tribunals. These records usually contain an abstract of the writ, or formal statement of the cause of action, which issued out of the Chancery under the king's seal. Some specimens of these writs preserved by Glanvill have been already given. As a rule they followed certain stereotyped forms, the judges refused to admit the validity of writs for which no precedent could be found. We find instances of new writs being introduced by the authority of the legislature[4], and some improvements and

[1] For the meanings of Common Law see above, p. 65, note 2.

[2] c. 17. Stubbs, Select Charters, p. 299.

[3] See above, p. 66.

[4] See the new writ given by the authority of the Council for the protection of the leaseholder, below, § 17, and the forms of writs provided by the Statute de Donis, below, Chap. IV. § 3.

CH. III. modifications of the old forms of action doubtless from time to time obtained recognition. By the Statute of Westminster II an attempt was made to extend the power of framing new writs[1]; this however was long confined within narrow limits, and did not produce the intended result of providing a legal remedy wherever experience had shown a real need of one. Strictly speaking, therefore, writs considered as a source of the Common Law may be referred either to Statute Law or to Judiciary Law, inasmuch as they derived their validity either from some express provision of the legislature, or from the fact of their recognition by the tribunals.

The decisions of the tribunals therefore now become the most important of the sources of law. Formal records are kept and studied, and a decision of a judge, especially if he be a man of weight, is treated as a precedent and followed in a similar case by another. Thus we constantly find in Bracton judicial decisions quoted as authorities for particular propositions[2]. Traces of the same practice are found in Glanvill. Records of cases adjudicated upon from the time of Richard I are in existence, and have been published amongst the documents issued by the Record Commission[3]. From this time forward the recorded decisions of the regular tribunals are looked to as authoritative statements of the law. And as from time to time new cases arise, calling for a new rule or a deduction from an old rule for which there is no precedent, the decisions of the tribunals come to constitute in the

[1] See the material part of this enactment given below, Chap. VI.

[2] See instances below, and Finlason's note on Reeves, Hist. of English Law, i. p. 300.

[3] The first publication was in 1811, under the name of Placitorum Abbreviatio. The collection edited by Sir F. Palgrave in 1835, and called Rotuli Curiae Regis, is more copious, and begins in the sixth year of Richard I. Mr. Bigelow of Boston, Massachusetts (Placita Anglo-Normanica, London, 1879), has collected various references to litigated cases to be found in historical records between the time of the Norman Conquest and Richard I. These are interesting as illustrating the gradual growth of technical procedure and legal forms, and appear in marked contrast with the regularity of the proceedings which seems to date from the reign of Henry II.

strictest sense of the term a source or cause of law. Judge-made or judiciary law[1] henceforth gradually displaces customary law.

(2) *Authoritative text-books.* Already in the time of Henry II the law had attained such a degree of uniformity throughout the country that a book was published with some claims to be called a systematic treatise on the law. Glanvill however rather presupposes the existence of a body of law than gives a complete exposition of it. It is a treatise rather on procedure than on the principles and rules of law which that procedure enforces. After Glanvill's time the elaboration of the law as a system proceeded with rapid strides. In the reign of Henry III the treatise of Henricus de Bracton was composed[2]. It purports to be a systematic exposition of the whole of English law, designed for the use of students and of judges. A great portion of the matter of the work is based on the sources of Roman law, or on the works of commentators[3]. There can be little doubt that at the time at which Bracton wrote a large amount of Roman law had been imported into the English system chiefly through the medium of clerical judges[4]. The jealousy so prevalent in later times between the common lawyers and the civilians had not yet arisen, and the newly appreciated treasures of the Roman law were doubt-

[1] For the characteristics of judiciary law see Austin on Jurisprudence, lect. xxxvii.

[2] Little is known of Bracton's life. He appears from entries in the Placitorum Abbreviatio to have served as an itinerant justice in Devonshire in 1246, 1252, and 1255. He also appears to have been an ecclesiastic, and there is a tradition that he was Archdeacon of Barnstaple. See Foss, Judges of England, ii. p. 251; Introduction to the Edition of Bracton, by Sir T. Twiss in the Rolls Series, pp. x–xii; Introduction to Bracton's Note-Book, by Prof. Maitland.

[3] Especially Azo. See a short treatise, 'Henricus de Bracton und sein Verhältniss zum Römischen Rechte,' by Dr. Carl Güterbock, Berlin, 1862, translated by Brinton Coxe, Philadelphia, 1866; Introduction by Sir T. Twiss, p. xxxiv; and the volume on 'Bracton and Azo' in the Selden Society's publications.

[4] Amongst the judges mentioned by Bracton are Martinus de Pateshull, Dean of St. Paul's; W. Ralegh, clericus; the Abbot of Reading; and the Bishops of Durham, Chester, and Carlisle. Güterbock, p. 37; Twiss, p. xxxvi.

less frequently resorted to to supply both matter and form for the decisions of an English judge[1]. Thus in incorporating a large portion of Roman law Bracton followed what was probably the prevailing tendency of the time. His work bears throughout traces of the influence of Roman law. Sometimes he inserts (not always appropriately) passages of the Institutes, Digest, or Code of Justinian; more often the form of the passage is slightly altered, but the substance remains. In arrangement and in phraseology, in casual words and turns of expression, the debt to the Roman lawyers is everywhere apparent. This is however less conspicuous in the extracts given below, relating to the law of land, than in most of the remainder of his work. The very different juristic conceptions prevailing in this branch of the law, which were due to feudalism, did not admit of any thorough application of the rules of Roman law. Many instances however will be found in the following extracts from Bracton of the application to English law of conceptions and terms borrowed from the Roman.

SECTION I.

Extracts from Statutes.

Magna Carta.

The edition of Magna Carta with which most editions of the Statutes commence is that issued in the ninth year of Henry III, A.D. 1225. The Charter was first issued by John in 1215: it was reissued in the first year of Henry III, 1216; again in 1217; and again in 1225. There are variations, in some cases of some importance, between the different editions. The following extracts contain the principal provisions of the Charter bearing upon the private law of land. It will be seen that the statute law of the reigns of John, Henry III, and Edward I is characterised throughout by marks of the

[1] See Güterbock, p. 37.

influence of the great lords (*domini capitales*). It was the interest of these great tenants *in capite* at once to restrict the oppressive rights of the Crown (and to that extent no doubt the inferior tenants participated in the benefit of the legislation), and also to protect and enhance the rights of lords of manors as against their tenants. The former characteristic is conspicuous in the following provisions of Magna Carta, the latter in the statutes of Merton, De Religiosis, De Donis, and Quia Emptores.

§ 1. *Relief.*

The following provisions fix the amount due by way of relief on the succession of the heir of the tenant, and the conditions under which it is to be exacted [1].

MAGNA CARTA (John, A.D. 1215), c. ii. Si quis comitum vel baronum nostrorum, sive aliorum tenentium de nobis in capite per servitium militare, mortuus fuerit, et, cum decesserit, haeres suus plenae aetatis fuerit et relevium debeat, habeat haereditatem suam per antiquum relevium; scilicet haeres vel haeredes comitis de baronia comitis integra per centum libras; haeres vel haeredes militis de feodo militis integro per centum solidos ad plus; et qui minus debuerit minus det secundum antiquam consuetudinem feodorum.

c. iii. Si autem haeres alicujus talium fuerit infra aetatem et fuerit in custodia, cum ad aetatem pervenerit, habeat haereditatem suam sine relevio et sine fine.

In the first charter of Henry III issued in 1216 and in the subsequent editions the latter article appears with the following addition:—

c. iii. Si autem haeres alicujus talium fuerit infra aetatem, dominus ejus non habeat custodiam ejus nec terrae suae, antequam homagium ejus ceperit; et postquam talis haeres fuerit in custodia, cum ad aetatem pervenerit, scilicet viginti unius anni, habeat haereditatem suam sine relevio et sine fine, ita tamen quod si ipse, dum infra aetatem fuerit, fiat miles, nihilominus terra remaneat in custodia domini sui usque ad terminum praedictum.

[1] As to reliefs, see above, pp. 40, 80.

CH. III. SECT. I. § 2.

TRANSLATION[1].

Chap. ii. If any of our earls or barons, or any other which hold of us in chief by knight's service, die, and at the time of his death his heir be of full age, and oweth to us relief, he shall have his inheritance by the old relief; that is to say, the heir or heirs of an earl, for a whole earldom, by one hundred pound[2]: the heir or heirs of a baron, for a whole barony, by one hundred marks; the heir or heirs of a knight for one whole knight's fee, one hundred shillings at the most; and he that hath less shall give less, according to the old custom of the fees.

Chap. iii. But if the heir of any such be within age, his lord shall not have the ward of him, nor of his land, before that he hath taken of him homage; and after that such an heir hath been in ward, when he is come to full age, that is to say, to the age of one and twenty years, he shall have his inheritance without relief and without fine; so that if such an heir, being within age, be made knight, yet nevertheless his land shall remain in the keeping of his lord unto the term aforesaid.

§ 2. *Guardian and Ward*[3].

MAGNA CARTA (1215), c. iv. Custos terrae hujusmodi haeredis qui infra aetatem fuerit, non capiat de terra haeredis nisi rationabiles exitus, et rationabiles consuetudines, et rationabilia servitia, et hoc sine destructione et vasto hominum vel rerum; et si nos commiserimus custodiam alicujus talis terrae vicecomiti vel alicui alii qui de exitibus illius nobis respondere debeat, et ille destructionem de custodia fecerit vel vastum, nos ab illo capiemus emendam, et terra committatur duobus legalibus et discretis hominibus de feodo illo, qui de exitibus respondeant nobis, vel ei cui eos assignaverimus; et si dederimus vel vendiderimus alicui custodiam alicujus talis terrae, et ille destructionem inde fecerit vel vastum, amittat ipsam custodiam, et tradatur duobus legalibus et discretis hominibus de feodo illo, qui similiter nobis respondeant, sicut praedictum est.

[1] The translations of the statutes given in this Chapter and in Chapter IV are taken from the Statutes of the Realm.

[2] The translation, which is that of the 'Inspeximus' of the Charter of 1225 in 25 Ed. I, is from the text 'haeres vel haeredes comitis de comitatu integro per centum libras, haeres vel haeredes baronis de baronia integra per centum marcas' etc.

[3] See above, pp. 41, 86.

c. v. Custos autem, quamdiu custodiam terrae habuerit, sustentet domos, parcos, vivaria, stagna, molendina, et cetera ad terram illam pertinentia, de exitibus terrae ejusdem; et reddat haeredi, cum ad plenam aetatem pervenerit, terram suam totam instauratam de carrucis et wainnagiis secundum quod tempus wainnagii exiget et exitus terrae rationabiliter poterunt sustinere [1].

In the charter of 1216 are added the words—et omnibus aliis rebus ad minus secundum quod illam recepit. Haec omnia observentur de custodiis archiepiscopatuum, episcopatuum, abbatiarum, prioratuum, ecclesiarum et dignitatum vacantium, excepto quod custodiae hujusmodi vendi non debent [2].

c. xxxvii. Si aliquis teneat de nobis per feodifirmam [3], vel per socagium, vel per burgagium, et de alio terram teneat per servitium militare, nos non habebimus custodiam haeredis nec terrae suae quae est de feodo alterius, occasione illius feodifirmae, vel socagii, vel burgagii; nec habebimus custodiam illius feodifirmae, vel socagii, vel burgagii, nisi ipsa feodifirma debeat servitium militare. Nos non habebimus custodiam haeredis vel terrae alicujus, quam tenet de alio per servitium militare, occasione alicujus parvae sergenteriae [4] quam tenet de nobis per servitium reddendi nobis cultellos, vel sagittas, vel hujusmodi.

Translation.

Chap. iv. The keeper of the land of such an heir, being within age, shall not take of the lands of the heir but reasonable issues, reasonable customs, and reasonable services, and that without destruction and waste of his men and his goods. And if we commit the custody of any such land to the sheriff, or to any other which is answerable unto us for the issues of the same land, and he make destruction or waste of those things that he hath in custody, we will take of him amends and recompense thereof, and the land

[1] By 3 Edward I, cap. 48, it is provided that if the guardian make a feoffment of the land the heir can recover against both guardian and feoffee by assize of novel disseisin, and the guardian shall lose the custody of the land. If the guardian be other than the chief lord, he is besides to be 'grievously punished by the king' (soit en greve peine denvers le roi).

[2] See these provisions re-enacted 3 Edward I, cap. 21.

[3] 'Fee farm,' that is, where a rent is reserved to the grantor in perpetuity out of the fee simple when it is granted away. See Butler's note (5) to Coke upon Littleton, 143 b, and Blackstone, ii. 43.

[4] As to petit serjeanty see above, p. 48.

CH. III. SECT. I. § 3.

shall be committed to two lawful and discreet men of that fee, which shall answer unto us for the issues of the same land, or unto him whom we will assign. And if we give or sell to any man the custody of any such land, and he therein do make destruction or waste, he shall lose the same custody; and it shall be assigned to two lawful and discreet men of that fee, which also in like manner shall be answerable to us as afore is said.

Chap. v. The keeper, so long as he hath the custody of the land of such an heir, shall keep up the houses, parks, warrens, ponds, mills, and other things pertaining to the said land, with the issues of the said land; and he shall deliver to the heir, when he cometh to his full age, all his lands stored with ploughs, and all other things, at the least as he received it. All these things shall be observed in the custodies of Archbishopricks, Bishopricks, Abbeys, Priories, Churches, and Dignities vacant, which appertain to us, except this that such custody shall not be sold.

Chap. xxxvii. If any do hold of us by fee-ferm, or by socage, or burgage, and he holdeth lands of another by knight's service, we will not have the custody of his heir, nor of his land, which is holden of the fee of another, by reason of that fee-ferm, socage or burgage; neither will we have the custody of such fee-ferm, or socage, or burgage, except knight's service be due to us out of the same fee-ferm. We will not have the custody of the heir, or of any land, by occasion of any petit serjeanty, that any man holdeth of us by service to pay a knife, an arrow, or the like.

§ 3. *Marriage.*

It has already been seen that till nearly the end of the twelfth century the right of the lord to dispose of his tenant in marriage applied only to female tenants. Glanvill does not speak of this right as a source of profit to the lord, but merely as a security against the lord being obliged to receive the homage of a hostile or unfriendly tenant[1]. That this was the origin of the practice appears clearly from the charter of Henry I[2]; nor could the lord arbitrarily refuse his consent, much less force his female tenant to marry against her will. In course of time, rights which were formerly based on purely

[1] See above, Chap. II. § 3 (4). [2] See above, p. 42, note 3.

feudal principles were retained in an exaggerated form merely because they became a source of profit to the lord. In this case the right to give consent to the marriage of a female tenant developed into the right to tender a suitable match, not only to the female tenant, but also to the male tenant if under age, a claim for which no feudal justification existed[1]. The penalty by which the lord's rights were enforced was finally fixed by the subjoined provision of the Statute of Merton.

CH. III. SECT. I. § 3.

MAGNA CARTA (1215), c. vi. Haeredes maritentur absque disparagatione, ita[2] tamen quod, antequam contrahatur matrimonium, ostendatur propinquis de consanguinitate ipsius haeredis.

STATUTE OF MERTON, 20 Hen. III, c. vi. De haeredibus per parentes vel per alios vi abductis vel detentis, ita provisum est; quod quicunque laicus inde convictus fuerit quod puerum[3] sic maritaverit, reddat perdenti valorem maritagii, et pro delicto corpus ejus capiatur et imprisonetur, donec perdenti emendaverit delictum, si puer maritetur, et praeterea donec domino regi satisfecerit pro transgressione; et hoc fiat de haerede infra quatuordecim annos existente. De haerede autem cum sit quatuordecim annorum vel ultra, usque ad plenam aetatem, si se maritaverit sine licentia domini sui, ut ei auferat maritagium suum, et dominus offerat ei rationabile maritagium ubi non disparagetur, dominus suus tunc teneat terram ejus ultra terminum aetatis suae, scilicet viginti et unius anni, per tantum tempus quod possit inde duplicem valorem maritagii recipere secundum aestimationem legalium hominum, vel secundum quod ei pro eodem maritagio prius fuerit oblatum sine fraude et malitia, et secundum quod probari poterit in curia domini regis.

De dominis qui maritaverint illos quos habent in custodia villanis vel aliis sicut burgensibus ubi disparagentur; si talis haeres fuerit infra quatuordecim annos, et talis aetatis quod consentire non possit, tunc si parentes conquerantur, dominus ille amittat custodiam usque ad legitimam aetatem haeredis; et omne commodum, quod inde perceptum fuerit, convertatur in commodum ipsius qui

[1] See above, p. 42, note 4.

[2] This proviso is somewhat significantly omitted in the Charter of 1216 and subsequent editions.

[3] Notice the extension to males.

CH. III. SECT. I. § 3. infra aetatem est, secundum dispositionem et provisionem parentum, contra dedecus ei factum. Si autem fuerit quatuordecim annorum et ultra, quod consentire poterit, et tali maritagio consenserit, nulla sequatur poena.

c. vii. Si quis haeres cujuscunque fuerit aetatis pro domino suo se noluerit maritare, non compellatur hoc facere, sed cum ad aetatem pervenerit, det domino suo et satisfaciat ei de tanto, quantum percipere posset ab aliquo pro maritagio, antequam terram suam recipiat, et hoc sive voluerit se maritare sive non; quia maritagium ejus qui infra aetatem est mero jure pertinet ad dominum feodi[1].

TRANSLATION.

MAGNA CARTA, chap. vi. Heirs shall be married without disparagement.

STATUTE OF MERTON, chap. vi. Of heirs that be led away, and withholden, or married by their parents, or by other, with force, against our peace, thus it is provided; That whatsoever layman be convict thereof that he hath so withholden any child, led away, or married, he shall yield to the loser the value of the marriage; and for the offence his body shall be taken and imprisoned until he hath recompensed the loser, if the child be married; and further until he hath satisfied our lord the king for the trespass; and this must be done of an heir being within the age of fourteen years. And touching an heir being fourteen years old or above, unto his full age, if he marry without licence of his lord to defraud him of the marriage, and his lord offer him reasonable and convenient marriage, without disparagement, then his lord shall hold his land beyond the term of his age, that is to say, of one and twenty years, so long that he may receive the double value of the marriage, after the estimation of lawful men, or after as it hath been offered him for the said marriage before, without fraud or collusion, and after as it may be proved in the King's Court. And as touching lords which marry those that they have in ward to villains, or other, as burgesses, where they be disparaged, if any such an heir be within the age of fourteen years, and of such age that he cannot consent to marriage, then if his friends complain of the same lord, the lord shall lose the wardship unto the age of the heir, and all the profit that thereof shall be taken shall be converted to the use

[1] See the Statute 3 Ed. I, cap. 22, by which these provisions of the Statute of Merton are re-enacted and extended.

of the heir being within age, after the disposition and provision of his friends, for the shame done to him; but if he be fourteen years and above, so that he may consent, and do consent to such marriage, no pain shall follow.

Chap. vii. If an heir, of what age soever he be, will not marry at the request of his lord, he shall not be compelled thereunto; but when he cometh to full age, he shall give to his lord and pay him as much as any would have given him for the marriage, before the receipt of his land, and that whether he will marry himself, or not; for the marriage of him that is within age of mere right pertaineth to the lord of the fee.

§ 4. *Widow's Dower.*

The additional provision made in the edition of 1217 to the provisions of the earlier issues of the Charter in respect of widows' rights fixed the law of dower on the basis on which it still rests. The general rule of law still is that the widow is entitled for her life to a third part of the lands of which her husband was seised for an estate of inheritance at any time during the marriage. At the present day there are means provided[1] which are almost universally adopted, of barring or defeating the widow's claim. The general rule of law however remains the same.

The history of the law of dower deserves a short notice, which may conveniently find a place here. It seems to be in outline as follows. Tacitus noticed the contrast of Teutonic custom and Roman law, in that it was not the wife who conferred a dowry on the husband, but the husband on the wife[2]. By early Teutonic custom, besides the bride-price, or price paid by the intending husband to the family of the bride[3], it seems to have been usual for the husband to make

[1] See 3 and 4 Will. IV, c. 105.

[2] 'Dotem non uxor marito, sed maritus uxori offert.' Tac. Germ. c. 18. Dos in the Roman sense was represented by the 'fader-fioh,' or gift by the father of the bride to the intending husband—the maritagium of the later law. See above, p. 101, note 2.

[3] See Laws of Ethelbert, 77; Ine, 31; Edmund, 1–4; Thorpe, Anc. Laws and Inst., fol. ed., pp. 9, 53, 108.

CH. III. SECT. I. § 4.

gifts of land or chattels to the bride herself. These appear to have taken two forms. In some cases the husband or his father[1] executed before marriage an instrument called 'libellum dotis,' specifying the nature and extent of the property to be given to the wife. Many forms of this instrument are preserved. The gift is sometimes made to the wife upon condition that if there is no issue of the marriage the property is to return to the heirs of the husband, sometimes the full property is vested in the wife[2]. Another and apparently among the Anglo-Saxons a commoner form of dower is the 'morning-gift.' This was the gift which on the morning following the wedding the husband gave to the wife, and might consist either of land or chattels[3]. It seems probable that in early times, if there was nothing in the form of gift to the contrary, the wife might, notwithstanding the marriage, alienate the property so given to her[4]. This power of disposing of the dower, if it existed, had ceased in Glanvill's time[5]. By the law as stated by Glanvill the man was bound to endow the woman *tempore desponsationis ad ostium ecclesiae*[6]. The dower might be specified or not. If not specified, it was the third part of the freehold which the husband possessed at the time of betrothal. If more than a third part was named, the dower was after the husband's death cut down to a third. A gift of less would however be a satisfaction of dower. It was sometimes permitted to increase the dower when the freehold available at the time of betrothal was small, by giving the wife a third part or less of subsequent acquisitions. This however must have been expressly granted at the time of

[1] Hence probably the species of dower called in later times 'ex assensu patris.'

[2] See Ducange, s. v. Dos.

[3] Morgen-gifu—pretium virginitatis.

[4] Kemble, Cod. Dipl. i. cx. By the Laws of Ethelbert (c. 81) it was provided that the morgen-gifu should devolve on the wife's paternal kindred if there were no issue of the marriage.

[5] Lib. vi. c. 3.

[6] 'Tenetur quisque tam jure ecclesiastico quam jure seculari sponsam suam dotare tempore desponsationis.' Glanvill, lib. vi. c. 1.

betrothal. A woman could never claim more than had been granted *ad ostium ecclesiae*. Dower too might be granted to a woman out of chattels personal, and in this case she would be entitled to a third part[1]. In process of time however this species of dower ceased to be regarded as legal, and was expressly denied to be law in the time of Henry IV[2]. A trace of it still remains in the expression in the marriage service, 'With all my worldly goods I thee endow.'

The proper remedy from the time of Glanvill, if the widow was wrongfully kept out of her dower, was by the real actions called the writ of right of dower, writ of dower, and of dower *unde nihil habet*; the last was only applicable when the widow was kept out of the whole of her dower. The first was applicable when she was deprived of part, and the second in all other cases. These forms of real actions were reserved in the statute[3] by which most kinds of real actions were abolished, but had long fallen into disuse, before the changes in procedure under the Judicature Acts, which superseded all the ancient forms of action.

MAGNA CARTA (ed. 1215), c. vii. Vidua post mortem mariti sui statim et sine difficultate aliqua habeat maritagium[4], et haereditatem suam, nec aliquid det pro dote sua, vel pro maritagio suo, vel haereditate sua quam haereditatem maritus suus et ipsa tenuerint die obitus ipsius mariti, et maneat in domo mariti sui per quadraginta dies[5] post mortem ipsius infra quos assignetur ei dos sua.

In the charter of 1216 are added the words,—nisi prius ei dos fuerit assignata, vel nisi domus illa sit castrum, et si de castro recesserit, statim provideatur ei domus competens in qua possit honeste morari quousque dos sua ei assignetur secundum quod praedictum est.

And in the edition of 1217 there is the further addition,—Assignetur autem ei pro dote sua tertia pars totius terrae mariti

[1] Glanvill, lib. vi. c. 2.

[2] Blackstone, ii. p. 134.

[3] 3 and 4 Will. IV, c. 27, s. 36; and see 23 and 24 Vict. c. 126, s. 26.

[4] i. e. her estate in frank-marriage (see above, p. 101, note 1).

[5] Called 'the widow's quarantine.' Blackstone, ii. p. 135.

CH. III. SECT. I. § 4.

sui quae sua fuit in vita sua, nisi de minori dotata fuerit ad ostium ecclesiae.

c. viii. Nulla vidua distringatur[1] ad se maritandum dum voluerit vivere sine marito, ita tamen quod securitatem faciat quod se non maritabit sine assensu nostro, si de nobis tenuerit, vel sine assensu domini sui de quo tenuerit, si de alio tenuerit.

TRANSLATION.

Chap. vii. A widow, after the death of her husband, incontinent, and without any difficulty, shall have her marriage, and her inheritance, and shall give nothing for her dower, her marriage, or her inheritance, which her husband and she held the day of the death of her husband; and she shall tarry in the chief house of her husband by forty days after the death of her husband, within which days her dower shall be assigned her, if it were not assigned her before, or that the house be a castle; and if she depart from the castle, then a competent house shall be provided for her in the which she may honestly dwell, until her dower be to her assigned, as it is aforesaid; and she shall have in the meantime her reasonable estovers of the common; and for her dower shall be assigned unto her the third part of all the lands of her husband which were his during coverture, except she were endowed of less at the church door.

Chap. viii. No widow shall be distrained to give herself in marriage, nevertheless she shall find surety that she shall not marry without our licence and assent, if she hold of us, nor without the assent of the lord, if she hold of another.

§ 5. *Scutage and Aids.*

During the Norman period a practice arose of making a composition in money for actual military service. This was called scutage or escuage[2]. Madox[3] finds traces of

[1] It seems to have been the practice for the lord to exact a fine on his female tenant's marriage, and sometimes to compel or distrain a widow to marry again in order to get the fine. See above, pp. 42, 84.

[2] The definite origin of scutage is assigned to the occasion of the expedition of Henry II to Toulouse in 1159. See Stubbs, Const. Hist. i. p. 456.

[3] Hist. Exch. ch. 16.

this practice as early as the reign of Henry I. It became very common in the reigns of Henry II, Richard I, and John. In the *Dialogus de Scaccario* (Henry II) *scutagium* is thus described: *Fit interdum, ut imminente vel insurgente in regnum hostium machinatione decernat rex de singulis feodis militum summam aliquam solvi, marcam scilicet vel libram unam, unde militibus stipendia vel donativa succedant. Mavult enim princeps stipendiarios quam domesticos bellicis opponere casibus. Haec itaque summa, quia nomine scutorum solvitur, scutagium nuncupatur* [1].

CH. III. SECT. I. § 5.

Every tenant *in capite* or immediate tenant of the Crown was bound either to supply the king with as many knights as he held knights' fees of the Crown, or to render an equivalent in money, the assessment of which must have been more or less arbitrary before this provision of Magna Carta. The fact of the tenant *in capite* doing personal service in the king's army, or paying or being duly charged with his escuage to the king, entitled him in his turn to escuage from his under-tenants by knight-service. Sometimes the amount so payable was fixed or ascertained in the charter of feoffment. But in many cases the uncertainty of the amount must have been felt as a great grievance, and hence the importance of this provision of Magna Carta. The significance of this chapter in its bearing on Constitutional History does not concern us here.

In the reissues of the Charter in the reign of Henry III the following articles were omitted. They were however revived by the Statute called 'Confirmatio Cartarum' (25 Edward I). The statute of Westminster I (3 Edward I, c. 36) ascertained the amount of aids to be taken by mesne lords, and the Statute 25 Edward III, ch. 5, c. 11, fixed those to be taken by the king [2].

MAGNA CARTA (ed. 1215), c. xii. Nullum scutagium [3] vel

[1] Stubbs, Select Charters, p. 201.

[2] Blackstone, ii. p. 65. See further as to scutage, below, § 11.

[3] Scutagium is properly distinguished from auxilium: sometimes how-

CH. III. SECT. I. § 5.

auxilium[1] ponatur in regno nostro, nisi per commune consilium regni nostri, nisi ad corpus nostrum redimendum, et primogenitum filium nostrum militem faciendum, et ad filiam nostram primogenitam semel maritandam, et ad haec non fiat nisi rationabile auxilium: simili modo fiat de auxiliis de civitate Londoniarum.

c. xv. Nos non concedemus de cetero alicui quod capiat auxilium de liberis hominibus suis, nisi ad corpus suum redimendum, et ad faciendum primogenitum filium suum militem, et ad primogenitam filiam suam semel maritandam, et ad haec non fiat nisi rationabile auxilium.

The text and translation of the statute 25 Ed. I. c. 6[2] is as follows:—

E. ausi avoms grante pur nous e pur nos heirs as Ercevesques, Evesques, Abbes, e Priurs, e as autres gentz de seinte eglise, e as Contes e Barons, e a tote la communaute de la terre, que mes pur nule busoigne tieu manere des aides, mises, ne prises, de nostre Roiaume ne prendroms, fors que par commun assent de tut le Roiaume, e a commun profit de meisme le Roiaume, sauve les auncienes aides e prises, dues e custumees.

Moreover we have granted for us and our heirs, as well to Archbishops, Bishops, Abbots, Priors, and other folk of holy church, as also to Earls, Barons, and to all the communalty of the land, that for no business from henceforth we shall take such manner of aids, tasks, nor prises, but by the common assent of the Realm, and for the common profit thereof, saving the ancient aids and prises due and accustomed.

§ 6. *Forfeiture*[3].

Magna Carta (1215), c. xxxii. Nos non tenebimus terras illorum qui convicti fuerint de felonia, nisi per unum annum et unum diem, et tunc reddantur terrae dominis feodorum.

ever the word is used in a large sense, as equivalent to any payment assessed on a knight's fee, and so including aids.

[1] See above, pp. 41, 82.

[2] See the Statutes Revised, 2nd ed. vol. i. p. 55.

[3] See above, p. 91

TRANSLATION.

Chap. xxxii. We will not hold the lands of them that be convict of felony but one year and one day, and then those lands shall be delivered to the lord of the fee.

§ 7. *Alienation*[1].

MAGNA CARTA (1217), c. xxxix. Nullus liber homo de cetero det amplius alicui vel vendat de terra sua quam ut de residuo terrae suae possit sufficienter fieri domino feodi servitium ei debitum quod pertinet ad feodum illud.

TRANSLATION.

Chap. xxxix. No freeman from henceforth shall give or sell any more of his land, but so that of the residue of the lands the lord of the fee may have the service due to him which belongeth to the fee.

§ 8. *Mortmain*[2].

MAGNA CARTA (1217), c. xliii. Non liceat alicui de cetero dare terram suam alicui domui religiosae ita quod illam resumat tenendam de eadem domo. Nec liceat alicui domui religiosae terram alicujus sic accipere quod tradat eam illi a quo eam receperit tenendam. Si quis autem de cetero terram suam alicui domui religiosae sic dederit, et super hoc convincatur, donum suum penitus cassetur, et terra illa domino suo illius feodi incurratur.

TRANSLATION.

Chap. xliii. It shall not be lawful from henceforth to any to give his lands to any religious house, and to take the same land again, to hold of the same house. Nor shall it be lawful to any house of religion to take the lands of any, and to lease the same to him of whom they were received to be holden. If any from henceforth so give his lands to any religious house, and thereupon be convict, the gift shall be utterly void, and the land shall accrue to the lord of the fee.

[1] For the meaning of this enactment and the history of the law of alienation, see below, § 14, and Chap. IV. § 5.

[2] For the law of mortmain and the construction of this enactment, see below, Chap. IV. § 2.

§ 9. *Rights of the Lord of a Manor over the Waste* [1].

STATUTE OF MERTON, 20 Henry III, c. iv. Item quia multi magnates Angliae, qui feoffaverint milites et libere tenentes suos de parvis tenementis in magnis maneriis suis, questi fuerunt quod commodum suum facere non potuerunt de residuo maneriorum suorum, sicut de vastis, boscis, et pasturis, quum ipsi feoffati habeant sufficientem pasturam, quantum pertinet ad tenementa sua: ita provisum est et concessum, quod quicunque hujusmodi feoffati assisam novae disseisinae deferant de communia pasturae suae, et coram justiciis recognitum fuerit quod tantam pasturam habeant quantum sufficit ad tenementa sua, et quod habeant liberum ingressum et egressum de tenementis suis usque ad pasturam suam, tunc inde sint contenti, et illi de quibus conquesti fuerint recedant quieti de hoc quod commodum suum de terris, vastis, boscis, et pasturis fecerint. Si autem dixerint quod sufficientem pasturam non habeant, vel sufficientem ingressum vel egressum, quantum pertinet ad tenementa sua, tunc inquiratur veritas per assisam. Et per assisam recognitum fuerit, per eosdem quod in aliquo fuerit impeditus eorum ingressus vel egressus, vel quod non habeant sufficientem pasturam et sufficientem ingressum et egressum sicut praedictum est, tunc recuperent seisinam suam per visum juratorum: ita quod per discretionem et sacramentum eorum habeant conquerentes sufficientem pasturam et sufficientem ingressum et egressum in forma praedicta; et disseisitores sint in misericordia domini regis, et dampna reddant sicut reddi debent ante provisionem istam. Si autem recognitum fuerit per assisam quod querentes sufficientem habent pasturam, cum libero et sufficienti ingressu et egressu ut praedictum est; tunc licite faciant alii commodum suum de residuo, et recedant de illa assisa quieti [2].

SECTION II.

EXTRACTS FROM BRACTON.

§ 10. *Growth of Judiciary Law.*

The following passage, taken in connexion with the extract from Glanvill's preface given in the last chapter (§ 1), illustrates what has been said above as to the development of the law at this period by means of recorded judicial decisions.

[1] See below, § 18 (2).

[2] For the translation, see below, p. 206.

HENRICI DE BRACTON, *De Legibus et Consuetudinibus Angliae.*

Lib. i. Pref. Cum autem fere in omnibus regionibus utantur legibus et jure scripto, sola Anglia usa est in suis finibus jure non scripto et consuetudine. In ea quidem ex non scripto jus venit quod usus comprobavit. Sed absurdum non erit leges Anglicanas (licet non scriptas) leges appellare, cum legis vigorem habeat, quicquid de consilio et de consensu magnatum et rei publicae communi sponsione, auctoritate regis sive principis praecedente, juste fuerit definitum et approbatum. Sunt autem in Anglia consuetudines plures et diversae secundum diversitatem locorum. Habent enim Anglici plurima ex consuetudine quae non habent ex lege, sicut in diversis comitatibus, civitatibus, burgis et villis, ubi semper inquirendum erit, quae sit illius loci consuetudo, et qualiter utantur consuetudine qui consuetudines allegant[1]. Cum autem hujusmodi leges et consuetudines per insipientes et minus doctos, (qui cathedram judicandi ascendunt antequam leges didicerint,) saepius trahantur ad abusum, et qui stant in dubiis et in opinionibus multotiens pervertuntur a majoribus, qui potius proprio arbitrio quam legum auctoritate causas decidunt, ad instructionem saltem minorum ego Henricus de Bracton animum erexi ad vetera judicia justorum perscrutanda diligenter, non sine vigiliis et labore; facta ipsorum, consilia et responsa, et quicquid inde notatu dignum inveni, in unam summam redigendo, sub ordine titulorum et paragraphorum (sine melioris sententiae praejudicio) compilavi, scripturae suffragio perpetuae memoriae commendanda.

TRANSLATION.

Whilst almost all other countries are governed by ordinances in writing and written law, in England alone the law and customs prevailing throughout the country are unwritten. In England indeed the law which has no written origin is that which usage has established. But it will not be preposterous to give to the laws of England, unwritten though they be, the name of laws, because whatever has been rightfully laid down and approved on the initiation of the royal authority, or that of the chief of the state, acting on the advice and assent of the chief men and the general approval of the community, possesses the force of law. But in England there are many and diverse customs varying in different places. For the English enjoy much by custom which

[1] As to local custom, see above, pp. 68, 74; below, Chap. V. § 6.

CH. III. SECT. II. § 10.

they do not enjoy by law; as for instance in different counties, cities, boroughs, and townships, where it is always necessary to ask, what the custom of that place is, and in what manner those who set up the custom can show that they have exercised it. Since however these laws and customs are frequently perverted by foolish and ignorant persons, who ascend the seat of judgment before they have learned the laws, and inasmuch as those who are doubtful and fluctuating in their minds are often swayed by their elders, who decide cases rather by their own arbitrary sentiments than by the authority of law, for the purpose of educating at least the younger generation, I, Henry de Bracton, have roused my soul to the diligent examination of the judgments of just men, not without nights of labour and much toil; I have brought together their acts, determinations, and opinions, and whatever else I found worthy of note in their proceedings, under one general treatise, ranking the various divisions under titles and paragraphs, without prejudice to any better opinion, so that by the instrumentality of writing they may be handed down to an everlasting remembrance.

§ 11. *Tenures.*

The following extracts give the outline of Bracton's division of Tenures. Tenures now fall into two great classes. There had always been a distinction in point of fact between the holding of land by a freeman and the beneficial enjoyment of land permitted to the non-free. In Bracton's time freehold tenure or the holding of land by free services had come to be opposed to the holding of land by non-free services or services unworthy of a freeman. What was formerly a distinction principally affecting the status of the holder comes now to be regarded as the basis of two different classes of rights of property. Dealing first with freehold tenures, Bracton proceeds to enumerate their principal classes,—knight-service, grand serjeanty, socage, and tenure by uncertain but non-military services. The nature of the tenure depends on the service to be rendered in respect of the land. The following passages seem to lead to the following principal conclusions.

(1) Where land is held of a mesne lord by knight-service the actual military service is due, not to the immediate lord,

but to the king[1]. The only exception to this rule seems to have been when the lord went with the king *in propria persona*. The theory seems to have been that for every knight's fee the service *unius militis* for forty days in every year, if called upon, or scutage in lieu thereof, was due to the Crown[2].

(2) Where military service is thus due to the king the tenure is knight-service, and the lord enjoys the valuable incidents of wardship and marriage.

(3) No services of whatever character rendered to the lord in his private capacity are sufficient, according to the better opinion, to give the tenure the character of tenure by knight-service, and consequently to cause the incidents of wardship and marriage to attach. The services must be '*propter exercitum regis et patriae tuitionem.*' In the case of freehold tenure where no military service is due a further distinction arises between tenure by uncertain services to be rendered to the lord, and socage tenure. These however probably were generally confounded together[3], and the distinguishing characteristic was evidently the one of most practical importance,—whether the lord was or was not entitled to wardship and marriage.

(4) Whether the land was held by knight-service or otherwise was a question of evidence to be decided first by reference to the charter by which the land might be burdened with military service or its equivalent, although it had been previously free from burdens, or freed from them, although previously so burdened: or if the charter was silent, regard must be had to the character and amount of the services customarily rendered in respect of the land in question, or of land in its neighbourhood. When, as was usually if not always the case (except with the king's own immediate tenants), no actual military service was rendered to the king

[1] See above, p. 35.

[2] See Coke upon Littleton, 69 a, and Madox, History of the Exchequer, chap. xvi; above, p. 131, and p. 61, note 3.

[3] Littleton expressly declares (s. 118) that every tenure that is not a tenure in chivalry is tenure in socage.

CH. III. SECT. II. § 11.

by any one in respect of the land held by knight-service [1], scutage was paid to the king in lieu thereof, to the amount assessed by the great Council, by his own immediate tenants by knight-service, whether such tenants were actually in possession of the land or not. It further appears that if a mesne lord went with the king to war or made satisfaction to the king in any manner in respect of such service, he in his turn might exact scutage from his tenants by knight-service to the amount assessed by the great Council, provided no tenant had either by himself or by deputy rendered actual service with the king in respect of the knight's fee for which the scutage was claimed [2].

Lib. iv. c. 28. fol. 207. Item dicitur liberum tenementum, ad differentiam ejus quod est villenagium [3], quia tenementorum aliud liberum aliud villenagium.

Item liberorum aliud tenetur libere pro [4] homagio et servitio militari, aliud in libero socagio cum fidelitate tantum, vel cum fidelitate et homagio secundum quosdam. Item liberorum aliud pura et libera et perpetua eleemosyna [5], quae quidem sunt tam in bonis hominum quam in bonis Dei; quia dantur non solum Deo

[1] In process of time a distinction seems to have arisen between the liability of tenants who held of the king *ut de corona* (that is, where the lands had actually been or were supposed to have been granted by the king or one of his predecessors to the tenant or his ancestor), and that of tenants who held of the king *ut de honore* (that is, where the king was temporarily or permanently entitled to the seignory in his capacity as lord paramount by virtue of escheat, wardship, &c.). The former class seem to have been considered to be strictly bound to *personal* attendance on the king, the latter not. Madox (Hist. of Exchequer, p. 454) gives two instances in the reign of Edward II of tenants holding *ut de honore* claiming on that ground exemption from personal service.

[2] A further exception occurred where the seignory of land, the tenants of which had not been accustomed to render military service, was granted by the king to a person to be held of the king by knight-service. In that case the grantee would be bound to render scutage, but could not in his turn exact it from his tenants. See the case of Roger de Sumervill, 27 Henry III, Madox, History of the Exchequer, p. 471. As to scutage generally, see Fitzherbert, Natura Brevium, 83, 84 a; Wright, Tenures, p. 120; Madox, Hist. of Exchequer, c. xvi; Coke upon Littleton, 72 b.

[3] For the meaning of villenagium in Bracton, see § 13.

[4] The land is to be held in return for, i.e. by homage and service.

[5] See above, p. 38.

et tali ecclesiae, sed abbatibus et prioribus ibidem Deo servientibus. Item est tenementum datum in liberam eleemosynam rectoribus ecclesiarum, quae pura est et libera et magis libera et pura, una quae datur ecclesiae nomine dotis in dedicatione et alia quae datur post dedicationem.

Lib. ii. c. 16. fol. 37. Item poterit quis feoffari ab alio per diversa genera servitiorum facienda, scilicet per servitium unius denarii, et reddendo scutagium, et per seriantiam unam vel plures. Et unde si tantum in denariis et sine scutagio vel seriantiis[1], vel si ad duo teneatur sub disjunctione, scilicet ad certam rem dandam pro omni servitio vel aliquam summam in denariis, id tenementum dici potest socagium[2]. Si autem superaddat scutagium et servitium regale licet ad unum obolum vel seriantiam, secundum quod superius dictum est, illud dici poterit feodum militare.

Lib. ii. c. 16. fol. 35 b. Item sunt quaedam servitia quae pertinent ad dominum capitalem, et quae consistunt in factionibus, et fiunt ex consuetudine, de termino in terminum, et de quibus oportet quod fiat mentio in scriptura[3], et alioquin peti non poterunt, ut si dicatur 'et faciendo inde sectam[4] ad curiam domini sui et haeredum suorum de quindena in quindenam, vel de tribus septimanis in tres septimanas, quolibet anno de termino in terminum.' Item 'faciendo inde tot aruras, et tot messuras, tot falcationes,' et quae omnia pertinent ad dominos feodi ex tenementis sic datis liberis hominibus, et proveniunt ex tenementis, et dici possunt feodalia sive praedialia servitia, et non personalia, nisi ratione praediorum et tenementorum. Item poterit quis feoffare alium per seriantium, quae quidem multiplex esse poterit, et unde quaedam pertinent ad ipsum dominum feoffantem, et quaedam ad ipsum regem, ut si dicatur, per servitium equitandi cum domino suo vel domina, qui proprie dicuntur *Rodknightes*, vel per servitia tenendi placita dominorum suorum, vel portandi brevia infra certa loca, vel pascendi leporarios et canes, vel mutandi aves, vel inveniendi arcus et sagittas, vel portandi; et de iis seriantiis non poterit certus numerus comprehendi. Et hujusmodi servitia omnia dici possunt intrinseca, quia in chartis et instrumentis sunt exprimenda et

[1] The tenure of grand serjeanty was usually, though not always, free from liability to scutage. Madox, Hist. Exch. xvi. p. 452.

[2] See above, p. 46.

[3] That is, in the writing which is the evidence of the grant; see below, § 12.

[4] Suit, attendance.

CH. III. SECT. II. § 11. dominis capitalibus remanebunt. Et cum propter exercitum regis et patriae tuitionem non fiunt, ideo ex talibus servitiis nullum competere deberet maritagium, nec custodia domino capitali, non magis quam de socagio. Contrarium autem habetur de quadam Abbatissa de Berking inter placita quae sequuntur regem [1] anno regni regis Henrici . . . coram W. de Raleighe, et quae recuperavit custodiam et maritagium de haerede cujusdam tenentis sui, qui tenebat tenementum suum in manerio de Berking per servitium equitandi cum ea de manerio in manerium; quod quidem Stephanus de Segrave non approbavit.

Sunt et alia genera seriantiae quae ad dominum capitalem non pertinent, sed ad dominum regem, pro exercitu regis ad patriae tuitionem vel defensionem, et hostium deprehensionem [2]: ut si quis ita feoffatus fuerit scilicet per seriantiam inveniendi domino regi unum hominem vel plures, ad eundum cum eo in expeditionem ad exercitum, equites vel pedites, cum aliquo genere armorum, et ex tali seriantia competit domino capitali sive de domino rege tenuerit, sive de alio, custodia et maritagium haeredis, quod quidem non esset tenendum in casibus praedictis. Illud idem servatur, si quis teneat per servitium inveniendi domino regi certis locis et certis temporibus unum hominem, et unum equum, et saccum cum brochia pro aliqua necessitate vel utilitate exercitum suum contingente.

Item sunt quaedam servitia quae dicuntur forinseca, quamvis sunt in charta de feoffamentis expressa et nominata, et quae ideo dici possunt forinseca, quia pertinent ad dominum regem, et non ad dominum capitalem, nisi cum in propria persona profectus fuerit in servitio, vel nisi cum pro servitio suo satisfecerit domino regi quocumque modo, et fiunt incertis temporibus, cum casus et necessitas evenerit, et varia habent nomina et diversa. Quandoque enim nominantur forinseca, large sumpto vocabulo, quoad servitium domini regis, quandoque scutagium, quandoque servitium domini regis, et ideo forinsecum dici potest, quia sit et capitur foris sive extra servitium quod sit domino capitali. Item scutagium, quod talis prestatio pertinet ad scutum, quod assumitur ad servitium militare. Item dicitur regale servitium, quia specialiter pertinet ad dominum regem et non ad alium, et secundum quod in Conquestu fuit adinventum [3], et hujusmodi servitia per-

[1] The King's Bench was that branch or department of the Curia Regis which was not fixed at Westminster, but which, in theory at least, followed the king wheresoever he might be in England. This was the proper style of the Court up to November 1, 1875.

[2] See above, p. 36.

[3] See above, Chap. I. sect. ii. § 1.

solvuntur ratione tenementorum et non personarum, quia ex tenementis proveniunt. . . . . Et quia tale servitium forinsecum non semper manet sub eadem quantitate, sed quandoque praestatur ad plus, quandoque ad minus, ideo de qualitate regalis servitii et quantitate fiat mentio in charta, ut tenens certum tenere possit quid et quantum persolvere teneatur: quod quidem dici poterit de sectis, quae pertinent ad dominum capitalem, cum possint ibi varia et diversa tempora denotari, de quibus fit mentio supra. Sed si sic dicatur, 'reddendo inde per annum tantum et faciendo tales sectas pro omni servitio, excepto regali servitio,' vel 'salvo forinseco,' tunc videndum erit imprimis si feodum illud in ipsa donatione forinsecum debuit ab initio vel non. Si autem nullum debuit ab initio, nec sit certum forinsecum in charta expressum, nunquam praestabitur, nec peti poterit propter incertitudinem. Si autem ab initio nullum, sed in ipsa donatione convenerit quod detur scutagium, et in charta exprimatur certum, erit omnino praestandum. Et sicut poterit donator liberius donare quam ipse tenuerit, et onerare seipsum et haeredes suos erga suos feoffatores, ita poterit suum feoffatum onerare ad plura servitia et ad alia, quam ipse teneatur feoffatori suo. Poterit enim de socagio facere servitium militare, et e converso, si ita convenerit ab initio inter ipsum et feoffatum suum. Sed quid si feodum feoffatoris non debeat forinsecum, et donator dederit pro forinseco, tunc refert utrum certum et expressum vel non. Si autem incertum, tunc tale quid peti non poterit; si autem forinsecum debuit ab initio, sed tamen in charta donatoris non exprimatur certum, videtur prima facie quod peti non potest. Sed revera sic erit intelligendum, quod tale et tantundem praestandum sit quantum praestant alii qui tenent tenementa in eadem villa et de eodem feodo per servitium militare.

TRANSLATION.

Book iv. chap. 28. fol. 207. Mention is sometimes made of a *free* tenement by way of distinction from that which is held in villenage, for of tenements some are free and some are villein tenements.

Also of free tenements some are held freely by homage and military service, some are held in free socage by fealty alone, or, as some say, by fealty and homage. Also of free tenements some are held in absolute and free and perpetual alms; these indeed are as much the property of man as of God, for they are given not only to God and to such a Church, but to the abbots and priors who there serve God. There is also the tenement which is given by the tenure of free alms to the rectors of churches, of which there

CH. III. SECT. II. § 11. are two kinds, one more absolute and free than the other. One is given by way of endowment at the dedication of the church, and the other after dedication.

Book ii. chap. 16. fol. 37. Also a person may be enfeoffed by another to hold by rendering different kinds of services; for instance by the service of paying one penny, and rendering scutage, and by one or more kinds of personal service. Hence, if the service consists only in paying money, and there be no scutage or serjeanty, or if the tenant be bound to two different things disjunctively, for instance to give a certain thing in lieu of all service, or a certain sum in money, in that case the tenement may be called a socage tenement. If however there be in addition scutage or service due to the king, even to the amount of no more than a halfpenny, or serjeanty, the tenement in that case may be called a military fee.

Book ii. chap. 16. fol. 35 b. Also there are certain services belonging to the chief lord which consist in the performance of certain duties. and are rendered according to custom at fixed times, and it is necessary that mention should be made of them in the charter, otherwise the lord will not be able to enforce them. For instance, if it be said 'and by the service of rendering for the said land suit to the court of the lord and his heirs every fifteen days, or every three weeks, in each year at fixed times.' Also 'by rendering therefor so many days' ploughing, reaping, or mowing.' All such services accrue to the lords of the fee from the tenements given under these conditions to free men, and issue from the tenements, and may be called services appertaining to the fee or to the land, and not personal services otherwise than in respect of lands and tenements. Also one may enfeoff another by services which may be of various kinds, and of which some belong to the lord who enfeoffs, and some to the king, as if the words are 'by the service of riding with his lord or lady, (these tenants are properly called Rodknights), or by the services of holding the pleas of their lords, or of serving writs within certain limits, or of feeding greyhounds or other dogs, or of caging hawks, or of finding bows or arrows, or carrying them,' and of these services no definite catalogue can be made. Services of this kind may all be called 'intrinsic,' because they must be expressed in charters and deeds, and then they will enure to the benefit of the chief lords. And when they have no relation to the royal army or the defence of the country, it follows that no right of marriage or wardship ought to accrue to the chief lord, any more than in the case of a socage tenement. But the contrary was held in the King's Bench in the —— year of King Henry before W. de Raleigh in the case of the Abbess of Berking, who recovered wardship and marriage from the heir of one of her tenants who held his tenement in the manor of Berking by the service of riding with her from manor to manor. This decision however was disapproved of by Stephen de Segrave.

There are two other kinds of services which belong not to the chief lord but to our lord the king, for the sake of the king's army in order to preserve and defend the kingdom and defeat its enemies. As if any one be enfeoffed as follows, that is to say by the service of finding for our lord the king one or more men, to march with him on an expedition as part of his army, whether as foot or horse soldiers with any kind of arms. From such service there accrues to the chief lord, whether he hold of our lord the king or of any other lord, the wardship and marriage of the heir, which ought not to be so held in the instances above given. The same consequence follows if any tenant holds by the service of finding for our lord the king at a certain place or time one man, or one horse, or a bag with a fastening pin for any necessary or useful purpose connected with the army.

Also there are some services which are called 'extrinsic,' although they are expressed and specified in the charter of feoffment; these may be called 'extrinsic,' for the reason that they appertain to our lord the king and not to the chief lord, unless when he has himself in his own person gone forth on military service, or unless when he has in any manner made satisfaction to our lord the king for his services. These services are rendered at times not fixed, when occasion or necessity arises, and they have various and different names. For sometimes they are called 'extrinsic,' the word being taken in a large sense as regards the service of our lord the king, sometimes they are called 'scutage,' sometimes 'royal service,' and the service may be called 'extrinsic' because it is rendered and received outside or beyond the service which is due to the chief lord. It may also be called 'scutage' because the rendering such service belongs to the shield or scutum which is used for military service. It is also called 'royal service' because it specially belongs to our lord the king and to no other, and is in accordance with the practice introduced at the Conquest, and services of this kind are rendered in respect of tenements and not of persons, because they issue out of tenements. . . . . . . And because such extrinsic service does not always remain the same in amount, but sometimes is rendered to a less, sometimes

CH. III. SECT. II. § 11.

to a greater amount, therefore mention should be made in the charter concerning the quantity as well as the quality of the royal service, so that the tenant may be able to know for certain what and how much he is bound to render; and this indeed may be said of the suit of court which belongs to the chief lord, since in the charter various and different times may be expressed concerning which mention has been made above. But if the words run thus, 'By the service of rendering for this tenement by the year so much, and performing such suits of court in lieu of all service excepting royal service,' then it will have to be seen in the first place whether from the fee comprised in the gift there was originally due extrinsic service or not. If there was no such service due originally, and there is no specific mention of extrinsic service in the charter, it shall never be rendered, nor can it be demanded by reason of uncertainty. But if there was originally no extrinsic service, but it has been agreed in the gift itself that scutage be rendered, and a definite amount of service is fixed in the charter, it shall assuredly be rendered. And as the donor may make a gift on terms more free than those under which he himself holds, and burden himself and his heirs as regards his feoffors, so he can burden his feoffee with a greater number and variety of services than those by which he is bound towards his feoffor. For he may make the tenure of the land military instead of socage, and the contrary, if this has originally been agreed between himself and his feoffee. But what if the feoffor's fee owes no extrinsic service, and the donor has made the gift in consideration of extrinsic service? The important question then is whether there is or is not a definite and express mention of extrinsic service in the gift. If the words are uncertain, then nothing of the kind can be demanded, if however extrinsic service was originally due from the tenement, but nevertheless there is no definite mention of it in the charter, it appears *prima facie* that no such service can be demanded. But in truth it must be understood thus, that service is to be rendered of the nature and amount which others render who hold tenements in the same township and of the same fee by military service.

§ 12. *A Common-Law Conveyance of a Freehold Estate.*
(1) *A Charter of Feoffment.*

The ordinary mode of granting an estate of freehold was by the process called a feoffment. A feoffment, as has been seen[1],

[1] See above, Chap. I. sect. iii. § 2.

consists of two parts. There must be (1) words of donation expressing the nature and extent of the interest to be taken by the feoffee, (2) livery of seisin, the ceremony fixed upon by law as that which is essential to pass the seisin, or possession as of freehold, from the feoffor to the feoffee. CH. III. SECT. II. § 12 (1).

The following extract is the specimen Bracton gives of a charter of feoffment. Though it was by no means necessary that the words of donation should be embodied in writing, it was usual, for the obvious object of preserving evidence of the grant, that a charter or deed of feoffment should be executed. Writing was first made essential to a feoffment by the Statute of Frauds [1].

BRACTON, lib. ii. c. 16. fol. 34 b. Fit autem donatio in scriptura per haec verba. Sciant praesentes et futuri quod ego talis dedi et concessi et hac praesenti charta mea confirmavi tali, pro homagio et servitio suo, tantam terram cum pertinentiis in tali villa . . . . . habendam et tenendam tali et haeredibus suis (generaliter vel cum coarctatione haeredum [2]) . . . . vel assignatis [3] . . . . . libere et quiete . . . . . reddendo inde per annum tantum ad certos terminos tales, et faciendo inde talia servitia et tales consuetudines . . . . . pro omni servitio consuetudine seculari exactione et demanda, (per quam generalitatem videtur expresse remittere omnia alia servitia, consuetudines, et demandas seculares, quae ad dominum pertinent de tenemento, licet hoc in charta expresse non contineatur).

TRANSLATION.

A gift in writing is made by the following words. 'Know all persons now and hereafter that I, A. B., have given and granted and by this present charter of mine have confirmed to C. D. in return for his homage and service so much land with its appurtenances in such a township to have and to hold to C. D. and his heirs' (either generally or with some limitation of heirs) 'or assigns, freely and peaceably, rendering for the same so much by the year at such and such fixed terms, and performing for the same such services and such customs in lieu of all service custom secular exaction and demand,' by which general expression

[1] 29 Car. II, c. 3.

[2] See below, Chap. IV. § 3.

[3] For the effect of these words see below, § 14.

CH. III. SECT. II. § 12 (2).

it appears that all other services customs and secular demands which belong to the lord from the tenement are expressly released, although no express words to this effect are contained in the charter.

(2) *Livery of Seisin.*

It is doubtful whether the doctrines relating to livery of seisin are mere applications of the rules of the Civil Law, or whether they are derived from primitive customs, of which the analogous rules of Roman Law may themselves be a development. Whatever may be the origin of the notion of livery of seisin [1], the following passage shows that the rules of Roman law were applied to define and regulate the doctrine. Bracton here imports certain principles from the civilians, especially from Azo [2], bearing on the theory of possession, and applies them to the doctrine of livery of seisin, which was the appropriate mode of transferring a freehold interest in lands from one person to another.

In order to acquire *possessio* two elements are necessary: (1) the consciousness of actual or possible physical control of the thing which is the subject of acquisition; (2) the *animus sibi habendi.* The requisites for the acquisition of *possessio* were to this extent common with the requisites for acquiring property by *traditio* or delivery; and the application of these rules gave rise to the feudal notion of investiture [3],—the clothing the donee with the actual possession of the land the subject of the grant.

Since, as has been seen, freehold interests were formerly the only interests in land known to the law, a grant of land is synonymous with a grant of a freehold interest in land, and the doctrines of Roman law as to conveying things movable

[1] It is probably Germanic. See Pollock and Maitland, Hist. of Eng. Law, ii. p. 84.

[2] See Güterbock, H. de Bracton und sein Verhältniss zum Römischen Rechte, pp. 59-70, and compare with the whole of the following extract the title in the Digest De Acquirenda vel Amittenda Possessione, lib. xli. tit. ii.

[3] See Spelman, sub voce.

by *traditio*, and things immovable by allowing the donee to enter on the vacant possession, gave rise to the principle that for passing a freehold interest in lands a ceremony was necessary by which the possession of the land itself should be given to the donee. This was livery or delivery of the seisin or possession of the land, and was effected either by the donor himself or his deputy. What did and what did not amount to 'livery of seisin' now becomes a curious question. Speaking generally, it must be the delivery of something, such as a clod of earth or a twig, on the land in the name of the whole, or it was sufficient if the two parties were actually present on the land and the one by word or act gave possession to the other. It was even effectual for the donor to bring the donee within sight of the land and to give him authority to enter, provided this were followed by the entry of the donee during the lifetime of the donor [1]. CH. III. SECT. II. § 12 2.

Great importance was attached to the notoriety of the transaction. That all the neighbours might know that *A* was tenant to *B* from the fact that open livery of seisin had been made to him, was of the utmost importance to *B* in order to protect and to enable him to assert his rights as lord. For in case of dispute as to the title to the lands, or the right to services, aids or reliefs, the fact of this open and notorious livery of seisin enabled the lord to appeal to the tribunal before which, since the reforms of Henry II, suits relating to land were commonly decided,—the verdict of twelve *legales homines de vicineto*, who would know themselves or have heard from their fathers the truth of the matter.

[1] See Coke upon Littleton, 48 b; where with characteristic refinement he distinguishes between livery in deed, or actual delivery of possession, and livery in law, where the transaction does not take place upon, but in sight of, the land, and is followed by the entry of the feoffee. In the case of livery not upon the lands, if the feoffee was prevented by violence or threats from entering, his estate might become completely vested by making in proper form every year 'continual claim.' See Littleton, lib. iii. c. 7.

CH. III. SECT. II. § 12 (2).

Bracton, lib. ii. c. 18. fol. 39. Item non valet donatio nisi subsequatur traditio, quia non transfertur per homagium res data, nec per chartarum vel instrumentorum confectionem, quamvis in publico fuerint recitata. Item neque per imaginariam traditionem, ubi corpore recedit et animo retinet possessionem, et vult potius quod res data cum eo remaneat, quam transeat ad donatorium, et unum agit et alterum agere simulat, sed tunc demum cum donator plenam fecerit seisinam donatorio per se si praesens fuerit, vel per procuratorem [1] et litteras si absens fuerit, ita quod charta donationis et litterae procuratoriae coram vicinis ad hoc specialiter convocatis legantur in publico, et etiam cum donator corpore et animo recesserit a possessione, si absens fuerit in ipsa traditione, sine aliqua spe et animo revertendi, ut dominus, et cum donatorius in possessione vacua extiterit corpore et animo [2] et cum voluntate retinendi possessionem, et quod unus desinat et alius incipiat possidere, quia donator nunquam desinit possidere, donec donatorius plenarie fuerit in seisina, nec jacebit seisina aliquo tempore medio vacua [3]. Videndum est primo quid sit traditio; et est traditio de re corporali propria vel aliena de persona in personam de manu propria vel aliena, sicut procuratoria, dum tamen de voluntate domini, in alterius manum gratuita [4] translatio. Et nihil aliud est traditio in uno sensu nisi in possessionem inductio de re corporali [5], ideo dicitur quod res incorporalis non patitur traditionem, sicut ipsum jus quod rei sive corpori inhaeret; et quia non possunt res incorporales possideri sed quasi, ideo traditionem non patiuntur sed quasi, nec adquiruntur nec retinentur nisi per patientiam et usum [6]. De re propria vel aliena ideo dicit,

[1] Compare Dig. lib. xli. tit. ii. 1. § 20.

[2] Compare the texts of Roman law: 'Adipiscimur possessionem corpore et animo neque per se animo aut per se corpore;' Dig. lib. xli. tit. ii. 3. § 1: 'Nulla possessio adquiri nisi animo et corpore potest;' Ib. 8.

[3] For the bearing of this principle that the freehold can never be in abeyance upon the rules of law relating to the conveyance of rights of future enjoyment, see below, Chap. V. § 3.

[4] Compare fol. 13: 'Item gratuita debet esse donatio et non coacta nec per metum vel vi extorta.'

[5] Compare Dig. lib. xli. tit. ii. 33: 'Fundi venditor etiamsi mandaverit alicui, ut emptorem in vacuam possessionem induceret, priusquam id fieret, non recte emptor per se in possessionem veniet.'

[6] As to the modes of acquiring incorporeal hereditaments, see below, § 18 (1). On the doctrine of the Roman lawyers as to quasi possessio or possession in an analogous sense of incorporeal things, or rights over the property of another, see Savigny's Treatise on Possession, translated by Sir E. Perry, pp. 130–134.

quod refert quis traditionem facere possit, et sciendum quod omnes qui donationem, etc. sive sit dominus sive non dominus. Si autem fiat traditio a vero domino, statim et sine mora incipit donatorius habere liberum tenementum, propter conjunctionem juris et seisinae [1] et mutuum utriusque partis consensum; et sufficit semel voluisse in ipsa traditione vel post traditionem, et quia res quae traditione nostrae fuerint, jure gentium nobis adquiruntur. Nihil enim tam conveniens est naturali aequitati quam desiderium domini volentis in alium rem suam transferre ratum habere [2]. Et nihil interest an ipse dominus per se tradat alicui rem suam datam, an alius voluntate ipsius sicut per procuratorem, si ipse praesens non fuerit, vel per nuntium, cum literis tamen procuratoriis patentibus, ut supradictum est in parte, continentibus voluntatem ipsius donatoris. Et in quo casu ostendantur litterae et charta, ut dici poterit, talis habuit et breve et charta, secundum quod Anglice dicitur, *hee had bothe writ and charter*. Et sive fiat traditio per ipsum dominum vel per procuratorem, et si cui fieri debeat traditio de aliqua domo per se, vel messuagio ratione alicujus fundi, eo animo ut donatorius totum fundum possideat usque ad certos terminos, cum omnibus juribus et pertinentiis suis, et ubi non est necesse omnes glebas circumire, nec ubique nec undique pedem ponere, fieri debet traditio per ostium et per haspam vel anulum, et sic erit in possessione de toto ex voluntate et aspectu et possidendi affectu [3]. Si autem nullum sit ibi aedificium, fiat ei seisina, secundum quod vulgariter dicitur, per fustim et per baculum, et sufficit sola pedis positio cum possidendi affectu ex voluntate donatoris, quamvis statim expletia non ceperit, poterit enim habere quis liberum tenementum ex traditione, quamvis statim non utatur, nec expletia capiantur, quia usus et expletia non multum operantur ad donationem. Valent tamen multotiens ad possessionis declarationem, et dici poterunt vestimenta donationum sicut traditio.

* * * * *

Item sufficit pro traditione corporali nuda voluntas domini ad alium, quasi mutata causa possessionis, dum tamen fiat cum solem-

[1] For, as observed above, p. 109, a person may be 'seised' by wrong, as when a wrongdoer turns out the rightful tenant he becomes 'seised' in his stead.

[2] Taken from the Institutes of Justinian, ii. i. § 40.

[3] 'Quod autem diximus et corpore et animo adquirere nos debere possessionem, non utique ita accipiendum est, ut qui fundum possidere velit omnes glebas circumambulet; sed sufficit quamlibet partem ejus fundi introire, dum mente et cogitatione hac sit, uti totum fundum usque ad terminum velit possidere.' Dig. xli. ii. 3. § 1.

CH. III. SECT. II. § 12 (2). nitate quod probatio non deficiat; ut si quis rem alicui locaverit vel concesserit ad terminum vitae vel annorum, et postea eidem vendiderit vel donaverit, licet eam ex tali causa primo non habuerit, eo tamen quod ipse dominus patitur eam ex tali causa vel alia quacunque apud eum esse, sua efficitur[1]. Eodem modo si ex nulla justa causa praecedente, sed si per intrusionem vel disseisinam sit aliquis in possessione rei alterius, et velit dominus proprietatis quod sua sit, sua erit, quamvis possessio apud verum dominum non fuerit: fingitur enim per voluntatem domini, quod res quasi ex eo et per manum suam ad detentorem pervenerit, possessio et dominium[2].

TRANSLATION.

Further a gift is not valid unless it be followed by delivery of possession, because the subject of the gift is not transferred by homage or by the execution of deeds or instruments, although they may have been read in public. Nor again is property transferred by an unreal delivery, when possession, though physically handed over, is intended to be retained, and when the giver means that the thing given should remain his own property rather than that it should pass to the donee, and when he does one thing and pretends to do another; but it is transferred only when the donor has given the donee full seisin by his own act if he be present, or by his attorney authorised in writing if he be absent, provided that the charter of donation and the letters of attorney be read in public before the neighbours specially assembled for the purpose, and also when the donor has both in act and intention withdrawn from possession (if he be not present at the actual handing over of possession), without any expectation or intention of returning as owner, and when the donee has been established in the vacant possession both in act and intention, and with the intention of retaining possession, and so that the one ceases and the other begins to hold

[1] Compare Dig. xli. ii. 3. § 19: 'Illud quoque a veteribus praeceptum est neminem sibi ipsum causam possessionis mutare posse. Sed si is, qui apud me deposuit vel commodavit, eam rem vendiderit mihi vel donaverit, non videbor causam possessionis mihi mutare, qui ne possidebam quidem.' Compare too the mode of conveyance by lease and release, i.e. where the lessee was in possession of land under a lease for years and then the lessor released the reversion to him by deed. See below, Chap. V. § 1.

[2] That is, a disseisor who was in by wrong might, since he had actually the seisin, accept a release of the rights of the disseisee (the rightful owner), and so acquire an indefeasible estate (see Blackstone, ii. p. 324, and above, p. 109).

possession, for the donor never ceases to hold possession until the donee is invested completely with the seisin, and the seisin will not lie vacant at any intermediate moment.

We must in the first place see what delivery is. Delivery is the voluntary passing to another of a corporeal thing belonging to the transferor or to another person, by his own proper hand or that of another person, as for instance of an attorney acting according to the will of the owner, into the hand of another person. And in one sense delivery is nothing else than the giving into possession of a corporeal thing. Therefore it is said that an incorporeal thing, such for instance as the mere right which inheres in a corporeal thing, does not admit of delivery: again, inasmuch as incorporeal things cannot be subjects of actual, but only of figurative possession, they are only acquired and held by subjection to or exercise of the right. The words 'belonging to the transferor or to another person' are used because it is important to consider who can make delivery, and it should be known that it is every one who is capable of making a gift, whether he be owner or not. If however the delivery be made by the true owner, forthwith and without delay the donee begins to have a freehold on account of the coincidence of the right and possession and the mutual consent of both parties, and it is enough once for all to have had the requisite intention, whether at the time of delivery or after delivery; and another reason is that delivery is a mode of acquiring property by the law of nature. For there is nothing so consonant to natural justice as that effect should be given to the intention of the owner when he wishes to transfer his property to another. And there is no difference whether the owner himself hands over to another the subject of the gift, or whether another person does it by his will; as for instance, if it be done through an attorney if the owner himself be not present, or by a messenger, provided he have letters patent of attorney, as has been before partly stated, containing the expression of the donor's will. And in that case the letters and the charter should both be shown, so that it may be said, as it is expressed in English, 'He had both writ and charter.' And whether the delivery be made by the owner himself or by his attorney, both in the case where delivery is to be made to any one of any house by itself, or of any messuage in respect of any land with the intention that the donee should possess the whole of the land up to certain boundaries, with all its rights and appurtenances, and in any case where there is no need that he should go round every field or tread with his feet the whole ground, delivery ought to be made by the door and by the hasp or ring, and thus the

CH. III. SECT. II. § 12 (2). donee will be in possession of the whole, by virtue of the intent and by looking at it and meaning to acquire possession. And if there be no building on the ground the seisin should be effected, as is commonly said, by the rod and staff, and the mere putting down the foot with the desire of possessing in accordance with the intention of the donor is enough, although no part of the produce is at once taken, for a man may have a free tenement by means of delivery although he do not immediately enjoy it or take any part of the produce, for actual enjoyment and taking some of the produce play no important part in the completion of the gift. They are however often of avail as evidence of possession, and may be called the outward and visible sign of a gift, just as delivery itself is.

The mere will of the owner is sometimes sufficient to effect the transfer of the corporeal tenement to another. The ground upon which the right to the possession rests is as it were changed; but this must be accompanied by some form sufficient to afford evidence of the intention of the transferor. For instance, if any one has leased and granted land to another for a term of life or years, and afterwards has sold or given the land to the same person, although at first the donee had a different ground of possession, so soon as the owner permits the land to remain in his possession by the title of sale or gift or otherwise it becomes the property of the donee. In the same way if at first there is no legal title to the possession, but a man is in possession of the property of another by intrusion or disseisin, and the owner of the property desires that it should be the property of the intruder, his it will be, although he was not the true owner who had the possession; for by a fiction the possession as well as the ownership is supposed to have been by the will of the lord, because the property has come into the possession of the disseisor as it were from the true owner and by his action.

§ 13. *Villenagium. Non-free Tenure* [1].

In early times, as has before been said, only freemen held property in land. Every person having an interest recognised and protected by law is of necessity a freeholder. The practice however of allowing villeins to continue to occupy their lands without interruption, and even to alienate and transmit their interests to their descendants, has given a new

[1] See Pollock, Land Laws, Note D.

sense to the word *villenagium*, which has now come to mean (1) the nature of a villein's interest in land, (2) the kind of interest which a villein has, though the land may be held by a freeman. Though there is some distinction, as pointed out in the text, between the rights which the lord would have against a villein and against a freeman holding in villenage, they resemble each other in this, that both hold at the will of the lord and can be turned out of the occupation of the land by him at any moment. Neither therefore can bring an assize, for this is a remedy applicable only to the freehold. There is nothing however to prevent the lord entering into a covenant with his villein, or freeman holding in villenage, to secure the continued enjoyment of the tenure. This covenant can be enforced by the villein, or freeman holding in villenage, and it appears that by a writ of covenant the *villenagium* itself might be recovered [1]. That is the first step towards the legal recognition of estates in copyhold, exactly identical, as will be seen, with the first step in the legal recognition of leasehold interests [2]. At this time the villein, or the freeman holding in villenage (except when he is protected by an express covenant under seal entered into by the lord), holds strictly at the will of the lord. The only restraints upon the will of the lord are those imposed by custom and moral or religious sanctions. The steps by which these customary practices gradually came to be recognised and enforced in courts of justice, and grew into legal rights, will be noticed in the fifth chapter.

BRACTON, lib. ii. cap. 7. fol. 36 a. Item potest quis dare tenementum quod ipse tenuit per servitium militare, tenendum in villenagium per villanas consuetudines et servitia, dum tamen certa et expressa.

Lib. iv. cap. 28. fol. 208. Item tenementorum aliud villenagium, et villenagiorum aliud purum aliud privilegiatum. Purum autem villenagium est, quod sic tenetur, quod ille qui tenet in

[1] But see as to these *conventiones* the opinion of Vinogradoff, Villeinage in England, p. 70.

[2] See below, § 17.

CH. III. SECT. II. § 13.

villenagio, sive liber sive servus, faciet de villenagio quicquid ei praeceptum fuerit, nec scire debeat sero quid facere debeat in crastino, et semper tenebitur ad incerta. Talliari autem potest ad voluntatem domini ad plus vel ad minus. Item dare merchetum ad filiam maritandam, et ita semper tenebitur ad incerta; ita tamen quod si liber homo sit, hoc faciat nomine villenagii et non nomine personae, nec enim tenebitur ad merchetum de jure, quia hoc non pertinet ad personam liberi sed villani. Si autem villanus fuerit, omnia faciat et incerta tam ratione villenagii quam personae, nec liber homo, si sic tenuerit, contra voluntatem domini villenagium retinere poterit, nec ipse compelli quod retineat nisi velit. Est etiam villenagium non ita purum sive concedatur libero homini vel villano ex conventione [1] tenendum pro certis servitiis et consuetudinibus nominatis et expressis, quamvis servitia et consuetudines sunt villanae. Et unde si liber ejectus fuerit, vel villanus manumissus vel alienatus, recuperare non poterunt ut liberum tenementum cum sit villenagium, et cadit assisa, vertitur tamen in juratam [2] ad inquirendum de conventione, propter voluntatem dimittentis et consensum, quia si querentes in tali casu recuperaverint villenagium [3], non erit propter hoc domino injuriatum propter ipsius voluntatem et consensum, et contra voluntatem suam jura ei non subveniunt, quia si dominus potest villanum manumittere et feoffare, multo potius poterit ei quandam conventionem facere, et quia si potest id quod plus est, potest multo fortius id quod minus est. Est etiam aliud genus villenagii quod tenetur de domino rege, a Conquestu Angliae, quod dicitur socagium villanum, et quod est villenagium, sed tamen privilegiatum [4]. Habent itaque tenentes de dominicis domini regis tale

[1] Conventio, 'covenant,' i.e. agreement by deed under seal, i. e. writing on paper or parchment sealed and delivered. Breve de conventione, 'writ of covenant.' Breach of a covenant always was a ground for an action at law.

[2] That is, the recognitors of the assize who had been summoned to decide the questions raised in the Assize of Novel Disseisin (see above, p. 110) were turned into a jury to determine on the fact of the existence of the alleged covenant. At this time the practice of determining questions by the voice of the recognitors of the assize was developing into trial by jury in civil proceedings generally. See Reeves, i. p. 354.

[3] From this it appears that by this form of action the villenagium itself, i.e. the right to hold the land under the obligation to render the accustomed services, could be recovered.

[4] This tenure is that from which the species of copyhold tenure known as tenure in 'ancient demesne' derived its origin. See Blackstone, ii. p. 98. Bracton (lib. i. cap. 11. fol. 7) describes what is probably the same

privilegium, quod a gleba amoveri non debent, quamdiu velint et possint facere debitum servitium, et hujusmodi villani sokmanni proprie dicuntur glebae ascripticii. Villana autem faciunt servitia sed certa et determinata. Nec compelli poterunt contra voluntatem suam ad tenenda hujusmodi tenementa, et ideo dicuntur liberi [1]. Dare autem non possunt tenementa sua, nec ex causa donationis ad alios transferre, non magis quam villani puri, et unde si transferri debeant, restituunt ea domino vel ballivo, et ipsi ea tradunt aliis in villenagium tenenda [2].

TRANSLATION.

Further a man may grant a tenement which he himself held by military service to be held in villenage by villein customs and services, provided that they are fixed and defined.

Further there is a species of tenement called a villein tenement [3]: and the tenure of villein tenements is sometimes pure villenage, sometimes privileged villenage. Pure villenage is where land is held on such terms that the tenant in villenage, whether he be free or a serf, shall do for his villein tenement whatever be commanded him, and has no right to know at night what he will have

class, as having been free men at the time of the Conquest, holding lands by free services, and as afterwards having received back their lands to be held by villein services, but retaining their personal status of freedom. As holders in villenage the assizes of novel disseisin and of mort d'ancestor were not available to them, but they might employ a remedy called by Bracton 'parvum breve de recto secundum consuetudinem manerii.' They were also protected collectively by writ of 'Monstraverunt' against an improper increase of their services. See Pollock and Maitland, Hist. of Eng. Law, ii. p. 370.

[1] The variety of customs prevailing in various districts gave rise to various species of tenure, which later lawyers found a difficulty in classifying. We find in later times that it was sometimes a matter of dispute whether a particular tenure was freehold or copyhold. Coke (Compleat Copyholder, xxxii) speaks of 'copyholds of frank-tenure which are most usual in ancient demesne. Though sometimes out of ancient demesne we shall meet with the like sort of copyholds, as in Northamptonshire there are tenants which hold by copy of court roll, and have no other evidence, and yet hold not at the will of the lord. These kind of copyholders have the frank-tenure in them, and it is not in their lords, as in case of copyholds of base tenure.' See Blackstone's tract, Considerations on Copyholds; and see below, Chap. V. § 6.

[2] See as to the mode of alienating copyholds, Chap. V. § 6.

[3] Villenage is used in this passage both in the sense of villein land and of villein tenure.

CH. III. SECT. II. § 13.

to do on the morrow; and he shall always be bound to uncertain services. Further he is liable to be taxed at the will of the lord to any extent. Further he is bound to pay a fine for the privilege of giving his daughter in marriage, and thus he will always be bound without defined limits, provided that, if he be a free man, he performs these duties as an incident of his tenure, not of personal status; and he will not by right be bound to pay the fine on marriage of a daughter, for this is appropriate to the personal status of a villein, not of a free man. But if he be a villein, he is bound to do all things, however undefined, both as an incident of his holding as a villein and of his personal status, nor can a free man, if he hold in this way, retain the villein tenement against the will of the lord, nor can he himself be compelled to retain it unless he desires to do so. There is also a holding in villenage not of such a pure type, whether the grant be to a free man or to a villein, by means of a covenant to be held for fixed services and customs named and expressed in the deed, although the services and customs are of villein nature. And if a free man or a villein who has received his freedom, or who has been conveyed to another person, is ejected from such a holding, they cannot recover the land as a free tenement because it is a villein tenement, and the assize would not lie. The assize may however be converted into a jury to inquire concerning the covenant, because of the intent and assent of the transferor; for if the complainants in such a case recover the villein tenement, there will not on this account be any wrong done to the lord because of his intent and assent, and the law does not come to the aid of the tenant contrary to the will of the lord; since if the lord is able to free the villein and to grant him a freehold, much rather can he make a covenant with him, for if the lord can do that which is more important, all the more can he do that which is less important.

There is also another kind of villein tenure which has been held of our lord the king ever since the Conquest of England. This is called villein socage, and it is a villein tenure but of a privileged kind. Thus the tenants of the demesne of our lord the king have this privilege, that they cannot be removed from the land as long as they are willing and able to render the services which they owe, and villein socmen of this kind are properly said to be bound to the land. Moreover they render villein services, but the services are fixed and ascertained. Nor can they be compelled contrary to their desire to hold tenements of this kind, and therefore they are called free. Further they cannot make a gift of their tenements, or transfer them to others by the title of gift any more than pure villeins can, and therefore if the tenements have to be transferred, the tenant surrenders them to the lord or his bailiff, and the lord transfers them to other persons to be held in villenage. CH. III. SECT. II. § 14.

§ 14. *Alienation.*

The probable early history of alienation, and the limitations to which it was subject in the interest of the family or of the heir, have already been sketched[1]. Every limitation on alienation based on the principles of the early customary law has disappeared by the time of Bracton. But with the predominating influence of the great lords, endeavours were made to impose other restrictions on the freedom of alienation.

It appears that about the time of the passing of the provisions quoted above[2] from Magna Carta, strenuous attempts were made in the interest of the great lords to prevent a tenant alienating any part of his land. These attempts however, as appears from the following passage, were not successful. The provision in Magna Carta given above appears to be the only restraint upon alienation of lands in fee simple ever recognised by law in the interests of the lord. When lands were held of a mesne lord, the effect of this provision seems to have been that if the lands were alienated contrary to the statute the heir of the alienor might enter upon the alienee and defeat his estate[3]. This it was hoped would prevent alienations of portions of the land to the damage of the interests of the lord. The law as to alienation in the case of lands held immediately of the king was different[4]. The subject is very obscure, but it appears probable, as is asserted by Sir E. Coke in his notes on the passage of Magna Carta, that before the reign of Henry III there was no greater restraint on the alienation of lands held in fee of the Crown

[1] See above, Chap. III. § 7.

[2] Cap. xxxix. (ed. 1217). See above, p. 133.

[3] Coke, 2 Inst. p. 66. [4] Ib. p. 65.

CH. III. SECT. II. § 14.

than in the case of lands held of a mesne lord[1]; that about this time it was established (whether by this provision of Magna Carta, as Sir E. Coke thinks, or not is doubtful) that the lands held immediately of the king could not be alienated without incurring liability to a fine for a licence of alienation. It continued for a long time to be a question whether such an alienation of lands without licence was a cause of forfeiture to the Crown, or whether the king could only distrain for the fine. This doubt was set at rest by 1 Edward III, st. 2, c. 12, by which it was provided that an alienation without licence of lands held of the king in chief should not be a cause of forfeiture, but a reasonable fine should be taken in the Chancery by due process. Henceforth for a licence of alienation by a tenant *in capite* the king was held to be entitled to a third part of the yearly value of the land, and for a fine upon alienation without licence to one year's value. These fines upon alienation were abolished by 12 Car. II, c. 24[2].

BRACTON, lib. ii. cap. 19. fol. 45. Sed posset aliquis dicere quod ex hoc quod donatorius ulterius dat et transfert rem donatam ad alios, quod hoc facere non potest, quia per hoc amittit dominus servitium suum, quod quidem non est verum, salva pace et reverentia capitalium dominorum. Et generaliter verum est, quod donatorius rem et terram sibi datam donare poterit cui voluerit, nisi ad hoc specialiter agatur in possessione ne possit. Cum enim quis tenementum dederit, certum dat tenementum tali modo, ut certas consuetudines recipiat et certum servitium, secundum quod superius dictum est. Et unde de jure plus petere non poterit, si habuerit quod convenit, et sic tollat quod suum fuerit et vadat. Non enim fit donatio tali modo quod habeat custodiam terrae et haeredis maritagium, sed quod habeat homagium et servitium, sed cum homagium habuerit et tale debeatur forinsecum[3] servitium quod domino capitali, debeatur relevium, et custodia terrae, et maritagium haeredis cum evenerint, et quae

[1] No special restraint is mentioned by Bracton. See Pollock and Maitland, Hist. of Engl. Law, i. p. 316.

[2] See First Report on the Dignity of a Peer, pp. 398–400, and for the later history of the law of alienation of lands, see below, Chap. IV. § 5.

[3] See above, § 11.

sequuntur, forinsecum sicut servitium domini regis; nunquam tamen habebit dominus capitalis ista simul, sed unum istorum tantum, cum evenerit, aut relevium, aut custodiam, et haeredis maritagium. Et bene poterit esse quod unum istorum semper eveniet, et aliud nunquam: et unde si dominus tantum relevium habeat, et teneat inde se contentum, quamvis plus valeant custodia et haeredis maritagium, et quia ubi quis tenetur ad duo sub disjunctione, unum solvendo vel faciendo liberatur, et unde cum quis capitalis dominus tenentem suum impedierit quod dare non possit, facit ei injuriam et disseisinam apertam, ex quo illum re sua et seisina uti non permittit. Tenens vero nullam facit injuriam domino suo ex tali donatione, quamvis damnum, cum ipse dominus habere possit relevium de suo feoffato et ejus haeredibus, et licet damnum facit, non tamen injuriosum erit praedicta ratione. . . . .

Si tenens meus fecerit donationem, quaeritur cui faciat injuriam;—non domino, quia dominus habet quicquid pertinet ad ipsum, et tenementum obligatum et oneratum, quicquid dicatur, et ad quemcunque pervenerit. Item nec feoffatus, quia nihil ad capitalem dominum quicunque feodum suum tenuerit, cum tenens sit tenens suus quamvis per medium. Item si dicat quod injuste ingressus est feodum suum, dico non, quia non est feodum suum in dominico sed tenentis illius, et dominus nihil habet in feodo nisi servitium, et sic erit feodum tenentis in dominico, et feodum domini in servitio, et si dominus prohibuerit ne tenens faciat voluntatem suam de tenemento suo quod tenet in dominico, sic intrat dominus in tenementum tenentis sui et facit ei disseisinam; nisi modus vel conventio in ipsa donatione adjecta aliud inducat, cum quilibet possit modum et conditionem in donatione sua apponere, et legem quae semper observabitur [1].

Lib. ii. cap. 35. fol. 81. Item eodem modo . . . . . poterit homagium . . . . . dissolvi et extingui in persona tenentis et convalescere in persona alterius, ut si tenens, cum homagium fecerit domino suo, se dimiserit ex toto de haereditate sua et alium feoffaverit tenendum de domino capitali, et quo casu tenens absolvitur ab homagio et extinguitur homagium, velit nolit dominus capitalis, et incipit in persona feoffati, qui obligatur propter tenementum quod tenet, quod est feodum domini capitalis [2].

[1] By the time of Littleton (see sect. 360) this condition, imposing a restraint on alienation, was held illegal. A partial restraint however was still permitted. In Bracton's time such restrictions were not uncommon, especially 'viris religiosis et Judaeis.' See fol. 13.

[2] This passage shows that it was possible before the Statute of Quia

CH. III.
SECT. II.
§ 14.

TRANSLATION.

But as regards the power of the donee to make a gift over and to transfer to another the property granted to himself, some might say that he cannot do so, because by this means the lord loses his service; this however is not true—with all respect to the chief lords be it said. And speaking generally, the truth is that the donee may grant the property and the land granted to him to whomsoever he pleases, unless there were some special provision against alienation at the time of the feoffment. For when any one makes a gift of a tenement, he gives away an ascertained tenement upon condition of receiving in exchange fixed customs and fixed services, in accordance with what has been said above. And he cannot rightfully claim anything more from the gift; let him therefore take what is his and go his way. For the gift is not made for the purpose of the donor's obtaining wardship and marriage of the heir, but for homage and service; nevertheless when the donor has the right to homage, and that kind of extrinsic service is due which belongs to the chief lord, then relief and the wardship of the land, and the marriage of the heir, shall become due when the occasion arises; and also incidents of tenure, as for instance the extrinsic service due to our lord the king; the chief lord however shall never have all these incidents at once, but one of them only when the occasion happens, either relief, or wardship and the marriage of the heir. And it may well be that one of these incidents may constantly happen and another never at all, hence if the lord have only a relief let him be content therewith, although wardship and the marriage of the heir are more valuable; and because when any one is bound to render one of two duties disjunctively, he discharges himself by paying or rendering one of them. Hence when any chief lord hinders his tenant from making a gift, he works him an injury and an open disseisin, in not suffering him to make use of his own property and his own seisin. The tenant however by such a gift works no wrong to his lord, although he does him harm; since the lord may have his relief from the feoffee of the tenant, and although the tenant may do the lord harm, yet the act will not be wrongful for the reason aforesaid. . . . .

Emptores for a freehold tenant to grant away *the whole* of his land to another, so as to place the grantee exactly in his own position, and to substitute him as tenant to the superior lord. The Statute of Quia Emptores (see below, Chap. IV. § 5) applied only to the case of a grant of a portion of his land by the tenant.

If my tenant makes a gift, it may be questioned to whom he works a wrong; not to the lord, for the lord has all that belongs to him; and he has the tenement bound and burdened whatever may be the words of gift, and into whosesoever hands it may come. Nor does the feoffee injure the lord's rights, because it matters nothing to the chief lord who holds his fee, since the actual tenant is his tenant, although there be an intermediate lord. Further if the lord allege that the tenant has wrongfully entered upon his fee, I say it is not so, because the fee is not the property of the lord but the tenant, and the lord has nothing in the fee except the services due to him, and thus the fee is the property of the tenant, but subject to services to the lord; and if the lord prohibits the tenant from doing what he pleases with the tenement which he holds in his demesne, this will be an entrance by the lord upon the tenement of his tenant, and will work a disseisin, unless any other consequence follows from any condition or covenant contained in the gift itself, for any one can annex terms and conditions to his gift, and thus create a rule of law which must always be observed.

Book ii. chap. 35. fol. 81. In the same way the tie of homage may be dissolved and extinguished as regards the person of the tenant, and attach to the person of another, as for instance where the tenant when he has done homage to his lord has altogether relieved himself of his inheritance and has enfeoffed another to hold of the chief lord, and in that case the tenant is released from the duty to render homage, and the homage is extinguished, whether with or against the will of the chief lord, and the tie attaches to the person of the feoffee, who is bound because of the tenement which he holds, because it is the fee of the chief lord.

§ 15. *Differences of Freehold Estates in respect of their Duration. Estates of Freehold and Estates less than Freehold. Conditional Gifts.*

As the necessary connexion between the personal status of freedom and the holding of land comes to be of less importance, the word 'freehold' gradually loses its original signification, and is confined to what was before only one of the principal attributes of freehold tenure. When the rights

CH. III. SECT. II. § 15.

over the land are given for a period the termination of which is not fixed or ascertained by a specified limit of time, the interest is a freehold interest. This is the usual sense of the word 'freehold' at the present day when opposed to 'leasehold' tenure. A trace of the older meaning remains in the opposition of 'freehold' to 'copyhold' tenure[1].

In the latter part of the following passages we find the groundwork of legal doctrines which attained afterwards to great complication and technicality, but which are comparatively plain as laid down by Bracton. These are—

(1) That a gift to *A* and his heirs is a *donatio simplex et pura* as opposed to a conditional gift, that under such a gift the donee *A* takes (to use the later expression) 'by purchase,' *ex causa donationis*, but that upon his death his heir takes by descent, that is, not directly from the donor, but as succeeding to and representing the donee. The effect of such a gift is therefore not to give one interest to *A* and another to his heir, but to give the whole interest to *A*, that is, an estate in fee simple descendible to his heirs general. In such a gift, as it is technically expressed, the word 'heirs' is a word of limitation, not of purchase. It is simply a mode of describing the nature and extent of the interest which is taken by *A*.

(2) If however other conditions or limitations are expressed in the gift, the estate given is, according to Bracton, to be modified thereby. Thus if an estate be given to a man and the heirs of his body, or to a man and his sons by a particular wife, the fee will in that case descend according to the modifications expressed in the gift; and if no such issue is born, the condition will not have been fulfilled, and the estate will revert to the donor. It does not appear from this passage within what limits this power of the donor to define interests to be taken under the grant was confined. Some of the instances given by Bracton would have been clearly inadmissible in later times. The law, as will be seen hereafter,

[1] See Chap. V. § 6.

took a more definite shape after the Statute De Donis Conditionalibus [1].

(3) It appears from this passage that what were afterwards known as remainders and estates of future enjoyment were regarded by Bracton as conditional estates. For instance, a gift to *A* and the heirs of his body, or, if they fail, then to *B* and the heirs of his body, &c., would, according to Bracton, give to *B* an estate in expectancy, to come into effect or enjoyment either on *A*'s dying without issue born, or on failure of *A*'s issue. This would in after times have been called a remainder [2]. Bracton speaks of it as a conditional gift. The prominence which Bracton gives to conditional estates is no doubt in a great measure owing to the full discussion of the nature and effect of conditions to be found in the sources of Roman law [3].

BRACTON, lib. iv. cap. 28. fol. 207. Videndum est igitur in primis de generibus tenementorum. . . . . Et sciendum quod liberum tenementum est id quod quis tenet sibi et haeredibus suis in feodo et haereditate, vel in feodo tantum, sibi et haeredibus suis. Item ut liberum tenementum, sicut ad vitam tantum vel eodem modo ad tempus indeterminatum, absque aliqua certa temporis praefinitione, scilicet, donec quid fiat vel non fiat, ut si dicatur, do tali donec ei providero. Liberum autem tenementum non potest dici alicujus quod quis tenet ad certum numerum annorum mensium vel dierum, licet ad terminum centum annorum, quae excedit vitas hominum. Item liberum non potest dici tenementum alicujus, quod quis tenet ad voluntatem dominorum precario, quod tempestive et intempestive poterit revocari, sicut de anno in annum, et de die in diem.

Lib. ii. cap. 5. fol. 13. Et sciendum quod multipliciter fit donatio; quandoque scilicet in feodo, quandoque in vita, quandoque ad feodi firmam [4], quandoque ad terminum vitae vel annorum. Si autem ad vitam qualitercunque, statim habet donatorius liberum tenementum, ut, si fuerit ejectus, recuperare possit

[1] See below, Chap. IV. § 3.

[2] See below, Chap. V. § 3.

[3] See especially Dig. xxxv. tit. 1. De Conditionibus et Demonstrationibus.

[4] For a gift in fee farm, see above, p. 123, n. 3.

CH. III. SECT. II. § 15.

per assisam novae disseisinae, et poterit ille cui sic data fuit terra illa, alteri dare, vel in feodo, vel ad vitam si voluerit, sed revocari poterit donatio[1]. Sed si ille, qui tenuerit ad vitam, sic et talibus verbis donationem fecerit de terra, quam ad vitam tenuerit, alicui, 'Do et concedo tali quicquid juris habeo in tali terra,' etsi qui dat liberum habeat tenementum, non tamen facit ei cui sic donatur liberum tenementum[2], quia dico, 'Do tibi jus meum,' hoc est terram talem ad vitam meam scilicet donatoris, non agitur ad vitam donatorii, et ideo donator licet liberum habuerit tenementum, donatorio tamen per haec verba liberum tenementum facere non potuit, quia si dixisset, 'Do tibi talem rem in dominico vel in feodo,' hoc non esset jus suum, sed injuria. Jus autem suum hoc fuit, dare illud quod habuit, scilicet terram dare ad vitam suam, scilicet donatoris et non ad vitam accipientis, quia hoc esset injuriosum et non justum, et ex hoc liberum tenementum habere non potuit.

Lib. ii. cap. 6. fol. 17. Donationum alia divisio scilicet quod alia simplex et pura, alia conditionalis, alia sub modo, uni facta, vel pluribus successive. . . . . . Simplex autem et pura dici poterit ubi nulla est adjecta conditio nec modus; simpliciter enim dari dicitur, quod nullo adjecto datur. Ut si dicatur, 'Do tali tantam terram in villa tali pro homagio et servitio suo, habendam et tenendam eidem tali et haeredibus suis de me et haeredibus meis, reddendo inde annuatim ipse et haeredes sui mihi et haeredibus meis tantum ad tales terminos pro omni servitio et consuetudine seculari et demanda,' ita quod certa sit res quae datur, et

[1] That is, if tenant for life makes a gift of an estate of greater duration than he himself possesses, the freehold passes, but the estate granted may be avoided after the death of tenant for life by the person entitled in remainder or reversion. The powers of a tenant for life to sell or lease lands have been greatly enlarged by the 'Settled Land Acts 1882–90,' the principal of which is 45 and 46 Vict. c. 38.

[2] This, however, was not law in later times. By such a grant as that supposed in the text, the grantee would become tenant *pur autre vie*, which is as much a freehold interest as is an ordinary estate for life. (See Blackstone, book ii. p. 120.) On the death of tenant *pur autre vie* in the lifetime of *cestui que vie* (the person during whose life the estate is to last), formerly the lands became the property of the first occupant. If the grant had been made to a man and his heirs, the heir took during the residue of the life of *cestui que vie*, and was called the *special occupant*. Blackstone, ii. p. 259. The Statute of Frauds, 29 Car. II, c. 3, followed by 14 Geo. II, c. 20, makes such estates subject to the will of tenant *pur autre vie*, and provides that, if not so disposed of, and there is no special occupant, the estate is to devolve upon the executors or administrators, and be dealt with as personal property.

certa servitia et consuetudines quae domino debentur, licet incerta sunt alia quae tacite remittuntur, 'et ego et haeredes mei warrantizabimus, acquietabimus, et defendemus in perpetuum talem et haeredes suos versus omnes gentes per praedictum servitium,' et sic acquirit donatorius rem donatam ex causa donationis, et haeredes ejus post eum ex causa successionis [1], et nihil acquirit ex donatione facta antecessori, quia cum donatorio non est feoffatus. . . . . Item augere poterit donationem et facere alios quasi haeredes, licet revera haeredes non sunt, ut si dicat in donatione, 'habendum et tenendum tali et haeredibus suis, vel cui terram illam dare vel assignare voluerit [2], et ego et haeredes mei warrantizabimus eidem tali et haeredibus suis, vel cui terram illam dare voluerit, vel assignare, et eorum haeredibus contra omnes gentes;' in quo casu si donatorius terram illam dederit vel assignaverit, si donatorius et haeredes sui defecerint, donator et haeredes sui incipiunt esse loco donatorii et haeredum suorum, et pro haerede donatorii erunt, quoad warrantizandum assignatis et haeredibus eorum, per clausulam contentam in charta primi donatoris, quod quidem non esset nisi mentio fieret de assignatis in prima donatione. Sed quamdiu primus donatorius superstes fuerit vel ejus haeredes, ipsi tenentur ad warrantiam, et non primus donator. Item sicut ampliari possunt haeredes sicut praedictum est, ita coarctari poterunt per modum donationis, quod omnes haeredes generaliter ad successionem non vocantur. Modus enim legem dat donationi, et modus tenendus est contra jus commune, et contra legem, quia modus et conventio vincunt legem, ut si dicatur, 'Do tali tantam terram cum pertinentiis in *N.* habendam et tenendam sibi et haeredibus suis quos de carne sua et uxore sibi desponsata procreatos habuerit.' . . . Quo casu, cum certi haeredes exprimantur in donatione, videri poterit, quod tantum sit descensus ad ipsos haeredes communes per modum in donatione appositum,

[1] In the technical language of later times the word 'heirs' in such a gift is a word of limitation, not of purchase; i.e. it is merely descriptive of the estate which the grantee takes. A gift to *A* and his heirs is equivalent to a gift to *A* in fee. If the words 'of inheritance' be omitted, the estate granted is only for life.

[2] This mention of assigns did not confer a right of alienation, which, as has been seen, existed already. In fact the phrase seems to have found its way into charters of feoffment from the habitual use of some similar expression in the old Anglo-Saxon charters; see above, pp. 13, 100. The practical effect, as Bracton points out immediately, seems to have been to extend the warranty of the donor for the protection of the assigns as well as the heirs of the donee. See Reeves, i. p. 320.

CH. III. SECT. II. § 15.

omnibus aliis haeredibus suis a successione penitus exclusis, quia hoc voluit donator. Et unde si hujusmodi haeredes procreati fuerint, ipsi tantum vocantur ad successionem, et si taliter feoffatus aliquem ulterius inde feoffaverit, tenet feoffamentum, et haeredes tenentur ad warrantiam[1], cum ipsi nihil clamare possunt nisi ex successione et descensu parentum, quamvis quibusdam videatur quod ipsi feoffati fuerint cum parentibus, quod non est verum[2]. Si autem nullos tales haeredes habuerit, revertetur terra illa ad donatorem per conditionem tacitam, etiam si nulla fiat mentio in donatione quod revertatur, vel si expressa mentio in donatione habeatur: et ita erit si haeredes aliquando extiterint et defecerint[3]. Sed in primo casu ubi nullus extiterit, semper erit res data donatorio liberum tenementum et non feodum. Item in secundo casu, quousque inceperint haeredes esse, est liberum tenementum[4], cum autem inceperint habere, incipit liberum tenementum esse feodum[5], et cum desierint esse, desinit esse feodum, et iterum incipit esse liberum tenementum[6], et ita nunquam ibi erit dotis exactio nisi fuerit donatio pura, quia de reversione expressa nunquam fiat mentio[7]. . . . .

Item esto quod sic dicatur in donatione, 'Do tali tantam terram

[1] See below, Chap. V. § 2.

[2] For the same principle applies as above, that the words are only descriptive of the estate taken by the grantee. The instance just given is that of an estate which would in later times have been called a special estate tail.

[3] A reversion, as will be shown at length below, Chap. V. § 3 (1), is not expressly granted, but is that portion of the estate of the grantor which he retains when he has made a grant of a smaller or lesser interest.

[4] That is, 'an estate for life.'

[5] This is an instance of what Blackstone calls an estate upon condition precedent; ii. ch. 10, p. 154.

[6] This, as will be seen in the next chapter, appears to have been ruled differently before 13 Edward I. The notion of a conditional estate had been by that time still further elaborated. The mere birth of issue was regarded as the happening of the condition so as to vest the fee in the donee, at all events so as to enable him to make a grant of the land in fee simple. The subsequent failure of issue to whom alone by the form of the gift the land could have descended would not affect the power of the donee to alienate after the fulfilment of the condition by the birth of issue. See preamble of De Donis, Chap. IV. § 3.

[7] Dower can never be claimed out of a conditional estate thus created, for there is always the chance of its reverting. So long as an estate granted to a man and the heirs of his body was regarded as conditional merely, and as subject to reversion to the lord in the event of the donee having no issue or of the issue failing, the widow of the donee had no

cum pertinentiis etc. habendum et tenendum sibi et haeredibus suis si haeredes habuerit de corpore suo procreatos;' si tales haeredes extiterint, quamvis defecerint, generaliter vocandi sunt omnes et in infinitum, quia satisfactum est conditioni[1]. Si autem nullus talis procreatus fuerit, semper erit res data liberum tenementum, et revertetur ad donatorem, omnibus aliis haeredibus exclusis, cum non sit conditioni satisfactum, et sic adjungitur conditio sub modo. Item fieri poterit donatio viro et uxori simul, et haeredibus uxoris tantum per modum donationis, et eodem modo viro et uxori et haeredibus viri tantum[2]. Item viro et uxori et haeredibus communibus si tales extiterint, vel si non extiterint tunc ejus haeredibus qui alium supervixerit. . . . .

Item poterit pluribus fieri donatio per modum simul et successive; ut si quis plures habeat filios, et sic fecerit primogenito

right to dower. When, however, the Statute De Donis converted these estates into estates of limited inheritance called 'estates tail,' the right to dower attached and could be claimed out of an estate tail as much as out of an estate in fee simple.

[1] And hence a gift 'viro et haeredibus suis de corpore procreatis,' was held to imply a condition, and to be the gift of the fee conditional on the donee having issue of his body. Such a gift, however, differed from that in the text in not being descendible to heirs general.

[2] Bracton here appears to confound two principles which as the law further developed were kept quite distinct. A person may make a disposition of his lands to *A* for a limited interest and give a further interest to another to come into enjoyment or possession after the death of the first donee. This is not to create a new heir, but to vest an estate immediately by gift in the second donee. It is the creation of what is called a remainder, a class of interest which will be further explained in Chap. V. § 3 (2). The person to whom a remainder is given takes directly from the person creating the remainder, and though the interest does not come into possession or enjoyment till after the termination of the interest of the first donee, the second donee does not in any sense take by devolution from the first donee. The first donee has a limited interest given to him which is terminated, and makes way for the enjoyment of the second donee. This case and the next are quite different from the other instances given by Bracton in the text, pp. 165, 166. Following apparently Anglo-Saxon custom (see above, pp. 13, 58, n. 2), it was held that in some cases the donor could restrict the devolution of the inheritance to certain persons or classes of persons. In the later development of the law, and probably in the time of Bracton, the application of this principle was confined to a gift to a man and his issue, technically called 'heirs of his body,' either generally, or of one sex, or to the issue by a particular wife. In this case, unlike the former, the inheritance is vested in the donee, and the issue take not directly from the donor, but by devolution from the donee.

CH. III. SECT. II. § 15.

donationem et dicat, 'Do *A* primogenito filio meo tantam terram etc. habendam et tenendam sibi et haeredibus suis de corpore suo procreatis, et si tales haeredes non habuerit, vel habuerit et defecerint, tunc terram illam do *B* filio meo postgenito [1], et volo quod terra ad ipsum *B* revertatur habendum et tenendum sibi et haeredibus suis quos de corpore suo procreatos habuerit, et si nullos tales habuerit, vel si habuerit et defecerint, tunc volo et concedo pro me et haeredibus meis quod praedicta terra revertatur ad *C* tertium filium meum, habendum et tenendum sibi et haeredibus suis quos de corpore suo procreatos habuerit, et sic de pluribus. Et si praedicti *A B C* sine talibus haeredibus de corpore suo procreatis decesserint, tunc volo quod praedicta terra revertatur ad me et ad alios haeredes meos,' quod quidem fieret sine expressione per tacitam conditionem, nisi donator aliud inde ordinaret. Item si largius fiat donatio, ut si dicatur, 'Do tibi tantum terrae etc. habendum et tenendum tibi et haeredibus tuis vel cui dare vel assignare in vita vel in morte legare volueris,' valet donatio propter voluntatem et consensum donatoris, quamvis contra legem terrae fieri videatur, et unde si legatarius primam habuerit seisinam, si haeres petat per assisam, legatarius contra assisam competentem habebit exceptionem de modo donationis: si autem legatarius extra seisinam petat ex causa testamentaria in foro ecclesiastico, obstabit ei regia prohibitio, ne judices ecclesiastici judicarent, quia non habent jurisdictionem nec coercionem ad judicium suum exequendum. Si autem in foro seculari agere voluerit, quamvis hoc sit inauditum, bene poterit per breve formatum, cum possit quis renunciare iis quae pro se et suis fuerint introducta, sine praejudicio aliorum [2]. . . . .

Item conditionum alia expressa et fit verbis negativis, ut si

[1] This would in later times have been called a vested remainder in tail. See Chap. V. § 3 (2).

[2] In this remarkable passage Bracton seems to suggest two modes by which the restriction upon the old Anglo-Saxon power of disposing of interests in lands by will might be evaded. Neither of these modes seems to have been ever adopted or recognised by the Courts of Common Law. A devise of lands was not recognised as conveying any legal interest to the devisee till after the legislation of Henry VIII. See Chap. VIII. As to the jurisdiction of the Ecclesiastical Courts in regard to legacies, see Blackstone, ii. 513, iii. 65. A writ of prohibition was the proper mode of preventing a Court exceeding the bounds of its jurisdiction. Glanvill (lib. xii. c. 21) gives a specimen of a writ of prohibition addressed to a plaintiff in the Ecclesiastical Court: 'Rex vicecomiti salutem. Prohibe R. ne sequatur placitum in curia Christianitatis quod est inter N. et ipsum de laico feodo ipsius R. in villa ipsa unde ipse queritur quod praefatus N. inde eum traxit in curia Christianitatis coram judicibus illis.'

dicatur, 'Si Titius haeres non sit, tu haeres esto[1],' vel 'Si tu haeredem de corpore tuo non habueris, tunc terra sic data revertatur ad tales,' unum vel plures, simul vel successive. . . . . . . CH. III. SECT. II. § 15.

Item poterit conditio impedire descensum ad proprios haeredes contra jus commune, ut si dicam, 'concedo tibi tantum terrae ad terminum x annorum, et post terminum revertatur ad me terra illa, et si infra terminum illorum x annorum decessero, concedo pro me et haeredibus meis quod terra illa tibi remaneat ad vitam tuam vel in feodo,' et sic facit conditio liberum tenementum et feodum, et tollit conditio haeredibus assisam mortis antecessoris, quia si illi prima facie habeant directam actionem, firmarius tamen habebit ex conventione exceptionem[2]. Item quod fuit ab initio liberum tenementum et ad vitam, per conventionem poterit mutari in terminum, ut si aliquis concedat alteri terram ad vitam, fieri poterit inter eos conditio, quod si tenens infra certum terminum obierit, quod haeredes tenentis vel assignati vel sui executores possunt terram sic datam tenere usque ad certum terminum, post mortem ipsius tenentis, et ita facit conditio de termino liberum tenementum, et e contrario, et dat exceptionem contra veros dominos et eorum haeredes. . . . . . Item dat exceptionem creditori contra debitorem verum dominum et haeredes ejus, si inter eos convenerit ab initio, quod si pecunia suo die solutum non fuerit, quod terra in vadium data remaneat creditori et suis haeredibus, ut infra de assisa mortis antecessoris de haerede Johannis Dacy[3].

Translation.

Bracton, book iv. chap. 28. fol. 207. I must then in the first place examine the different kinds of tenements. . . . . .

Now it is to be observed that a freehold tenement is that which a man holds to himself and his heirs in fee and in inheritance, or in

[1] This instance is taken almost verbatim from the Digest, De Vulgari et Pupillari Substitutione, xxviii. tit. vi. 1, and is not applicable to the law at the time of Bracton, the maxim being, 'Solus Deus haeredem facere potest, non homo.'

[2] As to the assisa mortis antecessoris, see above, p. 110. Notice the accurate use of the term 'exceptio' in the sense employed by the Roman lawyers. 'Conventio' is here used, somewhat inaccurately, to express a conditional grant. This grant of the fee would not have been held good in later times, for it would in effect have amounted to a contingent remainder without any particular estate of freehold to support it: see below, Chap. V. § 3 (2).

[3] See below, Chap. V. § 5 (2). The reference is to the report of some case.

CH. III. SECT. II. § 15. fee alone, to him and his heirs. Land is also held as freehold when it is held only for life, or for an indefinite period, without any fixed limit of time, as for instance until such a thing happens or does not happen, as if it be said 'I give to such a one until I provide for him.' But a tenement cannot be called a freehold which any one holds for a certain number of years, months, or days, though it be for a term of a hundred years, which exceeds the lives of men. Further, a tenement cannot be called a freehold which a man holds at the will of the lord and by favour, which may be revoked in season or out of season, as when a man holds from year to year or from day to day.

Lib. ii. chap. 5. fol. 13. And it should be known that a gift is made in many ways, sometimes for instance in fee, sometimes for life, sometimes in fee farm, sometimes for a term of life or years. But if it be made in any manner for life, the donee has at once a freehold, so that if he be ejected he can recover by the assize of novel disseisin, and he to whom the land was thus given can give it to another either in fee, or for life if he desires, but the gift is liable to revocation. But if he who has held for life makes a gift of the land which he holds for life to any one in such words as the following, 'I give and grant to such a one whatever right I have in such land,' although the donor has a freehold, he does not create a freehold in favour of the donee, because when I say 'I give you my right,' that means 'I give such and such land for the life of me the donor,' and there is no question about the life of the donee, and therefore although the donor has a freehold, nevertheless by these words he cannot create a freehold in favour of the donee, because if he had said 'I give you such land in demesne or in fee,' this would be a wrongful act and not the exercise of a right. His right was to give that which he had, that is to say to give the land for his life, that is for the life of the donor and not for the life of the donee, for the latter would be wrongful and not right, and under a grant for the donor's life the donee cannot acquire a freehold.

Book ii. chap. vi. fol. 17. There is another division of gifts; that is to say one kind is simple and absolute, another is conditional, another is restricted; and gifts may be made to one person or to several in succession. . . . . . A gift may be called simple and absolute when no condition or restriction is added, for that is said to be given absolutely when no terms are annexed to the gift. As if it be said 'I give such a one so much land in such a township in return for his homage and service, to have and to hold to the said —— and his heirs of me and my heirs, rendering for the same by the year for himself and his heirs to me and my heirs so much, at such terms, in discharge of all service and secular customs and claims,' so that the subject-matter of the gift be certain, and the services and customary rights which are due to the lord be ascertained, although other matters from which he is tacitly discharged may be uncertain, 'and I and my heirs shall warrant, acquit, and defend such a one and his heirs against all persons for the service aforesaid:' and thus the donee acquires the subject of the gift by the title of a grant, and his heirs after him by the title of descent, and the heir acquires nothing from the grant made to his ancestor, because he is not enfeoffed with the donee. . . . . . Further the donor can enlarge the gift and make other persons in a manner heirs, although they are not in reality heirs, as if he says in the grant 'to have and to hold to such a one and his heirs, or to whomsoever he may wish to grant and assign that land, and I and my heirs will warrant the said —— and his heirs and his donee or assign and their heirs against all persons;' in which case if the donee makes a gift or assignment of that land, then in case of the death of the donee and failure of his heirs it falls upon the donor and his heirs to take the place of the donee and his heirs, and to be in the position of the heir of the donee, so far as regards warranting the assigns and their heirs, by virtue of the clause contained in the charter of the first donor, which be it observed would not be the case unless mention had been made of assigns in the first grant. But so long as the first donee or his heirs survive, it is they who are bound to warranty, and not the original donor. Likewise as the class of heirs may be enlarged, as has been said above, so can it be restricted by the limitations expressed in the gift, and in that case the heirs general do not succeed. For the limitations fix the legal effect of the gift, and the limitations of the gift must be abided by contrary to common right, and contrary to the general law, because such limitations, when agreed on, override the general law, as if the words are 'I give such a one so much land with the appurtenances in *N.* to have and to hold to him and his heirs whom he may have begotten of his body by his wedded wife.' . . . . . In which case, since a restricted class of heirs is mentioned in the gift, it may be seen that the descent is only to the common heirs of husband and wife according to the limitations expressed in the gift, all other heirs of the husband being altogether excluded from the succession, because such was the intention of the donor. Hence it is that if heirs of this kind have been begotten, they alone are called to the succession, and if one who is enfeoffed in this manner has proceeded to enfeoff any one

CH. III. SECT. II. § 15.

else of the land, this feoffment holds good, and the heirs of the feoffor are bound to warranty, since they can claim nothing except by succession and descent from their ancestors, although some think that the heirs themselves have been enfeoffed together with their parents, which is not true. But if a feoffee to himself and the heirs of his body have no such heirs, the land will revert to the donor by an implied condition, even if there be no mention in the deed of gift of such reversion, or if there be such express mention; and this will be the case too, if heirs have at any time come into existence and have failed. But in the first case, where no heir has come into existence, the donee will always hold the property given as an estate for life and not as a fee. Also in the second case, until an heir has come into existence the estate is an estate for life; when however an heir has come into existence the life estate passes into a fee, and when there ceases to be any heir the fee also comes to an end and passes into an estate for life, and as a consequence such a gift will never support a claim of dower unless it be an absolute gift, because it is never the practice to make express mention of the reversion. . . . . .

Further suppose that the words used in the grant are 'I give to such a one so much land with the appurtenances etc. to have and to hold to him and his heirs if he have heirs begotten of his body;' if such an heir come into existence, although he fail, then the heirs general are entitled and for ever, because the condition has been satisfied. But if no such heir be begotten, the property the subject of the gift will always be an estate for life, and will revert to the donor to the exclusion of all other heirs, for the condition has not been satisfied. In this way a condition may be annexed to the gift under the form of a limitation. Further a gift may be made to husband and wife together, and by the limitations in the gift to the heirs of the wife only, and in the same way to the husband and wife, and to the heirs of the husband only. Also to the husband and wife and their common heirs if any such come into existence, or if there be none, then to the heirs of the survivor. . . . . .

Further a gift may be made to more persons than one at one time to follow in succession according to the limitations of the gift; as if a man has more sons than one and makes a gift to the eldest in the following terms, 'I give to *A* my eldest son so much land to have and to hold to him and his heirs begotten of his body, and if he have no such heirs, or if he have had heirs and they have failed, then I give that land to *B* my younger son, and I desire that the land should revert to *B* to hold to him and the heirs begotten of his body, and if he have had no such heirs, or if he have had heirs and they have failed, then I desire and grant for myself and my heirs that the aforesaid land should revert to *C* my third son, to have and to hold to him and his heirs begotten of his body, and so on. And if the aforesaid *A B C* have died without heirs begotten of their bodies, then I desire that the land aforesaid should revert to me and to my other heirs.' This indeed would happen without express words by an implied condition unless the donor were to direct otherwise concerning the land. Further if the gift be made in wider terms, as if it be said, 'I give to you so much land etc. to have and to hold to you and your heirs or to whomsoever you wish to give or assign it in your lifetime or to leave it at your death,' the gift is valid because of the intention and assent of the donor, although it appears to be opposed to the law of the land. Hence if the legatee be the first in obtaining the seisin and then the heir bring the assize, the legatee will be able to meet the action by a valid plea setting up the limitations of the gift. If however the legatee be not able to obtain possession, and asserts his claim by proceedings on the will in the Ecclesiastical Court, he will be met by the king's prohibition prohibiting the ecclesiastical judges from determining the suit, for they have no jurisdiction in such matters, nor have they any means of enforcing their judgments. If however he should desire to bring his action in the temporal Courts, though there is no precedent for such a proceeding, he might well do so by means of a special writ, since it was open to the testator to waive the benefit of a rule of law introduced for the benefit of himself or his heirs, provided that he does so without prejudice to others.

Further some conditions are express and are imposed by negative words, as if it be said, 'If Titius be not heir, you are to be heir,' or 'If you have no heir of your body, then let the land thus given revert to such and such,' one or more together or successively.

Further a condition may contrary to the ordinary course of the law prevent the land descending to the right heirs, as if I say, 'I grant to you so much land for a term of ten years, and after the term let that land revert to me, and if I die within the term of those ten years, I grant for me and my heirs that that land should remain to you for your life or in fee,' and thus by virtue of a condition an estate for life or fee is created, and the condition bars the heirs from their assize of *mort d'ancestor*, because if they have prima facie a right of action the tenant for years will nevertheless be able to plead the grant in bar to the assize. Further an estate which was originally a freehold for life, may by the terms of the grant be changed into a term of years: as

CH. III. SECT. II. § 16.

if one grant to another land for his life, a condition may be agreed on that if the tenant die within a certain period, the heirs or assigns or executors of the tenant can hold the land so granted for a certain term after the death of the tenant himself, and thus a condition can turn a term into a freehold and vice versa, and can give rise to a plea in bar against the lords and their heirs. . . . . . Further the creditors may have a plea in bar against the debtor (the real owner) and his heirs, if it has been agreed between them originally that if the money be not paid on the proper day the land given in pledge should enure to the creditor and his heirs, as in the case mentioned below, an assize of *mort d'ancestor* in the matter of the heir of John Dacy.

§ 16. *Tenancy by the Curtesy of England.*

The life interest which a husband has in certain events in the lands of which his wife was in her lifetime actually seised [1] for an estate of inheritance is called an estate by the curtesy of England. In order to give the husband title as tenant by the curtesy the wife must have had by him issue born alive capable of inheriting the lands [2]. The origin of the name is doubtful. It appears to be connected with *curia* [3], and to have reference either to the attendance of the husband as tenant of the lands at the lord's court, or to mean simply that under the circumstances mentioned the husband is acknowledged tenant by the Courts of England [4], the equivalent Latin expression being *tenens per legem Angliae*. The doubt referred to in the text as being entertained by Stephanus de Segrave is a curious instance of the discussion and criticism to which rules of law were subjected at this time [5].

[1] As to what amounts to an actual seisin, see Coke upon Littleton, 29 a.

[2] See Littleton, sect. 35. In gravelkind lands a man may be tenant by the curtesy without having had any issue.

[3] In ancient Scotch law the expression is 'curialitas.'

[4] As Gunderman (Englisches Privatrecht, p. 167) points out, this species of interest was not, as Littleton (sect. 35) asserts, peculiar to England, but is found also in France and Germany. For another explanation of the term see Pollock and Maitland, Hist. of Eng. Law, ii. p. 413.

[5] For further details as to the incidents of tenancy by the curtesy, see Blackstone, Book ii. p. 126.

CH. III. SECT. II. § 16.

Bracton, lib. v. cap. 30. fol. 437 b. Si quis cum haereditatem habuerit vel non habuerit uxorem duxerit habentem haereditatem vel maritagium[1] vel aliquam terram ex causa donationis, si liberos inter se habuerint ex justis nuptiis procreatos, si uxor praemoriatur, remanebit viro haereditas et terra sua tota vita ipsius viri, sive superstites fuerint liberi sive mortui, omnes, vel quidam; dum tamen semel aut vocem aut clamorem dimiserint quod audiatur inter quatuor parietes, si hoc probetur[2]. Et quod dicitur de primo viro dici poterit de secundo, si postmodum nupserit secundo viro, sive de primo viro haeredes habuerit apparentes sive non, plenae aetatis vel minoris aetatis, quod quidem injuriosum est secundum Stephanum de Segrave, maxime cum de primo viro haeredes habuerit, quod quidem sustinere posset si nullos habuerit, dicebat enim quod lex illa male intellecta fuit et male usitata, quia quod dicitur de lege Angliae intelligi debet de primo viro et eorum haeredibus communibus, et non de secundo, maxime cum haeredes apparentes extiterint de primo[3].

Translation.

If any one, whether he has an inheritance of his own or not, marries a wife who has an inheritance or land in frank marriage, or any land whatever by the title of grant, if they have issue of their own begotten in lawful wedlock, and the wife predeceases, the inheritance and her land will enure to the husband for his whole life, whether all or any of the issue survive the mother or not, provided that the issue has once uttered a sound or cry capable of being heard within four walls, and this be proved. And what has been said concerning the first husband shall hold good also of the second if she have afterwards married a second husband, whether or not she have an heir apparent by her first

[1] See above, p. 101, n. 2.

[2] This is characteristically put by Bracton as an essential condition. In later times crying was properly regarded as *evidence*, but not as necessarily the only evidence, of the child being born alive. It was usual in early times to evade the extreme difficulty which was experienced in adopting modes of deciding disputed facts by fixing on some one fact as the sole evidence of the thing to be proved. On the other hand, some one fact was often regarded as a conclusive index of the truth or falsehood of matter in dispute, admitting of no contradiction.

[3] The law was settled in accordance with the opinion of Stephanus de Segrave by the Statute of Westminster II, 13 Edward I, cap. 1. It was held that the Statute had made a change in the common law (Year Book, 30 Edward I, p. 126).

CH. III. SECT. II. § 17. husband, whether of full age or under age. But this according to Stephanus de Segrave is bad law, especially when she have heirs in existence by the first husband, though it might hold good if she have none, for he used to say that that law was misunderstood and misapplied, because what is said as to the curtesy of England ought to be understood to relate only to the first husband and their common heirs, and not to the second husband, especially when there exists an heir apparent by the first husband.

§ 17. *Terms of Years.*

In the following passage Bracton speaks of estates less than freehold. The characteristic of this class of interests in land is that the estate is sure to come to an end on the lapse of some specified time, however remote that time may be. The passage is very remarkable, as noting the precise point at which terms[1] of years came to be recognised as estates in land[2]. Before the change here mentioned the termor or lessee had no interest which the law would protect against third persons, nor indeed against the lessor, unless the interest in the lands rested on a *conventio*, or covenant by deed. It had been the practice from very early times to grant leases by deed[3], and in such a case, if the lessor wrongfully ejected the lessee, the lessee had his remedy by action on the covenant (*per breve de conventione*), as in the case of any other covenant under seal. The new writ which was introduced, as stated in this passage, afforded the lessee a remedy against his lord, whether the lease was by deed or not; and also gave him

[1] It should be observed that by the word 'term' is meant not only the period during which the interest lasts, but the interest or estate itself.

[2] The distinguishing characteristic of an estate in lands is that it consists of a collection of rights *in rem*, or rights available against all the world, as distinct from the other great class of rights, *jura in personam*, which are only available against some particular or determinate person or persons; e. g. rights arising from contract. See Austin, i. pp. 380–389, and below, Appendix to Part I, § 1. A more apt illustration of the distinction between rights *in personam* and rights *in rem* than that contained in the following passage cannot be found.

[3] See Madox, Formulare Anglicanum, Preliminary Dissertation, xx; Forms, Nos. cxxxv, ccxx, ccxxi, ccxxii; and see above, p. 49.

a right to protection against ejectment by a third person, and probably an additional remedy, by enabling the lessee to recover possession of the land, and not merely damages for breach of covenant. This was called the writ of *quare ejecit infra terminum* [1].

Thus the interest of the termor or lessee for years, instead of resting at best upon a covenant with his lessor, and therefore being enforceable only as against him, became a right of property which could be enforced against any wrong-doer, by a remedy analogous to that provided for a wrongful ouster of a freeholder from his possession. Thus these interests became estates or rights of property in land. There was however an important difference in the devolution of the estate on the death of the lessee. Under the earlier law, the persons, who, upon the death of the lessee within the term, would have been entitled to the benefit of the covenant, were the executors or administrators of the deceased, and therefore it was natural that this new estate or interest should descend, not to the heir-at-law, but to the personal representatives, the executors or administrators, of the lessee. Thus leasehold interests came to be classed with personal and not with real property [2].

Bracton, lib. ii. cap. 9. fol. 27. Si autem fiat donatio ad terminum annorum quamvis longissimum, qui excedat vitas hominum, tamen ex hoc non habebit donatorius liberum tenementum, cum terminus annorum certus sit et determinatus, et terminus vitae

[1] According to Fitzherbert the new writ was that of 'ejectio firmae,' but he appears to have made a mistake, 'ejectio firmae' being a later development of the writ of trespass. See Pollock and Maitland, Hist. of Eng. Law, ii. p. 109, and infra, p. 243. In the following passage of Bracton the recovery of the possession of the land is mentioned as if it were part of the extended remedy provided by the council. If so, the importance of the passage in the history of the recognition of leasehold interests is much increased. In later times it was doubted whether the judgment was not for damages merely, and not for the recovery of the term. It was, however, finally settled that in 'ejectio firmae' the term itself could be recovered. See Fitzherbert, Natura Brevium, 145 m; 1 Selwyn's Nisi Prius, Ejectment, p. 615; Doe d. Poole v. Errington, 1 Adolphus and Ellis, 756.

[2] See as to the further history of terms of years, below, Chap. V. § 1.

CH. III. SECT. II. § 17.

incertus, et quia, licet nihil certius sit morte, nihil tamen incertius est hora mortis. Poterit etiam quis terram alicui concedere ad terminum annorum, et ille eandem infra terminum illum alteri dare, vel eidem in feodo, et sic mutare unam possessionem in aliam, si firmarium feoffaverit [1]. Si autem alium, utraque possessio durabit, quia sese compatiuntur terminus et feoffamentum de eadem terra, quia ibi sunt diversa jura, ad feoffatum vero pertinet proprietas feodi et liberum tenementum, firmarius vero nihil sibi vindicare poterit nisi usum fructuum, scilicet quod libere uti possit et sine impedimento feoffati percipere usum fructuum [2]. Item dare poterit quis alicui terram ad voluntatem suam, et quamdiu ei placuerit de termino in terminum, et de anno in annum, et in quo casu ille qui accipit nullum habet liberum tenementum, cum dominus proprietatis rem sic concessam repetere possit sicut a precario [3].

Lib. iv. cap. 36. fol. 220. Nunc dicendum si quis ejiciatur de usufructu vel usu et habitatione [4] alicujus tenementi quod tenuerit ad terminum annorum ante terminum suum. Poterit enim quis in uno et eodem tenemento habere liberum tenementum et alius usumfructum et usum et habitationem. Solent aliquando tales, cum ejecti essent infra terminum suum, perquirere sibi per breve de conventione. Sed quia tale breve locum habere non potuit inter aliquas personas, nisi tantum inter illum qui ad firmam tradidit et ad terminum, et illum qui ceperit, nec alios obligare potest obligatio conventionis, et etiam quia inter tales personas vix vel non sine difficultate potuit terminari negotium, de consilio curiae provisum est firmario contra quoscunque dejectores per tale breve :

[1] A man may make a lease of his land to another for a term of years, and within that term grant the freehold to a third person or to the lessee. This latter proceeding would be technically called 'releasing' the reversion. As to the conveyance by lease and release, see below, Chap. V. § 3 (1), and Chap. VII.

[2] If the freeholder enfeoffs a third person of the land already held by the lessee, the possession of the lessee or termor will co-exist with the seisin of the freeholder. The lessee has the use of the soil, and the right to cultivate it and reap its produce, and for this purpose has exclusive possession. This however does not amount to seisin (see above, pp. 49, n. 1, 109), which must reside elsewhere, either in the lessor or in his feoffee.

[3] As to 'precarium,' see above, p. 30.

[4] These terms are borrowed from the Roman lawyers. See Justinian's Institutes, ii. Titt. iv. v. The Roman conception of the interest is very analogous to that of English law ; it implied the right of temporarily using a thing of which some other person was the dominus in such a way as not to interfere with his ultimate or reversionary right.

'Rex Vicecomiti salutem, Praecipe *A* quod juste et sine dilatione reddat *B* tantum terrae cum pertinentiis in tali villa quam idem *A* qui dimisit etc.' Vel sic, 'Si talis fecerit te securum etc., ut infra, ostensurus quare deforceat tali tantum terrae cum pertinentiis, in tali villa, quod talis dimisit ipsi tali ad terminum qui nondum praeteriit, infra quem terminum praedictus talis illud vendidit tali, occasione cujus venditionis ipse talis postmodum talem de praedicta terra ejecit ut dicit. Et habeas ibi etc. Teste etc.' Et si tale breve competat contra extraneum propter venditionem, multo fortius competat contra ipsum dominum qui dimisit et sine causa ejecit, quam contra extraneum qui causam habuit qualem qualem, si occasione venditionis ei factae venditor firmarium ejecit, vel aliter si alius ejecerit quam ille qui dimisit; et tunc sic, 'Quam *C* de *N* ei dimisit ad terminum qui nondum praeteriit, infra quem terminum praedictus *A* vel praedictus *C* ipsum *B* de eadem terra vel firma sua injuste ejecit ut dicit etc.' . . . Non magis poterit aliquis firmarium ejicere de firma sua quam tenentem aliquem de libero tenemento suo. Et unde si ille ejecerit qui tradidit, seisinam [1] restituet cum damnis, quia talis restitutio non multum differt a disseisina. Si autem alius quam qui tradidit ejecerit; si hoc fecerit cum auctoritate et voluntate tradentis, uterque tenetur hoc judicio, unus propter factum et alius propter auctoritatem. Si autem sine voluntate, tunc tenetur ejector utrique tam domino proprietatis quam firmario, firmario per istud breve, domino proprietatis per assisam novae disseisinae, ut unus rehabeat terminum cum damnis, et alius liberum tenementum suum sine damnis. Si autem dominus proprietatis tenementum ad firmam traditum alicui dederit in dominico tenendum, seisinam ei facere poterit salvo firmario termino suo [2]. Poterit enim eum inducere in seisinam vacuam, quantum ad ipsum et suos, et attornare [3] ei firmarium et servitium suum, dum tamen feoffatus non utatur, nec expletia capiat, maxime nec firmarium impediat uti, nec ipsum ejiciat.

CH. III. SECT. II. § 17.

TRANSLATION.

BRACTON, book ii. chap. ix. fol. 27. If moreover a gift be made for a term of years, though of exceeding length—longer than the

[1] 'Seisin' is here used improperly, as simply equivalent to possession.

[2] That is, if the freeholder wishes to convey the freehold to another, he can effect this notwithstanding the interest of the lessee. He can convey the reversion by 'grant,' or he can make livery of seisin and cause the farmer to attorn to the feoffee. See below, Chap. V. § 1.

[3] On the necessity of attornment on the part of the termor to complete the alienation of the freehold, see below, Chap. V. § 3 (1).

CH. III. SECT. II. § 17.

life of man—nevertheless this will not give the donee a freehold, since a term of years is fixed and ascertained, and the limit of life is uncertain, and because, although nothing is more certain than death, nothing is more uncertain than the time of death. Moreover if land be granted to a person for a term of years, the grantor may during the same term grant the same land to another or to the same person in fee, thus, if he enfeoffs the lessee, changing one kind of possession for another. If however he enfeoffs another, both kinds of possession will continue, because the term and the feoffment of the same land may well co-exist, since in that case there are different sorts of rights; the ownership of the fee and the freehold belong to the feoffee, while the lessee can claim nothing for himself except the usufruct, that is to say he may freely and without hindrance on the part of the feoffee take the produce. Further one may give to another land to hold at will, or so long as he pleases, from term to term, or from year to year, in which case the donee has no freehold, for the lord of the fee may reclaim land thus granted as from one holding by mere grace and favour.

Book iv. chap. 36. fol. 220. I must now speak of the case of a person being ejected from the use and occupation of any tenement which he holds for a term of years before the expiration of his term. For in one and the same tenement one man may have a freehold and another use and occupation. The usual remedy open to such lessees, when they are ejected before the expiration of their term, is by action of covenant. But inasmuch as this action was not available except as between lessor and lessee, and third persons could not be bound by the covenant, and even as between lessor and lessee it was an insufficient and inconvenient mode of determining the matter, by the advice of the Curia Regis a remedy was provided which the farmer could avail himself of as against any person whatsoever who should turn him out of possession. This was by means of the following writ: 'The king to the sheriff greeting. Command *A* that he duly and without delay do restore to *B* so much land with the appurtenances in such a township, from which the said *A* who demised the land to *B* (has wrongfully ejected him, etc.).' Or thus: 'If *A* gives proper security, summon *B* to show cause why he ejects and keeps ejected *A* from so much land with the appurtenances which *C* demised to *A* for a term which is not yet passed, and within the said term the said *C* sold the land to *B*, by reason of which sale the said *B* afterwards ejected *A* from the said land as he saith, etc.' And if such a writ is available against a stranger on account of a sale to him, much more is it available against the lord himself who demised to, and without reason ejected, the lessee, than against a stranger who had some sort of excuse if at the time of the sale made to him his vendor ejected the farmer, or if on any other ground any one other than the original lessor has ejected the lessee. In that case the writ speaks of 'the land which *C* of *N* demised for a term which has not yet expired, within which term the aforesaid *A* or *C* wrongfully ejected *B* from the said land as he alleges etc.' . . . No one can eject a farmer from his farm any more than he can eject a tenant from his freehold. Hence if it be the lessor who ejects the farmer let him restore the possession with damages, for such a right of restitution does not differ much from the case of disseisin. But if the ejector be some person other than the lessor, if he have done the wrong by the authority and at the bidding of the lessor, both of them are liable to judgment, one because he did the act, and the other because he authorised it. But if the act was done against the will of the lord, then the wrongdoer is liable both to the lord of the fee and to the farmer, to the farmer by the writ which I have mentioned, to the lord of the fee by the assize of novel disseisin, so that the one may recover the term with damages, and the other his freehold without damages. Further if the lord of the fee gives any one a tenement to hold in demesne which has been granted to another for a term of years, he may well grant to him the seisin without prejudice to the term of the farmer. For the lord may confer upon the grantee the seisin which he vacates so far as relates to himself and those claiming under him, and he can cause the farmer to attorn to the grantee and to render to him the services, provided always that the feoffee may not enter into occupation of the land itself, or take any part of its produce, and in particular may not hinder the farmer in his enjoyment, or eject him.

§ 18. *Servitudes.* (*Easements and Profits.*)

(1) *In General.*

The branch of our law which relates to the class of rights over land belonging to another (jura in alieno solo), called servitudes, is derived mainly from the Roman system. The principles here laid down by Bracton are in most cases taken direct from Roman sources, and, speaking generally, are still recognised as the basis of the law on this subject.

CH. III. SECT. II. § 18 (1).

The main characteristic of the rights in question is that they are either rights of using the land of another for certain defined and limited purposes, as, for instance, of riding or driving cattle across it; or rights of restraining the owner from using his land in certain definite ways, for example, the owner of a house with ancient windows has a right to prevent any owner of adjoining land doing anything upon his soil which may obstruct the access of light and air to the ancient window. The former class are called positive, the latter negative servitudes. It is convenient, though not perhaps strictly accurate, to speak of both classes as rights of user exercised over the land of another.

If the purposes for which the land of another is used merely tend to the more convenient enjoyment of another piece of land, the right is called an *easement*; if the right is to take a portion of the soil or the produce of the soil of another, the right is called a *profit à prendre*.

Bracton points out clearly the distinction between rights over the land of another which are *appurtenant*, or rights which are exercised over tenement *B* (called the *praedium serviens*) by the successive owners of tenement *A* (*praedium dominans*) as and being such owners,—and rights *in gross*, or rights which are not attached to the ownership of any piece of land[1]. Again, he points out correctly that the

[1] It appears to be the more correct view to confine the expression 'easement' to rights *appurtenant* to land. Whether there can be an easement properly so called not so appurtenant is a question which has been much discussed, but apparently never finally settled; although the dictum of Lord Cairns in Rangeley v. Midland Railway Company (1868), Law Reports, 1 Chancery, p. 310, that 'an easement must be connected with a dominant tenement' appears never to have been dissented from. (See Gale on Easements, 4th ed., p. 13, note d.) Such rights at all events partake of the nature of easements as far as regards their mode of creation, which must be by deed (Bird v. Higginson, 6 Adolphus and Ellis, 824; Wood v. Leadbitter, 13 Meeson and Welsby, 838). Probably however they do not possess the principal characteristic of an easement properly so called—the capacity of being asserted as against third parties. They are rights *in personam*, not rights *in rem*. (See Hill v. Tupper, 2 Hurlstone and Coltman, 121; Stockport Waterworks Company v. Potter, 3 ib. 300.) There is no question however that the law recognises *profits* 'in gross,' i.e. not appurtenant to lands, as rights *in rem*.

essence of the right consists in the power of restraining the owner of the servient tenement (that over which the rights are exercised) from putting into force his full rights of doing as he pleases with the land. He may not so use his land as to obstruct my right of passage over it, or of having water from his stream. His rights are however only limited by positive duties; that is, by certain duties imposed by known rules of law. User of land which causes damage to a neighbour does not necessarily amount to legal injury. The principles and the illustrations here given by Bracton are in the main applicable to the law at the present day.

With regard to the origin of servitudes, or the modes in which they may be acquired, Bracton correctly lays down the two modes which have always been recognised, *grant* (dominorum constitutio) and *prescription* (usus). Feoffment with livery was confined to granting freehold estates in land. It was not applicable to the class of rights in land under consideration. Hence the other principal mode of creating rights was adopted, namely writing under seal, and it became a principle that for the creation of a servitude (easement or profit) a grant by deed was necessary.

The other mode of acquiring servitudes is, according to Bracton, *per longum usum continuum et pacificum*. The user must have been as of right, not violent, or clandestine, or permissive. These principles, borrowed from the Romans, took root in our law. Only, as time went on, the notion of prescription[1] underwent a change. Long enjoyment of a

[1] It is important to bear in mind the distinction between local or particular custom and prescription. A local custom is where within the limits and subject to the restrictions recognised by the law (see Blackstone, i. p. 76) a practice has prevailed time out of mind in a particular district, creating certain special rights and duties peculiar to the dwellers in that district. Prescription is where a person possesses a right by reason of the fact of long and uninterrupted enjoyment, as of right, either by himself and his ancestors, or by himself and his predecessors in title (i. e. those who have preceded him in the ownership of the land in respect of which the right is claimed, and whose rights have by alienation or devolution become vested in him). See Blackstone, ii. p. 263.

CH. III. SECT. II. § 18 (1). right was not considered, as was the case in the Roman system, and as Bracton's language here implies, as itself a positive mode of acquisition, but only as evidence that at some period the owner of the soil had created the right in question by a lost or forgotten deed [1]. So far was this carried that, on

[1] Blackstone, ii. 265. This doctrine, arising from what at the present day we may venture to pronounce false historical notions, has produced a curious rule with regard to 'profits.' According to the legal theory, every profit, such for instance as a right of pasture on the lord's waste, must have originated in a grant by the lord. Therefore it can only be claimed by persons who are capable of taking by grant. Therefore it cannot be claimed, in virtue of a local custom or otherwise, by an indefinite body, such for instance as the inhabitants of a parish who are not a corporation (see Lord Hatherley's observations in Warrick v. Queen's College, Oxford, Law Reports, 6 Chancery Appeals, p. 724; and compare Goodman v. Mayor of Saltash, Law Reports, 7 Appeal Cases, 633). In fact the inhabitants have in many places exercised such rights of pasturage. And there can be little doubt that the practice has descended from very early times, and was in fact a recognised right in the community inhabiting the district before the idea arose that the soil was the property of the lord. To the same origin doubtless must be referred most of the rights of a similar character enjoyed by freeholders and copyholders. These rights did not as a fact originate in a grant, they were recognised at a time before the notion of the sole ownership of the lord came into existence; but because of the false historical theory that such rights must have been created by grant, it has become an established rule in our law that inhabitants, unlike freehold or copyhold tenants, cannot as such claim profits *in alieno solo*, and that a custom to exercise such alleged rights is invalid. Where the practice has been to exercise the privilege as of right from time immemorial, great practical injustice is often done by the operation of this rule of law. That inhabitants as such could not claim a right of common was formally decided in Gateward's case (6 Coke's Reports, 59 b) in 4 James I. It appears from the Act, 43 Eliz. c. 11, that such rights were at that time recognised, and that an Act of Parliament was thought necessary for their extinguishment (see Elton on Commons, p. 151). The Act provides for the reclamation of certain marshes wherein 'divers have common by prescription by reason of their resiancie and inhabitancie, whiche kynde of commons nor their interest therein can by the common law be extinguished or granted to bynde others whiche shoulde inhabite there afterwardes' (Statutes of the Realm, iv. 977). The inference would seem to be that the established rule of law is in fact a creation of the Elizabethan lawyers. See above, p. 8, note 2. Somewhat inconsistently, however, rights in the nature of easements are still recognised as capable of resting on local custom. For example, a custom for the inhabitants of a particular district to play lawful games on a certain piece of land was upheld in Fitch v. Rawlings,

proof of enjoyment for a considerable period, juries were directed to find that a grant had been made and lost, although distinct proof might be given that the enjoyment had originated in usurpation before that period[1]. A new species of prescription was introduced by the Prescription Act, 2 and 3 Will. IV, c. 71. By that Act exercise and enjoyment of the easement or profit for definite periods limited by the Act have the effect of creating an indefeasible title to the right in question[2]. CH. III. SECT. II. § 18 (I).

These rights were deemed so far to be of the nature of freehold rights as that the appropriate remedy for disturbance of their enjoyment was by the Assize of Novel Disseisin.

Bracton, lib. iv. cap. 37. fol. 220. Pertinent enim ad liberum tenementum jura sicut et corpora[3], jura sive servitutes diversis respectibus. Jura autem sive libertates dici poterunt ratione tenementorum, quibus debentur. Servitutes vero ratione tenementorum a quibus debentur[4], et semper consistunt in alieno et non in proprio, quia nemini servire potest suus fundus proprius[5], et nullus hujusmodi servitutes constituere potest nisi ille qui fundum habet et tenementum[6], quia praediorum aliud liberum aliud servituti suppositum. Liberum dici poterit quod in nullo tenetur vel astringitur praediis vicinorum. Si autem teneatur, dicitur servituti suppositum quod prius fuerat liberum, et hoc sive teneatur praedio sive tenemento alieno de voluntate et constitutione dominorum, vel propter servitium certum, vel propter vicinitatem, quia, si

2 Henry Blackstone, 393; and a custom to hold horse-races on a particular day on a moor, in Mounsey v. Ismay, 1 Hurlstone and Coltman, p. 729. Doubtless the recognition of profits as being claimable by custom would have been more detrimental to the interests of lords of manors than the recognition of mere easements.

[1] See Gale on Easements, p. 149.

[2] See Sections 1–3.

[3] See Justinian's Institutes, ii. tit. 2; and for the distinction between corporeal and incorporeal things, see below, Appendix to Part I, § 1 (II).

[4] And hence the expressions 'servient tenement,' 'dominant tenement' have taken root in our law to express respectively the land over which the right is exercised, and the land to the ownership of which the right is attached.

[5] 'Nulli res sua servit.' Dig. lib. viii. tit. ii. 26.

[6] Compare Dig. lib. viii. tit. iv. 1. § 1: 'Ideo autem hae servitutes praediorum appellantur quia sine praediis constitui non possunt.'

CH. III. SECT. II. § 18 (1).

fuerit incertum, ut si quis plus dederit aliquando minus, haec esset potius emptio herbagii quam pastura, et hoc erit potius personale quam praediale [1]. Item eodem modo si quis temporibus ad voluntatem suam. Item herbagium dici poterit si cui concedatur, quia non habet liberum tenementum ad quod pertinere possit. Et talis dici poterit constitutio qua domus domui, rus ruri, fundus fundo, tenementum tenemento subjungatur, et non tantum personae per se vel tenementum per se, sed uterque simul tam tenementum quam personae. Et ita pertinent servitutes alicui fundo ex constitutione sive ex impositione de voluntate dominorum. Item pertinere poterunt sine constitutione per longum usum continuum et pacificum et non interruptum per aliquod impedimentum contrarium ex patientia inter praesentes, quae trahitur ad consensum [2]. Et unde licet servitus expresse non imponatur nec constituatur de voluntate dominorum, tamen si quis usus fuerit per aliquod tempus pacifice sine aliqua interruptione nec vi nec clam [3] nec precario [4], quod idem est quod de gratia, ad minus sine judicio

[1] Bracton is here distinguishing what would in later times have been called rights appurtenant, or rights attached to and enjoyed by the successive owners of a dominant tenement, from rights in gross; see above, p. 182.

[2] The rule of Roman law was, as laid down by Ulpian (Dig. lib. xli. tit. iii. 10. § 1), 'Hoc jure utimur ut servitutes per se nusquam longo tempore capi possint, cum aedificiis possint.' That is, where a house (or other immovable thing) which has been acquired by *usucapio* has attached to it certain rights over the property of another, these servitudes are acquired together with the house, etc. But no servitude *per se* can be acquired by long user. The law appears to have been different in Cicero's time, but the possibility of acquiring servitudes by *usucapio* was abolished as inconsistent with the true principles of law by the Lex Scribonia, see Pothier, Dig. lib. xli. tit. vii. Compare Dig. lib. xli. tit. i. 43. § 1: 'Incorporales res traditionem et usucapionem non recipere manifestum est;' but the praetorian rule, allowing servitudes to be acquired by lapse of time, which was preserved in the codification of Justinian, practically abrogated the Lex Scribonia. The doctrines of Roman law as to the acquisition of rights of ownership over things are here adapted by Bracton to the acquisition of rights *in re aliena*. This took root in our law. The rights in question can be *acquired* by prescription. Rights of ownership over things cannot be so acquired, but the remedies (and now the rights, 3 and 4 Will. IV, c. 27, s. 34) of the true owner are extinguished by the lapse of a defined period.

[3] See Dig. lib. xliii. tit. xxiv. 1. 'Praetor ait, "Quod vi aut clam factum est, qua de re agitur, id quum experiendi potestas est restituas."' Compare xli. tit. ii. 6.

[4] 'Ait Praetor, "Quod precario ab illo habes, aut dolo malo fecisti ut desineres habere, qua de re agitur id illi restituas."' Dig. xliii. tit. xxvi.

disseisiri non potest; quia si violentia adhibeatur, nunquam erit jus disseisitoris propter temporis diuturnitatem, nisi per negligentiam ipsius qui vim patitur ex longa et pacifica et continua possessione inter praesentes, secus inter absentes[1], et talis seisina multipliciter poterit interrumpi[2]. Si autem fuerit seisina clandestina scilicet in absentia dominorum, vel illis ignorantibus, et si scirent essent prohibituri, licet hoc fiat de consensu vel dissimulatione ballivorum, valere non debet. Si autem precario fuerit et de gratia, quae tempestive revocari possit et intempestive, ex longo tempore non acquiritur jus, nec in casu proximo notato. Illud autem, quod de gratia est, ad voluntatem concedentis revocari poterit quocumque tempore, quod quidem non est in commodato. Potest etiam servitus ita constitui in proprio, ne liceat domino fundi pascere in suo proprio, et sic constituitur servitus in fundo alieno, aliquando ab homine, aliquando ex patientia et usu[3]. Et eodem modo imponitur quandoque a jure et nec ab homine nec ab usu, scilicet, ne quis faciat in proprio per quod damnum vel nocumentum eveniat vicino[4]. Nocumentum enim poterit esse justum, et poterit esse injuriosum. Injuriosum ubi quis fecerit aliquod in suo injuste contra legem vel contra constitutionem prohibitus a jure. Si autem prohiberi a jure non possit ne faciat, licet nocumentum faciat et damnosum, tamen non erit injuriosum,

2. Compare the rule of our law that continued enjoyment in order to give a title must be 'as of right,' 2 and 3 Will. IV, c. 71. As to 'precario,' see above, p. 30.

[1] Compare the Institutes of Justinian, lib. ii. tit. vi. pr. 'Immobiles [res] . . . inter praesentes decennio, inter absentes viginti annis [usucapiuntur].'

[2] The interruption must be of the right itself, not of the actual enjoyment. Interruption of the right destroys the prescription or custom (see Blackstone, i. 77); interruption of the actual enjoyment or user, however long continued, operates only as some evidence that the right has been abandoned or released.

[3] This is a correct description of 'negative' easements, where one person has, as owner of tenement *A*, the right to restrain the owner of tenement *B* from putting his land to uses which would, but for this special right, be legitimate. For example, *A* who has a house with an ancient window overlooking *B*'s land, can prevent *B* from building on his land so as to obstruct the access of light and air to the window. Compare Dig. lib. viii. tit. i. 15: 'Servitutum non ea natura est, ut aliquid faciat quis; veluti viridaria tollat, aut amoeniorem prospectum praestet, aut in hoc ut in suo pingat; sed ut aliquid patiatur aut non faciat.'

[4] This however is not properly a servitude at all, but part of the general rights attached to the possession of property. For the distinction between dominium and servitus see Austin, vol. ii. lect. xlviii.

CH. III. SECT. II. § 18 (1). licitum est enim unicuique facere in suo quod damnum injuriosum non eveniet vicino, ut si quis in fundo proprio construat aliquod molendinum, et sectam suam et aliorum vicinorum subtrahat vicino, facit vicino damnum et non injuriam, cum a lege vel a constitutione prohibitum non sit ne molendinum habeat vel construat[1]. Item a jure imponitur servitus praedio vicinorum, scilicet ne quis stagnum suum altius tollat per quod tenementum vicini submergatur. Item ne faciat fossam in suo per quam aquam vicini divertat, vel per quod ad alveum suum pristinum reverti non possit in toto vel in parte. Item ne quid faciat in suo quo minus vicinus suus omnino uti possit servitute imposita vel concessa, vel quo minus commode utatur loco, tempore, numero vel genere, qualitate vel quantitate. Et non refert utrum hoc omnino fecerit vel quod tantundem valeat: ut si quis habuerit jus eundi per fundum alienum, non solum facit disseisinam si viam obstruat, sed si ire non permittat omnino commode vel ad usum debitum. Item si reficere viam non permittat, ad viam enim pertinet refectio. Item eodem modo si omnino aquam non divertat, sed fossam faciat vel purgare non permittat; quia ad aquae ductum pertinet purgatio, sicut ad viam pertinet refectio. Item licet omnino non impediat, si fecerit tamen quo minus commode, facit disseisinam, ut si communiam habeat in certo loco cum libero et competenti ingressu et egressu, faciat quis fossatum et hayam, murum vel pallacium, per quod oportet me ire per circuitum, ubi prius ingressus sum per compendium, salvo tamen vicino jure suo si recenter ad querelam ejus qui injuriam passus est quod suum fuerit exequatur[2]. . . . Si autem debitum modum excedat quis, incontinenti repelli poterit, post tempus vero non nisi cum causae cognitione: et sic, ut praedictum est, poterit quis habere servitutem in fundo alieno et uti, nisi prohibeatur ex justa causa. Jura siquidem quae quis in fundo alieno habere poterit, infinita sunt.

[1] Bracton here correctly draws the distinction between *damnum*—mere damage or harm,—and *injuria*—an illegal act causing damage. Obstructing a beautiful prospect which I have always enjoyed from the windows of my house is, in the view of English law, a mere *damnum*; diminishing by obstruction the quantity of light and air which I receive through ancient windows is injuria. 'Sic utere tuo ut alienum non laedas' is said to be the maxim of our law. As Mr. Austin points out (ii. p. 829), if by 'laedas' is meant mere damage, the maxim is untrue as a legal proposition; if it means 'injury,' it tells us nothing, as it affords no explanation of the distinction between damage and injury.

[2] The case put is apparently the interruption of the easement by a third person. The owner of the tenement has apparently a right prior to that of the owner of the easement to a remedy against the wrongdoer.

TRANSLATION.

CH. III. SECT. II. § 18 (1).

BRACTON, book iv. chap. 37. fol. 220. There are certain rights which belong to a tenement—besides the ownership of the corporeal thing—these are from different points of view called rights or servitudes. They are called rights or franchises in reference to the tenements to which they appertain. They are called servitudes in reference to the tenements subject to the obligation; and they always consist in rights over another man's land and not over a man's own land, because no one can have a servitude over his own land, and no one can create a servitude of this kind but he who has lands and tenements, for some lands are free, others subject to a servitude. Land may be called free when it is in no respect bound or subservient to the lands of neighbours. If however it is so subservient, land which may before have been free is said to be subjected to a servitude, and this whether its subjection to the land or tenement of another be by the will and grant of the owners, or because of an ascertained obligation, or because of vicinage. The servitude must be ascertained, because if the right be uncertain, for instance if at one time the owner grant a person more pasture, at another less, this would be rather a purchase of the feed than a right of common of pasture, and would be a right in gross rather than one appurtenant to the land. The same consequence follows if the grant be to use the pasture at times of the grantor's own choosing. Also, if the grant be merely to a person, it should be called a right of herbage, because the grantee has no free tenement to which it can appertain. But that only can properly be called a grant of a servitude whereby one house, or estate, or farm, or tenement is made subservient to another, and not only when there is nothing but two persons and a single tenement: but both elements must co-exist, there must be two tenements and a grantor and grantee. And in this way servitudes can be made to appertain to any land by voluntary grant or reservation on the part of the owners. They may also appertain to a tenement without a grant by long and peaceable user uninterrupted by any hindrance interposed, and permitted to continue by parties who are on the spot, all which amounts to assent. Hence it follows that although a servitude may not be reserved or granted in express words by the owners of the soil, nevertheless if there has been any user extending over any considerable time, exercised in peace, without any interruption, and not by violence or stealth, or by virtue of a request, which is the same thing as by favour, the person enjoying the right

CH. III. SECT. II. § 18 (1). cannot be ousted of it at all events without the judgment of a court; but if the servitude be enjoyed by violence, the disseisor will never acquire the right by reason of the length of time for which it has been enjoyed, although it may be that through the negligence of the person ousted the right may be acquired by long and peaceful and uninterrupted possession, under the eyes of the parties; though it is otherwise in the absence of the parties; and a seisin so obtained can be interrupted in many different ways. And if the seisin be clandestine—that is to say in the absence of the owners, or without their knowledge, and if they would have been likely to forbid it if they had known,—it ought not to be of any avail, although the bailiffs of the land may have assented to or winked at it. Moreover if it was due to a mere act of grace and favour which may be revoked in season and out of season, no right is acquired by lapse of time; no more than in the case last mentioned. And where a thing is permitted as a mere favour it may be reclaimed at the will of the benefactor at any time; which however is not so where there is a contract for the loan of a chattel. A servitude too may be so created over a person's own land, as that the owner should not be permitted to feed cattle on his own land; and thus a servitude is created over another man's land, sometimes by act of party, sometimes by acquiescence and user. And in the same way it is sometimes imposed by law, and neither by act of party or by user, for instance that no one should do on his own land any thing by which damage or harm should result to his neighbour. For harm may be permitted by law, or it may be wrongful. It is wrongful when any one does any act on his own land wrongfully contrary to law or contrary to a grant, he being forbidden by law to do the act. But if he be not forbidden by law to do the act, although he does harm and causes damage, yet the act will not be wrongful, for it is lawful for any one to do upon his own land any thing which will not cause wrongful damage to his neighbour, as if any one erects a mill on his own land, and diverts from his neighbour his own custom and that of the neighbours, he thereby does his neighbour harm but not injury, since he is not forbidden either by law or covenant to have or erect a mill. Again there are servitudes which are imposed by law on neighbouring tenements, as for instance that a man should not raise the level of the water in his pool so high as to drown the land of his neighbour. Another instance is that a man may not make a ditch on his own ground so as to divert his neighbour's water, or so as to prevent it in whole or in part from flowing back into its ancient channel. Again a man may not do any act on his own land by which his neighbour is prevented from using altogether a servitude annexed to or granted over any land, or so as to prevent his convenient use of it in point of place, time, number or kind, quality or quantity. And it does not matter whether he does this directly or indirectly, as if any one has a right of passing and repassing over the land of another the servient owner does not only oust him of his right if he obstructs the way, but if he does not allow him to use the way with perfect convenience or for the proper object of the servitude. So again if he does not allow the way to be repaired, for a right of way carries with it the right of repairing the way. The same may be said although he may not divert a watercourse altogether, but only makes a ditch or prevents the cleaning out of the watercourse, for a right to a watercourse involves the right of cleaning out the watercourse, just as the right of way carries with it the right of repairing the way. Again although the servient owner do not obstruct the user of the servitude altogether, if he so act as to prevent its convenient use, he causes a disseisin, as if I have a right of common in an ascertained spot with free and sufficient ingress and egress, and any one erects a bank or hedge or wall or palisade, which obliges me to go a roundabout way where formerly I used a short cut; saving however to the neighbour his full right if he forthwith claim that which is his due on the complaint of the person who has suffered the wrong. . . . But if a person exceeds the limits of his right he can be forthwith restrained, but after a lapse of time only by judicial process, and thus as has been said above a person may have a servitude over another's land and enjoy it unless he be restrained on some legal ground. Indeed the kinds of rights which one person may have over the land of another are infinite in number.

(2) *Rights of Common.*

Rights of common have always been the most important class of profits, and amongst rights of common stands prominent that which Bracton here describes—common of pasture. Other rights of common are common of turbary, or of cutting turf for fuel to be burnt in a house; common of estovers, or of taking from another's land timber or underwood, heath, furze, fern, etc., to be used for fuel, litter, fodder

CH. III. SECT. II. § 18 (2). for cattle, or similar purposes; common of piscary, or the right of fishing in another's water. Of these rights by far the most important is the right of common of pasture.

Though there is much that is obscure in the history of rights of common, indications are not wanting which tend to confirm the view stated in the first chapter of the growth of manors. It was probably in consequence of the change there noticed that the common or uncultivated land of the township was, in process of time, regarded as the sole property of the lord of the manor and was called the lord's waste, and the old customary rights of the villagers came, as notions of strict legal rights of property were more exactly defined, to be regarded as rights of user on the lord's soil—as *jura in re aliena*[1]. Still the name remained, and attached, as is seen remarkably in the following passages, to the waste or uncultivated land itself, which was still usually called common land, as if the commoners had rights of property in common over the soil itself, instead of having simply rights *in alieno solo*.

An important consequence too of the old customary law is found in the fact that every freeholder holding lands within the manor had, as of right, common of pasturage on the wastes as incident to his lands. To every new feoffment therefore these rights would attach, and this continued to be the law till the passing of the Statute of Quia Emptores, in the eighteenth year of Edward the First. By that Statute a mesne lord could no longer make a feoffment of lands to be held of himself in fee; the freeholder therefore whose title rested on a grant subsequent to that Statute was no longer a tenant of the manor, and could claim no rights over the wastes of the manor as incident to his feoffment. The technical name for this class of rights of pasturage incident to freehold lands held of a manor before 18 Edward I is 'common appendant.'

[1] Compare pp. 6, 7, 17, 18, 45.

It seems from the following passage that often there were no exact limits as to the number of beasts which a commoner might put upon the waste land. Bracton however indicates that, at all events in the case of a new feoffment, the number must have some relation to the nature and size of the land, and to the prevailing customs. In later times the right of the freeholder holding lands of the lord of the manor came to be expressly defined [1]. He was entitled to have common of pasture for so many beasts useful in agriculture for tilling or manuring the soil, as his arable land would sustain during the winter. This is expressed technically as a right of common of pasture for all commonable cattle levant and couchant upon the lands. This class of rights of common of pasture enjoyed by the freeholders of the manor over the wastes of the manor as necessarily incident to their freeholds (called common appendant) is the most ancient and in early times by far the most important class of rights of common [2].

If the view above given of the history of these rights of common be correct, it will be seen that the rights of the commoners and the rights of the lord must in very early times have come in conflict. Already in the time of Glanvill we find the law recognised and protected by a regular form of action the right of the commoner, by enabling him to bring an assize of novel disseisin against any one who disturbed him in the enjoyment of his right of common [3]. Would this form of action protect the commoner against *any* curtailment of the land over which he exercised his rights by the lord? It seems that the fair inference to be drawn from Bracton's comment on the Statute of Merton (20 Henry III, cap. 4) is

[1] It will be borne in mind that wherever at the present day a freeholder holds in fee of the lord of a manor that relation must have been created previous to the eighteenth year of Edward I. See Chapter IV. § 5.

[2] See Mr. Joshua Williams' note on the case of Lord Dunraven v. Llewellyn (15 Queen's Bench Reports, 761; Elements of Real Property, 17th Ed., Appendix F), and see the judgment of Lord Hatherley in Warrick v. Queen's College, Oxford, Law Rep. 6 Ch. Appeals, p. 726.

[3] Glanvill, lib. xiii. cap. 37; above, p. 114.

CH. III. SECT. II. § 18 (2).

that the lord had no right independently of that Statute to appropriate any portion of the waste as against the freeholders having rights of common appendant[1]. The effect of that Statute was to establish the right of the lord to appropriate the land over which rights of common of pasture existed, provided he left sufficient for the tenants of the manor in convenient places, with proper means of access. This is the footing on which the law as to the respective rights of the lord and the freeholders of the manor has rested ever since. The Statute of Merton only applied to the rights of common of pasture enjoyed by freehold tenants of the manor over the wastes of the manor. Rights of common enjoyed by prescription or grant by persons other than the tenants of the manor were beyond its scope; nor did it apply to rights of cutting turf or peat (common of turbary), nor to rights of taking 'estovers,' such as wood, gorse, heath, or fern[2].

Rights of common, other than those enjoyed by freehold tenants of a manor as such, created by grant or prescription and attached to the ownership of lands, are called rights of 'common appurtenant.' Where, as is usually the case, the claim rests on prescription, it is said in technical language that the tenant in fee of the lands and all those whose estate he has[3] have enjoyed the right from time whereof the memory of man runneth not to the contrary, or during the period required by the Prescription Act[4].

A right of common may also be granted to a man and his heirs irrespective of the ownership of any land, and then it descends like an estate in fee simple, and is called a right of common 'in gross.'

Bracton points out in the following passage that the lord could not curtail the common over which rights of common appurtenant or in gross existed by any right derived either

[1] See Pollock and Maitland, Hist. of Eng. Law, i. p. 612.

[2] See Coke's Second Institute, 87.

[3] This is technically called prescribing in a *que estate*.

[4] 2 and 3 Will. IV, c. 71.

from the common law or from the Statute of Merton. A provision however of the Statute of Westminster II[1] placed prescriptive rights of common of pasture appurtenant upon the same footing as rights of common appendant. It should be observed that where the right of common can be traced expressly to a grant, which gives the right over a definite extent of waste ground, the lord cannot enclose or curtail the common as against his own express grant[2].

The above may be taken as an outline of the leading principles of the law relating to rights of common at the present day[3]. Much waste or common land has from time to time been enclosed under local Acts of Parliament, and various general provisions have been enacted providing machinery for enclosing commons, with compensation to the owner of the soil and the various persons interested in the land[4].

Bracton, lib. iv. cap. 38. fol. 222. Quoniam magis celebris est illa servitus per quam conceditur alicui jus pascendi, ideo primo dicendum est de illa quae dicitur communia pasturae. Commune autem nomen generale est, et convenit suis partibus sicut genus se habet ad suas species. Communia enim ex virtute vocabuli componitur ex una et cum, et subintelligitur alio, (id est) communia in alieno et una cum alio et non in fundo proprio, quia nemini servit suus fundus proprius ut supra[5]. Acquiritur enim communia multis ex causis. Scilicet ex causa donationis, ut si quis dederit terram cum pertinentiis et cum communia pasturae etc.[6] Item ex causa emptionis et venditionis, ut si quis communiam emerit in fundo alieno, ut pertineat ad tenementum suum,

[1] 13 Ed. I, c. 46, given below, Chapter IV. § 4.

[2] Approvement must now be sanctioned by the Board of Agriculture under 56 and 57 Vict. c. 57.

[3] The rights of *copyhold* tenants of the manor to common resting on the custom of the manor will be treated of in dealing with copyhold rights generally. See Chapter V. § 6.

[4] See Stephen, Commentaries, vol. i. pp. 641–645.

[5] Thus we see how the doctrines of Roman law coincided with the interest of the lord to reduce the rights of commoners to the character of *jura in alieno solo*. See above, p. 192.

[6] In this case the common of pasture would attach or be appurtenant to the land granted, in other words would be enjoyed by the grantee and his successors in title over land other than that granted.

CH. III. SECT. II. § 18 (2). licet sit de feodo alieno et diversa baronia, et ex constitutione dominorum fundorum. Item acquiritur ex causa dominorum fundorum, sicut per servitium certum [1]. Item ex causa vicinitatis, ut si quis cum vicino, et vicinus cum eo [2]. Item ex longo usu sine constitutione cum pacifica possessione, continua et non interrupta, ex scientia, negligentia, et patientia dominorum, non dico ballivorum, quia pro traditione accipiuntur, ita quod nec per vim nec clam nec precario ut supra. Et eisdem rationibus pertinere poterit communia ad liberum tenementum, in eo autem quod communia est nomen generale continens sub se plures species. Est enim communia in eo, quod dicitur pastura, de omni quod edi poterit vel pasci, large sumpto vocabulo vel stricte, large, ut si quis habeat in alieno communiam pasturae, scilicet herbagii, pessonae, sive glandis sive nucis, et quicquid sub nomine pessonae continetur. Item foliorum et frondium stricte, scilicet aliquod istorum unum vel duo. Item distingui poterit communia pasturae per tempora, ut si omni tempore vel certis temporibus et certis horis. Item per loca, ut si ubique, et per totum, sine aliqua exceptione. Excipiuntur tamen quaedam tacite, et quandoque expresse; sicut rationabilia defensa, et exigi non poterunt ratione pasturae, nisi specialiter concedantur, et non nisi post tempus, qualia sunt blada, prata, ligna, *Byngheys* sicut ad boves [3], item ad vaccas et vitulos suis temporibus, item ad oves multones et oves matrices, et agnos suis temporibus. Item nec in curia alicujus nec in gardinis, nec in viridariis, nec parcis vel hujusmodi. Item nec in dominicis alicujus, quae claudi possunt et excoli, nisi per modum certum constitutionis, et certis temporibus vel certis locis et determinatis et infra certa loca. Item ad certa genera averiorum, vel si ad omnimoda averia et sine numero, vel cum coarctatione et cum numero, vel ad certum genus averiorum. Item notandum quod non debet dici communia, quod quis habuerit in alieno sive pro precio, sive ex causa emptionis, cum tenementum non habeat ad quod possit communia pertinere, sed potius herbagium dici debet quam communia; cum hoc posset esse quasi

[1] This means apparently that a right of common may be granted by the lord in return for services to be rendered.

[2] As to common of vicinage, see below, p. 202, n. 2.

[3] Rights of common would *prima facie* be exercisable over waste land only. Of course they may be granted over any land, but this requires express mention in the grant. So also if there be a special right of common for any species of cattle other than the ordinary commonable cattle.

personale quid, sive certum dederit quis pro herbagio habendo, sive incertum[1]. Item communia dici poterit secundum quod stat in generali, secundum quod supra dictum est, habere jus fodiendi in alieno, aurum scilicet, et inde aurifodina dici potest locus iste. Item argentum et inde argentifodina, et sic de ceteris metallis[2]. Item jus fodiendi lapides, cretam, arenam, et turbam[3], et hujusmodi. Item communia et non herbagium, ut jus falcandi herbam vel brueram vel hujusmodi ad rationabile estoverium. Item eodem modo ad secandum in alieno bosco ad rationabile estoverium aedificandi, claudendi, et ardendi.

Ib. fol. 224. Nemo potest communiam pasturae clamare ut pertinentem ad liberum tenementum suum nisi ille qui liberum tenementum habet. Liberum autem dicitur ad differentiam villenagii et villanorum qui tenent villenagium, quia non habent actionem nec assisam, sed dominus cujus liberum tenementum villenagium fuerit[4].

Ib. fol. 225 b. (*Of defences by the tenant of the servient tenement to an assize of novel disseisin for disturbance of common rights.*) Item poterit tenens respondere contra assisam quod querens nullam communiam clamare potuit in tali loco, quia tenementum illud est suum separale, et quod illud includere possit et excolere pro voluntate sua, et inclusum habere omni tempore. Ad quod querens (si possit) doceat contrarium vel diversum per assisam, scilicet quod nullo tempore includi poterit, vel quod non nisi certis horis et temporibus[5]. Item respondere potest tenens et dicere quod ille qui queritur nullum omnino habet tenementum liberum, vel quasi, ad quod aliqua communia pertinere possit vel etiam mansiunculam. Item dicere potest quod nulla communia pertinet ad tale tenementum: quia illud fuit aliquando foresta, boscus, et locus vastae solitudinis et communia, et jam inde efficitur assartum, vel redactum est in culturam, et non debet

[1] This distinction was not recognised in later law. Common of pasture in gross, i.e. not appurtenant to any tenement, is recognised as a class of rights of common.

[2] The right to mines of gold and silver is by the common law of England part of the royal prerogative. Blackstone, i. 294.

[3] 'Turf,' or peat—the well-known right called common of turbary.

[4] As to the foundation of the claim of copyholders to rights of common, see Chapter V. § 6.

[5] This is one of the many allusions which this passage contains to rights of common pasturage enjoyed over lands at certain periods of the year, which at other times is the separate property of an individual. See above, p. 6.

CH. III. SECT. II. § 18 (2).

communia pertinere ad communiam, et ubi omnes de patria solebant communicare[1]. Ad hoc facit de Itinere W. de Ralegh in comitatu War. assisa novae disseisinae de communia pasturae si Augustinus, etc.[2] Eodem modo dici poterit de mariscis, et aliis vastitatibus in culturam redactis, quia ubi eadem ratio, ibi esse debet idem jus.

Ib. fol. 227. Item potest constitutio servitutis aliquando minui et restringi, ut si prius constituatur quod per totum et ubique, restringi poterit quoad certum locum. . . . Item quod prius sine numero, coarctari potest ad certum numerum. . . . Et eodem modo poterunt omnia praedicta augeri et ampliari, sed non contra voluntatem contrahentium; quia per hoc competeret assisa novae disseisinae domino tenementi, sed in contrarium per vim ageretur, sicut competeret assisa novae disseisinae de communia pasturae ei cui debetur servitus secundum modum et constitutionem servitutis. Est tamen quaedam constitutio quae dicitur constitutio de Merton, per quam etiam invito eo cui servitus debetur communia coarctatur, unde primo videndum est qualis est illa constitutio, et est talis[3]:—

Quia multi sunt magnates qui feoffaverunt milites et libere tenentes suos in maneriis suis de parvis tenementis, et qui impediti sunt per eosdem quod commodum suum facere non possunt de residuo maneriorum suorum, sicut de vastis, boscis, et pasturis magnis, desicut ipsi feoffati sufficientem habere possent pasturam, scilicet quantum ad tenementa sua pertinet: ideo provisum est et concessum ab omnibus, quod cum hujusmodi feoffati a quibuscunque de cetero arramaverint erga dominos suos assisam novae disseisinae de communia pasturae, de hoc quod aliquam partem tenementorum suorum excoluerint, si coram justiciariis cognoverint quod sufficientem habeant pasturam quantum ad tenementum suum pertinet cum libero ingressu et egressu, et chaceam de tenementis suis usque ad pasturam illam vel viam, tunc inde sint contenti, et illi de quibus tales questi sunt quieti sint de hoc quod commodum suum ita fecerint de terris, vastis, et pasturis suis. Si autem dixerint quod sufficientem pasturam non habu-

[1] The language of this passage and the principle here stated seem strongly to support the historical view that the idea that all the neighbouring inhabitants had equal rights over the soil of waste lands is the true origin of rights of common.

[2] This is the name of the case decided on the circuit in question.

[3] See the text of this statute as given in the Statutes of the Realm, above, § 9.

erint, quantum pertinet ad tenementa sua, cum sufficienti ingressu et egressu, tunc inde inquiratur veritas per assisam. Et si per assisam recognitum fuerit quod in aliquo impediverint ipsius domini ingressum vel egressum, vel quod habeant sufficientem pasturam[1], secundum quod praedictum est, tunc recuperent querentes seisinam suam per visum recognitorum, ita quod per discretionem et sacramentum eorundem habeant conquerentes sufficientem pasturam cum sufficienti et competenti ingressu et egressu, in forma praedicta, et disseisitores in misericordia, et damna reddant sicut prius reddi solent ante provisionem istam. Si autem recognitum fuerit per assisam quod querentes sufficientem habeant pasturam, cum libero ingressu et egressu secundum quod praedictum est, tunc licite faciant domini sui commodum de residuo, et in quo casu, si quis liber homo feoffatus fuerit per aliquem, et occasione alicujus assisae captae vel alia occasione, vel si non permiserit dominum suum includere, vel si, cum incluserit, hayas suas fregerit et fossata, et muros suos prostraverit per vim cui resisti non possit, competit domino breve domini regis in hac forma:—

Rex Vicecomiti salutem. Ostensum est nobis ex parte *A* quod cum in curia nostra coram nobis et consilio nostro sit provisum et concessum quod magnates Angliae et milites et alii qui liberos tenentes suos feoffaverint de parvis tenementis in maneriis suis commodum suum facere possint de residuo maneriorum suorum sicut de vastis, boscis et pasturis, si ipsi feoffati sufficientem habeant pasturam quatenus ad tenementa sua pertinet cum libero ingressu et egressu, et ipse *A* parcum suum per multum tempus jam inclusum habuit, boscum vel hujusmodi; *B* qui parvum tenementum habet in eadem villa, vel alia, et de feodo ipsius *A*, occasione cujusdam assisae novae disseisinae inter eosdem *A* et *B* nuper captae de communia pasturae ipsius *B* quam pertinere dixit ad liberum tenementum suum in eadem villa, non permittit ipsum *A* parcum suum habere inclusum, immo hayas suas frangit et fossata, desicut communiam pasturae habere poterit sufficientem extra parcum vel boscum illum, quatenus ad tenementum suum pertinet cum libero ingressu et egressu: et ideo tibi praecipimus quod assumptis tecum liberis et legalibus hominibus de proximo vicineto, per quos rei veritas etc., in propria persona tua accedas apud talem villam et per eorum sacramentum, etc., si praedictus *B* sufficientem possit habere pasturam extra praedictum parcum vel

[1] The text of the Statute of Merton, given above, p. 134, seems more accurate and intelligible than the reading given in this passage.

CH. III. SECT. II. § 18 (2).

boscum quatenus pertinet ad liberum tenementum suum in eadem villa cum libero ingressu et egressu vel non. Et si ita esse inveniris tunc eidem *A* pacem inde habere facias ne amplius, etc. Teste, etc.

Ad quod imprimis videndum est qualiter constitutio illa sit intelligenda, ne male intellecta trahat utentes ad abusum. Videri oportet utrum ille quem restringit constitutio, sit liber homo proprius vel alienus [1]. Si autem sit alienus non ei imponit legem constitutio [2], tum quia habet servitutem illam forte sicut ex consensu et conventione ubique, quae dissolvi non potest nec per contrarium voluntatem et dissensum, tum quia non feoffatus est per dominum soli, quod coarctari potest ad certum numerum et determinatum secundum quantitatem sui tenementi. Et unde in hoc casu si dominus soli et proprietatis sibi velit aliquid appropriare et includere, hoc facere non poterit sine voluntate et licentia praedictorum, et, si fecerit, per assisam recuperabunt [3]. Si autem fuerint libere tenentes proprii tunc refert qualiter fuerint feoffati, quia non omnes nec in omnibus per constitutionem restringuntur, et ideo videndum erit utrum feoffati fuerint large, scilicet per totum et ubique, et in omnibus locis, et ad omnimoda averia et sine numero, et ita tamen quod hujusmodi communia ad ipsos pertineat ratione feoffamenti, et non propter usum, tales non ligat constitutio memorata, quia feoffamentum non tollit, licet tollit abusum, et maxime propter consensum eorum voluntarium qui servitutem et communiam concesserunt [4]. Si autem communia

[1] That is, whether or not he be a tenant of the manor over the wastes of which the right of common is claimed.

[2] The Statute of Merton regulated the respective rights of the lord of the manor and his tenants over the waste. It did not affect the rights of persons who had rights of common appurtenant to freeholds outside the manor. The lord could not by this Statute enclose the waste so as to curtail rights of common appurtenant. By the Statute of Westminster II, 13 Edward I, c. 46 (see Chap. IV. § 4), the provisions of the Statute of Merton were extended to cover the relations of the lord and commoners having rights of common appurtenant.

[3] This passage throws light on the much disputed question whether this right of appropriation or approvement belonged to the lord at common law or rested on the Statutes of Merton and Westminster II. Bracton's authority, particularly valuable as being contemporary evidence, is express that the right rested on the Statute, and that except for the Statute the lord could not have 'approved' at all. See Coke's Second Institute, pp. 85, 474; Grant v. Gunner, 1 Taunton's Reports, p. 435; above, p. 194.

[4] This appears to mean that even in the case of freehold tenants of a manor, if rights of common had been expressly granted over the whole waste, &c., the lord could not approve so as to derogate from his express grant.

fuerit stricta cum numero averiorum certo et determinato, licet usus se largius et latius habuerit quam necesse esset, tales ligat constitutio, quod coarctentur ad certum locum et infra certum locum, dum tamen locus ille sufficiens sit et competens cum libero ingressu et egressu et competenti, quod non sit gravis nec difficilis. Competens autem debet esse locus, ita quod non longius distet sed propinquius assignetur. Item eodem modo si ita feoffatus fuerit quis, sine expressione numeri vel generis, sed ita, cum pastura quantum pertinet ad tantum tenementum in eadem villa, talem ligat constitutio sicut prius cum expressione; quia cum constet de quantitate tenementi, de facili perpendi poterit de numero averiorum et etiam de genere, secundum consuetudinem locorum. Item si qualitercunque usus fuerit vel feoffatus large vel stricte, si loco competenti usus fuerit, et sive coarctari possit sive non, non tamen coarctari debet cum damno et gravamine ad locum longius distantem, cum distantia inducunt incommoditatem. Et eodem modo coarctari non debet, nisi velit, si accessus sit difficilior. . . . Item tempus spectandum erit, scilicet quod tenementum tempore feoffamenti jacuit incultum, et quod tenementum redactum fuit in culturam [1]. Item quod tenementum [2] sit pratum, et quod inclusum et positum in defensum, cum nemo possit communiam petere in aliquo tenemento, quod excoli possit, vel includi, vel poni in defensum omni tempore vel saltem aliquo, et ex aliqua generali constitutione, ut si quis dicat, 'do tibi tale tenementum cum communia pasturae quae pertinet ad tantum tenementum in tali villa cum certo numero averiorum, vel sine numero,' hoc intelligendum erit de communia pasturae, quae communis esse debet, et pertinere ad liberum tenementum, hoc est non tenemento quod possit excoli, vel licito sed non omni vel aliter dum includitur vel ponitur in defensum tempore, vel si singulis annis possit includi et poni in defensum et excoli, vel alio quod possit includi, nisi hoc facit specialitas et modus constitutionis servitutis, vel longus usus continuus et pacificus [3]. Modus constitutionis servitutis, ut si dicat quis, 'do tibi tantam terram cum communia

[1] If the dominant tenement was uncultivated or waste land at the time of the feoffment, it seems that rights of common would not attach to it, unless expressly granted.

[2] Tenementum here means the servient tenement.

[3] The import of this passage seems to be that *prima facie* the right of common extends only over the waste or uncultivated lands properly so called, and not over lands which the tenant has the right to keep enclosed always or for some periods of the year. It was however not unusual for rights of common pasturage to exist over cultivated lands between harvest

CH. III. SECT. II. § 18 (2).

pasturae ad tot averia etc. per totam terram meam ubique in terris colendis, pratis, et clausis, et in omnibus locis,' et hoc non erit sic intelligendum quod omni tempore, nisi tantum temporibus competentibus, scilicet post blada asportata et faena levata; vel quando tenementum jacet incultum et ad waractum, vel si dicat expresse sic, 'ubique scilicet quando tenementum jacet incultum etc.' non propter hoc impediri debet dominus quin terram suam excolat quolibet anno si velit, quia non imponit sibi ipsi servitutem per hoc quin possit. Si autem ita dicat, 'cum pastura per totum et in omnibus locis, et secundo anno vel tertio in terra colenda, in terra colenda quando jacet ad waractum,' et adhuc idem erit ubi jacuerit ita ut dicitur, quia bene poterit esse quod nunquam jacebit, nec imponitur ei necessitas quod non colat, quia per hoc non includit se quin possit. Si autem sic dicat, 'omni tempore et in omnibus locis, scilicet quod secundo anno jaceat campus ad waractum vel incultus vel apertus, et quod tali tempore communiam habeat,' tali tempore excoli non possit nec includi, et maxime ubi hoc facit longus usus vel consuetudo a vicinis approbata et dominis, quae pro lege observari debet inter tales[1]. Item vel ubi hoc faciat vicinitas, et sine constitutione[2]. Poterit autem esse servitus personalis et realis[1]. Item personalis et realis certis horis

and seedtime, the lands being for the rest of the year enclosed for the protection of the growing crops. See Nasse, p. 46. This was called in later times common of shack: see Corbet's case, above, p. 7, n. 1. In the same way there might be rights of common pasturage over meadows after the removal of the hay-crop, until the grass began to grow again. And so where the system prevailed of cultivating the lands in common on the three-field or two-field system, that is, where the individual plots of the various landowners of the community were not divided from each other, but all were cultivated upon a common plan, being divided into two or three fields, one of which was left fallow every year, rights of common pasturage were often recognised over the fallow land. These rights of pasturage were however, as it would appear from this passage, exceptional, and must either be expressly granted, or proved as a local custom. See Nasse, pp. 46 50. These are amongst the rights which, owing to the fiction noticed above (p. 184), that they must originally have been created by grant, it has become impossible to sustain in a court of law unless they are claimed either by copyhold tenants of a manor under a custom, or by freeholders as appurtenant to their tenements. A custom for all the inhabitants of a district to turn out cattle on the waste, stubbles, meadows, or fallows, though doubtless the origin of the quasi-right, would be invalid.

[1] The whole of this passage is remarkable, as showing the great strength and vitality of common rights at this time.

[2] That is, the prescriptive rights of neighbours apart from any relationship of lord and tenant may be of the same character. There is a distinct

et certis temporibus. Item personalis tantum, et sic debetur personis et non tenementis, et quae proprie dici potest herbagium. Item localis et non certis personis, sicut alicujus universitatis, burgensium et civium [2], et omnes conqueri possunt et unus nomine universitatis. CH. III. SECT. II. § 18 (2).

TRANSLATION.

Inasmuch as the most common servitude is where a right of pasturage is granted to a person, I must in the first place treat of that right which is called 'common of pasture.' Now the term 'common' is a general expression, and is appropriate to the different divisions of these rights, just as a *genus* is related to its various *species*. For the word common is compounded of the words '*una*' and '*cum*,' and the word '*alio*' is understood, that is to say the right of common exists over another's land, and together with another person, and not over a person's own land; because a man's own land is never subject to a servitude in favour of its owner, as has been said above. Now a right of common is acquired by many titles. There is for instance the title

class of rights of common called common *pur cause de vicinage*. For instance, if there are adjoining wastes *A* and *B* belonging to different manors, a commoner who is entitled to put his cattle on common *A*, may be also entitled to have them permitted to stray into common *B*. In this case he is said to have common rights *pur cause de vicinage* in common *B*. The right of common is said to be more properly an excuse for a trespass.

[1] This points to the distinction between rights appurtenant to land, that is, enjoyed by the successive owners of a piece of land as and being such owners, and passing by alienation of the *praedium dominans*, and rights in gross, or rights (*in rem*, of property, available against third persons, opposed to rights *in personam*) not attached to the ownership of a *praedium dominans*, or as they were called later, rights 'in gross.' See above, p. 182, n. 1. Compare Dig. lib. viii. tit. i. 1: 'Servitutes aut personarum sunt, ut usus et ususfructus, aut rerum, ut servitutes rusticorum praediorum, et urbanorum.'

[2] Both rights of property in the land itself, and rights over the land of another, might be granted (apart from the Statutes of Mortmain) to a corporation. Therefore the rule that inhabitants as such cannot claim a profit *in alieno solo* (see above, p. 184, n. 1) does not apply where the rights are claimed in the name of a corporation. A corporation may claim such rights by prescription, because the rights might by legal possibility have originated in a grant. Bracton's language no doubt points to the actual historical origin of these rights, namely that they were local customs which became legalised. The theory of the later lawyers excluded from the category of legal rights all profits not capable of originating in a grant.

CH. III. SECT. II. § 18 (2).

of a gift of the land to which it is appurtenant, as if anyone gives land with its appurtenances and with common of pasture, etc. It may also be created by purchase and sale, as when one has bought a right of common over another's land so that it may be appurtenant to his tenement, although it be held of another fee and a different barony; and in that case it is created by the grant of the owner of the servient land. It may also be created by the lord of the land, as by means of fixed services. Also it may arise by reason of neighbourhood, as when one intercommons with his neighbour, and his neighbour with him. Also it may be acquired without a grant by user for a long time with peaceful, continuous, and uninterrupted enjoyment of the right, the lords (I do not say their bailiffs) knowing of it and neglecting to interfere; for this is regarded as equivalent to a legal transfer, provided the enjoyment has not been by violence, or clandestinely, or by request and permission as has been said above. In these various ways may a right of common of pasture be made appurtenant to a freehold tenement; it must however be remembered that common of pasture is a general name containing under it many species. For there may exist a right of common in whatever may be called 'pasture,' that is of everything on which animals may be fed, the word being taken in a broad sense or strictly; in a broad sense, as for instance if one has common of pasture over another's land of the herbage, fall of fruit, whether acorns or beechmast, or whatever comes under that designation. Strictly, as if the right of common be limited to leaves or branches, for instance to any one or two kinds of them. Also rights of common of pasture may be distinguished as to time; they may exist at all times, or only at certain times and certain hours. There may also be a distinction as to the places where they are to be enjoyed, as for instance whether they are to be exercised on the whole land and everywhere without any exception. Moreover, some places may be exempted from the exercise of the right tacitly, and some in express terms, as for instance in the case of reasonable enclosures, which cannot be claimed to be subject to rights of common of pasture unless they be specially granted, and then only after a certain time. Such are corn lands, meadows, woods, 'byngheys' for oxen, also for cows and calves at their season, also for wethers and ewes and lambs at their season. So neither can the right be exercised in anyone's curtilage or garden or lawn or park and so forth. Nor again does the right exist over demesnes which may be enclosed and cultivated, unless by the terms of an express grant, and at certain fixed times and places and within certain limits. Also there may be no limit either as regards the number or kind of beasts, or the right may be restricted to a certain number or to certain kinds of beasts. Further, it is to be observed that a right which a person has in another's soil either for payment or by purchase ought not to be called a right of common, because he has no tenement to which a right of common can appertain, but it ought rather to be called a right to the herbage than a right of common, since this may be as it were a kind of personal right, whether the price which the person has given for the right of herbage be ascertained or not. Also, following up what has been said above as to generic expressions, a right of digging in another man's land may be called a right of common, as for instance a right of digging gold, and hence the place may be called a gold digging. So with regard to silver and silver digging, and so of other metals. The same is the case with regard to digging stones, chalk, gravel, and turf, and things of that kind. Other instances of rights of common, which do not resemble the right of herbage, are rights of cutting grass or underwood for reasonable estovers. And the same observations apply to the right of cutting in another's wood reasonable estovers for the purpose of building, enclosing, or fuel.

Fol. 224. No one but a freeholder can claim common of pasture as appertaining to his freehold. Now a tenement is called freehold by way of distinction from a tenement held in villenage, and from one held by villeins, who hold villein tenements: for they have no right of action or assize, but only their lord who is the freeholder of the land held by them in villenage.

Fol. 225 b. Further, the tenant can defend the assize on the ground that the complainant has no right to claim any common in the place in question, because it is the defendant's separate tenement, and because he is entitled to enclose it and cultivate it as he pleases and keep it enclosed for ever. To which the complainant, if he can, may prove by means of the assize that the fact is contrary or different, for instance that at no time could the land be enclosed, or that it could be enclosed only at certain times and seasons. Further, the tenant may answer and say that the complainant has no free tenement at all, or anything resembling a free tenement, to which any right of common could appertain, not even so much as a hovel. Further, he may say that no right of common belongs to the tenement in question, because it was formerly a

CH. III. SECT. II. § 18 (2).

forest, a wood, or wild waste land and common to all, and afterwards in recent times enclosed and brought under cultivation, and that no right of common can lawfully appertain to land which is itself common, and which the whole community formerly used in common. For this there is authority in Augustin's case, which was an assize of novel disseisin of common of pasture on the circuit of W. de Ralegh in the county of Warwick. The same may be said in the case of marshes and other waste lands which have been brought under cultivation, for where the same principle applies the law ought to be the same.

Fol. 227. Further, the grant of a servitude may sometimes be curtailed and restricted, for instance a right which formerly prevailed over the whole of the lands and everywhere may be restricted to a particular part. . . . . . So what was at first unlimited in point of number of beasts may be limited to a certain number; . . . and in the same way all the above-mentioned rights may be enlarged and added to, but not contrary to the will of the parties; for in that case, on the one hand, an assize of novel disseisin would be open to the owner of the servient tenement, and on the other, if violence be done to the owner of the servitude, an assize of novel disseisin of common of pasture would be open to him according to the measure and definition of the servitude. There is however a certain ordinance called the Statute of Merton, whereby a right of common may be curtailed even against the will of him to whom the servitude is due; wherefore it is in the first place necessary to see what are the terms of that Statute, and they are as follows:—

Also because many great men of England, which have infeoffed knights and their freeholders of small tenements in their great manors, have complained that they cannot make their profit of the residue of their manors, as of wastes, woods, and pastures, whereas the same feoffees have sufficient pasture as much as belongeth to their tenements; it is provided and granted, That whenever such feoffees do bring an assize of novel disseisin for their common of pasture, and it is knowledged before the Justicers, that they have as much pasture as sufficeth to their tenements, and that they have free egress and regress from their tenement unto the pasture, then let them be contented therewith; and they on whom they have complained shall go quit for that they have made their profit of their lands, wastes, woods, and pastures; and if they allege that they have not sufficient pasture, or sufficient ingress and egress according to their hold, then let the truth be inquired by assize, and if it be found by the assize that the same deforceors have in any thing disturbed them of their ingress and egress, or that they had not sufficient pasture, as before is said, then shall they recover their seisin by view of the inquest, so that by their discretion and oath the plaintiffs shall have sufficient pasture, and sufficient ingress and egress in form aforesaid; and the disseisors shall be amerced, and shall yield damages as they were wont before this provision. And if it be certified by the assize that the plaintiffs have sufficient pasture with ingress and egress, as before is said, let the other make their profit of the residue, and go quit of that assize [1].

In that case if any free man has been enfeoffed by any one else, and on the occasion of the taking of an assize or on any other occasion it be alleged that he has either not permitted his lord to enclose, or that when the lord has enclosed he has broken down his hedges and embankments, and has thrown down his walls with overwhelming force, the lord may sue out a writ of our lord the king in the following terms:—The King to the Sheriff, greeting. It has been shown to us on behalf of *A* that although it has been provided and granted in our court before ourselves and our council that great men of England and knights and other persons who have enfeoffed their free tenants of small tenements within their manors may have the benefit of the residue of their manors, that is to say of the wastes woods and pastures, provided the feoffees have sufficient pasture so far as appertains to their tenements with free ingress and egress, and that the said *A* has kept his park or his wood or the like enclosed now for a long time, and that *B*, who holds a small tenement in the same township or in another, and of the fee of the aforesaid *A*, on the recent occasion of the taking of an assize of novel disseisin between the aforesaid *A* and *B* concerning common of pasture of the aforesaid *B*, which as he declared is appurtenant to his free tenement in the same township, refuses to allow the aforesaid *A* to keep his park enclosed, nay further breaks down his hedges and dyke, although he can have sufficient common of pasture outside that park or wood as much as appertains to his tenement with sufficient ingress and egress, therefore I command thee that, taking free and competent men of the nearest neighbourhood, by whom the truth of the matter etc., thou in thine own person shouldest go to that district and by their oaths etc. (ascertain) whether the aforesaid *B* can have sufficient pasture outside the aforesaid park

[1] To this point the translation is taken from Statutes of the Realm, and is from the text given above, § 9.

CH. III. SECT. II. § 18 (2). or wood as much as appertains to his tenement in the same district with free ingress and egress or not. And if thou findest this to be so, then cause the aforesaid *A* to be quieted in the matter that I hear no more, etc. Witness, etc.

In relation to this matter it should in the first place be observed how that ordinance is to be understood, lest if it be misunderstood a wrong use should be made of it. It should be observed whether he whom it is sought to bind by the ordinance is a free tenant of the lord of the waste or of another lord. If he be the tenant of another lord he is not affected by the ordinance, so as to be confined to a definite and limited number of beasts, according to the size of his tenement, both because he enjoys that servitude, it may be, by some title such as by consent and agreement, and this cannot be put an end to merely by an opposite intent and disagreement, and because the tenant was not enfeoffed by the lord of the soil. And it follows in this case that if the lord of the soil and of the manor desires to appropriate any part to himself and to enclose, he will not be able to do this without the consent and licence of the aforesaid foreign tenants, and if he does it they shall recover by the assize. If however the free holders are tenants of the manor then the question is in what manner have they been enfeoffed, because it is not every one who is restricted by the ordinance, nor does the restriction avail in all places, and therefore it must be observed what the extent of their rights is by the feoffment, whether it is in wide terms, as for instance over the whole waste and everywhere, and in all places, and for all manner of beasts, and without stint, and in that case, because common of this kind belongs to the tenants by reason of the feoffment and not by reason of usage, such tenants are not bound by the ordinance, for the ordinance does not destroy the effect of the feoffment, though it does prevent misuse of the right of common; and the ground on which this rule rests is the voluntary consent of those who have conceded the servitude and granted the right of common. If however the right of common was stinted to a fixed and determined number of beasts, but it has been used more widely and in excess of what was necessary, in such a case the ordinance applies to restrict them to a certain place and within certain limits, provided that that place is sufficient, and has free and sufficient ingress and egress, without impediment or difficulty. And the place ought to be sufficient, in the sense that the distance be not too great, but the pasturage should be assigned sufficiently near. Also in the same manner if a man be enfeoffed without any express definition of the number or kind of beasts, but in such words as 'with as much common of pasture as belongs to such a tenement in the same township' such a one is bound by the statute in the same way as in the former instance where there was express definition, because when the size of the tenement is fixed, the number and even the kind of beasts can easily be estimated according to the custom of the place. Further, in whatever way the feoffee has enjoyed the right—whether the terms of his feoffment be wide or restricted—if only he has enjoyed the right in a convenient place, and whether he can be restricted or not, he ought in no case to be put to loss and damage by being restricted to a place at an inconvenient distance—for distance is a cause of inconvenience—and in the same way he ought not to be restricted against his will by access being made more difficult. . . . . . Further, regard must be paid to the condition of things at the time, for instance to the fact that at the time of the feoffment the tenement lay uncultivated, and was afterwards brought under cultivation. Also that the (servient) tenement is a meadow, and that it is enclosed and fenced in, since no one can claim a right of common in any tenement which can be cultivated or enclosed or fenced in at all times or even at any time if the grant be in general terms; for instance if any one were to say, 'I give you such a tenement with common of pasture which belongs to such a tenement in such a township with a fixed number of beasts or without a fixed number'—this should be understood of common of pasture which ought to be common and to belong to a free tenement, and not to relate to a tenement which can be cultivated and enclosed and fenced in for the purpose either at a permitted time or at any time, or it may be in particular years, or which otherwise may be enclosed, unless the right be specially granted by the terms of the instrument creating the servitude, or exist by virtue of long and uninterrupted and peaceable enjoyment. Instances of a grant in special terms would be if one were to say, 'I give you so much land with common of pasture for so many beasts &c. over my whole land everywhere in cultivated land, meadows, closes and in all places,' and this must not be understood as applying to all times, but only to convenient times, that is to say after the corn has been carried, and the hay removed, or while the tenement lies uncultivated and fallow, or again if he say 'everywhere that is to say when the tenement lies uncultivated.' The lord ought not by such words to be prevented from cultivating his land in any year if he pleases to do so, because he does not by a grant of this kind impose upon himself any servitude so as to prevent the

CH. III. SECT. II. § 18 (2).

cultivation; and if the words are, 'with common of pasture over the whole and in all places and in the second or third year in tilled land, or in tilled land when it is lying fallow,' it will be the same thing as if the words are 'when it shall have lain fallow'—for it may well be that it will never so lie, nor is any obligation imposed upon the lord not to cultivate, and he does not by such words preclude himself from cultivating. But if the words are, 'at all times and in all places, that is to say that every second year the field shall lie fallow or untilled or unfenced, and that at such time he shall enjoy his right of common,' at such a time it cannot be cultivated or enclosed, and especially when this is the outcome of prolonged usage or custom approved of by the neighbours and the lords, for this should be regarded amongst such persons as a law. The same may be said when the practice arises from vicinage and without special grant. Moreover, the servitude may belong both to a person and to property; and it may belong to a person and to property at fixed hours and times. Moreover, it may belong to a person alone, and thus be owing to persons and not to tenements. Such a right may properly be called a right of herbage. Further, the servitude may be enjoyed by a particular locality and not by definite persons, as by the burgesses or citizens of any corporation, and in such a case the whole body may be the claimants, or one person in the name of the whole body.

CHAPTER IV.

LEGISLATION OF EDWARD I.

CH. IV.

THE reign of Edward I was a period of great legislative activity. The statutes passed in this reign introduced some important changes, which have affected the subsequent history and the present condition of the law. Beside the changes effected by new enactments, the regular action of the courts proceeds, and with it the development and definition of the law. The series of regular reports called the Year Books begins with the reign of Edward II, and contains reports of cases decided to the end of the reign of Edward III, and from the beginning of the reign of Henry IV to the end of that of Henry VIII[1].

The text-books of this reign, of which the principal are the treatises of Britton[2] and Fleta[3] (possibly the Mirror of

[1] See Reeves, ii. p. 229. There have been lately published in the series under the direction of the Master of the Rolls, from MSS. in the Libraries of Cambridge University, Lincoln's Inn, the Inner Temple, and the British Museum, twelve volumes called Year Books, containing reports of cases decided on the itinera of the judges and at Westminster between the 20th and 21st years of Edward I, and the 16th year of Edward III. See Preface to Year Books, 30 and 31 Edward I, p. x. The reports of the reign of Richard II are contained in a volume styled Bellewe's Reports.

[2] There is great doubt as to the authorship of Britton. Some have thought that the name is identical with Bracton, and that the work is merely an authoritative abridgment of Bracton; others have ascribed it to an independent writer. See Nichols, Britton, preface, pp. xviii–xxvii.

[3] So named because it was written by some lawyer, perhaps a judge, during imprisonment in the Fleet. (Fleta, preface.) See Pollock and Maitland, Hist. of Engl. Law, i. p. 189.

Justices is also to be ascribed to this reign[1]), add but little to the great treatise of Bracton. The treatise called Fleta carries the law down to a point later than the thirteenth year of the king, and contains comments on the changes in the law since Bracton wrote[2].

The changes of historical importance in the law relating to land which were effected by new legislation during this reign will be seen from the following statutes; the development of the common law effected by judicial decisions is reserved for the next chapter.

The statutes of this reign are usually in Latin, though some are in French, and in one case a chapter of a statute is partly in Latin, partly in French[3]. It seems impossible to lay down any principle by which the choice of the language was regulated. 'Both the Latin and French were the languages of the law, and probably were adopted according to the whim of the clerk or other person who drew up the statute[4].'

§ 1. *A Manor in the time of Edward I.*

The following Statute, though not making any change in the positive law relating to land, is valuable as showing clearly the legal conception of a manor in the time (probably) of Edward I. 'In myn opinion this statute was made sone after the barons' warre, the whyche ended at the battayle of Evesham, or sone after in the tyme of Kynge Henry the thyrde[5], where as many noblemen of bloud were slayne, and many fled that afterward were attaynted for the treason they did to the Kynge. And by reason thereof their castelles and manours were seased into the Kynge's handes. And so for

[1] See p. xxiv of the Introduction to the Mirror of Justices in Vol. VII. of the Selden Society's publications.

[2] The other treatises which were published in this reign were An Abbreviation of Bracton by Gilbert de Thornton, the Summa Magna and Parva of Radulph de Hengham, and a small tract called Fet Assavoir.

[3] Statute West. II. ch. 34.

[4] Reeves, ii. p. 228.

[5] From internal evidence the document would appear to be later than 13 Edward I. See p. 214, note 2.

want of reparations the castelles and the manors fell to ruine and in decaye. And when the Kynge and his counsayle saw that, they thought it was better to extende them and make the most profit that they coude of them, than to lette them fall to the grounde, and come to no manne's helpe and profyte. Wherefore Kynge Edwarde the first ordeyned this statute to be made the fourth year of his reigne, wherein is contayned many and dyvers chapters and articles, the which at that tyme was but instructions, how and what they shuld do that were commissioners or surveyours in the same.'—(Fitzherbert, Surveyinge, chap. i: A.D. 1539.) CH. IV. § 1.

EXTENTA MANERII, 4 Edward I, Stat. 1[1].

Inquirendum est de castris, et aliis edificiis fossatis circumdatis, quantum muri, edificia lignea et lapidea, plumbo vel alio modo cooperta, valeant, et pro quanto poterunt appreciari, secundum verum valorem eorundem murorum et edificiorum: et pro quanto edificia extra fossatum poterunt appreciari, et quantum valeant, una cum gardinis, columbariis, et omnibus aliis exitibus curiae per annum.

Item inquirendum est quot campi sunt in dominico[2], et quot acrae terrae sunt in campo, et quantum valet quaelibet acra per se per annum; item inquirendum est quot acrae prati sunt in dominico, et quantum valet quaelibet acra ad locandum per se per annum, et ad cujusmodi bestias et animalia pastura illa fuerit magis necessaria, et quot et quales possit sustinere, et quantum valet pastura cujuslibet bestiae et animalis per se per annum ad locandum.

Item inquirendum est de pastura forinseca, quae est communis[3], et quot et quas bestias et quot animalia et quae dominus [rex[4]] habere possit in eadem, et quantum valeat pastura cujuslibet bestiae et animalis per se per annum ad locandum.

[1] This is the date given in most editions of the Statutes. In 'Statutes of the Realm' (i. p. 242) it is included amongst the Statutes of uncertain date, and printed after the Statutes of Edward II. It was repealed by the Statute Law Revision Act 1863 (26 and 27 Vict. c. 125).

[2] See above, pp. 24, 49.

[3] See above, Chap. III. § 18 (2).

[4] Some MSS. omit this word, which is not inserted in 'Statutes at Large.' If it is rightly inserted, the passage would be in accordance with the view taken of the history of the rights of the king, above, p. 18.

CH. IV. § 1. Item inquirendum est de parcis et dominicis boscis quae dominus ad voluntatem suam poterit assartare et excolere [1], et quot acras in se contineant, et pro quanto vestura cujuslibet acrae poterit appreciari, et quantum fundus in se contineat et valeat quando prostratus fuerit, et quantum valet quaelibet acra per se per annum.

Item inquirendum est de boscis forinsecis, ubi alii communicant, quid de eisdem boscis dominus sibi possit appruare [2], et de quot acris, et pro quanto vestura cujuslibet acrae communiter possit appreciari, et quantum fundus valeat quando prostratus fuerit. Item inquirendum est utrum dominus de residuo boscorum praedictorum forinsecorum dare possit, et quantum valeant hujusmodi donationes et venditiones per annum.

Item inquirendum est de pannagio, herbagio, melle, oleribus, et omnibus aliis exitibus vivariorum, mariscorum, morarum, bruerarum, turbariarum, et vastorum, et quantum valeant per annum.

Item de molendinis, et piscariis separalibus et communibus, quantum valeant per annum.

Item de libere tenentibus [3] quibuscunque et forinsecis [4] vel extrinsecis, inquirendum est quot sunt libere tenentes, et qui, et quas terras, et quae tenementa, et quae feoda teneant, et per quod servitium, utrum per socagium, vel servitium militare, vel alio modo, et quantum valeant per annum et reddant per annum de redditu assisae [5], et qui tenent per cartam, et qui non [6], et qui tenent per antiquam tenuram, et qui per novum feoffa-

[1] This probably refers to the parks and other enclosures which had been made under the provisions of the Statute of Merton. See Chap. III. §§ 10, 18 (2).

[2] That is, what approvements can be made of woodlands, where rights of common are enjoyed by freeholders who are not tenants of the manor. This would seem to show that this document must be subsequent to the Statute 13 Edward I, c. 46. See below, § 4. For the meaning and derivation of 'appruare' see Glossary.

[3] See above, p. 48.

[4] 'Forinseci tenentes' are probably those tenants who hold of the lord of the manor as a fact, but whose tenements are not within the ambit of the manor, and who are therefore not tenants of the manor.

[5] 'Rents of assize are the certain rents of freeholders and ancient copyholders, because they be assized and certain, and doth distinguish the same from *redditus mobiles*, farm-rents for life, years, or at will, which are variable and uncertain.' Coke, Second Institute, 19.

[6] It is an important fact that at this time there were freeholders whose title did not rest on any grant. These were probably the representatives of the free proprietors of the times before the Conquest, who had not only

mentum. Item inquirendum est de praedictis libere tenentibus et qui sequuntur curiam de comitatu in comitatum, et qui non, et quid et quantum accidit domino post mortem talium libere tenentium.

Item inquirendum est de custumariis [1], quot sunt custumarii, et quantum terrae quilibet custumarius teneat, et quae opera et quas consuetudines faciant, et quantum valeant opera et consuetudines cujuslibet custumarii per se per annum, et quantum reddant de redditu assisae per annum praeter opera et consuetudines, et qui possint talliari ad voluntatem domini, et qui non.

Item inquirendum est de coterellis [2], quae cotagia et curtulagia teneant, per quod servitium, et quantum reddant per annum pro praedictis cotagiis et curtulagiis.

Item inquirendum est de placitis et perquisitis comitatuum, et curiarum forestarum, cum expeditatione canum, et quantum valeant per annum in omnibus exitibus.

Item inquirendum est de ecclesiis quae pertinent ad donationem domini [3] quot et quae sunt, et ubi, et quantum quaelibet ecclesia valet per annum per se, secundum veram estimationem illius.

Item inquirendum est quantum valeant heriota, nundinae, mercheta, consuetudines et servitia, operationes et consuetudines forinsecae, et quantum valeant placita et perquisita, fines et relevia, et omnia alia casualia quae accidere possunt in omnibus per annum.

TRANSLATION [4].

First, It is to be inquired of the castles and also of other buildings compassed about with ditches, what the walls, and

preserved their free status, but also had not become subject to other than a free tenure. See above, Chap. III. § 13.

[1] See above, p. 50; Chap. III. § 13; and below, Chap. V. § 6.

[2] See above, p. 50.

[3] 'Advowsons are either advowsons *appendant* or advowsons *in gross.* Lords of manors being originally the only founders, and of course the only patrons, of churches, the right of patronage or presentation, so long as it continues annexed to the possession of the manor, as some have done from the foundation of the church to this day, is called an advowson appendant: and it will pass or be conveyed, together with the manor, as incident and appendant thereto, by a grant of the manor only, without adding any other words. But where the property of the advowson has been once separated from the property of the manor by legal conveyance, it is called an advowson in gross, or at large, and never can be appendant any more; but is for the future annexed to the person of its owner, and not to his manor or lands.' Blackstone, ii. 22.

[4] See note 1, p. 122.

CH. IV. § 1. buildings of timber and stone, covered with lead, or otherwise, are worth, and how they may be prized according to the very value of the same walls and buildings, and for how much the buildings without the ditch may be prized, and what they be worth with the gardens [curtilages], dove houses, and all other issues of the court-yard, by the year.

It is to be inquired also how many fields are of the demesnes, and how many acres of land are in every field, and what every acre is worth by the year; also it is to be inquired how many acres of meadow are of the demesnes, and how many be in a field, and how much every acre by itself is worth by the year to be let, also how many acres of pasture there be, and for what beasts or cattle the same pasture is most necessary, and how many it will find, and of what manner, and what the pasture of every beast is worth to be let by the year.

Also it is to be inquired of foreign pasture that is common, how many and what beasts and cattle the lord[1] may have in the same, and how much the pasture of every beast is worth by the year to be let.

Also it is to be inquired of parks and demesne woods which the lord may assart[2] and improve at his pleasure, and how many acres they contain, and how much the vesture of an acre is worth; and how much the land is worth after the wood is felled, and how many acres it containeth, and how much every acre is by the year.

Also it is to be inquired of foreign woods, where other men have common, and how much the lord may improve to himself of the same woods, and how many acres, and for how much the vesture of every acre may be valued at, and how much the ground is worth yearly after that the wood is felled. And it is to be inquired whether the lord may give or sell anything of the residue of the foresaid woods, and what such gifts and sales are worth by the year.

Also it is to be inquired of pawnage[3], herbage[4] [of the town], honey, and all other profits of vivaries[5], moors, marshes, heaths, turbary, and waste, and how much they are worth by the year.

Also of mills and fishings several and common, what they be worth by the year.

Also it is to be inquired of freeholders, the which dwell without as well as within, that is to say, how many freeholders there be

[1] Or the king, see note 4, p. 213.

[2] Or clear.

[3] Or pannage, i. e. the right to feed pigs or other beasts in woods on beech-mast, acorns, &c.

[4] See above, p. 186.

[5] Vivaria = warrens.

and who they are, and what manner lands and tenements, and what fees they hold, and by what services, whether it be by socage or knight service, or otherwise, and what they are worth, and pay yearly of rent of assise, and who hold by charter, and who not, and who by old tenure, and who by new feoffment. Also it is to be inquired of the said free tenants, which do follow the court from county to county [1] and which not, and what and how much falleth to the lord after the death of such free tenants. CH. IV. § 2.

It is to be inquired also of customary tenants, that is to wit, how many there be, and how much land every of them holdeth, what works and customs he doth, and what the works and customs of every tenant be worth yearly, and how much rent of assise he pays yearly, besides the works and customs, and which of them may be taxed at the will of the lord, and which not.

It is also to be inquired of cottagers, that is to say, what cottages and curtilages they hold, and by what service, and how much they do pay by the year for all their cottages and curtilages.

It is also to be inquired of pleas and perquisites of the counties and of the courts of the forest, with lawing of dogs [2], and how much they be worth by the year in all issues.

It is also to be inquired of churches that belong to the lord's gift, how many there be, and what, and where, and how much every church is worth by the year after the true estimation of the same.

It is also to be inquired what be the value of herriots, fairs, markets, customs, services, and foreign works and customs; and what the pleas and perquisites [of courts], fines, and reliefs, and all other casualties are worth by the year, that may fall in any of these things.

§ 2. *Alienation in Mortmain.*

It appears from the following Statute that the provision in Magna Carta [3] given in the last chapter was construed as an absolute prohibition against granting lands to religious houses. The prohibition is now extended so as to prevent any alienation of lands '*per quod ad manum mortuam deveniant.*' Lands

[1] So in the margin of 'Statutes at Large,' which seems correct.

[2] i. e. mutilating the foot so as to prevent the dog chasing game. Spelman, s. v. Expeditatio.

[3] Cap. 43. ed. 1217; above, Chap. III. § 9.

CH. IV. § 2. were said to come into a 'dead hand' when they were held not by an individual tenant, but by a corporation or body[1]. This expression was probably first applied to the holding of lands by religious bodies or persons who, being 'professed,' were reckoned dead persons in law. It then came to be applied to the holding of lands by corporations as opposed to individuals, whether the corporation were ecclesiastical or lay, sole or aggregate.

An attempt was made soon after the passing of this Statute to evade its provisions by bringing collusive actions for the recovery[2] of land, in which the 'religious men and other ecclesiastical persons' sued the tenant, who thereupon by arrangement made default. This was held not to be within the Statute of 7 Edward I, the words of that enactment applying only to the case of acquisition of lands by gift or other alienation, and not to recovery by process of law. To stop this practice it was enacted by the Statute of Westminster II that in such a case a jury should determine whether the claimant had right over the land demanded or not. If not, the land claimed was to be forfeited to the lord of the fee, and the same penalty was attached to the attempt of a tenant to protect himself against his lord by setting up crosses in his land and so pretending to avail himself of the privileges of the Templars and Hospitallers[3]. The restriction

[1] A corporation is a fictitious person invested by the law with the attribute of perpetuity. This fictitious person may be (1) a corporation aggregate, that is, may consist of many individual persons united together by the law, the aggregate thus formed continuing for ever by a perpetual succession of individual members: such as the mayor and commonalty of a city, the head and fellows of a college, the dean and chapter of a cathedral church. Such a body can only act in its corporate capacity by the use of the 'common seal.' The two characteristics of a corporation aggregate are that it possesses perpetual succession and a common seal. (2) A corporation sole is where a person and his successors in infinitum fill a definite office or station which confers a special status or collection of rights and duties, such as the king, a bishop, or the parson of a parish. See Blackstone, i. p. 469.

[2] The tenant against whom the action was brought was technically said to 'suffer a recovery.'

[3] 13 Edward I, c. 33. See Coke's Second Institute, p. 432.

as to holding lands in mortmain might at all times have been dispensed with by licence from the Crown and the mesne lords if any. In later times, when the power of the Crown to dispense with the provisions of statutes had become an important constitutional question, the right of the Crown to grant licences to alien or take lands in mortmain was made to rest on the Statute 7 and 8 Will. III, c. 37; and by the same Statute all necessity for the consent of the mesne lords was removed. Several exceptions have been introduced in favour of particular corporations or classes of corporations by Act of Parliament, as for instance the Universities and Colleges of Oxford and Cambridge, limited companies, and many others. When however no licence has been obtained from the Crown or been conferred by Act of Parliament, the old rule of law still prevails [1].

STATUTUM DE VIRIS RELIGIOSIS, 7 Edward I, Stat. 2. c. 13.

Rex Justitiariis suis de Banco [2], salutem. Cum dudum provisum fuisset [3] quod viri religiosi feoda aliquorum non ingrederentur sine licentia et voluntate capitalium dominorum de quibus feoda illa immediate tenentur; et viri religiosi postmodum nihilominus tam feoda sua propria quam aliorum hactenus ingressi sint, ea sibi appropriando et emendo, et aliquando ex dono aliorum recipiendo, per quod servitia, quae ex hujusmodi feodis debentur, et quae ad defensionem regni ab initio provisa fuerunt, indebite subtrahuntur, et domini capitales escaetas suas inde amittunt; nos super hoc pro utilitate regni congruum remedium provideri volentes, de consilio praelatorum, comitum et aliorum fidelium regni nostri de consilio nostro existentium, providimus, statuimus, et ordinavimus, quod nullus religiosus aut alius quicunque terras aut tenementa aliqua emere vel vendere, aut sub colore donationis aut termini vel alterius tituli cujuscunque, ab aliquo recipere, aut alio quovis modo, arte vel ingenio, sibi appropriare praesumat,

[1] See now The Mortmain and Charitable Uses Act 1888, 51 and 52 Vict. c. 42, which repeals the older Statutes and consolidates the law on the subject.

[2] This Statute is in the form of a writ or ordinance addressed to the Justices of the Common Pleas.

[3] By Magna Carta, c. 43; above, p. 133.

CH. IV. § 2. sub forisfactura eorundem, per quod ad manum mortuam terrae et tenementa hujusmodi deveniant quoquo modo. Providimus etiam quod si quis religiosus aut alius, contra praesens statutum, aliquo modo, arte vel ingenio, venire praesumpserit, liceat nobis, et aliis immediatis capitalibus dominis feodi taliter alienati, illud infra annum a tempore alienationis hujusmodi ingredi et tenere in feodo et haereditate. Et si capitalis dominus immediatus negligens fuerit, et feodum hujusmodi ingredi noluerit infra annum, tunc liceat proximo capitali domino mediato feodi illius, infra dimidium annum sequentem, feodum illud ingredi et tenere, sicut praedictum est; et sic quilibet dominus mediatus faciat, si propinquior dominus in ingrediendo hujusmodi feodum negligens fuerit, ut praedictum est. Et si omnes hujusmodi capitales domini hujusmodi feodi, qui plenae fuerint aetatis, et infra quatuor maria, et extra prisonam, per unum annum negligentes vel remissi fuerint in hac parte, nos statim post annum completum a tempore quo hujusmodi emptiones, donationes, aut alias appropriationes fieri contigerit, terras et tenementa hujusmodi capiemus in manum nostram, et alios inde feoffabimus per certa servitia nobis inde ad defensionem regni nostri facienda; salvis capitalibus dominis feodorum illorum wardis, escaetis, et aliis ad ipsos pertinentibus, ac servitiis inde debitis et consuetis.

Et ideo vobis mandamus quod statutum praedictum coram vobis legi et de cetero firmiter teneri et observari faciatis. T. R. apud Westmonasterium xv° die Novembris anno etc. septimo.

Translation.

The king to his Justices of the Bench greeting. Where of late it was provided that religious men should not enter into the fees of any without licence and will of the chief lord of whom such fees be holden immediately, and notwithstanding such religious men have entered as well into their own fees as into the fees of other men, appropriating and buying them, and sometimes receiving them of the gift of others, whereby the services that are due of such fees and which at the beginning were provided for defence of the realm, are wrongfully withdrawn, and the chief lords do leese[1] their escheats of the same, We therefore to the profit of our realm intending to provide convenient remedy, by the advice of our prelates, earls, barons, and other our subjects, being of our council, have provided, made, and ordained, that no person religious or other, whatsoever he be, that will buy or sell

[1] Lose.

any lands or tenements, or under the colour of gift or lease, or that will receive by reason of any other title, whatsoever it be, lands or tenements, or by any other craft or engine[1] will presume to appropriate to himself under pain of forfeiture of the same, whereby such lands or tenements may anywise come into mortmain. We have provided also that if any person, religious or other, do presume either by craft or engine to offend against this statute, it shall be lawful to us and other chief lords of the fee immediate to enter into the land so aliened within a year from the time of the alienation, and to hold it in fee as an inheritance. And if the chief lord immediate be negligent, and will not enter into such fee within the year, then it shall be lawful to the next chief lord immediate of the same fee to enter into the same land within half a year next following, and to hold it as before is said; and so every lord immediate may enter into such land if the next lord be negligent in entering into the same fee as is aforesaid. And if all the chief lords of such fees, being of full age, within the four seas, and out of prison, be negligent or slack in this behalf for the space of one whole year, we, immediately after the year accomplished from the time that such purchases, gifts, or appropriations hap to be made, shall take such lands and tenements into our hand, and shall infeoff other therein by certain services to be done to us for the defence of our realm, saving to the chief lords of the same fees their wards and escheats, and other things to them belonging, and the services for the same due and accustomed. And therefore we command you that ye cause the foresaid statute to be read before you, and from henceforth to be kept firmly and observed. Witness Myself at Westminster the 15th day of November, the seventh year of our reign.

Statute of Westminster II, 13 Edward I, c. 32.

Cum viri religiosi et aliae personae ecclesiasticae implacitent aliquem, et implacitatus fecerit defaltam, ob quam tenementum amittere debeat, quia Justitiarii hucusque tenuerunt quod, si implacitatus fecerit defaltam per collusionem, ut cum petens occasione Statuti[2] per titulum doni aut alterius alienationis seisinam de tenemento consequi non posset, per illam defaltam consequeretur, et fieret fraus Statuto; ordinatum est per Dominum Regem et concessum quod in hoc casu, postquam defalta facta fuerit, inquiratur per patriam[3] utrum petens habeat jus in sua petitione

[1] Or 'device.'

[2] 7 Edward I, c. 13; above, p. 219.

[3] i. e. by a jury; see p. 154.

CH. IV. § 3. aut non. Et si compertum fuerit quod petens jus habet in sua petitione, procedatur ad judicium pro petenti, et recuperet seisinam suam. Et si jus non habuerit incurratur tenementum proximo domino feodi, si illud petat infra annum a tempore inquisitionis captae. (*The remaining provisions of the chapter are similar to those of the Statute 7 Edward I.*)

TRANSLATION.

When religious men and other ecclesiastical persons do implead any, and the party impleaded maketh default, whereby he ought to leese[1] the lands, forasmuch as the justices have thought hitherto that if the party impleaded make default by collusion, that where the demandant by occasion of the statute could not obtain seisin of the land by title of gift or other alienation, he shall now by reason of the default, and so the statute is defrauded; it is ordained by our lord the king and granted, that in this case after the default made it shall be inquired by the country whether the demandant had right in the thing demanded, or no. And if it be found that the demandant had right in his demand, the judgment shall pass with him and he shall recover seisin; and if he hath no right the land shall accrue to the next lord of the fee, if he demand it within a year from the time of the inquest, &c.

§ 3. *Estates Tail.*

With the reign of Edward I we arrive at the period when the influence of the lords of manors (*domini capitales*) upon legislation was most strongly felt. The Statute of Westminster II consists of fifty chapters dealing with various branches of the law; the first of them is known as the Statute *De Donis Conditionalibus*. The object of this enactment was, as stated in its text, to protect inheritances, and to lessen the danger of the lord's right of escheat being defeated or indefinitely postponed by the alienation of the tenant.

The technical expression 'conditional gift' has been already explained in commenting on the passage of Bracton given above[2]. It has been already seen that in Bracton's time a gift accompanied by words of procreation, as, for instance, to a man and the heirs of his body, or to a man and his wife and the heirs of their bodies, and similar expressions, was held to

[1] Lose.

[2] See Chapter III. § 15.

be an estate of inheritance conditional on issue being born; until this event happened the interest was in effect merely an estate for life. It was, strictly speaking, an estate descendible to the class of heirs mentioned in the gift, if such there should be. If therefore a donee, holding to himself and the heirs of his body, made an alienation of his land, his heirs, Bracton tells us, would be bound to warranty, that is, to uphold the gift, inasmuch as they could only claim by descent from their ancestor and take nothing by the original gift. These estates therefore, upon the happening of the condition, differed from ordinary estates in fee simple only in the restricted character of their devolution to the class of heirs named in the gift. So soon as the condition was performed by the birth of issue, the tenant could alienate and convey an estate in fee simple. So if the donee of such an estate committed treason, the fee simple would, after birth of issue, be forfeited. This would not have been the case if the descent had been secured by virtue of the form of the gift. The power of alienating the whole would as a matter of course involve the power of alienating particular rights over the land, such as granting a rent payable out of it, or charging it with debts so as to bind successors in title. If however the land was not alienated, it would descend not according to the ordinary rules affecting inheritances, but according to the mode expressed in the gift. It can hardly be doubted that this strained construction was put upon such gifts in order to favour the practice of alienation, which was dear to the common lawyer and to the great mass of landowners, though abhorrent to the *domini capitales*.

It was to restrain the practice of alienating these conditional estates, and so at once to prevent the lord losing the benefit of escheat upon failure of the descendants of his feoffee, and to protect the interests of the heir, that the Statute *De Donis Conditionalibus* was passed. In order to effect this object it was provided that such an alienation should not defeat the devolution of the estate to the heir, but that in the event of the tenant of a conditional estate alienating, the heir on the

CH. IV. § 3. decease of his ancestor might recover the estate from the feoffee, or any person claiming under him. It was further provided that where the tenant had made a feoffment in fee, having had issue born, who had subsequently died, the original donor (or lord) might recover the land from the feoffee by the same form of remedy as he might have employed before the Statute to recover land which his tenant had conveyed away for an estate in fee without having had issue born.

The effect of this Statute was to create a new species of estates of inheritance, which, except under certain special circumstances, could not be alienated so as to defeat the expectant interest of the issue specified in the gift, or postpone the reversion of the lord. There was, it is true, no direct provision restraining the grant in fee simple of such estates. No forfeiture or other immediate penalty would be incurred either by feoffor or feoffee. But inasmuch as the feoffor could only give a title valid against himself and not as against his issue or his lord after his own decease, the fee simple which he would convey to the feoffee would be insecure and precarious, and liable to be defeated by the issue of the feoffor, or after failure of the issue, by the lord or original donor. An estate in fee which was thus liable to be defeated was called in later times a *base fee*[1].

The provision of the Statute that the will of the donor as expressed in the charter should for the future be observed was held by the tribunals to have the following interpretation :— Wherever lands were granted by words which before the Statute would have created a conditional gift of one of the kinds specified in the Statute, such a gift would now pass an estate of less extent than a fee simple. Thus, suppose *A*, tenant in fee simple, made a grant to *B* and the heirs male of his body. This limitation, which before the Statute would

[1] This expression is usually applied at the present day to the estate created by the alienation of tenant in tail not in possession without consent of the 'Protector' (see below, p. 255), in which case he bars his own issue, but not remaindermen or reversioners. See 3 and 4 Will. IV, c. 74, § 35.

have been a fee simple conditional on *B* having a son born, was now held to convey a special kind of estate of inheritance, namely an estate descendible only to heirs male. This was considered to be a smaller estate than a fee simple which was capable of descending to heirs general, i. e. collateral as well as lineal. This secondary species of fee has ever since this Statute been designated *an estate tail*, *feudum talliatum* [1], being a portion of an estate *taillé*—cut off—from the fee. Hence it came to be established that when *A*, tenant in fee simple, had made the grant above mentioned he had not granted away all that he had to grant, some interest or estate was left in him still, the fee simple in fact was not gone; but inasmuch as the right of present enjoyment had been parted with for an estate which would last as long as *B* and his male line continued, the fee simple was what was called an estate in reversion, as opposed to one in possession. *B*'s estate was called an estate *in fee tail*, an estate cut off from the larger estate; and in technical language the effect of the above grant would be, that *B* would have an estate in fee tail in possession, *A* would have an estate in fee simple in reversion expectant upon the determination of the estate tail [2]. The difference between an *estate* in reversion and a mere *possibility* should be noticed. After the Statute, and the judicial interpretation of it above explained, *A* would have an estate or definite interest known to the law, which he could if he pleased convey by the proper mode and vest in another person. Before the Statute he would merely have had the possibility or chance of the fee simple escheating to him on failure of *B*'s

[1] This expression, which occurs in the Statute of Westminster II itself, 13 Edward I, c. 46, is also found in use at an earlier date. See Pollock and Maitland, Hist. of Eng. Law, ii. p. 19, n. 6.

[2] This conclusion seems not to have been reached at once. In a note to a case in 31 Edward I (Year Book, p. 384) it is said that 'in a gift in frank-marriage the reversion is always saved and supposed, but in a gift in tail the reversion is not saved if the reversion be not expressly saved in the charter.' No doubt it was usual in charters to express that the land on failure of the issue of the donee should revert to the donor and his heirs.

CH. IV. § 3. male issue; and this is not a present disposable right known to the law, but is merely a possibility of obtaining such a right[1]. In consequence of the recognition of this new estate or interest in lands—the estate tail—it became possible to create interests in lands of a much more complicated character than before. When a person had granted away the fee simple he had disposed of all that he had to grant, and could make no further valid disposition of his property. But now that an interest was recognised intermediate between the estate for life and the estate in fee simple, it became possible to grant lands as follows—to *A* for life, and after the expiration of that interest (or, more shortly, remainder) to *B* and the heirs of his body, remainder to *C* and his heirs. Here the ultimate gift to *C*, though passing to him at once an estate, would be merely an estate in expectancy, that is the enjoyment of it would be postponed, not only till *A*'s death, but also till after the failure of *B*'s lineal descendants. We shall see how the great restriction imposed on alienation by this Statute was broken in upon by the action of the tribunals. The further history of estates tail is reserved for the next chapter[2].

Statute of Westminster II, 13 Edward I, c. 1.

De Donis Conditionalibus.

In primis, de tenementis[3] quae multotiens dantur sub conditione, videlicet, cum aliquis dat terram suam alicui viro et ejus uxori

[1] An escheat is however sometimes improperly called a reversion.

[2] See Chap. V. § 2.

[3] 'This is the only word which the said Statute of W. 2, that created estate tail, useth; and it includeth, not only all corporate inheritances which are or may be holden, but also all inheritances issuing out of any of those inheritances, or concerning or annexed to or exercisable within the same, though they lie not in tenure, therefore all these without question may be entailed. As rents, estovers, commons or other profits whatsoever granted out of land, or uses, offices, dignities which concern lands or certain places may be entailed within the said statute because these savour of the realty. But if the grant be of an inheritance merely personal, or to be exercised about chattels, and is not issuing out of land, nor concerning any land or some certain place, such inheritances cannot be entailed, because they savour nothing of the realty.' Coke upon Littleton, 19 b. See instances, ibid.

et haeredibus de ipsis viro et muliere procreatis [1], adjecta conditione expressa tali, quod si hujusmodi vir et mulier sine haerede de ipsis viro et muliere procreato obissent, terra sic data ad donatorem vel ad ejus haeredem revertatur; in casu etiam cum quis dat tenementum in liberum maritagium quod donum habet conditionem annexam, licet non exprimatur in carta doni, quae talis est, quod si vir et mulier sine haerede de ipsis viro et muliere procreato obierint, tenementum sic datum ad donatorem vel ad ejus haeredem revertatur; in casu etiam cum quis dat tenementum alicui et haeredibus de corpore suo exeuntibus, durum videbatur, et adhuc videtur hujusmodi donatoribus et haeredibus donatorum quod voluntas ipsorum in donis suis expressa non fuerit prius nec adhuc est observata. In omnibus enim praedictis casibus post prolem suscitatam et exeuntem ab ipsis quibus tenementum sic fuit datum conditionaliter, hucusque habuerunt hujusmodi feoffati potestatem alienandi tenementum sic datum, et exhaeredandi de tenemento exitum ipsorum contra voluntatem donatorum et formam de dono expressam: et praeterea cum deficiente exitu de hujusmodi feoffatis, tenementum sic datum ad donatorem vel ad ejus haeredem reverti debuit per formam in carta de dono expressam, licet exitus, si quis fuerit, obisset, per factum et feoffamentum ipsorum, quibus tenementum sic fuit datum sub conditione, exclusi fuerunt hucusque de reversione eorundem tenementorum, quod manifeste fuit contra formam doni sui: propter quod Dominus Rex, perpendens quod necessarium et utile est in praedictis casibus apponere remedium, statuit, quod voluntas donatoris secundum formam in carta [2] doni sui manifeste expressam de caetero observetur, ita quod non habeant illi, quibus tenementum sic fuit datum sub conditione [3], potestatem alienandi

[1] To bring the gift within the Statute to the words of inheritance must be added words 'of procreation.' It must be expressed that the heirs are to be the actual issue of the donee or donees. The Conveyancing Act 1881 (44 and 45 Vict. c. 5) makes the words 'in tail' sufficient without the words 'heirs of the body.'

[2] The Statute was soon extended by judicial interpretation so as to cover gifts when the words of donation were only spoken as well as when they were embodied in a charter. 'Note, that if one demand land by formedon (see below, p. 228, n. 3) either in the "reverter" or in the "descender," it is not necessary that he have any evidence of the form, except matter in pais' (facts on which the jury may rest their verdict), 'for although he have not any charter, he shall be received to aver by good matter in pais that the thing was thus given.' Year Book, 20 Edward I, p. 130.

[3] The Courts seem to have held in the beginning of the reign of

CH. IV. § 3. tenementum sic datum, quo minus ad exitum illorum quibus tenementum sic fuerit datum remaneat post eorum obitum, vel ad donatorem, vel ad ejus haeredem, si exitus deficiat per hoc quod nullus sit exitus omnino, vel si aliquis exitus fuerit, per mortem deficiet, haerede hujusmodi exitus deficiente. Nec habeat de caetero secundus vir hujusmodi mulieris aliquid in tenemento sic dato per conditionem post mortem uxoris ejus per legem Angliae [1], nec exitus de secundo viro et muliere successionem haereditariam, sed statim post mortem viri et mulieris quibus tenementum sic fuit datum post eorum obitum, vel ad eorum exitum, vel ad donatorem, vel ad ejus haeredem, ut praedictum est, revertatur. [[2] Et quia in novo casu novum remedium est apponendum, fiat impetranti tale breve [3]: 'Praecipe *A* quod juste, etc. reddat *B* tale manerium cum pertinentiis, quod *C* dedit tali viro et tali mulieri et haeredibus de ipsis viro et muliere exeuntibus:' vel 'Quod *C* dedit tali viro in liberum maritagium cum tali muliere, et quod post mortem praedictorum viri et mulieris praedicto *B* filio praedictorum viri et mulieris descendere debet per formam donationis praedictae ut dicit:' vel 'Quod *C* dedit tali et haeredibus de corpore suo exeuntibus, et quod post mortem ipsius talis praedicto *B* filio praedicti talis descendere debet per formam donationis, etc.' Breve per quod donator habet recuperare suum, deficiente exitu [4], satis est in usu in Cancel-

Edward II that the word 'heirs' was left out of the Statute by mistake of the clerk, and that the Statute was binding not only on the donee but on his heirs in infinitum. See Reeves, ii. 200. Thus lands granted after the passage of this Statute to a man and the heirs of his body could never, except as explained in the next chapter, be alienated so as to defeat the interest of the heir by descent, or the reversion of the donor. This however was the only restriction upon alienation; and therefore an alienation in fee simple by tenant in tail conveyed the estate to the donee, subject to the rights of the reversioner or remainderman upon failure of the issue in tail, and to that of the issue, to avoid the gift by bringing the action called formedon in the 'reverter,' 'remainder,' or 'descender.'

[1] As to tenancy per legem Angliae, or by the curtesy, see above, Chap. III. §. 16.

[2] The words between brackets are repealed by the Statute Law Revision Act 1887 (50 and 51 Vict. c. 59).

[3] This was called the writ of 'formedon (*forma doni*) in the descender,' and was the appropriate remedy when the heir of tenant in tail, upon whom the estate tail had descended, sought to recover against the alienee of a preceding tenant in tail. It was in the nature of a writ of right, differing from it in being applicable to the recovery of an estate tail, the writ of right being for the recovery of the fee.

[4] This writ was called the writ of formedon in the reverter. No

laria [1].] Et sciendum, quod hoc statutum quoad alienationem tenementi contra formam doni imposterum faciendam locum habet, et ad dona prius facta non extenditur. Et si finis super hujusmodi tenemento imposterum levetur, ipso jure sit nullus, nec habeant haeredes hujusmodi, aut illi ad quos spectat reversio, licet plenae sint aetatis, in Anglia, et extra prisonam, necesse apponere clameum suum [2].

TRANSLATION.

First, concerning lands that many times are given upon condition, that is, to wit, where any giveth his land to any man and his wife, and to the heirs begotten of the bodies of the same man and his wife, with such condition expressed that if the same man and his wife die without heir of their bodies between them begotten, the land so given shall revert to the giver or his heir; in case also where one giveth lands in free marriage, which gift hath a condition annexed, though it be not expressed in the deed of gift, which is this, that if the husband and wife die without heir of their bodies begotten, the land so given shall revert to the giver or his heir; in case also where one giveth land to another and the heirs of his body issuing, it seemed very hard and yet seemeth to the givers and their heirs, that their will being expressed in the gift was not heretofore nor yet is observed. In all the cases aforesaid after issue begotten and born between them, to whom the lands were given under such condition, heretofore such feoffees had power to aliene the land

mention is made of the writ of formedon in the remainder, by which the remainderman could recover; e.g. where lands were granted to *A* in tail remainder to *B* in fee, *A* aliens for an estate in fee simple to *C* and dies without issue. *B* recovers against *C* by the form of the original gift creating the estate tail. According to Reeves (ii. p. 201) this writ first appears early in the reign of Edward II. A specimen however of a writ of formedon in the remainder, the remainder being expectant upon a joint estate for lives (not upon an estate tail), is to be found in the Year Book, 30 Edward I, p. 180.

[1] The Chancery was the 'officina brevium,' the office from which the writs were issued under the Great Seal. The duties of the Chancellor and his clerks in this respect were simply ministerial, they had no power to give validity to a new form of writ, except so far as that power was conferred upon them by the Statute of Westminster II, c. 24. See below, Chap. VI, and Blackstone, iii. p. 49.

[2] The effect of a fine in barring estates tail, that is, enabling the tenant in tail to alienate for an estate in fee simple, was not permitted till the Statute 32 Hen. VIII, c. 36 (Blackstone, ii. 355); and as to the history of the law relating to the necessity of putting in a claim to avoid an interest being barred by a fine, ibid. p. 354.

CH. IV. § 3. so given, and to disinherit their issue of the land, contrary to the minds of the givers, and contrary to the form expressed in the gift. And further, when the issue of such feoffee is failing, the land so given ought to return to the giver or his heir by form of gift expressed in the deed, though the issue, if any were, had died; yet by the deed and feoffment of them, to whom land was so given upon condition, the donors have heretofore been barred of their reversion of the same tenements which was directly repugnant to the form of the gift: wherefore our lord the king, perceiving how necessary and expedient it should be to provide remedy in the aforesaid cases, hath ordained, that the will of the giver according to the form in the deed of gift manifestly expressed shall be from henceforth observed, so that they to whom the land was given under such condition shall have no power to aliene the land so given, but that it shall remain unto the issue of them to whom it was given after their death, or shall revert unto the giver or his heirs if issue fail, either by reason that there is no issue at all, or if any issue be, it fail by death, the heir of such issue failing[1]. Neither shall the second husband of any such woman from henceforth have anything in the land so given upon condition after the death of his wife, by the law of England, nor the issue of the second husband and wife shall succeed in the inheritance, but immediately after the death of the husband and wife, to whom the land was so given, it shall come to their issue or return unto the giver or his heir as before is said. [And forasmuch as in a new case new remedy must be provided, this manner of writ shall be granted to the party that will purchase it[2]. . . . The writ whereby the giver shall recover when issue faileth is common enough in the Chancery.] And it is to wit that this statute shall hold place touching alienation of land contrary to the form of gift hereafter to be made, and shall not extend to gifts made before. And if a fine be levied hereafter upon such lands it shall be void in the law, neither shall the heirs or such as the reversion belongeth unto, though they be of full age, within England, and out of prison, need to make their claim[3].

[1] Or rather 'either by reason of an absolute default of issue or of its subsequent extinction.' Challis on Real Property, p. 231.

[2] The English version of the Statutes preserves the forms of the writs in the original Latin. See above, p. 212, and below, p. 240, n. 1.

[3] Except as regards the power of tenant in tail to alienate the inheritance, or to lose it by forfeiture or other involuntary alienation, an estate tail resembles an estate in fee simple. Tenant in tail is at liberty to *use*

§ 4. *Rights of Common Appurtenant.*

It has been already observed[1] that the Statute of Merton had no application where persons outside the manor and not tenants of the lord enjoyed, as appurtenant to their freehold tenements, rights of common of pasture over the wastes of the manor. The object of the following enactment was to extend the principles of the Statute of Merton to commoners having such rights of common. These rights of common are called rights of common *appurtenant*, as opposed to the rights of common of pasture enjoyed by the freehold tenants of the manor, which are rights of common *appendant*. It is worthy of observation that the rights of common here contemplated must have rested on ancient custom; it could not have been supposed by the framers of this Statute that the right had at some former date been granted by the lord, according to the theory of later lawyers[2].

Statute of Westminster II, 13 Edward I, c. 46.

Cum in statuto edito apud Merton concessum fuerit, quod domini boscorum, vastorum, pasturarum, appruare[3] se possent de boscis, vastis et pasturis illis, non obstante contradictione tenentium suorum, dummodo tenentes ipsi haberent sufficientem pasturam ad tenementa sua, cum libero ingressu et egressu ad eandem, et pro eo quod nulla fiebat mentio inter vicinum et vicinum, multi domini boscorum, vastorum, et pasturarum, hucusque impediti extiterunt per contradictionem vicinorum sufficientem pasturam habentium; et quia forinseci[4] tenentes non habent majus jus communicandi in bosco, vasto, aut pastura alicujus domini, quam proprii tenentes ipsius domini; statutum est de caetero quod Statutum apud Merton provisum inter dominum et tenentes suos locum habeat de caetero inter dominos boscorum, vastorum, et pasturarum, et vicinos, ita quod domini hujusmodi

the land as he pleases, unlike tenant for life he is not liable for waste, he can cut timber, open mines, and generally deal with the land at his pleasure. So the husband of tenant in tail, having had inheritable issue, is entitled to an estate by the curtesy, and the widow of tenant in tail to dower.

[1] Chap. III. § 18 (2). [2] See above, p. 184. [3] See Glossary, s. v.

[4] Freeholders not tenants of the manor.

CH. IV. § 4. vastorum, boscorum, et pasturarum, salva sufficiente pastura hominibus suis et vicinis, appruare se possint de residuo. Et hoc observetur de his qui clamant pasturam tanquam pertinentem ad tenementa sua. Sed si quis clamat communam per speciale feoffamentum vel concessionem ad certum numerum averiorum, vel alio modo quam de jure communi habere deberet, cum conventio legi deroget, habeat suum recuperare, quale habere deberet per formam concessionis sibi factae. Occasione molendini ventritici, bercariae, vaccariae, augmentationis curiae necessariae aut curtilagii, de caetero non gravetur quis per assisam novae disseisinae de communa pasturae. Et cum contingat aliquando, quod aliquis jus habens appruare se, fossatum aut sepem levaverit, et aliqui noctanter vel alio tali tempore, quo non credant factum suum sciri, fossatum vel sepem prostraverint, nec sciri poterit per veredictum assisae aut juratae qui fossatum aut sepem prostraverint, nec velint homines de villatis vicinis indictare de hujusmodi facto culpabiles, distringantur propinquae villatae circum adjacentes, levare fossatum aut sepem ad custum proprium, et dampna restituere. Et cum aliquis jus non habens communicandi usurpet communam tempore quo haeredes extiterint infra aetatem, vel uxores sub potestate virorum suorum existentes, vel pastura sit in manu tenentium in dotem, per legem Angliae [1], vel aliter ad terminum vitae, vel annorum, vel per feodum talliatum [2], et pastura illa diu usi fuerint, multi sunt in opinione quod hujusmodi pasturae debent dici pertinere ad liberum tenementum, et quod hujusmodi possessori competere debet actio per breve novae disseisinae, si hujusmodi pastura deforcietur; sed de caetero tenendum est quod habentes hujusmodi ingressum a tempore quo currit breve mortis antecessoris [3], si antea communam non habuerunt, non habeant recuperare per breve novae disseisinae si fuerint deforciati.

TRANSLATION.

Whereas in a statute made at Merton it was granted that lords of wastes, woods, and pastures might approve the said wastes, woods, and pastures, notwithstanding the contradiction of their

[1] See above, Chap. III. § 16.

[2] See above, p. 225, n. 1.

[3] That is, 'a coronatione regis Henrici III.' 'But the said long possession is great evidence and strong presumption of the right of common, and stabitur praesumptioni donec probetur in contrarium.' Coke, ad loc., 2nd Inst. p. 477. For the fiction by which continued enjoyment was held to be evidence of a grant, see above, p. 184.

tenants, so that the tenants had sufficient pasture to their tenements, with free egress and regress to the same; and, forasmuch as no mention was made between neighbours and neighbours, many lords of wastes, woods, and pastures have been hindered heretofore by the contradiction of neighbours having sufficient pasture; and because foreign tenants have no more right to common in the wastes, woods, or pastures of any lord, than the lord's own tenants; It is ordained that the statute of Merton, provided between the lord and his tenants, from henceforth shall hold place between lords of wastes, woods, and pastures and their neighbours, saving sufficient pasture to their tenants and neighbours, so that the lords of such wastes, woods, and pastures may make approvement of the residue. And this shall be observed for such as claim pasture as appurtenant to their tenements. But if any do claim common by special feoffment or grant for a certain number of beasts, or otherwise, which he ought to have of common right, whereas covenant barreth the law, he shall have such recovery as he ought to have had, by form of the grant made unto him. By occasion of a windmill, sheepcote, deyry, enlarging of a court necessary, or courtelage, from henceforth no man shall be grieved by assise of novel disseisin for common of pasture. And where sometime it chanceth, that one having right to approve doth then levy a dyke or an hedge, and some by night or at another season when they suppose not to be espied do overthrow the hedge or dyke, and it cannot be known by verdict of the assise or jury who did overthrow the hedge or dyke, and men of the towns near will not indict such as be guilty of the fact, the towns near adjoining shall be distrained to levy the hedge or dyke at their own cost, and to yield damages. And where one, having no right to common, usurpeth common, what time an heir is within age, or a woman is covert, or while the pasture is in the hands of tenants in dower, by the courtesy, or otherwise, for term of life or years, or in fee tail, and have long time used the pasture, many hold opinion that such pastures ought to be said to belong to the freehold, and that the possessor ought to have action by a writ of novel disseisin if he be deforced of such pasture; but from henceforth this must be holden that such as have entered within the time that an assise of mortdauncester hath lien, if they had no common before, shall have no recovery by a writ of novel disseisin if they be deforced.

§ 5. *Alienation. The Statute of 'Quia Emptores.'*

CH. IV. § 5. The history of the law of alienation has already been touched upon [1]. We have seen that in the Anglo-Saxon time in the case of bookland the power of alienation depended upon the limitations contained in the 'book,' and was usually unrestricted. There does not appear to be any reason to suppose that this freedom of alienation, so far as it was effected *inter vivos*, was ever materially curtailed, until the passing of the Statute De Donis, except by the article of Magna Carta, already given [2], and the establishment of the right of the Crown to grant licences for alienation by tenants *in capite*. No licence was required by law as a condition of the validity of the alienation of lands held of a mesne lord. We gather indeed from Bracton that this freedom of alienation was a matter which was contested by the great lords in his day. In Bracton's view [3] the lord could only fairly claim his service and homage. He must not push his rights further. The fact that it might be more advantageous to him to prevent a change of tenants was not sufficient to deprive the tenant of his right of alienation. Let the lord 'take that which was his and go his way [4].' It seems that at the beginning of the reign of Edward I the barons determined on attempting, where they could not prevent alienation altogether, at all events to diminish the loss sustained by the granting out of lands by their tenants to be held of themselves by subinfeudation.

It seems that before the passing of this Statute, where *A* held land in fee simple of *B*, *A* might have granted to *C* the whole of those lands to be held of *B*; and such a grant would operate to create a tenancy between *C* and *B* [5]. This relation, however, could not at the common law (that is, independently of the Statute presently to be mentioned) have been effected

[1] See Chap. III. § 14.

[2] See Chap. III. § 7.

[3] Lib. ii. c. 19. s. 2. fol. 46. Above, Chap. III. § 14. p. 160.

[4] 'Tollat quod suum fuerit et vadat.' Bracton, fol. 45; above, p. 158.

[5] Coke, 2nd Inst. p. 65; and see above, p. 159, n. 1.

by a grant by *A* to *C* of *part* of the lands held by *A*. At common law, a feoffment made by *A* to *C* of a portion of his lands would in every case have created anew the relation of lord and tenant, with all the incidents attaching to that relation, as between *A* and *C*. In this case there would be no immediate relation of lord and tenant between the chief lord and *C*. The advantageous rights of the lord over the land would consequently be diminished. The land thus aliened would not escheat to the chief lord on the failure of the heirs of the alienee, nor would the lord be the guardian of the lands or of the body of the heir.

To preserve these rights it was in the eighteenth year of Edward I enacted that every alienation in fee simple, whether of the whole or of a part of the land, should have the effect of substituting the alienee for the alienor in relation to the chief lord; the alienee simply stepping into the place of the alienor, and being subject to all the duties and obligations under which he held the land of his lord. The primary object of this enactment was to prevent the loss arising to the lords of manors from subinfeudation, or subdivision of the tenements held of them. Consequently, whenever at the present day a freehold tenant in fee simple holds of a mesne lord, the separation of the freehold from the domain must have occurred at a date anterior to the eighteenth year of Edward I. From this time forward every alienation of land in fee simple presents the characteristics of a complete out and out transfer, the transferee stepping for all purposes into the place of the transferor. Gradually by successive alienations the tie between the chief lord and the freeholder becomes weakened. In socage tenure, when no rent was payable and no value attached to the service, there was no motive for keeping up the empty ceremony of fealty, and thus in many cases the relation of lord and tenant became altogether obliterated. Finally, when all the valuable incidents attaching to knight-service were abolished, and the tenure itself converted into socage by the Statute of Charles (12 Car. II, c. 24) the relation between

CH. IV. § 5. the freeholder and his lord fell into abeyance, and the freeholder became for all practical purposes owner of the soil. Thus at the present day in the great majority of cases no intermediate lord is recognised between the freeholder and the crown, except where the freehold is within the known precincts of a manor, and the relation between the freeholder and the lord of the manor has been kept up by the recognition of mutual rights and duties, such as payment of rent, or rendering heriots or other duties to the lord.

Statute of Westminster III, 18 Edward I, c. 1.

Statutum Domini Regis de terris vendendis et emendis.

Quia emptores terrarum et tenementorum de feodis magnatum et aliorum in praejudicium eorundem temporibus retroactis multotiens in feodis suis sunt ingressi, quibus libere tenentes eorundem magnatum et aliorum terras et tenementa sua vendiderunt, tenenda in feodo sibi et haeredibus suis de feoffatoribus suis et non de capitalibus dominis feodorum, per quod iidem capitales domini escaetas, maritagia, et custodias terrarum et tenementorum de feodis suis existentium saepius amiserunt, quod quidem eisdem magnatibus et aliis dominis quam plurimum durum et difficile videbatur, et similiter in hoc casu exhaeredatio manifesta; Dominus Rex in Parliamento suo apud Westmonasterium post Pascha anno regni sui decimo octavo, videlicet in quindena Sancti Johannis Baptistae, ad instantiam magnatum regni sui, concessit, providit, et statuit, quod de cetero liceat unicuique libero homini terram suam seu tenementum sive partem inde pro voluntate sua vendere, ita tamen quod feoffatus teneat terram illam seu tenementum de eodem capitali domino [1] et per eadem servitia et consuetudines, per quae feoffator suus illa prius tenuit.

c. ii. Et si partem aliquam earundem terrarum seu tenementorum alicui vendiderit, feoffatus illam teneat immediate de capitali domino, et oneretur statim de servicio quantum pertinet sive pertinere debet eidem domino pro particula illa, secundum quantitatem terrae seu tenementi venditi; et sic in hoc casu decidat capitali domino ipsa pars servicii capienda per manum feoffatoris, ex quo feoffatus debet eidem capitali domino juxta quantitatem

[1] That is, the next immediate lord, of whom the feoffor himself holds.

terrae seu tenementi venditi de particula illa servicii sic debiti esse intendens et respondens. CH. IV. § 5.

c. iii. Et sciendum est quod per praedictas venditiones sive emptiones terrarum seu tenementorum, seu partis alicujus eorundem, nullo modo possunt terrae seu tenementa illa in parte vel in toto ad manum mortuam devenire arte vel ingenio contra formam statuti super hoc dudum editi [1]. Et sciendum quod istud statutum locum tenet de terris venditis tenendis in feodo simpliciter tantum [2]; et quod se extendit ad tempus futurum. Et incipiet locum tenere ad festum Sancti Andreae proximo futurum.

TRANSLATION.

c. i. Forasmuch as purchasers of lands and tenements of the fees of great men and other lords have many times heretofore entered into their fees, to the prejudice of the lords, to whom the freeholders of such great men have sold their lands and tenements to be holden in fee of their feoffors and not of the chief lords of the fees, whereby the same chief lords have many times lost their escheats, marriages, and wardships of lands and tenements belonging to their fees, which thing seems very hard and extreme unto those lords and other great men, and moreover in this case manifest disheritance, our lord the King in his parliament at Westminster after Easter the eighteenth year of his reign, that is to wit in the quinzine of Saint John Baptist, at the instance of the great men of the realm granted, provided, and ordained, that from henceforth it should be lawful to every freeman to sell at his own pleasure his lands and tenements or part of them, so that the feoffee shall hold the same lands or tenements of the chief lord of the same fee, by such service and customs as his feoffor held before.

[1] 7 Edward I, De Viris Religiosis; above, p. 219.

[2] See Year Book, 22 Edward I, p. 641: 'Note that a man may enfeoff another to hold to him and the heirs of his body begotten, to be holden of him (the feoffor) by a certain service by the year; and in this case there is no need that he be enfeoffed to hold of the chief lord of the fee: for the Statute Quia Emptores terrarum etc. is understood of the case of one enfeoffing another in fee simple and not in fee tail.' Hence, if a tenant in fee simple makes an alienation for an estate tail, or an estate for life, the tenant in tail or the tenant for life holds of the alienor in respect of his reversion in fee. It is otherwise, however, if the alienor parts with his whole estate, leaving no reversion in himself; as for instance, if he grants an estate by way of remainder in fee expectant on the determination of the estate for life, or in tail. (Coke, 2nd Inst. p. 504.)

CH. IV. § 5. c. ii. And if he sell any part of such lands or tenements to any, the feoffee shall immediately hold it of the chief lord, and shall be forthwith charged with the services for so much as pertaineth or ought to pertain to the said chief lord, for the same parcel, according to the quantity of the land or tenement so sold; and so in this case the same part of the service shall remain to the lord, to be taken by the hands of the feoffee, for the which he ought to be attendant and answerable to the same chief lord according to the quantity of the land or tenement sold for the parcel of the service so due.

c. iii. And it is to be understood that by the said sales or purchases of lands or tenements, or any parcel of them, such lands or tenements shall in no wise come into mortmain, either in part or in whole, neither by policy ne craft, contrary to the form of the statute made thereupon of late. And it is to wit that this statute extendeth but only to lands holden in fee simple, and that it extendeth to the time coming. And it shall begin to take effect at the Feast of Saint Andrew the Apostle next coming.

The effect of the Statute of Quia Emptores upon the form of charters of feoffment can be clearly traced by comparing the following form with that given above [1].

Sciant praesentes et futuri quod Ego Johannes Elys de Sheldone dedi concessi et hac praesenti carta mea confirmavi Domino Willielmo de Charneles de Bedeworth totum pratum meum quod habui de Willielmo de Burthate cum fossis et hayis libertatibus et cum omnibus suis pertinenciis et emolumentis quae aliquo modo seu causa de dicto prato mihi vel haeredibus meis accidisse potuissent . . . .
Habendum et tenendum praedictum pratum cum omnibus suis pertinenciis praedictis sibi dicto Willielmo et haeredibus suis et suis assignatis, de capitalibus dominis feodi, libere, haereditarie, pacifice, et in perpetuum quiete, reddendo et faciendo eisdem servicia eis inde debita et consueta [2]. Ego vero dictus Johannes

[1] Chapter I. p. 61.

[2] If a rent be reserved to the grantor, as was not uncommon, this cannot operate as the creation of a rent *service*, for that would be contrary to the Statute. If, however, the grant be in tail or for life a rent service may be created; for the Statute is no bar to the creation of a tenure as between the reversioner in fee and the tenant of a smaller or particular freehold estate. Where a rent service is created, the lord or reversioner has always the right to distrain for the rent in arrear. Where on a grant in fee simple a rent is reserved to the grantor, this is not a rent *service* but

et haeredes mei et mei assignati praedictum pratum cum fossis et hayis et cum omnibus suis pertinentiis prout supradictum est praedicto Willielmo et haeredibus suis et suis assignatis warrantizabimus acquietabimus et in perpetuum defendemus. . . . . CH. IV. § 5.

Hiis testibus etc.

Datum apud Oldecotenhale die Sabbati proxima post purificationem beatae Mariae Virginis, anno regni Regis Edwardi vicesimo quarto.—*Madox, Formulare Anglicanum, No. cccxxxiii.*

a rent *charge.* It is in fact equivalent to a re-grant from the donee in fee simple of a charge upon the lands. In order to give the person entitled to the rent the right to distrain, it was necessary, before the Statute 4 George II, c. 28, that there should be a special clause in the deed by which the rent is created to that effect. If there was no clause of distress the rent was called a rent *seck* (reditus siccus). The appropriate remedy for the recovery of a rent, before the abolition of real actions, was by Assize of Novel Disseisin.

CHAPTER V

COMPLETION OF THE COMMON OR EARLIER LAW.

CHAP. V. By the end of the reign of Edward I the main outlines of the law relating to land are complete. There is no statute producing an organic change in the law, such as was effected by the statutes of *De Donis* and *Quia Emptores*, till the reign of Henry VIII. During the period extending from the reign of Edward I to the reign of Henry VIII, the changes in the law are to be looked for chiefly in the action of the regular tribunals, and in the growth of a wholly new set of principles affecting land created by the new jurisdiction of the Chancellor. The latter will be discussed in the next chapter. The present will be confined to an examination of the development of certain particular classes of rights during the period above mentioned.

The sources of our knowledge of the law for this period are (1) the official reports of cases decided by the common law tribunals contained in the Year Books[1]; (2) authoritative

[1] The reports in the Year Books are written in the strange jargon called law-French. Documents such as records of proceedings in court, charters, the text of statutes (most commonly, see above, p. 210), were in Latin. French was formerly the oral language in which all *viva voce* proceedings were conducted. By 36 Edward III, Stat. 1. c. 15, after reciting that a reason why the laws were so ill obeyed was that they were 'pleaded, showed, and judged in the French tongue, which was much unknown in the realm, so that people which do implead or be impleaded in the king's court and in the courts of other have no knowledge nor understanding of

text-books, of which Littleton's work on Tenures [1], published in the reign of Edward IV, is the most important. The principal classes of rights in relation to land which require notice as attaining further development during this period are—leasehold interests; estates tail; rights of future enjoyment; estates in joint tenancy, and tenancy in common; rights of creditors over the lands of their debtors; and copyhold estates.

§ 1. *Leasehold Interests.*

The early history of leasehold interests or estates for years has already been noticed, and reference has been made to the change effected in the reign of Henry III, by which leasehold interests were erected into a distinct kind of estate or property in land [2]. This interest or property is less than freehold, it is wanting in the great characteristic of freehold—uncertainty as to the period at which the rights will come to an end. It is essential to a leasehold, or, as it is often called, a *chattel* interest in land, that the period of its termination should be fixed from the beginning, or at least be capable of being fixed.

that which is said for them or against them by their serjeants or other pleaders,' it was provided that 'all pleas which shall be pleaded in any courts whatsoever shall be pleaded, showed, defended, answered, debated, and judged in the English tongue, and that they be entered and inrolled in Latin.' Reports of proceedings still continued to be in French till the reign of Elizabeth, and the practice lingered on till the close of the seventeenth century. It was however prohibited by an Act of Parliament passed in the time of the Commonwealth, anno 1650, cap. 37.

[1] Thomas de Littleton, of Frankley in Worcestershire, appears to have been made a Justice of the Common Pleas in 1466, and to have died in 1481. His work was probably written late in life, and is addressed to his son Richard, who went to the bar. He was the first to attempt a systematic classification of the law relating to land, and his work has formed the basis of all subsequent treatises. The earlier editions are remarkable in the history of typography as well as in that of law. Many translations of Littleton's text were made in later times, one of which was adopted by Sir E. Coke, and has since gone by his name. Sir E Coke was also the most distinguished of many annotators of Littleton, and the 'reputation of the commentary has to some extent overlaid and obscured the intrinsic merit of the original.' See Encyclopædia Britannica, s. v. Littleton.

[2] See above, Chap. III. § 17.

CHAP. V. § 1. The rights under consideration present characteristics wholly different to freehold interests as to the mode in which they are created, the kind of interest which may be given, the mode in which they devolve on the death of the person entitled, and the remedy by which the right is vindicated.

The proper mode of granting an estate for years at common law[1] is by words of demise followed by the entry of the lessee. The appropriate words of the grant are *demisi concessi et ad firmam tradidi*—demise, grant, and to farm let. The lessee is sometimes called the *termor*, sometimes, from the main object of the transaction, the *farmer*.

It was not necessary that the words of demise should be in writing until the passing of the Statute of Frauds (29 Car. II, c. 3), which rendered writing necessary for the validity of all leases, except those for a term not exceeding three years, and fulfilling certain conditions as to rent.

In order to complete the interest of the lessee, it is, at common law, necessary that the words of demise should be followed by his entry on the lands. The words of demise, spoken or written, confer a right to enter, technically called an *interesse termini*, but the lessee does not become actually tenant in possession until he has made entry upon the land demised.

Leasehold interests, requiring no livery of seisin, may at common law be created so as to take effect in possession or enjoyment at a future time. This is impossible in freehold interests except in the case of remainders[2]. A lease to commence next Christmas conveys a perfect right to the lessee to enter at Christmas, and to hold for the specified term.

Again, leasehold interests are not subject to the rules affecting the devolution of freehold interests. Before the change recorded by Bracton[3], the only parties who could under any circumstances have claimed the benefits of a lease

[1] In this chapter the expression 'common law' is applied to the rules of the older law, which have in some cases been modified or supplemented by subsequent legislation, to be afterwards noticed.

[2] See below, § 3.

[3] See above, Chap. III. § 17.

on the death of the lessee were his executors or administrators [1], and that only when the lease rested on an express covenant by deed. Hence, when leasehold interests became rights of property (or rights available not only against the lessor, but also against all the world), it was natural that they should not be brought under the rule of primogeniture, but should pass under the will to the executors of the deceased, or, in the case of intestacy, to the administrator, with the rest of the chattels. Thus leasehold interests came to be classed with personal property. Since however they are rights over things immovable, they received the mongrel name of 'chattels real,' and cannot be excluded from a treatise professing to deal with real property.

The nature of the remedy provided for the ejected leaseholder, *contra quoscunque dejectores*, has already been stated [2]. The writ then devised, however, left the lessee without remedy in two cases. First, not having the freehold, he was liable to be ousted by the successful plaintiff in a collusive action against the lessor, in which the lessor allowed judgment to go against him by default, or, as it was technically called, suffered a recovery. A partial remedy for this injustice was provided by the Statute of Gloucester [3], but the leaseholder was not wholly protected against a proceeding of this nature till the Statute 21 Henry VIII, c. 15. Secondly, if the lessor ejected the lessee, and then enfeoffed a third person, the lessee could not bring his writ of *quare ejecit infra terminum* against the feoffee, because *he* was not the ejector; nor against the lessor, because *he* was not in possession. A further remedy was therefore necessary, and a writ was devised, being a development of the writ of trespass and called the writ of *ejectio firmae*, which was available in the case supposed against the feoffee [4]. This proceeding was by a series of fictions (now abolished)

[1] The administrator is the person appointed, formerly by the Ecclesiastical Court, now by the Probate Division of the High Court of Justice, to administer and distribute the personal property of the intestate.

[2] See Chap. III. § 17.

[3] 6 Edward I, c. 11. See Coke upon Littleton, 46 a.

[4] See Pollock & Maitland, Hist. of Engl. Law, ii. p. 109.

CHAP. V. § 1. extended, till, in the form of the action of ejectment, it became the appropriate means of asserting the right to the possession of land under whatever title, and took its place as the statutory substitute for all the forms of real actions.

Thus the interest of the lessee for years was gradually protected at all points, and took its place as a distinct class of rights of property.

An important class of interests, of the nature of estates for years, should be mentioned here. These are estates at will, estates from year to year, and estates at sufferance.

A tenancy at will is where the land is held by the tenant so long as lessor and lessee please that the tenancy should continue. No notice from either party is necessary to terminate a tenancy at will strictly so called; any act by either party, affording to the other proper evidence of his determination that the tenancy should no longer continue, is sufficient. The chief characteristics of this tenancy will be found in the extract from Littleton given below.

The inconveniences of tenancies at will induced the tribunals to provide some means of giving greater security to a tenant who held under no regular lease for years. The circumstances of the letting—especially the character of the rent, whether payable yearly, half-yearly, quarterly, or otherwise—are looked to, in order to ascertain the nature of the interest which the parties intended to create. Most commonly the reservation of an annual rent and payment of any part of it is held to constitute what is called a tenancy from year to year. Such a tenancy can usually be put an end to only at the end of the current year of the tenancy, by either party giving at least half a year's previous notice to quit[1]. Other modifications of tenancies at will, such as

[1] 'This kind of lease was in use as long ago as the reign of Henry VIII.' Blackstone, ii. p. 147, note, citing Year Book, T. 13 Hen. VIII, 15, 16. The requisite length of notice was altered in the case of agricultural or pastoral tenancies by the Agricultural Holdings Act 1875 (38 and 39 Vict. c. 92) to one year; and this provision is re-enacted subject to variation by agreement in the Agricultural Holdings Act 1883 (46 and 47 Vict. c. 61).

quarterly, monthly, or weekly tenancies, can be created, depending in each case upon evidence as to the terms of the letting.

Tenant at sufferance is where a lessee whose term has expired holds on after its expiration. He is in the position of one who has come in rightfully, but holds on without any right. He cannot however be treated as a trespasser by the true owner before entry made upon him. Any recognition by the owner will convert him into a tenant at will; and, if he has held previously under a regular lease, it requires but slight evidence to lead to the inference that a tenant at sufferance has been converted into a tenant from year to year on the terms of his previous holding so far as they are applicable.

Terms of Years.

BRITTON[1], lib. v. chap. xiv. § 8. Ceo mot, terme, se estent ausi bien a terme de vie cum a terme des aunz. Mes cil qi ne lest for qe a terme des aunz, tut feist il le les a terme de c. aunz, si il ne lest for qe les esplez, et retient vers ly le fee et le dret et le fraunc tenement, si avaunt le les le out; et ceo qe il retient lerra a soen heir cum il morra; ou sauntz tort fere al fermer porra il doner et aliener a estraunge persone; ou al fermer mesmes purra il relesser chescune manere de dreit et quiteclamer, et feffer, sauntz oster primes le fermer de sa seisine tele quele[2]; et aussi ne purra il mie fere a autre estraunge persone, si le fermer de soen gré ne se cheve al purchaceour[3]; car la seisine del alienour sei continue touz jours par le fermer, qi use sa seisine en le noun soen lessour.

[1] See above, Chap. IV. p. 211, note 2. The text and translation are taken from Nichols' edition.

[2] The farmer or lessee is not seised, for he has no freehold interest (see above, p. 160), but is only possessed; nor is the freeholder actually seised, for he has parted with the possession. 'The possession of the termor or lessee constitutes the seisin of the freeholder.' Hence the reversion lies in grant, not in livery; i. e. can be granted by deed with attornment (see next note). At the same time the freeholder can, with the consent of the lessee, come on the land and make livery of the freehold to a third person; in which case the freehold in possession passes, and not merely the reversion.

[3] Until the Statute 4 Anne, c. 16, ss. 9, 10, the grant of a freehold reversion expectant on a term of years must have been completed by the attornment or acknowledgment of the grantee by tenant for years. The necessity of attornment was done away with by that Statute.

CHAP. V. § 1.

TRANSLATION.

The word 'term' extends as well to a term of life as to a term of years. But he who leases only for a term of years, although he make the lease for a term of a hundred years, leases the profits only, and retains to himself the fee and the right and the frank tenement, if he had them before the lease; and all that he retains he will leave at his death to his heir, or he may, without doing any wrong to the farmer, give and alien it to a stranger; or he may release and quit claim every sort of right to the farmer himself, and enfeoff him, without first ousting the farmer of his seisin, such as it is. This he cannot do to a stranger, unless the farmer of his own consent will attorn to the purchaser; for the seisin of the alienor is all along continued by the farmer who enjoys his seisin in the name of his lessor.

LITTLETON'S TENURES, lib. i. chap. vii. sect. 58. *Tenant for Term of Years.* Tenaunt pur terme dez ans est lou home lessa terres ou tenementes a un autre pur terme de certeins ans solonques le nombre dez ans que est accorde perentre le lessour et le lessé: et quant le lessé entra per force de le lees, donques il est tenaunt pur terme dez ans. Et si le lessor en tiel cas reserva a luy un annuell rente sur tiel lees, il poet eslier a distreigner pur le rente en les tenementes lessez, ou il poet aver une accion de dette pur les arrerages envers le lessee. . . . .

Sect. 59. Et est assavoir, que en lees pur terme dez ans per fait ou sauns fait, il ne besoigne ascun liverë de seisin destre fait a le lessé, mes il poet entrer quanques il voet per force de mesme le lees. Mes de feoffementes faitz en pays, ou dones en le taille, ou leses pur terme de vie, en tielx cases ou franktenement passera, si ceo soit per fait ou sauns fait, il covient daver un liverë de seisin.

Sect. 60. Mes si home lessa terrez ou tenementes per fait, ou sauns fait, a un pur terme dez ans, le remaindre oustre a un autre pur terme de vie, ou en le taille, ou en fee, donques en tiel case il covient que le lessour fait un liverë de seisin a le lessé pur terme dez ans, ou autrement riens passera a ceux en le remaindre, coment que le lessee entra en les tenementes. Et si le termor en tiel cas entra devant ascun liverë de seisin fait a luy, donques est le franktenement et auxi la revercion en le lessour: mes si soit fait liverë de seisin a le lessee, donques est le franktenement ove le fee a ceux en le remaindre, solonques la fourme del graunt et la volunte de le lessour.

Chap. viii. sect. 68. Tenaunt a volunte est ou terres ou tenementes sont lesses per un home a un autre, a aver et tener a luy a la volunte le lessour, per force de quel lees le lessé est en possessione, en tiel cas le lessé est appelle tenaunt a volunte, pur ceo que il nad ascun certeyn sure estate, qar le lessour luy poet oustre a quel temps quil luy plerroit: unquore si le lessé embleia la terre, et le lessour apres lembleier, et devaunt que les blees sont matures luy ousta, unquore le lessé avera les blees, et avera frank entre, egresse, et regresse a scier et de carier les blees, pur ceo que il ne savoit a quel temps son lessour voilloit entrer sur luy. Autrement est si tenaunt pur terme dez ans qui conust le fyn de son terme embleia la terre, et le terme est finye devaunt que les blees sont matures; en ceo cas le lessour, ou celuy en le revercion avera les blees, pur ceo que le termour bien conust le certeynte de son terme et quant sa terme serroit fynye.

Sir E. Coke's Translation.

Chap. vii. sect. 58. Tenant for term of years is where a man letteth lands or tenements to another for term of certain years, after the number of years that is accorded between the lessor and the lessee. And when the lessee entereth[1] by force of the lease, then is he tenant for term of years; and if the lessor in such case reserve to him a yearly rent upon such lease, he may choose for to distrain[2] for the rent in the tenements letten, or else he may have an action of debt for the arrearages against the lessee. . . . . .

Sect. 59. And it is to be understood, that in a lease for years, by deed or without deed, there needs no livery of seisin to be made to the lessee, but he may enter whensoever he will by force of the same lease. But of feoffments made in the country[3], or gifts in tail, or leases for term of life; in such cases where a freehold shall pass, if it be by deed or without deed, it behoveth to have livery of seisin.

[1] Entry is necessary in order to complete the interest of the lessee. Before entry the lessee has an interest called an *interesse termini*, that is, an indefeasible right of entry, which may be asserted by his executors or administrators if he die without having entered.

[2] The right to distrain for rent in arrear is incidental to the relation of lessor and lessee. Whatever movable things are upon the demised tenements, whether belonging to the lessee or not, are liable to distress, with certain specified exceptions—beasts of the plough, materials used in trade, etc. See Coke upon Littleton, 47 a; and see Agricultural Holdings Act 1883 (46 and 47 Vict. c. 61), sects. 44, 45.

[3] A conveyance 'en pais' is an ordinary conveyance, see Chap. III. § 12, as opposed to a conveyance by fine, recovery, &c.

CHAP. V. § 1.

Sect. 60. But if a man letteth lands or tenements, by deed or without deed, for term of years, the remainder[1] over to another for life, or in tail, or in fee, in this case it behoveth that the lessor maketh livery of seisin to the lessee for years, otherwise nothing passeth to them in the remainder, although that the lessee enter into the tenements. And if the termor in this case entereth before any livery of seisin made to him, then is the freehold and also the reversion in the lessor. But if he maketh livery of seisin to the lessee, then is the freehold together with the fee to them in the remainder, according to the form of the grant and the will of the lessor.

Chap. viii. sect. 68. Tenant at will is, where lands or tenements are let by one man to another, to have and to hold to him at the will of the lessor[2], by force of which lease the lessee is in possession. In this case the lessee is called tenant at will because he hath no certain nor sure estate, for the lessor may put him out at what time it pleaseth him. Yet if the lessee soweth the land, and the lessor, after it is sown and before the corn is ripe, put him out, yet the lessee shall have the corn, and shall have free entry, egress, and regress to cut and carry away the corn, because he knew not at what time the lessor would enter upon him[3].

[1] See below, § 3.

[2] This estate is at the will of both parties, and therefore the lessee, like the lessor, can put an end to it without notice.

[3] 'And this is not only proper to a lessee at will, that when the lessor determines his will that the lessee shall have the corn sown &c., but to every particular tenant that hath an estate incertain, for that is the reason which Littleton expresseth in those words "because he hath no certain nor sure estate"; and therefore if tenant for life soweth the ground and dieth, his executors shall have the corn, for that his estate was uncertain and determined by the act of God. And the same law is of the lessee for years of tenant for life. . . . If tenant *pur terme d'autre vie* soweth the ground and *cesty que vie* dieth, the lessee shall have the corn. . . . But if the lessee at will sow the ground with corn &c., and after he himself determine his will and refuseth to occupy the ground, in that case the lessor shall have the corn, because he loseth his rent. And if a woman that holdeth land *durante viduitate sua* soweth the ground and taketh husband, the lessor shall have the emblements, because that the determination of her own estate grew by her own act.' Coke, Comment. ad loc. 55 b. The crops to which a tenant whose estate is terminated is thus entitled are called *emblements*. See Blackstone, ii. pp. 122, 145. Now, by 14 and 15 Vict. c. 21, sect. 1, where a tenancy determines by reason of the death or cesser of estate of any lessor entitled for his life, or other uncertain interest, instead of claims to emblements the tenant is to continue to occupy until the end of the then current year.

Otherwise it is, if tenant for years, which knoweth the end of his term, doth sow the land, and his term endeth before the corn is ripe; in this case the lessor or he in the reversion shall have the corn, because the lessee knew the certainty of his term, and when it would end.

§ 2. *Estates Tail.*

'Tenant in fee tail,' says Littleton [1], 'is by force of the Statute of Westminster II, cap. 1.' The mode in which that Statute created what was in effect a new species of estate has already been explained [2]. The various attributes of estates tail became the constant subject of judicial decision, and introduced a vast amount of complexity into the law relating to land. The tendency of the courts was to extend the provisions of the Statute so as to embrace other cases besides those mentioned in its text. Wherever to the words of inheritance were added words of procreation,—wherever it was expressed directly or indirectly that the lands were to go to the heirs who were the issue of the body of the donee, the case was held to fall within the limits of the Statute [3].

There were four principal classes of estates tail recognised: estates in tail general, estates in tail special, estates in tail male, and estates in tail female. An estate in tail general was where an estate was given to a man or woman and the heirs of his or her body generally, in which case the estate descended to the legitimate descendants of the donee without

[1] Sect. 13.

[2] See Chap. IV. § 3.

[3] 'If therefore either the words of inheritance or the words of procreation be omitted, albeit the others are inserted in the grant, this will not make an estate tail. As if the grant be to a man and the *issue of his body*, to a man and his *seed*, to a man and his *children*, or *offspring;* all these are only estates for life, there wanting the words of inheritance, *his heirs*. So on the other hand a gift to a man, and his heirs *male*, or *female*, is an estate in fee simple, and not in fee tail; for there are no words to ascertain the body out of which they shall issue. Indeed, in last wills and testaments, wherein greater indulgence is allowed, an estate tail may be created by a devise to a man and his *seed*, or to a man and his *heirs male;* or by other irregular modes of expression.' Blackstone, ii. p. 115. See Conveyancing and Law of Property Act 1881 (44 and 45 Vict. c. 41), sect. 51.

CHAP. V. § 2. restriction to the issue of any particular marriage. An estate in special tail was where the lands were descendible only to a limited class of lineal descendants, as where lands were given to *A* and the heirs of his body by *C* his present wife. If no such heirs were born, the estate on the death of *A* reverted to the donor; and as on the death of *C* the wife without issue this must necessarily be the case, *A* becomes, after that event, what is technically called 'tenant in tail after possibility of issue extinct.' Gifts in frank-marriage differed only from these gifts in special tail in being free from all liability to service to the donor until the fourth generation of tenants [1].

An estate in tail male was where by the form of the gift the descent was restricted to lineal male descendants [2]. An estate in tail female was where the descent was restricted to lineal female descendants. These two latter classes of entails, though not within the express words of the Statute of Westminster II, were recognised, according to Littleton, by the equity of the Statute [3].

Inasmuch as the estate of tenant in tail was, according to the metaphorical expression of the lawyers, 'carved out of,' that is, less than an estate in fee simple and different from it [4],

[1] Littleton, sects. 16, 17, 19.

[2] This was settled in a case which arose in 18 Edward III (Year Book, p. 46). Gift to *A* and the heirs male of his body. *A* had issue a daughter, who had issue a son; question, whether *A*'s grandson could succeed *per formam doni*. Held that he could not, the gift being of a more restricted character than an estate which is given generally to heirs of the body. (Reeves, ii. p. 336.)

[3] Sect. 21. When a particular case does not fall within the express terms of a statute, but the judge, conceiving that the legislator in pursuance of his general design would have embraced the case if it had been present to his mind, acts as if it was covered by the statute, the case is said to fall within the 'equity of the statute.' See Austin, ii. p. 596.

[4] An estate tail is said to be less than a fee simple, because the law regards as a disposable interest the possibility of enjoying the lands after the determination, by failure of issue or otherwise, of the estate tail. There is no estate larger than a fee simple, because the law does not regard the possibility of the enjoyment of the estate after the failure of heirs general as a disposable interest. Littleton, sect. 18.

it followed that if tenant in fee simple made a gift in tail, such a gift was not within the Statute of Quia Emptores, but a tenure was created between tenant in tail and tenant in fee simple, the former *holding of* the latter[1]. CHAP. V. § 2.

It must be borne in mind that estates tail are only known in freehold interests, and that there can be no estate tail in a chattel-interest, such as a term of years.

The history of the alienation of estates tail is connected with the difficult and obsolete doctrine of warranty[2], of which the Courts took advantage to break in upon the policy of the law as conceived by the great barons who procured the enactment of the Statute of Westminster II. The effect of a warranty accompanying a gift of an estate of inheritance was to oblige the warrantor or donor to defend the possession of his donee. If the donee was ousted by a claimant establishing a superior title, the warrantor was bound to give the donee or his representatives lands of value equal to those of which he had been deprived. The burden of this obligation would descend to the heirs of the warrantor (at least to the extent of preventing the heir from disputing his ancestor's gift), and the benefit of it to the heirs of the donee[3]. This principle would have been sufficient, if applied to estates tail, to have enabled a tenant in tail, by alienating his land with a warranty, to have given the purchaser an estate which his heir could not defeat. It seems, however, to have been held early in the reign of Edward II[4] that, if tenant in tail aliened the land with warranty, the heir of the tenant in tail was not bound by his ancestor's alienation and warranty (that is, could defeat the estate of the donee or his heirs by claiming in opposition to the gift of the ancestor), unless he had *assets* (lands in fee simple equivalent to those which had been granted away) by descent from his ancestor[5]. On the other hand, if he had

[1] Littleton, sect. 19.

[2] For the early history of the doctrine of warranty see above, p. 80, n. 1.

[3] Littleton, sect. 697. [4] Reeves, ii. pp. 200, 203.

[5] Littleton, sect. 712. Reeves shows (ii. p. 204) that this rule of law is probably an extension of the provisions of the Statute of Gloucester

CHAP. V. § 2. assets, the ordinary rule prevailed, and the heir of the warrantor was bound by his ancestor's warranty. And if the warrantor was a prior tenant in tail, who had died without issue, upon which, according to the limitations of the estate, the land went over to a subsequent tenant in tail, such last tenant in tail was bound by the warranty of his predecessor, even though there were no assets. This was called *collateral* as opposed to *lineal* warranty[1].

The doctrine that the issue of the tenant in tail was bound by his ancestor's alienation with warranty only in cases where he had assets by descent greatly narrowed the power of effectual alienation possessed by the tenant in tail. And it must be remembered that even where such alienation was binding on the issue, it would not bind the lord or donor so as to bar him of his reversion[2] in the event of the failure of issue of the donee in tail.

Thus the Statute de Donis, as interpreted by the Courts, put an effectual check to the practice of free alienation of estates, where, as was commonly the case, words of procreation were added to the words of inheritance.

As time went on, the great inconvenience of such a restriction was strongly felt. Titles were insecure, for an old entail, of which nothing was known, might be brought to light; nor would any period of enjoyment, however long, afford an answer to such a claim. 'Farmers were ousted of their leases, creditors defrauded of their debts.' The free alienation of land was restrained, a grievance which was probably felt with increasing severity in consequence of the impoverishment of the landowners caused by the wars of the Roses. The king, too, suffered by the protection against forfeiture which the practice afforded to the issue of a traitor. Thus all members

(6 Edward I, c. 3) as to alienation of tenants by the curtesy. See Littleton, sect. 724.

[1] Reeves, ii. p. 340.

[2] And this reversion is now a definite estate or interest, not a mere possibility of the lands escheating. It is a reversion in fee expectant on the determination of the estate tail. See below, § 3.

of the community, except perhaps the great landowners themselves, were interested in obtaining a relaxation of the practice of strictly entailing lands which had grown up under the provisions of the Statute of Westminster II[1].

Although feigned recoveries, or fictitious suits in which a writ of right was brought by a third person against the tenant, who thereupon suffered judgment to pass against him, had long been known as a mode of conveying lands, it was for some time thought that the heir of tenant in tail was not bound by a judgment so obtained against his ancestor. 'In the reigns of Henry IV and Henry V some doubts began to be entertained whether a recovery suffered by tenant in tail was not good against the issue[2].' These doubts continued without being finally determined during the reign of Henry VI. They were at length set at rest by the introduction of a series of fictions, by virtue of which it was feigned that a gift with warranty had been made by the original donor of the tenant in tail, that a claim was made to the lands by a person having a title superior to that of the original donor, and that tenant in tail received from the

[1] 'But the true policy and rule of the common law in this point was in effect overthrown by the Statute *De Donis Conditionalibus*, which established a general perpetuity by Act of Parliament for all who had or would make it, by force whereof all the possessions in England in effect were entailed accordingly, which was the occasion and cause of the said and divers other mischiefs. And the same was attempted and endeavoured to be remedied at divers parliaments, and divers bills were exhibited accordingly (which I have seen), but they were always on one pretence or another rejected. But the truth was that the lords and commons, knowing that their estates tail were not to be forfeited for felony or treason, as their estates of inheritance were before the said Act (and chiefly in the time of Hen. III, in the Barons' War), and finding that they were not answerable for the debts or incumbrances of their ancestors, nor did the sales, alienations, or leases of their ancestors bind them for the lands which were entailed to their ancestors, they always rejected such bills, and the same continued in the residue of the reign of E. I and the reigns of E. II, E. III, R. II, H. IV, H. V, and H. VI, till about the 12th year of E. IV,' &c. Sir Anthony Mildmay's Case, Coke's Reports, 6. 40 a. See Blackstone, ii. 116.

[2] Reeves, ii. 573.

CHAP. V. § 2. original donor an equivalent for the lands of which he was deprived by the judgment. Further, the supposed original donor was made a party to the suit, and, upon his failing to defend his fictitious gift, he and his heirs were barred of their reversion. This was the course adopted, though possibly not for the first time, in the famous 'Taltarum's Case'[1] (12 Edward IV). A translation of the pleadings is given below. From this time till 1834 (3 and 4 Will. IV, c. 74) it became the common practice for tenant in tail to 'suffer a recovery;' that is, by a proceeding similar to that adopted in Taltarum's case, to convert his estate into a fee simple. In effect, therefore, wherever an estate tail was given, tenant in tail might, so soon as he came of age, by this process give to another an estate in fee simple, which by arrangement might then be re-conveyed to himself, and thus he was enabled to cut off, bar, or defeat the expectations of his own issue, and the interests of all persons claiming after him in remainder or reversion. After a statute passed in the reign of Henry VIII, the same result might have been effected by a fine[2].

By the above-mentioned statute (3 and 4 Will. IV, c. 74) fines and recoveries were abolished, and tenant in tail may now, by a deed enrolled in the Chancery Division of the High Court of Justice, alienate his lands for any estate in fee simple or otherwise[3], and thus defeat the expectations of his own issue and of all remaindermen and reversioners[4].

The only additional restriction imposed upon the alienation of an estate tail is that the consent of the person who is called the Protector of the settlement is necessary to its being effectually barred. Alienation by tenant in tail without this consent binds his own issue, but not remaindermen

[1] As to this name, see Pollock, Land Laws, p. 87, and Law Quarterly Review, vi. p. 280.

[2] See above, p. 229, note 2.

[3] Except that in the case of a lease not exceeding twenty-one years at a rack-rent, or not less than five-sixths of a rack-rent, no enrolment is necessary. Sect. 41.

[4] Or persons entitled to a remainder or reversion. See § 3.

or reversioners, and creates what is called a 'base fee[1].' The Protector of the settlement is usually the tenant for life in possession; but the settlor of the lands may appoint in his place any number of persons not exceeding three to be together Protector during the continuance of the estates preceding the estate tail[2]. The practical effect therefore of an estate tail at the present day is to prevent the alienation of lands for a valid estate of inheritance in all cases till tenant in tail comes of age[3]. After this, his power of disposing of the lands differs from that of tenant in fee simple only in the mode in which it is exercised, and in the necessity, where the estate is not in possession, for the consent of the Protector. There is a special exception in the Statute of tenants in tail after possibility of issue extinct[4].

Translation of the Pleadings in Taltarum's Case.

YEAR BOOK, 12 EDWARD IV, 19.

In a Writ of Entry on the Statute of Richard[5], '*Ubi ingressus non datur per legem etc.*,' sued against one J. Smith, the defendant said[6] that the plaintiff ought not to have his action, for that before the alleged entry one T. B. was seised of the tenements &c. in fee, and gave them to one W. Smith to have and to hold to him and the heirs of his body begotten; by force whereof he was

[1] See above, p. 222. A perfect specimen of a 'base fee' is to be found in George Eliot, 'Felix Holt.'

[2] Sect. 32.

[3] It is almost the universal practice, when lands are brought into strict settlement upon a marriage, to give an estate for life to the husband, followed by an estate tail to the eldest (unborn) son. Consequently the lands cannot be alienated for an estate in fee simple until the son attains the age of twenty-one. In order to effect an alienation then, it is necessary that father and son should both join. The lands, if not alienated, are the freehold of the father for his life, the son having the inheritance. The effect of such an arrangement upon family relations is a point worthy of the consideration of the legislature, in considering the important question of the retention of estates tail as an interest recognized by law.

[4] 3 and 4 Will. IV, c. 74. s. 18.

[5] 5 R. II, c. 8.

[6] Defendant justifies the entry by showing a title derived from T. B., who enfeoffed W. S. for an estate in tail general, from whom the lands descended through R. to the defendant.

seised, and had issue one Richard, and died seised, and the tenements descended to Richard; and he entered and was seised, and had issue the said J. Smith, and died seised, and the tenements descended to the said J.; and the plaintiff claiming by colour of a deed of feoffment before the gift &c. entered, upon whose possession the said J., as son and heir of the said R. at the time of the alleged entry, entered, &c.; upon which entry the plaintiff has grounded this action. To which the plaintiff says[1] that well and true it is that the said T. B. gave the tenements ut supra &c.; but he says that the said W. had issue one Humfrey the elder (son), and the said R. the younger, and died; after whose death H. entered and was seised by form of the gift, &c.; and being so seised, one T. Taltarum sued a writ of right against the said Humfrey, returnable, &c. On which day the parties appeared, and the said T. Taltarum counted[2] of his possession, and the said H. made defence, and vouched to warranty one R. King, who was ready, and entered into the warranty, and joined issue on the mere right; and the said Taltarum imparled[3] (with him), and then returned (into court), and the tenant by the warranty did not return, but in contempt of court made default, by which the said T. T. had final judgment against the said H., and he over against the tenant by the warranty[4], by force whereof the said Taltarum entered and was seised, &c.; and then the said H. died without heir of his body, and then Taltarum enfeoffed the present plaintiff, whereby he was seised when the defendant entered. To which the defendant said[5], that well and true it is that the

[1] The plaintiff, in order to displace the title thus set up by the defendant, replies that W. S. had an elder son, H, to whom the lands descended, that Taltarum brought a writ of right against H., that H. vouched R. K. to warranty, that R. K. made default, that Taltarum consequently recovered against H., became seised, and enfeoffed the plaintiff.

[2] This is the *narratio*, count, or formal statement of the plaintiff's claim in his 'declaration.'

[3] That is, by leave of the Court the two parties retire to discuss the matter.

[4] For the recovery of lands of equal value by way of compensation.

[5] The defendant rejoins that before Taltarum's proceedings H. made a gift to Tregos in fee (which would be a valid conveyance though liable to be avoided after H's death, see above, p. 224), that Tregos availed himself of this grant for the purpose of giving back to H. and his wife an estate in special tail, which by the death of the wife became an estate tail after possibility of issue extinct (above, p. 250), that Taltarum's proceedings defeated only the last-mentioned estate, and that after the death of H., R. entered as heir of the body of W. S. by virtue of the gift made to W. S. by T. B.

said W. had issue Humfrey the elder and R. the younger, and died; and that after his death the tenements descended to Humfrey as son and heir, and he entered and was seised as son and heir by the form of the gift, &c. But he says [1] that the aforesaid Humfrey, before the writ purchased [2] &c., enfeoffed one Tregos of the said lands in fee, &c.; the which Tregos, before the writ purchased, gave the tenements to the said H. and to one Jane his wife, to have and to hold to them and to the heirs of their bodies begotten, the remainder to the right heirs of the said H. in fee, &c., by force of which they were seised, &c., and then Jane died, after whose death H. was sole seised of the said tenements as tenant in tail after possibility (of issue extinct). And, while he was so seised, the said Taltarum sued the said writ of right, and recovered against the said H. in the manner and form as alleged; the which H. continually after the said judgment during his life was seised of the said tenements by force of the gift made to him and to his wife, and died without heir of his body. After whose death the said R., as brother and heir of the said H. begotten of the body of W., entered and was seised by force of the gift made to W., and died seised; and the tenements descended to the said J. Smith, and he entered and was seised by force of the gift, &c.; without this [3], that the said T. Taltarum, after the said recovery in the life of the said H., entered on the said tenements, as he has alleged; and without this, that the said H. had any other estate in the said tenements on the day of the purchase of the writ of right or afterwards,

[1] The defendant by this pleading does not question the effect of the recovery by Taltarum, but sets up other matter, namely, a prior alienation in fee by Humfrey, and a re-grant in special tail by the feoffee to Humfrey and his wife. His contention is, that it is this estate only which is defeated by Taltarum's recovery, and not the original estate tail given to W. Smith.

[2] That is, before Taltarum's suit. 'Purchasing' a writ was the usual expression for commencing an action by suing out a writ, for which the usual fees must be paid, notwithstanding the provision of Magna Carta (c. 40), 'Nulli *vendemus* rectum aut justitiam.'

[3] 'Absque hoc.' The technical term by which the denial of a material allegation of the plaintiff was introduced in the kind of plea called a special traverse. The defendant denies that there was any such recovery by Taltarum as that alleged in the plaintiff's replication, except the recovery stated and admitted in the preceding part of the defendant's rejoinder. This, with other like mysteries of the older form of pleading, was made unnecessary by the Common Law Procedure Act 1852 (15 and 16 Vict. c. 76).

CHAP. V. § 2. except that by force of the gift made to him and to his wife, &c.; and without this, that the said Taltarum was seised of the said tenements as of fee and of right in the time of the king, as he has alleged, and that the said recovery is false and feigned in law[1].

[1] The important point in these pleadings is the allegation of the recovery by Taltarum on the default of King, who had been vouched to warranty. The fiction is that King is the donor, and that he had made the original gift in tail with warranty, and in consequence of his being vouched, and accepting the challenge, he is in effect substituted as the defendant in Taltarum's suit. When therefore he makes default, Taltarum is enabled to recover the lands and dispose of them to the plaintiff for an estate in fee simple. Humfrey, the tenant in tail, would in his turn be entitled to recover against King, who had failed in making good the title of his donee. This of course was a mere fiction. It appears to have been assumed on both sides that if the case had not been complicated by the other entail, which according to the defendant had been created before the recovery by Taltarum (and the case was on this point decided in defendant's favour), that that recovery would have been good, inasmuch as the ousted tenant in tail would have had his recompense against the vouchee; for this is the ground on which the Court base their judgment. This is the point which makes Taltarum's Case so important a turning-point in the history of the law of estates tail. It established, not expressly, but by implication, that the Courts would allow a tenant in tail to 'suffer a recovery,' that is, to procure a plaintiff to bring a fictitious action against tenant in tail, or, more usually, against some person to whom tenant in tail had granted an estate for the express purpose of being made defendant in the proceedings. This grantee was technically called the 'tenant to the *praecipe* or writ.' A writ of right for the recovery of an estate in fee simple was thus brought collusively by the plaintiff against the tenant to the *praecipe*, who vouched to warranty the donor (the tenant in tail), and he in his turn vouched to warranty another person supposed to be *his* donor, usually the crier of the court. The necessary steps would then be taken to try the matter as between the plaintiff and the last vouchee; then followed the farce of 'imparling,' and the default of the second vouchee, the recovery of the fee by the plaintiff, the judgment that the vouchee should recompense the tenant in tail for his default, and the conveyance of the fee by the successful plaintiff to the ousted tenant in tail. (See form in Blackstone, ii. appendix 5.) Thus wherever by proper words a tenancy in tail was created, as for instance where lands were given to *B* and the heirs of his body, remainder to *C* in fee, it was in the power of *B*, on his attaining full age, to 'suffer a recovery;' or, in other words, to turn his estate tail into an estate in fee simple, thereby causing the land to descend to heirs collateral as well as lineal, barring the reversion in fee to the lord, and defeating the expectations of all persons having estates limited to take effect subsequently to the estate tail. That the legislature should so long have abstained from substituting a simpler method, such as was at last applied in 1833, for a process so cumbrous and

§ 3. *Interests in Futuro. Reversions and Remainders.*

In close connexion, speaking historically, with the doctrine of estates tail is that of future interests or estates in expectancy. An estate in expectancy, or, more accurately, a right of future enjoyment of lands [1], is distinguished from an estate in possession, or an estate of present enjoyment. The actual enjoyment or possession of lands is in the former case postponed until the lapse of a specified time, or the happening of some specified event. On the other hand, these estates differ from mere chances or possibilities of rights, inasmuch as they are distinct and definite interests known to the law, capable of alienation by the appropriate methods, and devolving at the death of the person entitled upon his representatives. Thus in the case of a gift of lands to *A* for life, and after his decease to *B* and his heirs, *B* has an estate in fee simple in the lands, postponed in point of possession or enjoyment till after the death of *A*, but yet a present interest which he can dispose of in the proper method, and which will descend to his heir. On the other hand, the expectation of *C*, eldest son of *D* tenant in fee simple, of succeeding to his father's lands, is not an interest recognized by the law, it is merely the hope or chance of having certain rights at some future time. If *C* dies before his father, his eldest son succeeds, not as representing him, but as heir to *D* the grandfather. CHAP. V. § 3 (1).

At present we are only concerned with such interests of future enjoyment as belong to the class of freehold rights over land. These are of two kinds, *reversions* and *remainders*.

(1) *Reversions.*

Where a freeholder grants away some estate smaller than that which he has himself, he has, in the metaphorical language of the law, an interest left in him, which, though

so expensive, is one of the most startling of the many marvellous instances in our system of law reforms delayed mainly through the indifference or ignorance which prevails so widely with respect to legal questions.

[1] See Fearne's treatise on Contingent Remainders, p. 2.

CHAP. V. § 3 (1). not immediately an interest of present possession or enjoyment, will become such so soon as the smaller preceding interest has expired. Thus, where a tenant in fee simple has created an estate in tail, for life, or for years, he has left in him a present estate, which will come into possession or enjoyment on the expiration or sooner determination of the estate tail, the estate for life, or the estate for years. The smaller estate thus granted is called the 'particular' estate. 'A reversion,' says Sir E. Coke, 'is where the residue of the estate always doth continue in him that made the particular estate[1].'

It has already been observed, that between the reversioner and the tenant of the particular estate a *tenure* exists—the latter *holds of* the former[2]. Hence, before the Statue 4 Anne, c. 16, the attornment of the tenant was necessary to complete the grant of the reversion; otherwise, the tenant would have had a new lord imposed upon him without his consent.

The proper mode of conveying or disposing of the reversion is by *grant*, that is, grant by *deed*, or writing on paper or parchment *sealed* and *delivered*. Suppose *A* has the reversion in fee simple expectant on an estate tail, or on an estate for life, or on an estate for years. He can by a simple deed of grant create any number of estates tail, or estates for life, or estates for years out of his reversionary interest, and dispose of them as he pleases. He can deal with the reversionary interest just as he can deal with an interest in possession, only he cannot give livery of seisin, for the simple reason that he has it not to give, inasmuch as he is not in actual possession of the lands. This however is subject to the exception that the reversioner is in one sense seised when the particular estate is only a lease for years[3]. The lessee for years is, as has been said above, not *seised* of the lands, but only *possessed* of the term. Seisin, as has been seen, implies

[1] Coke upon Littleton, 22 b.

[2] See above, p. 237, n. 2.

[3] See above, § 1.

(1) actual possession, (2) possession as of freehold. Where therefore there is a particular estate of leasehold tenure, the reversioner, if he can obtain the consent of the lessee to come on the land for the purpose, can pass his interest by feoffment, accompanied by livery of seisin. In this case, however, he grants, not the reversion, but the freehold in possession. CHAP. V. § 3 (1).

When a reversioner desires, not to grant his reversion to a third person, but to convey it to the person who already has the particular estate, he is said to *release* the reversion[1]. This he may do by deed. Supposing therefore, in the case above put, *A*, tenant of the reversion in fee, should execute a deed releasing his interest to tenant in tail, tenant for life, or tenant for years, the reversion in fee would coalesce with the particular estate in tail, for life, or for years. This coalescing of a smaller estate with a larger is called *merger*, the rule being that where the same person becomes entitled to two estates, the one of which is to take effect in possession during the continuance or immediately on the determination of the other, the smaller one is *merged* or swallowed up in the larger. So in the above cases, each of the tenants in possession, tenant in tail, tenant for life, and tenant for years, becomes at once tenant in fee simple in possession. The same effect is produced by the surrender of the particular estate to the reversioner. The particular estate merges in the larger reversionary estate.

Thus, as the law became more refined, new modes of conveying lands from one person to another were introduced, destined, with some modifications to be hereafter noticed, to supersede in practice the old feoffment, fine, and recovery.

If *A*, tenant in fee simple, wished to convey the lands to *B*, he might make a lease to him of the lands in question, upon which *B* would enter, and was then at once capable of taking a release by deed of the reversion in fee[2]. This was called

[1] See the passage from Britton quoted above, § 1. The word 'release' is the proper technical expression for this class of conveyances.

[2] See Littleton, sect. 459.

CHAP. V. § 3 (2). conveyance by lease and release, and became in later times the usual mode of conveying lands. Its later history will be noticed hereafter[1].

A conveyance of the reversion might also be made to a stranger. In this case it was formerly necessary that the tenant of the particular estate, whether in tail, for life, or for years, should *attorn* to the grantee of the reversion, in other words, acknowledge him as the person of whom the lands were held. The necessity for attornment was done away with by 4 Anne, c. 16, sects. 9, 10. Thus two new modes of conveying the immediate freehold were added, *lease and release*, and *grant and attornment*.

(2) *Remainders* (*Vested and Contingent*).

The other kind of future interests which can arise at common law in freeholds are called *remainders*. A remainder differs from a reversion in this, that while a reversion is an estate of future enjoyment not expressly created by, but resulting from, the alienation of a 'particular' estate, a remainder is created by express words at the same time as the particular estate, and is so limited as to come into enjoyment or possession so soon as the particular estate comes to an end. In Sir Edward Coke's words[2], a remainder is 'a remnant of an estate in lands or tenements, expectant on a particular estate created together with the same at one time.'

As has been seen, a tenure exists between the reversioner and the tenant of the particular estate. This is not the case as between the remainderman (or person to whom the remainder is given), and the tenant of the particular estate.

In order that a freehold remainder may be effectually created at common law, it is necessary that the seisin or freehold possession should be vested in the grantee of the particular estate, or, if the particular estate be an estate for years, in the remainderman, and that at the same time the remainder

[1] See Chapter VII. § 3.

[2] Coke upon Littleton, 143 a.

should pass to the person entitled after the donee of the particular estate. This was a consequence of the great importance attached to the preservation of notoriety as to the person entitled to the freehold. Hence it was that the doctrine arose that a freehold interest in possession must pass instantly from donor to donee, that, as it was sometimes expressed, it could not be for an instant in abeyance. The only mode of conveying such an interest was by feoffment with livery of seisin, or by the fictitious processes of fine or recovery. It was however possible for the tenant in fee simple, in making a grant, to divide the interest which passed from him among two or more persons, so that one should take immediately after the interest of the other came to an end. There must be no interval between the end of the first interest and the commencement of the second; the instant the first determines, the second begins. Thus, suppose *A*, tenant in fee simple, makes a feoffment accompanied by livery of seisin to *B* for his life, and after the termination of that estate, or (more shortly) with *remainder* to *C* and the heirs of his body, with remainder to *D* and his heirs, the gift would operate as expressed, and the various estates come into enjoyment, one after the other, upon the determination of the preceding estate in each case. The ultimate limitation in fee is of course liable to be barred or cut off by the tenant in tail suffering a recovery. On the other hand, *A* cannot, at common law, make a feoffment to *B* for life, to commence in point of enjoyment at any future period, for instance, the day after to-morrow, nor can he provide that the remainder limited to *C* shall take effect six months after the death of *B*. An estate in remainder must according to the rules of the common law, come into possession or enjoyment at once, as soon as the particular estate upon which it is limited comes to an end.

It follows, from the very definition of a remainder above given, that so soon as the fee simple is parted with, the donor has given away all that he has to grant, and can make no ulterior disposition. A remainder limited to take effect after

CHAP. V. § 3 (2). a fee simple estate is simply void. Nor is the case altered when, as has been pointed out above, the estate in fee simple is liable to be terminated by the happening of some specified event. For instance, if an estate be granted to *A* and his heirs so long as he continues unmarried, this estate will come to an end upon *A*'s marriage; but the rule that a remainder cannot be limited after a fee simple would, *at common law*[1], prevent the settlor from making any ulterior gift, such as 'and from and after the marriage of *A* to *B* and his heirs.' Nor again would the common law permit an estate to be granted to *A* for life, provided that if *A* should marry *B*, the estate should go to *C*. This would not be a remainder or grant of a remnant of an estate within Sir E. Coke's definition, but the creation of an estate in derogation of a previous estate, and this was not permissible at common law[2]. In like manner the established rule, that the benefit of a condition can only be reserved in favour of the donor or his heirs, operated to prevent the creation of any ulterior estate, to take effect on the happening of any future event. Though a person may, on making a grant of lands, reserve to himself and his heirs a right of re-entry on the happening of any specified event, he cannot reserve this right in favour of a stranger. *A* grants lands to *B* and his heirs on condition of his rendering rent annually; upon non-payment, *A* enters and defeats the estate

[1] See Fearne on Contingent Remainders, 8th ed. p. 12. The employment of uses, both before and after the Statute of Uses, to create interests of this character, and the effects of the recent Statute 40 and 41 Vict. c. 33, will be explained hereafter. (See Chaps. VI. and VII.)

[2] See Butler's note to Fearne, Contingent Remainders, p. 383; Sugden's note to Gilbert on Uses, p. 177. It would seem however that there would be no objection at common law to a grant to *A* until marriage with *B* and then to *C*. Here the estate would be an estate determinable upon the specified event, and in any case would not be more than a life estate, there being no words of inheritance in the grant, see above, p. 165, n. 1. Such a grant would therefore be a conditional limitation (see above, pp. 162, 163), and on the happening of the event the estate would terminate in accordance with the limitation, and this estate, being a particular estate, and not a fee simple, there is nothing to prevent the estate to *C* taking effect by way of remainder. See Fearne, p. 13, and Butler's note, ibid.

of *B*. But such a condition and right of entry cannot be reserved in favour of *C*. Thus it appears that the only mode of creating rights of future enjoyment in freeholds at common law is by way of remainder — a remainder being confined within the limits of Sir E. Coke's definition. CHAP. V. § 3 (2).

The doctrine of remainders at common law came in process of time to be subject to a further complication, which should be noticed here [1]. Hitherto remainders have been treated as present or vested interests where the enjoyment is postponed till the lapse of a certain specified time or the happening of some specified event. A distinction subsequently arose between remainders where an estate of future enjoyment was given to a definite existing person upon an event certain to happen, and where an estate of future enjoyment was created in favour of a person not existing, or not ascertained, or was to come into effect upon an event which might or might not happen. In the former case the remainder is said to be vested, in the latter it is said to be contingent.

In the case of a vested remainder nothing interferes with the enjoyment of the remainderman, except the fact that the property is in the hands of the tenant of the particular estate. All that has to happen, in order that the remainderman may come into enjoyment of the property, is the termination of the particular estate. Of course it may be that the person entitled to the remainder may as a fact never come into the enjoyment of the property, as, for instance, where lands are given to *A* for life, remainder to *B* for life, and *B* dies before *A*, but this does not affect the fact that *B*'s interest, so long as it exists, is a vested remainder [2].

[1] The history of contingent remainders is obscure. It seems from the case in the Liber Assisarum given below, p. 271, that in one form they were recognized as early as the reign of Edward III. However, the passage from Littleton below, p. 273, and the cases in the Year Books referred to by Mr. Joshua Williams (Principles of Real Property, p. 325, 17th ed.), show that their recognition was not firmly established till a later period. It seems however convenient to give a sketch of the general rules relating to contingent remainders in this place.

[2] 'It is not the uncertainty of ever taking effect in possession that

CHAP. V. § 3 (2).

On the other hand, in the case of a contingent remainder, according to the rules of the common law, something must happen besides the determination of the particular estate before the interest created can come into actual enjoyment. If the remainder be limited to a person unborn or not ascertained, as, for instance, if lands be given to *A* for life, remainder to the unborn son of *B* in tail, in order that the contingent remainder may take effect, *B* must have a son born, or at least begotten [1], in the lifetime of *A*. So soon as this happens, the remainder vests in the son of *B*. In other words, the future interest, which before was a contingent, now becomes a vested remainder. So if lands are given to *A*, remainder to the heirs of B [2], *B* must die in *A*'s lifetime, for *nemo est haeres viventis*; and if *B* survives *A* for ever so short an interval, his heir will never take, otherwise there would be a period during which the freehold would be in abeyance [3]. So if lands are given to *A* and *B* jointly for life, remainder to the survivor in fee, so soon as one dies, the contingent remainder which the other had is turned into a vested remainder, which again by the operation of the doctrine of merger coalesces with the life estate [4], and the survivor becomes entitled to an estate in fee simple in possession. So again, if lands be given to *A* till *C* returns from Rome, then to *B* and his heirs, this is a contingent remainder [5], for the

makes a remainder contingent; for to that, every remainder for life or in tail is and must be liable; as the remainderman may die, or die without issue before the death of the tenant for life. The present capacity of taking effect in possession, if the possession were to become vacant, and not the certainty that the possession will become vacant before the estate limited in remainder determines, universally distinguishes a vested remainder from one that is contingent.' (Fearne on Contingent Remainders, p. 216.)

[1] See Williams on Real Property, p. 332, and Stat. 10 and 11 Will. III, c. 16.

[2] This seems to have been the earliest form in which contingent remainders were recognized. See the case from 30 Lib. Ass. below.

[3] The practical effect of the common law rules has been greatly modified by the Statute 40 and 41 Vict. c. 33 as to contingent remainders created after August 2, 1877. See below, Chap. VII.

[4] As to 'merger' see above, p. 261.

[5] See above, p. 264, n. 2.

estate upon which the expectant interest is limited to take effect is determinable on an event which may never happen. On the other hand, if the interest were expressed to take effect after the death of *A* or upon *C*'s return from Rome, whichever might first happen, the estate would be a vested remainder, for it is certain that *A* will die.

The principles above laid down will suffice to explain the rule which prevails in the case of contingent remainders, that inasmuch as the freehold can never be in abeyance, 'every contingent remainder of an estate of freehold must have a particular estate of freehold to support it.' Thus not only must every contingent remainder of a freehold be ready to *vest*, that is to become a complete right either of present or of future enjoyment (an estate in possession or a vested remainder) as soon as the preceding estate comes to an end, but that preceding estate must itself, at common law, be an estate of freehold. Lands cannot, at common law, be given to *A* for ten years, remainder to the unborn son of *B* [1].

The subjoined passage from Littleton shows that in his time the doctrine of contingent remainders was not firmly established. It cannot be said that in the above cases 'the remainder is in him to whom the remainder is entailed, before livery of seisin is made to him that has the freehold.' No doubt in the case of a gift to *B*, remainder to the heirs of *C*, the person who is the heir presumptive or apparent, that is who would be the heir if the ancestor were to die at once, has a chance, or possibility, or expectation of the right becoming his, but it is not such a right as the law regards as vested, that is as completely created—it is wanting in the main characteristic of a vested or completely created right, for there is no determinate person to take it.

Contingent remainders may be created in favour of unborn persons, provided only that the person who is to take the estate comes into existence before the preceding particular estate comes to an end. So soon as the designated person is

[1] See Williams on Real Property, p. 330.

CHAP. V. § 3 (2). born, the estate vests in him. Thus an estate might be given by way of remainder to an unborn person for life or in tail, subject only to the rule that no interest could be given to the unborn child of an unborn person [1]. For instance, if an estate be given to *A* for life, remainder to his unborn son in tail, remainder to *C* in fee, the first remainder is contingent, that is, it does not become a completely vested interest, for the reason above given, till *A* has a son born. So soon as this happens the interest is no longer contingent, but vested or complete, and the son of *A* has a vested remainder in tail, an interest which is ready to come into possession or enjoyment as soon as *A*'s life estate determines. On the other hand, *C* has an interest which is vested or complete from the moment of its creation.

Now if, before *A* has a son born, his life estate determines by death, forfeiture or otherwise, or if he acquire the fee by taking a conveyance from *C* of his interest, in which case before the birth of a son his life estate would merge or become united to or lost in the fee simple, or if before the same event he convey his life interest to *C*, in all the above cases the contingent remainder would, as the law formerly stood, have been destroyed, and no after-born son of *A* would take any interest at all. This liability to be destroyed by the happening of any of the above events was the great characteristic of contingent remainders, and the ingenuity of conveyancers was exercised to prevent so inconvenient a result. A recent change in the law has removed the liability to destruction to which contingent remainders were subject by reason of the forfeiture, surrender, or merger of any preceding estate of freehold [2].

The same act renders contingent remainders alienable *inter*

[1] See Fearne, Contingent Remainders, p. 502. This rule, which has long been firmly established, has taken the place of, and perhaps may be historically traced to, the somewhat unintelligible doctrine laid down by Sir E. Coke, that a possibility upon a possibility is never admitted by intendment of law. See Williams on Real Property, p. 334.

[2] 8 and 9 Vict. c. 106. s. 8.

vivos[1]. Formerly the change or contingency was not considered an appropriate subject of alienation *inter vivos*, though it fell within the rights capable of being disposed of by will. At the present day, if lands are given to *A* for life, remainder, if *C* be living at his decease, to *B* and his heirs, *B* may dispose of his contingent interest during the lives of *A* and *C* by alienation *inter vivos*, or by will[2], or, upon his decease intestate, the contingent remainder will descend to his heir[3].

There is one rule of construction of great technicality, but at the same time of much practical importance, which should be noticed in connexion with the doctrine of remainders. It has been seen that in a grant to *A* and his heirs, or to *A* and the heirs of his body, the words 'heirs,' 'heirs of his body,' or their equivalents, are words of limitation and not of purchase[4]; they are merely descriptive of the estate taken by *A*, and do not express that any estate is conveyed to *A*'s heir. The same rule applies although the words of the grant may appear to convey expressly an estate to the heirs by way of remainder. Thus, if a gift be made to *A* and after his decease to his heirs, or to *A* for life and after his decease to *B* for life (or to *B* and the heirs of his body), with an ultimate remainder to the heirs of *A*, the above rule operates to prevent the vesting of any estate in the heir directly by the gift; *A* (in the last case) has two estates, one for life in possession, the other in fee in remainder; if the intermediate estate of *B* be taken away, merger[5] takes place, and *A* becomes tenant in fee in possession. This doctrine is known by the name of the 'rule in Shelley's case[6],' and may be stated as follows:—Wherever there is a limitation to a man which if it stood alone would convey to him a 'particular' estate of freehold, followed by a limitation

[1] Sect. 6.

[2] Fearne, Contingent Remainders, 366, note. 7 Will. IV and 1 Vict. c. 26. s. 3.

[3] 3 and 4 Will. IV, c. 106. s. 1.

[4] See above, pp. 162, 166, n. 2.

[5] See above, p. 261.

[6] See Williams on Real Property, p. 316.

CHAP. V. § 3 (2). to his heirs or to the heirs of his body (or equivalent expressions) either immediately, or after the interposition of one or more other particular estates, the apparent gift to the heirs or heirs of the body is to be construed as a limitation of the estate of the ancestor, and not as a gift to his heir[1].

The conception of a 'remainder' is probably peculiar to English law, and is closely connected with the notions of estate and tenure. The tenant of lands has not the full property, but only an estate or interest of greater or less extent or duration. An estate in fee simple is considered as an aggregate out of which any number of smaller estates may be derived or carved; so long as the fee simple itself is not parted with, it is retained as a present interest or right, though the enjoyment or possession of it is postponed. So the interests which are parted with are regarded as present rights postponed in point of enjoyment. Roman law did not admit of the simultaneous existence in different persons of separate rights of future and present enjoyment over the same subject-matter, except perhaps in the case of *dominium*, and the so-called *jura in re aliena* (*ususfructus*, *emphyteusis*, etc.). Where these rights existed, the interest of the *dominus* was closely analogous to an English reversion. In French law, as it stood before the Code Napoleon, and in the systems derived from it (e. g. the law of Lower Canada), it is possible to create future interests by way of *substitution*. A thing may be given *inter vivos* or by will to *A*, subject to a condition that he should on the happening of a specified event, as for instance at his own decease, hand it over to *B*. In this case a *substitution* is created in favour of *B*. *A* is regarded as the complete proprietor, subject only to the charge of handing over the thing to *B* and to all that is involved in this obligation; for instance, he may not alienate, charge, or destroy the thing which is the subject of the substitution. *B*, on the other hand, has no present right, he has merely the hope

[1] See Littleton, sect. 719, Coke's Commentary, *ad loc.*, and Williams on Real Property, pp. 316-322.

or expectation of becoming the proprietor of the thing if he survives *A*. If he die, living *A*, nothing passes to his heirs; but if he survives *A*, he becomes upon *A*'s death full proprietor. The doctrine of *substitutions* formed a large and important chapter in the early French law, but was wholly abolished by the Code Napoleon, Article 896[1]. CHAP. V. § 3. (2)

BROOKE'S ABRIDGMENT[2], *Done and Remainder*, § 2.

TRANSLATION.

30 LIBER ASSISARUM[3], p. 47. H. was seised of tenements in Winchester devisable by will by custom[4], where there is also a custom that he who is seised by devise cannot make alienation by warranty or otherwise which shall be a bar to the remainder-man, or reversioner. H. devised to Alice his wife for term of life, remainder to Thomas his son for term of life, so that the said Thomas should make no gift or alienation so as to bar the remainder to the nearer heirs of the blood of the children (*propinquioribus haeredibus de sanguine puerorum*) of the said H. after the death of the said Thomas. And H. had also issue Maud (who had issue Isabel), and Edmund elder brother of Thomas. And then H. the devisor died, and afterwards E. the elder son died without issue. Alice the mother entered by the devise and died seised, and then Thomas entered and aliened in fee with warranty to the tenant in the assize[5], and Maud died. And Isabel her daughter, plaintiff in the assize, made claim, and took the door of the messuage now in demand into her hands by the hasp[6]. And Thomas afterwards died without issue, and Isabel

[1] See some excellent observations on the English conception of an 'estate' and its consequences in Markby, Elements of Law, p. 154; and see Pothier, Traité des Substitutions, artt. 1-6.

[2] Brooke's Abridgment is a compilation and arrangement of the cases reported in the Year Books and early Reports, and was published in the year 1568; Reeves, iii. 814.

[3] A volume of Reports of the reign of Edward III, numbered according to the year of the reign.

[4] See above, p. 48.

[5] i. e. the defendant. The case turns on whether upon the proper construction of the devise the remainder in fee vests in Thomas, who would then have conveyed it to the defendant, or in Isabel.

[6] As to 'continual claim' and its effect in preserving to the person disseised the right of actual entry, see Littleton, lib. iii. c. 7. s. 414.

CHAP. V. § 3. (2) entered upon the alienee, and he ousted her, and she brings the assize, and it is said that those who are the heirs of H. shall not have the remainder by force of the words *propinquioribus haeredibus de sanguine puerorum*[1], for it is not limited to his heirs, but to the next in blood of his children, so that his children themselves shall not have the land by the remainder, but the children of the children.

(*Wilby.*) A man leased to *A* for term of life, remainder to his next of blood, and had issue two sons; the elder has issue and dies, tenant for life dies, the younger brother shall have the land and not the issue of the elder brother, for the younger brother is nearer of blood to his father the devisor than is the son of the elder son, for the one is his own son, and the other is only the son of his son, and yet the son of his elder son is his heir, but not his next of blood.

(*Seaton.*) If H. had had many sons and daughters who had issue and died, the remainder vests in the heir of each of the children of H., since he is *proximus &c. de sanguine puerorum*, which extends to the heirs of all the children of H.; but if the daughter of H. had issue when the tenant for life died, and the son of H. had no issue at that time, the issue of the daughter of H. shall have the remainder of the whole; and notwithstanding the son of H. should have issue afterwards, that issue should have nothing, for it was vested in the other before, and he in whom the remainder vests when it falls retains it[2]. It is otherwise in the case of a descent, as where there is a descent to a daughter, and afterwards a son is born, the son ousts the daughter. With a remainder it is different.

(*Fincheden.*) If land be leased for term of life, remainder to the right heirs of J. and N.[3], and then J. have issue and die, and then tenant for life dies, and the heir of J. enter, and then N. die, the heir of N. shall have nothing, because he was not the heir when the remainder fell[4].

(*Fish.*) If there be a brother and sister, and the land be leased for term of life, remainder to the right heirs of the brother, and he die, and the tenant for life dies, the sister enters, and then

[1] And therefore that the defendant, alienee of Thomas, had no title, although Thomas was the heir of the heir of H.

[2] See above, p. 266.

[3] It will be observed that this is a contingent remainder. *Nemo est haeres viventis.* These words in the case in the text are sufficient to convey an estate in fee to the heir of J.

[4] See above, p. 266.

the wife of the brother is delivered of a son begotten by the brother in his lifetime, the son shall not have the land, but the sister, who is aunt to him, shall retain it, because the land was vested in her before, since where a remainder or any other purchase vests in any person it shall continue in such possession.

And then the assize was awarded. And so observe that by this award the daughter of the daughter, plaintiff in the assize, shall have the remainder, and not the alienee of T., since the remainder never vested in T. as heir of E., who was heir of H. the devisor; for it was said that by those words—to the next in blood of his children—that the child himself should take nothing, but another of the blood of the same child whichever be nearer, and the plaintiff recovered by the award: *quod nota.*

LITTLETON'S TENURES, lib. iii. c. 13, sect. 720. Item jeo ay oye dit, que en temps le Roy Richard le second, il y fuist un Justice de le Comen Banke, demurrant en Kent, appelle Rykhill, qui avoit issue divers fitz, et son entent fuist, que son eisne fitz averoit certeyn terres et tenementes a luy, et a les heires de son corps engendres, et pur defaute dissue, le remeyndre a le second fitz, &c., et issint a le tierce fitz, &c., et pur ceo quil voille que nul de ses fitz alieneroit ou ferroit garrauntie pur barrer ou leder les autres queux serront en le remeyndre, &c., il fist faire tiel endenture a tiel effecte, scil. que les terres et tenementes furent dones a son eisne fitz sur tiel condicion, que si leisne fitz alienast en fee, ou en fee taille, &c., ou si ascun de ses fitz alienast, &c., que adonques lour estate cessera et serroit voyde, et que adonques mesmes les terres et tenementes immediate remeyndront a le second fitz, et a les heires de son corps engendres, &c., sur mesme la condicion, scil. que si le ii fitz alienast, &c., que adonques son estate cessera, et que adonques mesmes les terres et tenementes immediat remeyndront al tierce fitz et a les heires des son corps engendres, et sic ultra, le remeyndre as autres de ses fitz, et lyverë de seisin fuist fait accordant.

Sect. 721. Mais il semble per reason que toutes tielx remeyndres en la fourme avauntdit faitez sount voides et de nul value, et ceo pur trois causes. Une cause est, pur ceo que chescun remeyndre que commence par un fait, il covient que le remeyndre soit en luy a qui le remeyndre est taillé per force de mesme le faits quant[1] le lyverë de seisin est fait a luy qui avera le frank-

[1] A later reading generally adopted is 'avant.' See Sir E. Coke's translation.

CHAP. V. § 3 (2). tenement, car en tiel case la nessance et le estre de le remeyndre est per le lyverë de seisin a celuy qui avera le franktenement, et tiel remeyndre ne fuist al second fitz, al temps de lyverë de seisin en le cas avauntdit, &c.

Sect. 722. La seconde cause est, si le primier fitz alienast les tenementes en fee, donques est le franktenement et le fee simple en lalienè, et en nul autre, et si le donour avoit ascun reversion, par tiel alienacion, la revercion est discontinue; donques coment per ascun reason poet estre, que tiel remainder commencera son estre et sa nessance immediate apres tiel alienacion fait a un estraunge, qui ad per mesme lalienacion franktenement, et fee simple? Et auxi si tiel remeyndre serroit bon, adonques purroit il entrer sur lalienè, lou il navoit ascun manere de droit avant lalienacion, que serroit inconvenient.

Sect. 723. La tierce cause est, quant la condicion est tiel, que si leisne fitz alienast, &c., que son estate cessera ou serroit voyde, &c., donques apres tiel alienacion, &c. poet le donour entrer per force de tiel condicion, &c., comme il semble, et issint le donour et ses heires en tiel cas doient pluis tost aver la terre que le second fitz, qui navoit ascun droit devant tiel alienacion, &c.; et issint il semble que tielz remeyndres en le cas avauntdit sont voydes.

Sir E. Coke's Translation.

Sect. 720. Also, I have heard say, that in the time of King Richard the Second there was a justice of the Common Place[1] dwelling in Kent, called Richel, who had issue divers sons, and his intent was, that his eldest son should have certain lands and tenements to him, and to the heirs of his body begotten; and for default of issue, the remainder to the second son, and so to the third son: and because he would that none of his sons should alien or make warranty to bar or hurt the others that should be in the remainder, he causeth an indenture to be made to this effect, viz. that the lands and tenements were given to his eldest son upon such condition, that if the eldest son alien in fee, or in fee tail, or if any of his sons alien, that then their estate should cease and be void, and that then the same lands and tenements immediately should remain to his second son and to the heirs of his body begotten, *et sic ultra*, the remainder to his other sons, and livery of seisin was made accordingly.

[1] Or Common Pleas.

Sect. 721. But it seemeth by reason that all such remainders in the form aforesaid are void and of no value, and that for three causes. One cause is, for that every remainder which beginneth by a deed it behoveth that the remainder be in him to whom the remainder is entailed by force of the same deed, before the livery of seisin is made to him that shall have the freehold [1]; for in such case the growing and the being of the remainder is by the livery of seisin to him that shall have the freehold, and such remainder was not to the second son at the time of the livery of seisin in the case aforesaid.

Sect. 722. The second cause is, if the first son alien the tenements in fee, then is the freehold and the fee simple in the alienee, and in none other; and if the donor had any reversion, by such alienation the reversion is discontinued: then how by any reason may it be that such remainder shall commence his being and his growing immediately after such alienation made to a stranger, that hath by the same alienation a freehold and fee simple? And also if such remainder should be good, then might he enter upon the alienee, where he had no manner of right before the alienation, which should be inconvenient.

Sect. 723. The third cause is, when the condition is such, that if the elder son alien, that his estate shall cease or be void, then after such alienation may the donor enter by force of such condition, as it seemeth [2]; and so the donor or his heirs in such case ought sooner to have the land than the second son, that had not any right before such alienation; and so it seemeth that such remainders in the case aforesaid are void.

§ 4. *Joint Tenants, Tenants in Common, Coparceners.*

Another class of rights which attained greater precision during the interval under consideration, and assumed the characteristics which they have possessed ever since, are those which are enjoyed by two or more persons who are simul-

[1] This however is contrary to the authority of the case given above. According to this doctrine, no contingent remainder, such as is created by a grant to *A* for life, remainder to the heir of *B*, could be valid.

[2] It is an inflexible rule of common law that the benefit of a condition can only be reserved in favour of a donor or his heirs. *A* cannot, in a lease to *B*, impose a condition that on non-payment of rent *C* may enter. See above, p. 264.

CHAP. V. § 4. taneously entitled to rights of property over the same piece of land. From the earliest times it must have been common for two or more persons to have undivided interests of some kind in land [1]. By the time of Littleton three kinds of undivided ownership had come to be distinguished as having different attributes. The persons entitled are called *joint tenants, tenants in common, coparceners.* The main characteristics of this class of rights will sufficiently appear from the subjoined extracts. The point of resemblance between the three kinds is that the co-owners have no separate estate or interest in any distinct portion of the land over which they have simultaneously rights of property, they are each interested, according to the extent of their share, in every part of the whole land and its proceeds.

LITTLETON'S TENURES [2], lib. iii. c. 3. s. 277. *Joint tenants* are as if a man be seised of certain lands or tenements, and infeoffeth [3] two, three, four, or more, to have and to hold to them for term of their lives, or for term of another's life, by force of which feoffment or lease they are seised; these are joint tenants.

Sect. 280. And it is to be understood, that the nature of joint tenancy is, that he which surviveth shall have only the entire tenancy according to such estate as he hath, if the jointure be continued. As if three joint tenants be in fee simple, and the one

[1] In Bracton the general term 'participes' is applied to such persons under whatever title they hold (fol. 428; Reeves, i. p. 447). It was said of such a tenant 'totum tenet et nihil tenet, scilicet totum in communi et nihil separatim per se.' In the Statute 34 Edward I, stat. 1, certain provisions are made 'de conjunctim feoffatis,' providing for the case where a tenant in an assize of novel disseisin pleaded that another was seised jointly with him.

[2] The extracts from Littleton's text given above are sufficient as specimens of the language in which he wrote. The following extracts are from the translation adopted by Sir E. Coke.

[3] Joint tenants differ from parceners or coparceners in the mode in which their interest is created. Joint tenancy must commence in consequence of alienation *inter vivos* or by will, an estate in coparcenary arises by devolution *ab intestato* to daughters, sisters, &c., or sons in gavelkind tenure. All the joint tenants must owe their estate to the same title, that is, the feoffment or other instrument of alienation must operate to convey a co-extensive interest, at the same time, to all the joint tenants. See Blackstone, ii. 180.

hath issue and dieth, yet they which survive shall have the whole tenements, and the issue shall have nothing[1]. And if the second joint tenant hath issue and die, yet the third which surviveth shall have the whole tenements to him and to his heirs for ever. But otherwise it is of parceners; for if three parceners be, and before any partition made the one hath issue and dieth, that which to him belongeth shall descend to his issue. And if such parcener die without issue, that which belongs to her shall descend to her co-heirs, so as they shall have this by descent, and not by survivor as joint tenants shall have.

Sect. 281. And as the survivor holds place between joint tenants, in the same manner it holdeth place between them which have joint estate or possession with another of a chattel real or personal. As if a lease of lands or tenements be made to many for term of years, he which survives of the lessees shall have the tenements to him only during the term by force of the same lease. And if a horse or any other chattel personal be given to many, he which surviveth shall have the horse only[2].

Sect. 282. In the same manner it is of debts and duties, for if an obligation be made to many for one debt, he which surviveth shall have the whole debt or duty. And so is it of other covenants and contracts.

Sect. 283. Also there may also be some joint tenants which may have a joint estate, and be joint tenants for term of their lives, and yet have several inheritances. As if lands be given to two men and to the heirs of their two bodies begotten, in this case the donees have a joint estate for term of their two lives, and yet they have several inheritances: for if one of the donees hath issue and die, the other which surviveth shall have the whole by the survivor for term of his life, and if he which surviveth hath also issue and die, then the issue of the one shall have the one moiety and the issue of the other shall have the other moiety of the land, and they shall hold the land between them in common, and they are not joint tenants, but are tenants in common. . . .

[1] This is the essential characteristic of joint tenancy, distinguishing it both from coparcenary and from tenancy in common.

[2] There is and always has been by the Common Law an exception in the case of property jointly owned for purposes of trade: the maxim being, 'Jus accrescendi inter mercatores locum non habet.' And in some other cases (e. g. that of joint mortgagees), although the legal estate 'survives,' the beneficial interest is by the rules of Equity regarded as belonging to the representatives of the deceased joint tenant.

CHAP. V. § 4.

Sect. 287. Also if there be two joint tenants of land in fee simple within a borough where lands and tenements are devisable by testament [1], and if the one of the said two joint tenants deviseth that which to him belongeth by his testament, and dieth, this devise is void [2]. And the cause is, for that no devise can take effect till after the death of the devisor, and by his death all the land presently cometh by the law to his companion which surviveth, by the survivor, the which he doth not claim, nor hath anything in the land by the devisor, but in his own right by the survivor according to the course of law, and for this cause such devise is void. But otherwise it is of parceners seised of tenements devisable in like case of devise.

Sect. 288. Also it is commonly said that every joint tenant is seised of the land which he holdeth jointly *per my et per tout*; and this is as much as to say as he is seised by every parcel and by the whole, and this is true, for in every parcel and by every parcel and by all the lands and tenements he is jointly seised with his companion [3].

Sect. 290. Also, joint tenants (if they will) may make partition [4] between them, and the partition is good enough, but they shall not be compelled to do this by law, but if they will make partition of their own will and agreement, the partition shall stand in force.

Sect. 291. Also if a joint estate be made of land to a husband and wife and to a third person [5], in this case the husband and wife

[1] See above, pp. 48, 68.

[2] A joint tenant, though he can make an effectual alienation *inter vivos*, cannot do so by will. For the effect of alienation by a joint tenant during his life see sect. 292, below.

[3] And yet, as Sir Edward Coke points out in his commentary on this passage, one of two joint tenants cannot dispose by feoffment, or otherwise, of more than a moiety of the lands; nor is the estate of a joint tenant affected by the escheat or forfeiture of the interest of his co-tenant.

[4] By a deed of partition. In this point joint tenants differ from coparceners, who were compellable to make partition by a proceeding called a writ of partition (Littleton, sect. 247). By the statutes 31 Henry VIII, c. 1; 32 Henry VIII, c. 32 this proceeding was made available for joint tenants. In later times the old writ of partition was in practice superseded by the jurisdiction of the Court of Chancery enforcing partition amongst joint tenants, upon a bill for the purpose being filed by one of them, and the old writ was finally abolished by Statute 3 and 4 Will. IV, c. 27. s. 36.

[5] As to the effect of a gift to a husband and wife and their heirs see Williams on Real Property, p. 285.

have in law in their right but a moiety, and the third person shall have as much as the husband and wife, viz. the other moiety. And the cause is for that the husband and wife are but one person in law[1]. . . . CHAP. V. § 4.

Chap. iv. sect. 292. *Tenants in common* are they which have lands or tenements in fee simple, fee tail, or for term of life, and they have such lands or tenements by several titles, and not by a joint title, and none of them know of this his several, but they ought by the law to occupy these lands or tenements in common, and *pro indiviso* to take the profits in common[2]. And because they come to such lands or tenements by several titles and not by one joint title, and their occupation and possession shall be by law between them in common, they are called tenants in common. As if a man infeoff two joint tenants in fee, and the one of them alien that which to him belongeth to another in fee, now the alienee and the other joint tenant are tenants in common, because they are in such tenements by several titles, for the alienee cometh to the moiety by the feoffment of one of the joint tenants, and the other joint tenant hath the other moiety by force of the first feoffment made to him and to his companion. And so they are in by several titles, that is to say by several feoffments.

Sect. 296. But if lands be given to two men, and to the heirs of their two bodies begotten, the donees have a joint estate for term of their lives; and if each of them hath issue and die, their issue shall hold in common. But if lands be given to two abbots, as to the abbot of Westminster and to the abbot of St. Albans, to have and to hold to them and to their successors, in this case they have presently at the beginning an estate in common and not a joint estate. And the reason is, for that every abbot or other sovereign of a house of religion, before that he was made abbot or sovereign, was but as a dead person in law, and when he is made abbot he is as a man personable in law, only to purchase and have lands or tenements or other things to the use of his house, and not

[1] It appears doubtful whether this rule has or has not been modified by the effect of the Married Women's Property Act, 1882; see *Re March* L.R. 27 Ch. D. 166 and *Re Jupp* L.R. 39 Ch. D. 148.

[2] Thus if lands are given to two to hold as tenants in common and one dies, his heir holds in common with the other. So one tenant in common may have a different estate from another—one may have the estate for years, another in fee, another for life, &c. The only essential characteristic is that the land itself should not be divided.

to his own proper use as another secular man may, and therefore at the beginning of their purchase they are tenants in common; and if one of them die, the abbot which surviveth shall not have the whole by survivor, but the successor of the abbot which is dead shall hold the moiety in common with the abbot that surviveth.

Sect. 298. Also if lands be given to two to have and to hold, scil. the one moiety to the one and to his heirs, and the other moiety to the other and to his heirs, they are tenants in common[1].

Sect. 299. Also if a man seised of certain lands infeoff another of the moiety of the same land without any speech of assignment or limitation of the same moiety in severalty at the time of the feoffment, then the feoffee and feoffor shall hold their parts of the land in common.

Lib. iii. c. 1. sect. 241. *Parceners* are of two sorts, to wit, parceners according to the course of the common law, and parceners according to the custom. Parceners after the course of the common law are where a man or woman seised of certain lands or tenements in fee simple or in tail hath no issue but daughters and dieth, and the tenements descend to the issues, and the daughters enter into the lands or tenements so descended to them, then they are called parceners, and be but one heir to their ancestor. And they are called parceners because by the writ which is called *breve de participatione facienda* the law will constrain them that partition shall be made among them[2]. And if there be two daughters to whom the land descendeth, then they be called two parceners, and if there be three daughters they be called three parceners, and four daughters four parceners, and so forth.

[1] Whether any particular gift creates a joint tenancy or a tenancy in common is a question of construction. The general rule at common law was in favour of a joint tenancy, as is seen from the first instance in sect. 296. It might have been expected that that gift would have simply created a tenancy in common in fee simple. In order to create a tenancy in common it is necessary that there should be words which either expressly or by necessary implication mean that the inheritances are to be several; as in the text, 'to the heirs of their *two* bodies begotten.' A gift however in these terms to a man and a woman capable of marrying each other would create a joint tenancy. In the later period of the law the rule has been different, and the inclination of the Court of Chancery was to construe limitations as much as possible in favour of tenancy in common.

[2] See above, p. 276, n. 3.

Sect. 254. And note that none are called parceners by the common law but females or the heirs of females which come to lands or tenements by descent; for if sisters purchase lands or tenements, of this they are called joint tenants and not parceners.

Sect. 265. Parceners by the custom are where a man seised in fee simple or in fee tail of lands or tenements which are of the tenure called gavelkind within the county of Kent hath issue divers sons and die, such lands or tenements shall descend to all the sons by the custom, and they shall equally inherit and make partition by the custom, as females shall do, and a writ of partition lieth in this case as between females. But it behoveth in the declaration to make mention of the custom [1]. Also such custom is in other places of England, and also such custom is in North Wales.

§ 5. *Creditors' Rights.*

No branch of the law is of greater practical importance than that which relates to the rights which creditors gradually acquired of having recourse to the land of their debtors for the payment of their debts. In the first place, the creditor might acquire rights over the debtor's land in consequence of a judicial proceeding either in the ordinary courts of common law, or under the extraordinary jurisdictions created by the Statute of Merchants, 13 Edward I, stat. 3, and the Statutum de Stapulis, 27 Edward III, stat. 2. c. 9. Secondly, a debtor might, without the intervention of any judicial proceedings, give the creditor the security of his land for a debt.

(1) *Remedies by Legal Process.*

After obtaining a judgment in his favour in an action at common law. the creditor was enabled by one of the provisions of the Statute of Westminster II (13 Edward I, c. 18) to choose whether to have execution upon the goods of the debtor by the writ which is still called the writ of *fieri facias* or to have a writ commanding the sheriff to 'deliver to him [all the chattels of the debtor saving only his oxen and beasts

[1] That is, in pleading it must be stated that the land is of the custom of gavelkind.

CHAP. V. § 5 (1). of his plough, and [1]] the one half of his land, until the debt be levied upon a reasonable price or extent.' This power of the creditor to seize and sell half the debtor's land is now [2] extended to the whole. The writ by which this is effected has ever since the Statute of Westminster II been called the writ of *elegit*.

The Statutes Merchant and Staple [3] were designed to give creditors who were merchants a speedier and more effectual mode of proceeding to recover debts than was afforded by the common law. The merchant creditor was empowered to summon his debtor before the 'Mayor of London or before some chief warden of a city or of another good town where the king shall appoint [4],' and obtain from him an acknowledgment or recognizance of the debt and of the day at which it would become due. This acknowledgment was then formally drawn up, and if the debt was not paid it might be enforced against the person and property of the debtor. As to the debtor's lands, 'the merchant shall have such seisin of the lands and tenements delivered unto him or his assigns that he may maintain a writ of novel disseisin if he be put out, and of redisseisin also as of freehold, to hold to him and his assigns until the debt be paid [5].'

It should be observed that these remedies by elegit and statute merchant bound the lands from the date of the judg-

[1] The remedy by elegit against the goods of the debtor after having long been disused was revived in 1880 in consequence of the discovery that it afforded a more ample protection to the creditor in the case of the bankruptcy of the debtor. By the Bankruptcy Act of 1883 the writ of elegit is no longer to affect goods; and the words of the Statute of Westminster II quoted in the text 'all' to 'and' are repealed (46 and 47 Vict. c. 52. s. 169).

[2] 1 and 2 Vict. c. 110. s. 11.

[3] The Statute of Acton Burnell, de Mercatoribus, 11 Edward I, followed by 13 Edward I, stat. 3, and the Statutum de Stapulis, 27 Edward III, stat. 2.

[4] 13 Edward I, stat. 3. The jurisdiction given by 27 Edward III, stat. 2, is to be exercised by the Mayor and Constables of the Staple. See for the places where the Staple is to be kept, ib. c. 1.

[5] 13 Edward I.

ment in the former case, and of the recognizance in the latter. The creditor might pursue his remedy against the lands although they had come to the hands of the heir of the debtor, or of a purchaser. Thus by the above provision a new kind of interest in lands was in effect created, and accordingly we read of *tenancy* by statute merchant, statute staple, and elegit [1].

The interest of such a tenant devolved at his decease not upon his heir but upon his executors or administrators, and so far partook of the nature of personalty. On the other hand, the estate had the characteristic of freehold that it had no fixed period of termination, and that the appropriate remedy in case of ouster was the assize of novel disseisin [2].

Besides the remedies available to the creditor against the debtor himself, the creditor might also in some cases take proceedings against the heir to whom the debtor's lands had descended. It appears that in early times the heir was bound to satisfy the debts of his ancestor out of the lands which descended to him, so far as the personalty was not sufficient for the purpose [3]. By the time of Edward I the liability of the heir for the debts of his ancestor seems to have been confined, except as regards debts due to the Crown, to those secured by deed (called specialty debts) in which the heir was expressly named [4]. For such debts an action at law has always been maintainable by the creditor against the heir. The liability of the heir in this respect was by a later statute extended to the devisee of the debtor [5]. But it was not till

[1] See Coke upon Littleton, 289 b.

[2] See above, Chap. II. § 9.

[3] Glanville, lib. vii. c. 8: 'Si vero non sufficiunt res defuncti ad debita persolvenda, tunc quidem haeres ipse defectum ipsum de suo tenetur adimplere; ita dico si habuerit aetatem haeres ipse.' See also Bracton, 61 b.

[4] See Britton, 64 b: 'For we will that none be bound to pay the debt of his ancestor, whose heir he is, to any other but to us, unless he be thereto especially bound by the deed of his ancestor.'

[5] 3 and 4 William and Mary, c. 14. s. 2, repealed by 11 Geo. IV and

CHAP. V. § 5 (2). 1807 that any mode was provided by which creditors could realise out of the lands of the debtor in the hands of the heir or devisee their debts which were not secured by deed binding the heir or devisee. By 47 Geo. III, c. 74, the fee simple estates of deceased *traders* were rendered liable to the payment of all debts, 'as well debts due on simple contract as on specialty;' and in 1833 (3 and 4 Will. IV, c. 104) the same rule was applied to the estates of all deceased persons, reserving however a priority to specialty creditors. This priority was abolished by 32 and 33 Vict. c. 46. The mode in which effect is given to the provisions of these statutes is by having the real estate of the deceased *administered* by the Chancery Division of the High Court in a suit instituted by a creditor, and the proceeds applied to the payment, first of debts, and then of legacies[1].

(2) *Mortgages.*

The second class of creditors' rights above noticed exist when, without the intervention of any legal process, the debtor has voluntarily given his land as security for the debt.

This practice is very ancient. Pledges of land are often mentioned in Domesday. In the time of Glanvill pledges of land were of two kinds, *vivum vadium* and *mortuum vadium*. Where a *vivum vadium* was created, the land was conveyed to the creditor to be held by him for a certain time, during which the rent and profits went towards the discharge of the debt. In a *mortuum vadium* there was no such arrangement as to the profits. The latter class of security was looked on as a species of usury, and, though not absolutely prohibited, rendered the creditor liable to the penalties of usury. It appears however that upon payment of the debt the debtor might recover the land just as in the case of a pledge

1 Will. IV, c. 47, which gives a more extended remedy against the devisee. As to a devise, see Chap. VIII.

[1] See Williams on Real Property, pp. 256–259.

of a personal chattel[1]. In the time of Littleton a mortgage had become a species of estate upon condition. The land was conveyed, usually by feoffment, by the debtor to the creditor, subject to the condition that on repayment of the loan by a certain day the feoffor (the debtor) might re-enter. On the failure of the feoffor to perform the condition, the law refused to regard the fact that the real nature and intent of the transaction was that the land should be held by the feoffee merely as a security for a debt, and insisted on the enforcing of the rules relating to estates upon condition in all their strictness, holding that the estate was thereupon vested absolutely in the feoffee.

In later times, when the jurisdiction of the Chancellor was firmly established, the rights and duties of mortgagor and mortgagee recognised by Equity became wholly different from those recognised by Law[2]. In form the transaction is

[1] 'Quandoque res immobiles (ponuntur in vadium) ut terrae et tenementa et redditus. . . . Item quandoque invadiatur res aliqua in mortuo vadio quandoque non. Mortuum vadium dicitur illud cujus fructus vel redditus interim percepti in nullo se acquietant. . . . Cum vero res immobilis ponitur in vadium ita quod inde facta fuerit seisina ipsi creditori, et ad terminum, aut ita convenit inter creditorem et debitorem quod exitus et redditus interim se acquietent, aut sic quod in nullo se acquietent. Prima conventio justa est et tenet. Secunda injusta est et inhonesta, quae dicitur mortuum vadium, sed per curiam domini regis non prohibetur fieri, et tamen reputat eam pro specie usurae. Unde si quis in tali vadio decesserit, et post mortem ejus hoc fuerit probatum, de rebus ejus non aliter disponetur quam de rebus usurarii. . . . Notandum tamen quod ex quo aliquis solverit id quod debuit, vel solvere se obtulit competenter, si creditor ulterius vadium penes se maliciose detinuerit, debitor ipse se inde curiae conquerens tale breve habebit: Rex vicecomiti salutem. Praecipe N. quod juste et sine dilatione reddat R. totam terram vel terram illam in illa villa quam ei invadiavit pro centum marcis ad terminum qui praeteriit ut dicit, et denarios suos idem recipiat, vel quam inde acquietavit ut dicit, et nisi fecerit summone eum per bonos,' &c. Glanvill, lib. x. cc. 6, 8, 9; and in xiii. 26, an account is given of the 'recognition' to ascertain whether land in dispute was held 'ut de feodo, an ut de vadio.'

[2] 'Equity' means the law administered by the Court of Chancery before Nov. 1, 1875, in so far as such law differed from the law administered in the Courts of Common Law. When on that date all the Courts were amalgamated, the distinction between Equity and Law in the

CHAP. V. § 5 (2).

still at the present day a conveyance of the lands, subject to a condition for re-entry, or more commonly to an agreement for reconveyance by the mortgagee to the mortgagor, on payment of the debt on a certain day, and to a proviso that, until default in payment of the debt, the mortgagor is to remain in possession [1]. So far as the legal estate, or interest at common law, is concerned, the ordinary rules governing conveyances of land apply; no notice is taken of the object of the transaction; the mortgagor, who remains in possession, is considered to have an interest in the nature of a term until default made in the payment of the debt; after default, the whole legal property in the land passes irrevocably to the mortgagee, with all its incidents. For instance, a mortgagor, after default in payment of the mortgage debt, cannot, except under the special powers created by the Conveyancing and Law of Property Act 1881 [2], make a valid lease of the lands without the concurrence of the mortgagee. In Equity, however, the real nature of the transaction is regarded, and even after default is made, notwithstanding the terms of the instrument creating the mortgage, the mortgagee will be made to reconvey the land to the mortgagor on payment of debt, interest, and costs. The right which remains in the mortgagor is called his *equity of redemption* (right to redeem), and is in fact the ownership of the land subject to the mortgage debt [3].

LITTLETON'S TENURES, lib. iii. c. 5. sect. 332. (*Of Estates upon Condition.*) Item, if a feoffment be made upon such condition that if the feoffor pay to the feoffee at a certain day forty pounds of

former sense of the terms came to an end, and the rules of Equity whenever they come into conflict with rules of Law are paramount and are administered alike by all Courts.

[1] The Conveyancing and Law of Property Act, 1881, provides a statutory form of mortgage in which these conditions are included by implication (44 and 45 Vict. c. 41. s. 26, and Third Schedule).

[2] By this Act, 44 and 45 Vict. c. 41. s. 18 a mortgagor in possession may now without the concurrence of the mortgagee make valid agricultural and mining leases subject to the conditions therein specified.

[3] See further as to mortgages, Williams on Real Property, part iv. chap. ii.

money, that then the feoffor may re-enter; in this case the feoffee is called tenant in mortgage, which is as much to say in French as *mort gage*, and in Latin *mortuum vadium*. And it seemeth that the cause why it is called mortgage is, for that it is doubtful whether the feoffor will pay at the day limited such sum or not: and if he doth not pay, then the land which is put in pledge upon condition for the payment of the money is taken from him for ever, and so dead to him upon condition. And if he doth pay the money, then the pledge is dead as to the tenant. CHAP. V. § 5 (2).

Sect. 333. Also as a man may make a feoffment in fee in mortgage, so a man may make a gift in tail in mortgage, and a lease for term of life, or for term of years in mortgage. And all such tenants are called tenants in mortgage according to the estates which they have in the land.

Sect. 337. Also if a feoffment be made upon condition that if the feoffor pay a certain sum of money to the feoffee, then it shall be lawful to the feoffor and his heirs to enter; in this case if the feoffor die before the payment made, and the heir will tender to the feoffee the money, such tender is void, because the time within which this ought to be done is past. For when the condition is, that if the feoffor pay the money to the feoffee, this is as much to say as if the feoffor during his life pay the money to the feoffee; and when the feoffor dieth then the time of the tender is past. But otherwise it is where a day of payment is limited, and the feoffor die before the day, then may the heir tender the money as is aforesaid, for that the time of the tender was not past by the death of the feoffor. Also it seemeth that in such case, where the feoffor dieth before the day of payment, if the executors of the feoffor tender the money to the feoffee at the day of payment, this tender is good enough; and if the feoffee refuse it, the heirs of the feoffor may enter. And the reason is for that the executors represent the person of their testator.

Sect. 339. Also if the feoffee in mortgage before the day of payment which should be made to him makes his executors and die, and his heir entereth into the land as he ought, it seemeth in this case that the feoffor ought to pay the money at the day appointed to the executors, and not to the heir of the feoffee, because the money at the beginning trenched to the feoffee in manner as a duty, and it shall be intended that the estate was made by reason of the lending of the money by the feoffee, or for some other duty; and therefore the payment shall not be made to the heir as it seemeth, but the words of the condition may be such as the payment shall be made to the heir. As if the condition were that if the feoffor pay to the feoffee or to his heirs such a sum at such a day, there after the death of the feoffee if he dieth before the day limited, the payment ought to be made to the heir at the day appointed [1].

§ 6. *Copyhold Tenure.*

It has been already seen that, at the time of Domesday, besides the *liberi homines* there was commonly a large class of persons of an inferior status, residing within the limits of the manor and bound as a general rule to render services upon the domain lands of the lord [2]. The various names which prevailed at the time of Domesday and earlier cease to be recognised, and we hear only of *villani*, villeins.

When a villein was attached to a particular manor, it followed a a matter of course that he had a permanent habitation, and the means of supporting himself and his family by the occupation of a plot of ground. This must have been the practice long before the Conquest, and was continued when the customary law of land was modified by the changes wrought by the Norman rule. When the judicial institutions of the country took the form in which they appear in the reign of Henry II, there was no *forum* in which the villein could assert his right to his land, at all events as against the lord. The courts baron of the manors were only for the freeholders of the manor, and the Curia Regis was in one point of view but the supreme court baron of the nation, and only took cognizance of freehold rights. The villein had no *locus standi* in either. At the same time, as has been pointed out in the third chapter, it became the practice to regard not so much the status of the villein, as the nature of his interest in land arising from the character of the

[1] Littleton proceeds (sects. 340–343) to consider where the debt is to be paid or tendered. He recommends the feoffor to fix some definite place in the instrument creating the mortgage, otherwise the feoffor will be bound to seek the feoffee if he be anywhere within the realm of England.

[2] See above, Chap. I. pp. 50–52 and Chap. III. § 13.

services rendered to the lord, and thus freemen came to hold land 'in villenage,' and were little or no better off as to legal rights than the born villeins. The only legal protection, which either the villein or the freeman holding in villenage seems to have had against the lord in Bracton's time, was where the lord entered into a covenant with the tenant in villenage[1]. CHAP. V. § 6.

The lawyers described the position of the tenant in villenage by the expression that he held his land at the will of the lord[2]. But, as a matter of fact, the customs and practices which prevailed in the various manors tended to protect and perpetuate the interests of this class of tenants. Custom fixed the rights of the lord, the amount of service to be rendered to him, the heriots upon the death of the tenant, the fine on the admittance of a new tenant, the mode of succession and devolution of the lands to the tenant's eldest or youngest son or to all the sons alike, and so forth. These customs, though the institutions of the country afforded no means of enforcing them as against the lord[3] by judicial action, were deeply rooted in the habits of the people, and in all probability the lord who ventured to set them aside and deprive the villein of his customary rights must have been exceptionally grasping and defiant of public opinion. Thus it is that throughout the period extending from Bracton to Edward IV we hear this class of tenants spoken of as if they had a recognised and legally protected interest in lands. Sir E. Coke[4] points out that 'in H. V. 11 they be called copiholders, in 14 H. IV. 34 tenant *per le verge*, and in 42 E. III. 25[5] tenant *per role*

[1] See above, Chap. III. § 13.

[2] 'For it is no more to say, "I hold the tenements in villenage of the Dean" &c., than to say, "I hold the tenements at the will of the Dean" &c.;' i. e. both are modes of describing the nature of the holding, not the status of the holder. Year Book, 20 Edw. I, p. 40.

[3] It appears that as against a wrong-doer other than the lord the villein might sue by petition in the manor court. See Littleton, sect. 76, below.

[4] Coke upon Littleton, 58 a.

[5] 'A Prior brings a suit of trespass against one J. for breaking his close

CHAP. V. § 6. *solonque le volunt le seignior*, and in statute of 4 E. I, called Extenta Manerii, they are called *custumarii tenentes*[1].'

It appears that the tenants in villenage were present at the manorial courts, not on a level with the freeholders or free suitors to the court,—who were the *pares curiae*, the judges of the court, by whose equal voice all matters were decided,—but in an inferior position. The customary heir would appear at the court and humbly request admittance to the land of his deceased father on payment of the customary dues; the tenant who had sold his holding in villenage would appear and surrender his land to the lord or his steward, and the purchaser would request admittance. These and similar transactions are recorded on the rolls of the court. The rolls of the court therefore contain the evidence of the customs of the manor, the authorised copy of the entry on the rolls of the court delivered to the tenant in his muniment of title, and gives him his name of 'copyholder.'

Thus in dealing with this class of tenants the court baron assumed a new form, which comes to be distinguished from the original court baron, and to be called the Customary Court Baron or Customary Court. The freeholders are not, generally speaking, suitors at the Customary Court, except perhaps when questions arise upon the customs of the manors affecting their interests[2]. The functions of the court are administrative rather than judicial. The copyholders or 'homage' are not *pares curiae*. Their principal function is to make presentments upon matters concerning their interests

and carrying away his goods, to wit, corn, and the defendant pleaded that the land was his frank-tenement, and they were at issue; and it was found by verdict that the said J. held the land of the Prior by copy of court roll at the will of the Prior; for that it was villein-land (niefeterre); and for that J. would not perform the services for the land, the Prior seized it,' &c.

[1] See above, Chap. IV. § 1.

[2] See Bacon's Abridgment, Court Baron. See, on the question of the historical reality of the distinction between the Court Baron and the Customary Court, Maitland's Introduction to Vol. II of the Selden Society's Publications, p. lxiv.

and the customs of the manor. Their powers vary according to the customs of different manors. In some there is a custom for the lord to enclose, or to grant portions of the waste to hold as copyhold, with the assent of the homage, which is usually expressed by a sworn jury of copyholders. The lord, or more commonly the steward, presides over the court; it is his duty to receive and record the presentments of the homage.

Gradually the interest of the copyholder came to be recognised by the regular tribunals. The great step seems to have been the recognition of the right of the tenant in villenage to maintain an action of trespass against his lord[1]. Thus incidentally and gradually the courts of common law came to recognise and enforce the customs which had grown up in different manors; for example, the custom of allowing the eldest son to succeed his father in his holding, or of admitting as tenant the person to whom the previous holder had sold his rights. As the character of the rights depended upon the customs proved to prevail in the different manors, the rights of copyholders varied accordingly. We find various customs as to the rules of descent, duration of interest, modes of alienation, extent of power of user and otherwise, prevailing in different manors, the customs of each manor constituting the law prevailing therein. Except where altered by special custom, copyholds, as to duration of interest, time of enjoyment, mode of descent, joint tenancy and tenancy in common, in general resemble freehold interests.

Copyhold tenure presents in the main the same characteristics at the present day. Land held by copyhold tenure is always parcel of, and included in, a manor. The lord of the

[1] It was held in a case reported in the Year Book, 7 Edward IV, p. 19, that this was the appropriate remedy, and not a writ of subpoena, i. e. an application to the jurisdiction of the chancellor. It would appear from this case and the passage in Littleton (sect. 77, see below), that at this time various attempts were made to secure legal protection for the interest of the copyholder.

CHAP. V. § 6. manor has the freehold, the copyholder holds 'at the will of the lord according to the custom of the manor.' The evidence of the nature and extent of his rights is to be looked for, primarily, in the court rolls of the manor. To these reference is made for ascertaining the various dues (fines, heriots [1], quit rents [2], and the like) which the copyholder must render to the lord. Here also is found the evidence of the mode of descent, mode of alienation, rights of the surviving husband or widow of the tenant [3], rights of the copyholder to common on the wastes of the manor [4], and so forth. For the lord being the freeholder, his rights of ownership remain untouched, except so far as they are limited by the copyholder's rights which have supervened. But inasmuch as the most important of the rights of ownership, the right of exclusion, is vested in the copyholder, a curious conflict sometimes arises. In some manors the copyholder may not cut timber or open mines, for these are rights belonging to the lord; but the lord cannot come upon the land to exercise them [5].

[1] See as to heriots, Western v. Bailey, Law Reports 1897, 1 Queen's Bench, p. 86.

[2] '*Quieti reditus* because thereby the tenant goes quit and free of all other services.' Blackstone, ii. 42.

[3] The right of the widow of the copyhold tenant is called *freebench*. It resembles in most points dower of freeholds, except that usually it only attaches to the copyholds which the husband has at the time of his decease. Williams on Real Property, p. 457.

[4] The rights of common enjoyed by the copyholders are similar to those annexed to freehold tenements, and differ only in the title on which they rest. While the freeholder can only claim common appurtenant to his freehold by virtue of a grant or by prescription, the copyholder's right rests on the custom of the manor. In order to establish such customary right of common, the copyholder must adduce evidence of the general practice prevailing in the manor, and is not limited to prove that the right has been attached by grant or prescription to his own particular tenement.

[5] There is a species of tenure prevailing, especially in the north of England, called customary freehold. It has been much discussed whether a customary tenant, who is said to hold by copy of court roll but not at the will of the lord, is properly a freeholder—whether, in other words, the freehold is in the lord, or in the tenant. The better opinion appears

The copyholder has the free right of alienation, but the mode of alienation preserves curiously the history of the interest. The copyholder first surrenders the land to the lord, and the lord then admits (and may be compelled to admit) the nominee of the copyholder upon payment of the accustomed fine, if any[1]. CHAP. V. § 6.

In some manors there is a custom to entail lands, in others no such custom exists. If there is no such custom, an estate of copyhold given to a man and the heirs of his body will create a fee simple conditional, and, like an estate in fee simple conditional in freeholds before De Donis, may be alienated on the happening of the condition[2]. Copyholds not being affected by the statute De Donis, the power of creating estates tail in copyhold lands must rest on a custom to entail. In like manner the power of barring the entail formerly depended on custom, and was effected either by a customary recovery or preconcerted forfeiture and regrant, or in some cases by a simple surrender[3]. Since the Act for the Abolition of Fines and Recoveries (3 and 4 Will. IV, c. 74) an estate tail in copyholds can be barred by a simple surrender with the concurrence of the protector where there is one.

The change in the position of the copyholder is thus summed up by Sir Edward Coke[4]: 'For, as I conjecture, in the Saxons' time, sure I am in the Normans' time, these

to be that, generally speaking, the freehold is in the lord, though it may be in some cases in the tenant; and whether this is so or not is a question of fact to be ascertained by evidence as to the nature and extent of the rights possessed by the tenant. See above, p. 155, n. 1, Williams on Real Property, pp. 428–430, and Pollock and Maitland, Hist. of Eng. Law, i. pp. 377–389.

1 Formerly the proper remedy when admittance was refused was by application to the chancellor. See Spence, Equitable Jurisdiction, i. p. 648. The usual course in modern times has been to obtain a mandamus from a court of law.

2 See above, Chap. IV. § 3, and Doe d. Spencer v. Clark, 5 Barnewall and Alderson's Reports, p. 458.

3 See Williams on Real Property, p. 435.

4 Compleat Copyholder, sects. 8, 9.

CHAP. V. § 6. copyholders were so far subject to the lord's will, that the lords upon the least occasion (sometimes without any colour of reason, only upon discontentment and malice, sometimes again upon some sudden fantastick humour, only to make evident to the world the height of their power and authority), would expel out of house and home their poor copyholders, leaving them helpless and remediless by any course of law, and driving them to sue by way of petition. But now copyholders stand upon a sure ground; now they weigh not their lord's displeasure, they shake not at every sudden blast of wind, they eat, drink, and sleep securely; only having a special care of the main chance, to perform carefully what duties and services soever their tenure doth exact, and custom doth require: then let lord frown, the copyholder cares not, knowing himself safe, and not within any danger. For if the lord's anger grow to expulsion, the law hath provided several weapons of remedy; for it is at his election either to sue a *subpoena*[1], or an action of trespass against the lord. Time has dealt very favourably with copyholders in divers respects.'

It might have been expected that so anomalous a class of rights as that which constitutes copyhold tenure would before the present time have been assimilated to the other forms of property in land. This however has not been done. Copyholds might at any period have been enfranchised (or converted into freeholds) by the conveyance of the freehold by the lord to the copyholder, or extinguished by surrender of the copyhold by the tenant to the lord. Various Acts[2] have in recent times created facilities for this process by providing means for the assessment and commutation of the lord's rights and otherwise; and at the present day either lord or copyholder may compel enfranchisement by taking the proper steps through the action of the Board of Agriculture[3].

[1] This is the technical expression for proceedings in Chancery. See Chap. VI.

[2] Now consolidated by 57 and 58 Vict. c. 46.

[3] 52 and 53 Vict. c. 30.

Where copyholds have not been enfranchised (and there is still a large though gradually decreasing amount of land subject to copyhold tenure) the rights are still regulated entirely by custom. And inasmuch as the characteristics of this form of property depend entirely upon custom, they must have prevailed from a time whereof the memory of man runneth not to the contrary. In practice this means that the customary usages should be shown to have existed as far back as available evidence goes, from which the legal inference arises that they have existed from time immemorial, that is, ever since the first year of Richard I [1].

LITTLETON, c. ix. sect. 73. (*Tenant by Copy.*) Tenant by copy of court roll is as if a man be seised of a manor within which manor there is a custom, which hath been used time out of mind of man, that certain tenants within the same manor have used to have lands and tenements, to hold to them and their heirs in fee simple, or fee tail, or for term of life, at the will of the lord according to the custom of the same manor.

Sect. 74. And such a tenant may not alien his land by deed, for then the lord may enter as into a thing forfeited unto him. But if he will alien his land to another, it behoveth him after the custom to surrender the tenements in court into the hands of the lord, to the use [2] of him that shall have the estate, in this form, or to this effect:—A. of B. cometh into this court and surrendereth in the same court a mease into the hands of the lord to the use of C. of D. and his heirs or the heirs issuing of his body, or for term of life, &c. And upon that cometh the aforesaid C. of D. and

[1] This date seems to have become fixed as giving a definite meaning to the expression 'time whereof' &c., in consequence of its having been fixed by the Statute of Westminster I (3 Edw. I, cap. 39) as the period of limitation in the case of a writ of right. Evidence therefore which shows that the custom alleged could not have prevailed in the time of Richard I has been held sufficient to show that the custom is not a legal one (see Bryant v. Foot, Law Reports, 3 Queen's Bench, 497). This principle however, notwithstanding the requirements of logic, must not be applied to copyholds; since, as has been seen, it cannot be maintained as an historical fact that copyhold estates existed at that time.

[2] It should be observed that a surrender to the *use* of the alienee has nothing to do with the uses of land discussed below in Chaps. VI. and VII.

CHAP. V. § 6. taketh of the lord in the same court the aforesaid mease [1], &c. To have and to hold to him and to his heirs, or to him and to his heirs issuing of his body, or to him for term of life at the lord's will, after the custom of the manor, to do and yield therefore the rents, services, and customs thereof before due and accustomed, and giveth the lord for a fine &c., and maketh unto the lord his fealty [2].

Sect. 75. And these tenants are called tenants by copy of court roll; because they have no other evidence concerning their tenements, but only the copies of court rolls.

Sect. 76. And such tenants shall neither implead, nor be impleaded for their tenements by the king's writ. But if they will implead others for their tenements, they shall have a plaint entered in the lord's court in this form or to this effect: A. of B. complains against C. of D. of a plea of land, viz. of one messuage, forty acres of land, four acres of meadow, &c., with the appurtenances, and makes protestation to follow this complaint in the nature of the king's writ of assize of mort d'ancestor at the common law, or of an assize of novel disseisin, or formedon in the descender at the common law, or in the nature of any other writ, &c.[3]

[1] And the lord is bound to admit the surrenderee.

[2] The law still requires surrender by the tenant and admittance by the lord or his steward either in or out of the Customary Court or assemblage of copyholders. No copyholder however need be present at a Customary Court. If the surrender be made out of court it was formerly necessary that the transaction should be mentioned or presented at the next court. This is no longer the case, an entry on the court rolls being sufficient. Admittance may now take place out of the manor and without holding a court (57 and 58 Vict. c. 46. s. 84). Formerly, when copyholds were devised, a previous surrender by the copyholder to the use of his will was necessary. This is so no longer (55 Geo. III, c. 192. s. 1); nor is it necessary, as formerly, that the devisee should bring the will into the Customary Court and claim admittance; now a delivery of a copy of the will to the lord or his steward is sufficient.

[3] The action of ejectment was as applicable to the recovery of the possession of copyholds as of freeholds, and took the place of the remedy here described. The same fictions were applied to the one as to the other—a fictitious lease to a fictitious plaintiff by the person who was the real claimant, fictitious entry and fictitious ouster by a fictitious wrongdoer, and permission to the real defendant to defend on the terms of his admitting the truth of the above fictions. See above, Chap. III. § 17, and Blackstone, iii. pp. 200–206.

Sect. 77. And although that some such tenants have an inheritance according to the custom of the manor, yet they have but an estate but at the will of the lord according to the course of the common law. For it is said, that if the lord do oust them, they have no other remedy but to sue to their lords by petition; for if they should have any other remedy they should not be said to be tenants at will of the lord according to the custom of the manor. But the lord cannot break the custom which is reasonable in these cases. CHAP. V. § 6.

But Brian, chief justice, said, that his opinion hath always been, and ever shall be, that if such tenant by custom paying his services be ejected by the lord he shall have an action of trespass against him[1]. And so was the opinion of Danby, chief justice, in 7 Ed. 4[2]. For he saith, that tenant by the custom is as well inheritor to have his land according to the custom as he which hath a freehold at the common law.

[1] Year Book, 21 Edw. IV, 80.

[2] Ibid., 7 Ed. IV, 18.

APPENDIX TO PART I

§ I. *Place of the Law of Real Property in the English System.*

(I)[1] In the preceding chapters the growth of the Common Law relating to land has been traced to the point at which it may be said that it has attained to its full development. The changes in the law of land which remain to be noticed are mainly due to the operation of Equity and Statute Law, working upon, and professing to leave unaltered to a great extent, the basis of the Common Law. At this point therefore it will be convenient to present in a tabular form a summary of the principal heads of arrangement or classification under which it appears that English private law may most appropriately be divided, with a view to show the place occupied in the English system by the law of land. By *private law* is meant that branch of the law which deals with the rights and duties[2] of persons considered in their private or individual capacity, as opposed to the rights and duties which are possessed by and incumbent on persons or bodies of persons considered as filling public, i. e. political or constitutional positions or offices, or which have relation to the whole political community, or to its magistrates and officers. Under *private law*, for example, are placed the class of rights and duties relating to property over things, or arising from § 1.

[1] The numerals relate to the various members of the classification shown below, Table I.

[2] For an analysis of the ideas involved in the words 'right' and 'duty' see Austin, Jurisprudence, especially lects. xii, xiv, xvi, xvii.

§ 1. contracts or civil injuries; under *public law* the rights and duties of the king, parliament, judges, and criminal law [1].

(2) The rights and their corresponding duties which form the matter of English private law are first to be divided into two great classes, differing from each other in respect of the persons on whom the duties, which correlate to the right, are incumbent. A person may have a right the essence of which consists in the fact that *all* other persons whatsoever are under a duty corresponding to the right; or he may have a right the essence of which consists in the fact that the corresponding duty is incumbent on some one or more *determinate* person or persons. An example of the first class of rights is the right of property which a person has in or over a piece of land or a herd of cattle. *All* other persons whatsoever are bound to abstain from acts injurious to his power of dealing as he pleases with his own. In other words, he may enjoy, use, and, if he pleases, if the thing is perishable, use up, the thing which is the subject [2] of the right, subject only to certain general limitations, and also to certain special limitations prevailing in particular cases, where his rights are limited by conflicting rights possessed

[1] Mr. Austin objects to the classification of law as public law and private law. See Austin, Jurisprudence, i. pp. 69, 70; ii. lect. xliv. The distinction however is convenient, is generally recognised by continental jurists, and appears to rest on a fundamental distinction in the nature of the rights constituting the two classes. See Professor Holland, Elements of Jurisprudence, pp. 78-82.

[2] I follow Austin in speaking of that over which the right is exercised, usually but not always a *thing* (i. e. a permanent external object, not a person, see lect. xiii), as the *subject* of the right. This seems more in accordance with the ordinary use of language than to apply the word 'subject,' as is usual with German jurists, to the *person* possessing the right. See Austin, ii. p. 736. Sometimes a person may be the *subject* of a right, e.g. the master has a right over the servant which entitles him to legal remedies against any one who wrongfully deprives him of the services of the servant; sometimes the right *in rem* cannot be said to have any subject properly so called at all, e.g. the right to personal security, or to a good name and reputation. See Austin, i. p. 48. Professor Holland styles the person possessing the right 'the person of inherence,' and that over which the right is exercised the 'object' of a right. Jurisprudence, p. 63.

by other persons over the same subject[1]. Rights of this class have received the name of rights *in rem*, an expression which means, *not* rights over things, but rights *available against all the world*, i.e. where a duty is incumbent on all persons whatsoever to abstain from acts injurious to the right[2]. § 1.

(3) Opposed to rights *in rem*, or rights available against all the world, is the other great class of rights, namely rights which are available only against some particular or determinate person or persons. These are called rights *in personam*, which is an abridged expression for rights *in personam certam* or *determinatam*. The principal, though not in our law the only, sources of these rights are *contracts* and *injuries*[3]. When one person has entered into a contract with another, as, for instance, when he is bound by a promise to pay money, to deliver goods on a certain day, not to carry on a trade within a given area, a legal tie is created as between these two parties, the one has a right against the other, the one

[1] See above, Chap. III. § 18.

[2] The expression *jus in rem*, or *jus in re*, is not found in the classical jurists. The expression '*in rem*' is however used by them in opposition to '*in personam*.' 'En effet l'expression *in rem* désigne communément dans la langue du droit romain, une disposition générale, sans acception de personne : et l'expression *in personam* désigne une disposition appliquée spécialement à une personne déterminée.' Ortolan, Justinien, iii. § 1956. See, as to actiones *in rem* and *in personam*, above, p. 71, n. 2. In our own law a judgment which is available in evidence against all the world is called a judgment *in rem*. See Austin, ii. p. 990 ; and on the general distinction between rights *in rem* and rights *in personam*, i. pp. 46, 380-389 ; Holland, Jurisprudence, p. 92 and Chaps. XI, XII.

[3] This points to the distinction between what are called by Austin *primary* and *secondary* or *sanctioning* rights (see i. p. 45, and ii. lect. xlv) ; and by Professor Holland *antecedent* and *remedial* (Jurisprudence, p. 93 and Chap. XIII). The latter are those which arise from injuries or violations of primary rights. The former class are those which do not arise from injuries, but are created by the appropriate mode or title provided by law. Using 'injury' in a large sense, the rights constituting the second class arise from violations of rights *in rem*, or *torts*, and also from violations of rights *in personam*, or breaches of contract or trust. It will be seen that all rights *in rem* and some rights *in personam* are primary, while all secondary rights are rights *in personam*.

§ 1. is under a duty towards the other, and no third party or stranger to the contract shares either in the right or in the duty. So when any right, whether *in rem* or *in personam*, is violated, a new right *in personam* arises. If my right of excluding all persons from my house or field is violated by a trespasser, a new right as against that individual trespasser accrues to me, namely a right to adopt the appropriate remedy provided by the law. So when a person is bound by contract to deliver goods on a future day, or not to carry on a trade within a given area, the breach of the contract gives rise in each case to new and distinct rights, rights to pursue the proper legal remedy against the wrong-doer. It will be seen at once that rights *in personam* comprise some of the most important branches of the law, but they are here mentioned only to be excluded, since it is clearly not under that head that the law relating to land will be found.

(4) The law dealing with rights *in rem* may be called—using the term 'property' in a large sense—the law of property, or the law dealing with property-rights. The word 'property' is used in so many senses [1] as to be nearly useless for juristic purposes. One of its best known applications is where it is applied to any collection of rights *in rem*, as distinct from rights *in personam*. The Roman lawyers marked the difference between the two branches of law by the words *dominium* and *obligationes*. If the word 'property' were not so ambiguous, one might venture to suggest that the 'law of property,' or 'of property-rights,' should be substituted for the obscure expression *rights in rem*.

(5) Rights *in rem* may be subdivided into two great classes in respect of their *subjects*. By the *subject* of a right is meant the thing, if any, over which the right is exercised [2]. My house, horse, or watch is the subject of my right of property. There are however some rights *in rem* which

[1] See the principal of these enumerated, Austin, ii. pp. 817–820.

[2] See above, p. 300, n. 2.

cannot properly be said to have any subjects, or to be exercised over any definite things. These will be noticed presently. § 1.

(6) The great distinction next to be mentioned between two classes of rights *in rem*, differing in respect of their subjects, is peculiar to English law and the systems derived from it. In Roman law and the systems to which it has given rise there is no such fundamental distinction between the law relating to land and the law relating to things movable, as to necessitate a separate treatment for each branch. It is otherwise in English law, and the outline of its history which has been given in the preceding chapters will account for this characteristic of our system.

The distinction therefore under consideration is between rights *in rem*, which have for their subject things real, that is to say, things immovable—in other words, land and all that is permanently affixed thereto[1]; and rights *in rem*, which have for their subject things personal or movable[2]. Speaking generally, though not with entire accuracy, the former class of rights constitutes the matter of the law of 'real property,' the latter the matter of the law of 'personal property.' There is however one important class of rights over land, as has already been seen, which belongs to the category of personal property[3].

(7) There is further a miscellaneous class of rights *in rem* which cannot be said to be rights over land, or indeed to have any subjects at all, but which possess some characteristics common to rights over land[4]. For instance, such of them as are descendible, devolve not, as is the case with

[1] Whether or not a thing can be said to be permanently affixed to land is a frequent subject of litigation, and there is a multitude of cases deciding in particular instances whether things are or are not 'fixtures,' and whether they are therefore to be treated as personal or as real property. See the term 'fixtures' explained in the case of Hallen v. Runder, 1 Crompton Meeson and Roscoe's Reports, p. 276.

[2] See Blackstone, ii. ch. 2.

[3] See above, Chap. V. § 1.

[4] See Blackstone, ii. ch. 3; and see Coke's note on the word 'tenements' in the Stat. West. II, Coke upon Littleton, 19 b; above, p. 226, n. 3.

§ 1. personal property, to executors or administrators (see 8), but to heirs. These rights therefore are usually treated along with rights over land. Amongst the principal of this class of rights are *advowsons*—*advocationes*, or the right of presentation to an ecclesiastical benefice[1]; and *franchises*—where 'a royal privilege or branch of the king's prerogative is subsisting in the hands of a subject[2].' For example, the rights to have 'waifs, wrecks, estrays, treasure-trove, royal fish, forfeitures, and deodands[3]' are franchises, which must rest on royal grant, or prescription which presupposes a grant. To this class too belong *dignities*, such as a peerage, which is the subject of grant by patent conferring the title with limitations similar to the limitations in an ordinary conveyance of land. Peerages may also be created by writ or royal summons to attend the house of peers; this, if acted upon, invests the person summoned with a dignity descendible to his heirs[4]. Another instance of the class of rights in question is found in *offices* which are now seldom hereditary. An office tenable for life, such as a college fellowship, is considered a freehold interest. The class of rights under consideration is by Blackstone and others included under the class of *incorporeal hereditaments*, together with another class which may be more conveniently referred to a different head. I have therefore marked them as *Incorporeal hereditaments A*.

(8) Rights over things movable, and rights which, though not over things movable or indeed over things at all, are yet classed with such rights, inasmuch as they are rights *in rem*[5], and, where they are descendible, devolve on executors or administrators (for example, patent rights, copyrights), lie beyond the scope of the present treatise.

(9) Having now pointed out briefly the place in the English system occupied by rights *in rem*, we pass to the im-

[1] See above, p. 215, n. 3. [2] See Blackstone, ii. p. 37.

[3] See for the explanation of these terms, and the royal prerogative in regard to them, Blackstone, i. ch. 8.

[4] See Blackstone, i. p. 400. [5] See Austin, i. p. 400.

mediate subject of the present treatise. At the head of his classification of rights over land Blackstone places the distinction between *corporeal* and *incorporeal hereditaments*[1]. Unsatisfactory as this nomenclature is, it points to a fundamental distinction between two classes of rights *in rem* which it is convenient to take at the outset of a systematic discussion of the law of land. The distinction is between rights over land which entitle their possessor to speak of the thing as his own, and rights over land which is in ordinary language the property of another. It will be sufficient to style the former *rights of ownership*, the latter *rights in alieno solo*. § 1.

The word 'ownership' is here used as applicable to that class of rights which entitle the person having them to speak of the subject of the rights as his own. The great characteristic of these rights, according to Mr. Austin, is that the person having them may put the thing which is the subject of the right to uses which, though not unlimited (for no rights of user are wholly unlimited), are yet indefinite[2]. Generally speaking, and within limitations more or less wide, tenant in fee, tenant for life, tenant for years[3] can use the thing which is the subject of the right as he pleases—can do what he will with his own.

(10) Opposite to these rights of indefinite user is the class of rights the very essence of which consists in the fact that the person having the right can only put the land which

[1] Book ii. ch. 2. It should be remembered that Blackstone in his classification of rights followed to a great extent the masterly 'Analysis of the Law' of Sir Matthew Hale.

[2] See Austin, lect. xlvii, xlviii; 'For the present I mean by property or dominion every right in and over a thing, which is indefinite in user, as distinguished from *servitus*.' ii. p. 821; and see Holland, Jurisprudence, p. 132.

[3] I do not forget that in common parlance we distinguish between tenant for years and the freeholder by saying that the former has the possession or occupation of the land, and that the latter only is the owner. But it is impossible to attempt to invest any word in common use with a technical meaning without running counter in some instances to popular usage. At all events a tenant-farmer talks of 'my farm' and has the exclusive right of possession.

§ 1. is the subject of it to uses of a strictly defined and limited character[1]. A person who has a right of way over his neighbour's land can only use the land for the purpose of crossing it on foot or with horses or cattle, according to the nature of the right, which depends on the terms of the original grant by which it has been created, or on the extent to which the user has, as a matter of fact, been enjoyed for the time required by law to create the right. The rights which the creditor has under certain circumstances over his debtor's land may also be referred to the class of rights *in alieno solo.*

(11) These rights *in alieno solo* comprise a large portion of the rights called by Blackstone *incorporeal hereditaments*[2]. In fact the classes of rights *in alieno solo* styled *easements*

[1] See Austin, lect. xlix; Holland, Jurisprudence, pp. 146–148.

[2] The division of hereditaments into corporeal and incorporeal, though deeply rooted in our legal phraseology, is most unfortunate and misleading. The confusion is inherited from the Roman lawyers (see Justinian, Inst. ii. tit. 2), but has been made worse confounded by our own authorities. The Romans, misled by the double sense of *res*, unhappily distinguished *res corporales* and *res incorporales*, the former being things 'quae tangi possunt, veluti aurum, vestis,' the latter mere rights, 'quae in jure consistunt.' It is obvious that this is mere confusion, the two ideas not being *in pari materia*, or capable of being brought under one class, or of forming opposite members of a division. Following the Romans, our lawyers distinguished between hereditaments as meaning the actual corporeal land itself, and another kind of hereditaments as not being the land itself but 'the rights annexed to or issuing out of the land.' A moment's reflection is sufficient to show that the distinction is untenable. The lawyer has nothing whatever to do with the material corporeal land, except so far as it is the subject of rights. It is the distinction between different classes of rights, and not between land on the one side and rights on the other, that he is concerned with. In such phrases as 'the land descends to the heir,' what is meant is, not that something happens to the land itself, but that a particular class of the ancestor's rights in relation to the land descends to the heir. The names 'corporeal and incorporeal' are most unfortunate, because if by 'corporeal' is meant 'relating to land,' then a large class of incorporeal hereditaments are also entitled to the name; if by 'incorporeal' is meant that they are mere rights, then all hereditaments are incorporeal, because the lawyer is only concerned with different classes of rights. In reality however it appears that the names point to different classes of rights, as indicated in the Table. See Austin, ii. pp. 707, 708.

and *profits*, marked *Incorporeal hereditaments B*, together with those marked in the Table as *Incorporeal hereditaments A*, seem to constitute the class of rights which Blackstone designates by that name. § 1.

(12) Taking incorporeal hereditaments in the narrower sense, as equivalent to the classes of rights *in alieno solo* named *easements* and *profits*, the principal characteristics of this class of rights have already been discussed [1]. The principal rights recognised by the law as easements properly so called are rights of *way*, i. e. of going over the land of another on foot, on horseback, or with carriages or cattle, in a certain line, or for certain purposes; *water-courses*, for example, where a person has the right to divert a flow of water to which, except for this special right, the owner of the *praedium serviens* would be entitled; the right to discharge water or other matter upon a neighbour's house or land [2]; the right to restrain a use of land which obstructs the access of light and air to an 'ancient' window.

(13) Of profits, the principal are *rights of common* of various kinds, which have already been sufficiently dealt with [3]; *rents* (the right to a rent issuing out of the land, unconnected with the relation of landlord and tenant) may be classed under the same head [4]; as also might *tithes* have been before the Act for their commutation (6 and 7 Will. IV, c. 71).

(14) It appears to be more accurate to class *creditors' rights* under the head of rights *in alieno solo*; though in the earlier stages of our law, as has been seen above, the tendency in the case of mortgages was to make the right of the creditor after default absolute. As legal ideas progress and become more refined, the notion that the land is only a security for the debt comes into prominence, and regulates the real rights of the

[1] See above, Chap. III. § 18.

[2] 'Ut stillicidium vel flumen recipiat quis in aedes suas vel in aream, vel non recipiat.' Just. Inst. ii. tit. iii. § 1.

[3] See above, Chap. III. § 18 (2).

[4] As to rents, see above, p. 238, n. 2.

TABLE I

(N.B. The figures relate to the preceding paragraphs.)

THE LAW OF ENGLAND DEALING WITH PRIVATE RIGHTS AND THEIR CORRESPONDING DUTIES (1).

- Private Rights.
  - Rights IN REM (2).
    i.e. Rights available against all the world—
    Property Rights (4)—
    divided in respect of their subjects (5) into
    - Rights over Things *Real = Immovable* (6).
      - Rights of *Ownership* (*Corporeal Hereditaments*) (9).
        - Descendible to heirs (Subjects of Tenure) (15).
          - Freeholds (17).
          - Copyholds (18).
        - To Executors or Administrators, Leasehold Interests or *Chattels real* (16).
      - Rights *in alieno solo* (10).
        - *Incorporeal Hereditaments B* (11).
          - *Easements* (12).
          - *Profits* (13).
        - Creditors' Rights (14). *Mortgages*, *Elegit*, &c.
    - Not over Things *Real* (7), (but treated along with them). *Incorporeal Hereditaments A.* (*Advowsons*, *Franchises*, *Dignities*, *Offices*, &c.).
    - Over Things *Personal* = *Movable* (8).
    - Not over Things *Personal* (8), but treated along with them, (e.g. *Patents*, *Copyrights*).
  - Rights IN PERSONAM (3).
    i.e. Rights available against some particular or determinate person or persons.

parties, and the creditor is reduced to his true position of having simply a right *in alieno solo*[1]. § 2.

(15)–(18) The distinctions resting upon the mode of devolution of rights over land, or between land the subject of tenure properly so called (15) and chattels real[2] (16), the historical distinction between freehold (17) and copyhold (18)[3], and between the various kinds of freeholds resting on the differences in the services due from the tenant to his lord[4], have been sufficiently explained in the preceding pages.

§ 2. *Rights over Things Real classified in respect of their duration.*

The conception of an 'estate' in lands is a peculiar characteristic of English law. It is regarded, as has been seen, as an interest falling short of complete ownership, but capable of differences in extent or duration. Thus where an interest is given to *A* for life, and after his death to *B* for life, and after his death to *C* in fee, all these interests are regarded as *estates*, varying in duration or extent, and in the time of their coming into possession or enjoyment[5]. The interest or right passes at once to the successive grantees. The grantor is regarded, not as parting with the whole ownership to *A*, with a proviso that after *A*'s death it is to go to *B*, and after *B*'s death to *C*, but as carving out of his estate two smaller interests or estates, and then as having still the fee simple or inheritance to give away, the grant of which exhausts all the interest in the lands which he has to bestow, which yet does not amount to the complete ownership of the land[6]. Thus the fee simple is regarded as the largest estate—the nearest approach to absolute ownership—which the law recognises; an estate tail,

[1] See above, Chap. V. § 5.
[2] See above, Chap. III. § 17, and Chap. V. § 1.
[3] See above, Chap. III. § 13, and Chap. V. § 6.
[4] See above, pp. 45–49.
[5] See below, Table III.
[6] See above, p. 60, and Austin's Jurisprudence, ii. p. 866.

TABLE II

RIGHTS OVER THINGS REAL CLASSIFIED IN RESPECT OF THEIR DURATION.

- Where the interest devolves upon successors (heirs) in infinitum; i. e. where there is no assignable event, certain to happen, upon which the rights will come to an end. FREEHOLD ESTATES OF INHERITANCE
  - Estates descendible to heirs general (collateral as well as lineal). *Estates in Fee Simple*[1].
  - Estates descendible only to lineal descendants. *Estates Tail*[2]
    - (*a*) General, (*b*) Male,
    - Special. Female.
- Where the interest does not devolve &c.; i. e. where there is some assignable event &c.
  - Where the time of the happening of the event is uncertain. FREEHOLD ESTATES NOT OF INHERITANCE
    - Created by voluntary alienation
      - *Estates for life*[3].
      - Estates *pur autre vie*, or granted to last during the life of another[4].
    - Not created by voluntary alienation
      - *Dower*[5].
      - *Curtesy*[6].
  - Where the time of the happening of the event is certain, or can be made certain from its beginning. ESTATES LESS THAN FREEHOLD, *Leasehold Estates*, (*Chattels real*), Herein of Estates *at Will*, *From year to year*, *On sufferance*[7].

[1] Above, pp. 60, 95. [2] Chap. IV. § 3, V. § 2. [3] Above, p. 163. [4] Above, p. 164. [5] Chap. III. § 4. [6] Chap. III. § 16. [7] Chap. V. § 1.

an estate for life, an estate for years are regarded as smaller or shorter interests, which cannot exist without the fee simple at the same time residing in some person other than him who has the smaller or 'particular' estate. § 3.

The classification given in Table II is in effect that of Blackstone in his chapters on Freehold Estates of Inheritance, Freeholds not of Inheritance, and Estates less than Freehold[1]. It is sufficient to refer in the foot-notes to the Table to the passages in the preceding chapters where the various rights have been explained. It should be observed that all the interests in question which are capable of being created by grant may be conditional, i. e. may either actually come to an end, or be liable to be put an end to by the grantor, on the happening of some (specified but uncertain) event[2].

§ 3. *Rights over Things Real classified in respect of the time of their enjoyment.*

Table III shows the classification of rights given by Blackstone in his chapter on 'Estates in Possession, Remainder, and Reversion[3].' In anticipation of explanations which will be given in Chapters VI, VII, and VIII, I have thought it convenient to oppose to the class of rights in question arising at common law, the class of rights of future enjoyment which do not arise at common law, the nature of which it would be at present premature to discuss. A glance at the Table will show the strange complication which prevails in this branch of English law, owing partly to historical causes, partly to the extreme technicality of lawyers whose minds were deeply imbued with the realist philosophy.

[1] Book ii. chaps. vii, viii, ix.

[2] See Blackstone, book ii. ch. x, and above, p. 264.

[3] Book ii. ch. xi. See also Austin's Jurisprudence, lect. liii, and above, Chap. V. § 3.

TABLE III

RIGHTS OVER THINGS REAL CLASSIFIED IN RESPECT OF THE TIME OF THEIR ENJOYMENT.

- Present rights of present enjoyment.
- Present rights of future enjoyment.
  - Rights arising at Common Law
    - Resulting from a grant or other alienation of a particular estate. *Reversions*[1].
    - Created expressly by grant or other alienation
      - Necessarily limited on (i. e. expressed to take effect in enjoyment immediately on the determination of) a particular estate. *Remainders*[2].
        - Where the enjoyment of the estate awaits only the end of the particular estate[3]. *Vested remainders.*
        - Where the enjoyment of the estate awaits not only the end of the particular estate but also the happening of some uncertain event, or the right is to vest in some person unborn or unascertained at the time of the creation of the interest[4]. *Contingent remainders.*
      - Not necessarily limited on a particular estate. *Leasehold interests in futuro.*
  - Rights not arising at Common Law
    - Created by instrument operating under Statute of Uses[5].
      - Rights similar to those capable of arising at Common Law. *Vested and Contingent Remainders and Leasehold interests in futuro created under Statute of Uses.*
      - Rights incapable of arising at Common Law.
        - Freeholds in futuro. *Springing uses.*
        - Freeholds arising in derogation of Freeholds. *Shifting uses.*
    - In Equity[6]. (Follow same rules as last class.)
    - By Will[7]. *Executory Devises.* (Follow same rules.)

[1] See above, Chap. V. § 3 (1). [2] Chap. V. § 3 (2). [3] See above, p. 263. [4] See above, p. 264. [5] See below, Chap. VII. § 2. [6] See below, Chap. VII. § 4. [7] See below, Chap. VIII.

PART II

THE MODERN LAW OF REAL PROPERTY

CHAPTER VI

ORIGIN AND EARLY HISTORY OF USES OR EQUITABLE INTERESTS IN LAND

It is not easy to discover at what time the practice first arose of attaching to the alienation of land a trust or confidence that the alienee should hold the lands to the *use* of the donor, or of some third person named by him. When 'uses' are first noticed in the records of our law they appear as the result of established and well-known practice [1]. Yet it was long before the obligation of a 'use, trust, or confidence' was recognised by any tribunal. It is true that the ecclesiastical courts at one time enforced conscientious obligations, entertaining suits *de fidei laesione*, but this jurisdiction is said to have been taken away from them in cases arising between laymen as to civil matters in the reign of Henry III [2]. If therefore a feoffment was made to *A to the use* of *B*, or, in other words, in trust and confidence that *A* would permit *B* to enter and occupy, or receive the fruits and profits of the lands, there were no *legal* means of compelling *A* to carry out this trust. It was simply a conscientious obligation. No doubt such obligations were enforced by the authority of the confessor, and regarded with special favour by the Church. CH. VI.

[1] See as to the origin of Uses, Pollock and Maitland, Hist. of Engl. Law, ii. pp. 228 and 231 seq.

[2] Spence's Equitable Jurisdiction, i. p. 118.

CH. VI. There seems no reason to question the commonplace of the text-books, that the practice of giving lands by way of use or trust was largely resorted to in order to enable ecclesiastical corporations to evade the Statutes of Mortmain [1].

Various conjectures have been made as to the origin of the recognition of the binding character of a trust, confidence, or use thus created. The clergy from early times recognised breach of faith as a matter of which the ecclesiastical courts would take cognizance. It is probable that some of the doctrines of Roman law greatly aided towards the establishment of the system of uses of land as a definite interest distinct from the legal estate. A strong analogy in some points to the system of uses is presented by the Roman distinction between legal and beneficial ownership [2]. It was possible under the Roman system, before the changes introduced by Justinian, for a thing to have two owners. There was the legal owner, the dominus *ex jure civili*, or *ex jure Quiritium*, who was the complete owner in the view of the older law—who alone could dispose of or claim the thing by the processes recognised by the older law. He might however in certain cases pass to another the beneficial ownership without affecting his own legal rights in the view of the older law. If, for instance, the owner of a *res mancipi*—for example, a slave—sold the slave to another, and to the completion of the transaction there was alone wanting the appropriate ceremony of *mancipatio*—delivery accompanied by certain forms—the legal title remained unaffected, what passed to the

[1] See Blackstone, ii. 271.

[2] Compare Gaius, Comm. ii. 40: 'Sequitur ut admoneamus apud peregrinos quidem unum esse dominium, ita aut dominus quisque est, aut dominus non intellegitur. Quo jure etiam populus Romanus olim utebatur: aut enim ex jure Quiritium unusquisque dominus erat, aut non intellegebatur dominus: sed postea divisionem accepit dominium, ut alius possit esse ex jure Quiritium dominus, alius in bonis habere. Nam si tibi rem mancipi neque mancipavero, neque in jure cessero' (the appropriate modes of conveyance under the older law), 'sed tantum tradidero, in bonis quidem tuis ea res efficitur, ex jure Quiritium vero mea permanebit,' etc.

purchaser was simply the beneficial, or, as it was barbarously called by the commentators, *bonitarian* ownership[1]; in virtue of which the purchaser could in effect, by calling in aid the later Praetorian jurisdiction, assert and exercise practically all the rights of the real owner, only he could not employ the older and more cumbrous procedure of the *jus civile*.

This analogy however does not carry us further than the separation of the idea of legal ownership, or ownership at the common law, from beneficial ownership, that is ownership unrecognised by the older law, but the advantages of which can practically be asserted by calling in aid another power distinct from that of the magistrate enforcing the older law. The distinction between the two kinds of ownership was abolished by Justinian[2].

Another analogy was found in the Roman idea of *ususfructus*[3], or the right to the temporary enjoyment of a thing, as distinct from the ownership of, or absolute property in it. This analogy however fails at several points. There is no binding relation between the owner and the usufructuary, by which the former is compelled to hold to the use of the latter. The relation between the two rather resembles that of a tenant for life, or other limited owner, and the reversioner in fee.

Another analogy is found in the doctrines relating to *fidei-commissa*[4]. The legal restrictions on successions and legacies led in the later period of the Republic to the practice of a testator instituting an heir, and at the same time requesting him to dispose of the whole or a portion of the property in a particular way, for example to hand over the inheritance or a legacy to a person who was not a Roman citizen, and therefore by the strict rule of the

[1] The classical expression for this beneficial ownership was 'in bonis habere' (see last note). Pothier, Dig. xli. tit. 1. ad init., distinguishes between 'dominium bonitarium' and 'in bonis habere.'

[2] Cod. lib. vii. tit. 25, 'De nudo jure Quiritium tollendo.'

[3] See Just. Inst. ii. tit. 4.

[4] Ib. tit. 23.

CH. VI. *jus civile* incapable of taking it directly. Till the time of Augustus there appears to have been no legal obligation on the person to whom this trust was committed. Justinian says of these *fidei-commissa*, as they were called, '*Nullo vinculo juris, sed tantum pudore eorum qui rogabantur, continebantur* [1].' Afterwards the obligation came to be recognised as one capable of being enforced in the proper court [2], and a Praetor fidei-commissarius was appointed to administer this branch of jurisdiction. At Rome 'trusts' could only be created by will, and under the later law the distinction for all practical purposes between *fidei-commissa* and legacies disappeared.

Whatever may be the true account of the origin of the recognition of uses, it appears that the practice of conveying lands to uses prevailed to a great extent as early as the reign of Edward III [3]. It seems to have been not unusual for lay persons to make fraudulent feoffments of their lands to evade their creditors. The result was that the creditor could not have execution for his debt, the land being in the hands not of the debtor but of his feoffee. The transaction being a collusive one, the debtor would receive from his feoffee the profits of the lands without the burdens attaching to legal ownership. This was restrained by the statute 50 Edward III, c. 6 [4]. In the reign of Richard II a similar practice seems to

[1] Inst. l. c. pr.

[2] 'Augustus . . . jussit consulibus auctoritatem suam interponere. Quod . . . paulatim conversum est in assiduam jurisdictionem,' etc. Ib. 1.

[3] The term 'ad opus' is found in a Curia Regis Roll of 6 Hen. III, and the earliest use of the French equivalent 'oeps' appears to be in the statute 7 Richard II, c. 12:—'Et outre ceo est auxint assentuz qe si ascun alien eit purchacez ou desore purchase ascun benefice de seinte esglise, dignite, ou autre, et en propre persone preigne possession dicelle, ou loccupie de fait deinz mesme le Roialme, soit il *a son oeps* propre ou *al oeps dautri*,' etc. 'And moreover it is assented, that if any alien have purchased, or from henceforth shall purchase any benefice of Holy Church, dignity, or other thing, and in his proper person take possession of the same, or occupy it himself within the realm, *whether it be to his own proper use, or to the use of another*,' etc. Revised Statutes, second edition, p. 147.

[4] 'Item pur ceo qe diverses gentz inheritez des diverses tenementz, creanceantz diverses biens en monoie ou en marchandise des plusours gentz de Roialme, *donnent lour tenementz et chateux a lour amys par collusion*

have been adopted in order to protect disseisors and other wrongdoers from the claims of the rightful owners of the land[1]. In the same reign the practice of evading the Statutes of Mortmain by giving lands to a feoffee to hold to the use of a religious corporation was effectually restrained by 15 Richard II, c. 5, given below. If therefore the practice of conveying lands to uses originated in the desire of the clergy to evade the Statutes of Mortmain, the device received a final check by this enactment. It seems, however, that the advantages of being the beneficial instead of the legal owner of lands were appreciated to such a degree that the practice, although it ceased to fulfil its original purpose, became more and more widely spread.

The use of lands came to be regarded as an interest wholly distinct from the legal estate, and free from all the burdens which attached to the tenancy at common law. If a person

davoir ent les profitz a leur volente, et puis senfuent a la fraunchise de Westminster ou Seint Martyn le Grant en Loundres ou autres tielx places privilegeez, et illoeques vivent long temps a grant countenance dautry biens et des profitz des ditz tenementz et chateux, tanqe les ditz creditours serront molt leez de prender une petite parcelle de lour dette et relesser le remanant, ordeigne est et assentuz qe si purra estre trovez qe tielx douns soient issint faitz par collusion qe les ditz creditours eient execution des ditz tenementz et chateux auxi avant come nul tiel doun nent euste este faite.' 'Because that divers people possessed by inheritance of divers tenements, borrowing divers goods in money or in merchandize of divers people of this realm, do give their tenements and chattels to their friends, by collusion thereof to have the profits at their will, and after do flee to the franchise of Westminster, of St. Martin le Grand of London, or such other privileged places, and there do live a great time with a high countenance of another man's goods and of the profits of the said tenements and chattels, till the said creditors shall be bound to take a small parcel of their debt, and release the remnant; it is ordained and assented, that if it be found such gifts be so made by collusion, that the said creditors shall have execution of the said tenements and chattels, as if no such gift had been made.' Statutes of the Realm, p. 398. See 2 Richard II, stat. 2. c. 3.

[1] The statute 1 Richard II, c. 9, is directed against the practice of persons wrongfully in possession of land, by disseisin or otherwise, making feoffments of such lands to persons so powerful that the rightful claimants of the land, 'for great menace that is made to them, cannot nor dare not make their pursuits.' In this case the 'great man' would hold the lands to the *use* of the wrongdoer.

CH. VI. who had only the *use* of lands (the legal title being vested in another person who was *seised to his use*), committed treason or felony, the lands were not subject to escheat or forfeiture; he who had the use owed no dues or service to the lord; his creditor could not take the lands in execution for debt[1]; nor could a rival claimant bring an action against him without the risk of the legal owner intervening and setting up his own legal title. On the other hand, he who had the *use* would have the full enjoyment of the lands, the feoffee to the use would allow him to be in possession and to reap the profits, and he could dispose of and sell his interest without the necessity of the cumbrous ceremony of livery of seisin, or of any formal conveyance. Further, he could create interests wholly unknown to the common law, and could even direct the devolution of the interest by his will. It is true that neither the interest of *cestui que use*, as the beneficiary was called[2], nor that of his alienee was protected or recognised by law; but in this case, as so often in the history of our law, usage laid the foundation of what afterwards became legal rights, and uses of land protected only by the obligations of conscience and good faith, of which the clergy were the guardians, were, it is said, by the time of Henry V the rule rather than the exception throughout the country[3].

Thus a new species of interest in lands grew up differing wholly from any right recognised by the common law. What then was the foundation of the right of a person having a use, or, in other words, what was the nature of the obligation incumbent upon the person holding to the use?

At first, so far as is known, it appears to have rested simply on moral or religious obligation. There was no court or public functionary of any kind whereby the use would be

[1] Except in cases within 50 Edward III, c. 6.

[2] If *A*, tenant in fee simple, makes a feoffment to *B* and his heirs to the use of *C* and his heirs, *B* is called *feoffee to uses*, *C cestui que use*. These names will in future be employed to denote respectively the bare legal owner and the beneficiary.

[3] See Spence, Equitable Jurisdiction, i. p. 441, note c.

protected. The only external authority by which the duty was enforced was that of the confessor. The common law courts knew nothing of *cestui que use,* and the ecclesiastical courts were powerless to help him. It so happened that, at the very time at which the practice of conveying land to uses was becoming prevalent, a new jurisdiction was rising into importance, administering justice outside the pale of the common law. This was the jurisdiction of the Chancellor.

The ordinary functions of the Chancellor were of a very ancient date. As the keeper of the Great Seal, all grants and letters patent passed under his supervision. All original writs, by which actions at law were commenced, were issued out of Chancery and sealed with the royal seal. But in issuing these writs the functions of the Chancellor were simply ministerial. He had no judicial authority. He could frame no new writ to meet a new state of circumstances. He was a prominent member of the Council, though subordinate to the great Justiciar so long as that office existed[1]. As time went on the position of the Chancellor increased in importance[2]. His close relations with the King armed him with a large measure of the royal power. His position as a great ecclesiastic made him solicitous for the interests of the Church, and familiar with the Canon and Civil Law.

In early times when the various functions of the different departments of state were ill-defined, it was the common practice for persons aggrieved, especially when for any reason they could not avail themselves of the ordinary process of law, to present petitions to the Council or to the King for redress. If a poor man was oppressed by one who, as often happened, was powerful enough to set the ordinary process of law at defiance, the remedy was to be sought from the King or the Council, who alone were strong enough to do right. Or again, if a case arose in which no writ lay, and consequently in which there was no remedy to be had at common

[1] See Dialogus de Scaccario, I. v, Stubbs, Select Charters, 171, 177.

[2] See Spence, Equitable Jurisdiction, i. pp. 117, 334, 355.

CH. VI. law, recourse could be had to the King or Council as the supreme depositaries of power. It appears that in the reign of Edward I it became usual for the King to refer such of these petitions as were addressed directly to him to the Chancellor[1]. In the twenty-second year of Edward III a writ or ordinance was issued directing that for the future all such matters as were of grace should be referred to the Chancellor or to the Keeper of the Privy Seal[2]. Hence the practice arose of presenting petitions directly to the Chancellor, upon which the Chancellor made decrees, giving or withholding redress according to principles which were certainly not always those of the common law.

This practice, which dates from the end of the reign of Edward III, or the beginning of that of Richard II, may be taken to be the cause of the rise of the judicial functions of the Chancellor[3]. Upon petitions thus presented, the Chancellor would, if he thought fit, issue a writ, called a writ of *subpoena*, in the name of the King, commanding the person complained of to appear and answer the matter alleged against him and abide by the order of the court. This was called the writ of *subpoena* from the usual addition of the words *sub poena centum librarum*. This penalty however was not commonly exacted, but from the earliest times it seems to have been the practice to enforce the decrees of the Chancellor by *attachment*, that is, by arrest and imprisonment for contempt of court[4]. Thus the Chancellor, unlike the courts of common law, had power to order things to be done, to decree that a contract should be performed, that property should be given up, that a thing creating a nuisance should be removed. From the writ above mentioned, the common expression in the older law books for a proceeding in Chancery is a 'writ of subpoena.'

The materials on which our knowledge of the early history

[1] See Spence, Equitable Jurisdiction, i. p. 335. [2] Ib. p. 337.

[3] See Select Cases in Chancery (Selden Society), pp. xvi. seq.

[4] See Spence, Equitable Jurisdiction, i. pp. 338, 369.

of the jurisdiction of the Chancellor is based are very scanty. But very few cases decided by the Chancellor found their way into the Year Books[1]. Amongst the public records are some petitions to the King referred to the Chancellor in the reign of Edward I[2]. There have been also published three volumes of Calendars of Proceedings in Chancery in the time of Queen Elizabeth, to which are prefixed earlier Petitions to the Chancellor, some of which date from the reign of Richard II. And a further volume of Select Cases in Chancery between the years 1364 and 1471 has been recently published by the Selden Society. The grounds upon which redress was sought are of a very miscellaneous character. The burden of all the petitions is that a grievance has been sustained, for which, for one reason or another, no remedy can be had at the common law. CH. VI.

Probably the most usual ground on which complaints to the Chancellor were based was that the person whose acts were complained of was too powerful to be touched by the common law. Cases of this kind at first formed the chief bulk of the Chancellor's work, but by the end of the fifteenth century they had passed from his jurisdiction to that of the Council. But there was another and an increasing ground for the interference of the Chancellor. This was the inadequacy of the common law to meet the wants of an advancing community. Practices had become common giving rise to what were considered to be rights and duties, upon the faith of which men acted, but which were wholly unrecognised by the common law. An attempt had been made by the statute of 13 Edward I, c. 24, to adapt the procedure of the common law to new cases as they arose. By that statute it was provided that 'whensoever from henceforth it shall fortune in the Chancery that in one

[1] The case given below from the Year Book of 18 Edward IV appears to have been decided by the Chancellor sitting alone, that in 7 Edward IV to have been before the Chancellor and the Judges of the Common Pleas and King's Bench.

[2] See Lord Campbell, Lives of the Chancellors, vol. i. p. 186.

case a writ is found, and in like case falling under like law and requiring like remedy is found none, the clerks of the Chancery shall agree in making the writ, or the plaintiffs may adjourn it until the next Parliament, and let the cases be written in which they cannot agree, and let them refer themselves until the next Parliament, [and] by consent of men learned in the law a writ shall be made, lest it might happen after that the Court should long time fail to minister justice unto complainants.' This statute did not immediately produce any great effect. The new writs, though framed in the Chancery, were adjudicated upon by the common law judges, who were tied and bound by precedent, and refused to recognise rights which had never been recognised before.

There was therefore abundant room for a new tribunal. Conspicuous among the practices which the common law refused to recognise, but which still were commonly observed, was that of giving lands to be held to uses. Here therefore was a field for the jurisdiction of the Chancellor. There are however but few traces of the early jurisdiction of the Court of Chancery affecting uses of lands. Nevertheless it is easy to see a combination of influences which brought the practice under the protection of the Chancellor. The obligation being one morally binding, resting on good conscience and good faith, would fall within his cognizance as an ecclesiastic. His clerical character, habituating him to search into men's consciences and motives, rendered his tribunal far fitter than a jury for ascertaining the intention accompanying the outward act of transferring lands[1]. The practice before the statute of Richard II would also recommend itself to him as beneficial to the interests of the Church. And uses of lands being wholly unrecognised by the common law, and yet the practice having attained the force of a custom, and many interests depending upon it, the Chancellor would be resorted to as the depositary of the unde-

[1] See as to this the report of the case in the Year Book, 4 Edward IV, given below.

fined prerogatives of the Crown, in an age when the limits of the administrative, legislative, and judicial functions were not clearly marked out. CH. VI.

The earliest known application recorded as having been made to the Chancellor to protect uses of lands occurs apparently in the reign of Richard II, at some date later than 1393[1]. As yet, however, the jurisdiction was not regularly established, and in the reign of Henry IV the Commons complained that many grantees and feoffees in trust alienated and charged the tenements granted, for which there was no remedy, and they prayed that one might be provided by Parliament[2]. Towards the end of the reign of Henry V and in the reigns of Henry VI and Edward IV complaints of breach of trust become more common[3]. It was during these reigns that the jurisdiction of the Court of Chancery affecting uses of lands began to be systematised, and to follow regular rules.

It is necessary at this stage to keep clearly in view the two opposing but related interests—that of *feoffee to uses*, or, to use a more modern expression, trustee, and that of *cestui que use*, or the person beneficially interested[4].

The feoffee to uses is alone recognised by the common law as entitled to the land. It is from him that every alienee who is to take a legal interest must receive his title; he, and he only, is recognised as the tenant to the lord; his treason alone is the cause of forfeiture; for his debts alone can the land be taken in execution. The law knows nothing of any third person who is free from the burdens while he reaps the profits of the tenancy.

Supposing however that the feoffee attempts to exercise his legal right by alienating or charging the lands, he would, at the time we are now speaking of, be restrained from doing so, by the extra-legal, or, if the expression may be allowed, supra-legal power of the Chancellor,—a power, as has been seen,

[1] Select Cases in Chancery (Selden Society), p. 48.

[2] Spence, Equitable Jurisdiction, i. p. 443.

[3] See Cases, Nos. 117, 118, 122, 135, 138, 143 and 147 in the Select Cases in Chancery.

[4] See above, p. 320, n. 2.

CH VI. stronger than the law. Further, the Chancellor having power not only to restrain wrong-doing, but to command the performance of acts, would order the feoffee to do any lawful acts of disposition which *cestui que use* may require of him. He would be constrained to convey his legal interest to *cestui que use* or his heir, or to a purchaser from him [1]; to convey to the person named in *cestui que use*'s will [2]; to make the provision required by him for his family; to make a portion for his wife, or for payment of his debts [3]; and to prosecute all actions necessary for the protection of *cestui que use*'s interest [4].

The earliest conception of a use was, as has been seen, a trust binding on the conscience of the feoffee, a personal obligation upon him. It followed that on the death of the feoffee the heir who succeeded him was discharged of the trust, no conscientious obligation affecting *him* ever having been created. But in the reign of Edward IV, if not earlier, the heir of the feoffee was held to take the lands subject to the same trusts as his ancestor held them [5]. The

[1] See the petition (2) given below; and see Cal. i. p. xc; ii. pp. xxi, xxviii, xxxi, xxxvi.

[2] Rothanhale v. Wychingham, Cal. ii. p. iii. This is one of the earliest cases in the reign of Henry V. It states a feoffment made in the sixth year of Richard II, the feoffor declaring by a separate deed his will to be that after his death the feoffees should hold the lands to the use of the feoffor's wife for life and his son in fee. The son disposed of his interest by his will, and the object of the petition is to force the feoffees to carry out the dispositions of the father's settlement and the son's will. See also Cal. ii. p. xxxviii; i. p. xxi, &c.

[3] Cal. ii. pp. xxiii, li.

[4] Cal. i. p. xlviii.

[5] See Goold v. Petit, and Saundres v. Gaynesford, temp. Henry VI (Cal. ii. pp. xxviii, xxxviii). In both these cases it is sought to compel the heir of feoffee to uses to make a conveyance to *cestui que use*. See however Year Book, 8 Edward IV, 6: 'And it was moved whether a subpoena would lie against the executor or against the heir [of feoffee to uses]. And *Choke* said, that he on one occasion sued out a subpoena against the heir of a feoffee to uses, and the matter was discussed at great length. And the opinion of the Chancellor and of the Justices was that it did not lie against the heir, wherefore he sued out a bill in Parliament. *Fairfax*: Cest matter est bon store pur disputer apres quant les auters veignent.' And see Year Book, 22 Edward IV, 6; where in answer to an observation by the Chancellor that records existed in the Chancery of cases where

same rule was extended to the case of a person taking by alienation for valuable consideration from the feoffee, and having notice of the use[1]. A purchaser for valuable consideration without notice[2] held the lands free from the obligation, and in that case the only remedy of *cestui que use* would be against the feoffee personally. In like manner the lord who came into possession on an escheat, the creditor upon an *elegit*, or the husband or wife by virtue of curtesy or dower, held the land free and discharged from the use.

In tracing the history of the law of uses it is necessary shortly to enumerate the chief characteristics of uses before the legislation to be noticed in the next chapter. It follows from what has been said as to the origin of uses, that the feoffee to uses must be an individual capable of the conscientious obligation. Hence a body corporate is incapable of holding to the use of any one. Nor were aliens, or persons attainted, or the king[3], capable of holding to a use.

The Court of Chancery in establishing rules regulating the interest of *cestui que use* in some respects followed the rules of law, in others departed from them. 'Equity follows the law' in respect of uses principally in holding these interests to be subject to the same rules as to the duration and devolution of the estate as in the case of the legal interest. For instance, if a feoffment be made to *B* and his heirs to the use of *C* and

subpoenas had been granted against the heirs of feoffees to uses, Hussey, Chief Justice, states that all the judges had agreed thirty years before that a subpoena would not lie against the heir. The Chancellor however said that if the law was as stated by Hussey, 'donques est grand folie pur enfeoffer autres en mon terre.'

1 Year Book, 5 Edward IV, 7 b: 'If J. enfeoffed A. to his own use, and A. enfeoffed R., although he purchased for valuable consideration, if A. gave R. notice of the intent of the first feoffment, he (R.) is bound under pain of a writ of subpoena to perform the will of J.'

2 If no valuable consideration passed, notice of the use was implied.

3 Gilbert on Uses, ch. i. sect. 1. It was to avoid the consequences of this rule that it was provided by the statute 1 Richard III, c. 5, that where Richard was enfeoffed to uses jointly with other persons the land should vest in the co-feoffees; where he was the sole feoffee, it should vest in *cestui que use*. Blackstone, ii. p. 332.

CH. VI. his heirs, or to the use of *C* and the heirs of his body, or to the use of *C* for life, or to the use of *C* for ten years, *C* would have an equitable estate in fee which would descend to his eldest son, or to all his sons in gavelkind lands [1], or to his youngest in borough English [2]; or an estate tail, which might be further limited so as to be an estate in tail special or general, male or female; or an estate for life; or an estate for years, which upon *C*'s dying within the term would devolve upon his executors [3].

On the other hand, the wife or husband of *cestui que use* was not entitled to dower or curtesy [4], nor was the lord entitled to escheat on failure of heirs, nor, except so far as certain changes were introduced by legislation, was the king entitled to forfeiture, or the creditor to take the lands in execution [5].

But the widest difference between the rules of common law and those which prevailed in the Court of Chancery is to be found in the manner in which uses of lands could be created or transferred. The simplest and most ordinary way of creating a use has already been referred to. For example, *A*, tenant in fee simple, makes a feoffment to *B* and his heirs, to the use of *C* and his heirs. Uses might also be created by a fine or recovery levied or suffered to an expressed use. In these cases uses are said to be created by a conveyance operating by way of *transmutation of possession* [6]; that is, they accompany one of the recognised modes of conveying the seisin at common law—feoffment, fine, or recovery. An expression of the intention of the donor that the donee should hold the lands granted to certain uses was sufficient to burden the donee with the duty of holding to the use of *cestui que use*.

[1] See Breggeland v. Calche, Cal. ii. p. xxxvi.

[2] 'If tenant in borough English enfeoff one to the use of himself and his heirs, the younger son shall have the subpoena, and not the heir general.' Year Book, 5 Edward IV, 7 b.

[3] Sugden's Gilbert on Uses, ch. i. sect. 2. 1.

[4] Ib. pp. 48, 49.

[5] Ib. ch. i. sect. 2. 5, 6.

[6] Ib. ch. i. sect. 5, and Introduction, p. xlvii.

But in some cases uses were said to be raised by implication; that is, though no use was expressed in the grant, yet the circumstances were such that the Chancellor would declare that the donor intended the donee to hold, not for his own benefit, but as donee to uses. This arose principally in the case where the feoffment or other conveyance was made without consideration, that is, without an adequate motive. In this case the doctrine of the Court of Chancery was that the intention of the donor must have been that the donee should hold not for his own benefit, but for the use and benefit of the donor. The use was said to *result* or come back to the donor[1]. Two kinds of consideration alone were regarded as affording a sufficient motive; these were *blood* or *money*. Blood, or, in other words, natural affection felt towards a near relative, would be sufficient to vest in a son, brother, nephew, or cousin, the beneficial as well as the legal interest, if the intention of the donor were expressed in a deed[2]. This however commonly took the form of a *covenant to stand seised*, to be presently noticed. The other consideration was money[3], and here, so long as the conveyance is expressed to be made for a money consideration, the amount is immaterial; it is, at all events, sufficient evidence of the intention of the donor to part with the beneficial as well as the legal interest in the lands. If no proper evidence of either of these motives existed, the beneficial interest *resulted* or came back to the donor. It was in fact only an instance of the practice which seems to have become very common about the time of the Wars of the Roses, so that 'the use of the country to deliver lands to be safely kept has made the mere delivery of possession no evidence of right without a valuable consideration[4].' This however did not apply to the case of a grant for life or years.

Uses raised by a conveyance operating by transmutation of possession are distinguished from uses raised without any such

[1] Sugden's Gilbert on Uses, ch. i. sect. 5. 1; sect. 6, p. 117.
[2] Ib. p. 93. [3] Ib. p. 94. [4] Ib. p. 125.

CH. VI. transmutation. Under certain circumstances a person, though he had done nothing which would be regarded at common law as a parting with his legal interest, was constrained by the Chancellor to hold to the use and benefit of another. This arose principally in the two cases of *bargains and sales*, and of *covenants to stand seised.*

A bargain and sale was where the legal owner entered into an agreement with a purchaser for the sale to him of his interest, and the purchaser paid, or promised to pay, the money for the land. The transaction would not be complete at law without a legal conveyance; but in Equity a use was 'raised' in favour of the purchaser, the bargainor was in the view of the Chancellor the bare legal owner, holding to the use and for the benefit of the bargainee [1].

A covenant to stand seised was where a person by deed agreed to stand seised to the use of some near relation—son, brother, nephew, or cousin. In this case the consideration of natural affection was sufficient to raise a use in favour of the covenantee [2].

When by any of the above methods the interest of *cestui que use* had been created, that interest might, without any formality, by words or acts evidencing the intention, be transferred by *cestui que use* to any one capable of taking a use.

Another mode by which uses could be raised or transferred was by will. An instance will be found below of a feoffment made on a death-bed to the use of a will. After the death of the feoffor the feoffee would be constrained to hold to the uses declared. Thus if *A* made a feoffment to *B* and his heirs to the uses declared by his last will, and declared a use in favour of *C* and his heirs, the use would, until *A*'s death, result or come back to him. Upon *A*'s death *C* could claim by virtue of the will to be the equitable or beneficial owner. So a use vested in *cestui que use* could be devised by him. For example, if *cestui que use* devised that his feoffees should alien

[1] Sugden's Gilbert on Uses, pp. 94-98.

[2] Ib. pp. 92-94.

the land for payment of his debts, the creditors might compel them in the Court of Chancery to do it[1]. Thus by the medium of uses the power of disposing of interests in lands by will was for all practical purposes regained, and was so firmly established as to withstand the attempt made in the reign of Henry VIII to restrain it by legislation[2]. It should be remembered that no formality, not even writing, was required to establish a will; any evidence of the expression of the intention of a testator would be sufficient to raise a use by which the next legal owner would be bound.

Various consequences as to the capacity of dealing with the beneficial interest in lands followed upon the introduction of uses besides those above pointed out. Of these the most important were—(1) that a man might convey the beneficial interest in lands to himself. This practice, as has been before observed, was largely resorted to in troublous times when a freehold tenant wished to retain the benefits, and escape the burdens, attaching to the legal estate in lands. (2) A man might convey a beneficial interest to his wife. The Chancellor did not consider himself bound by the stringent doctrine of the common law that a married woman was incapable of holding separate property. A use declared in favour of a woman would be enforced whether the woman was married at the time or married afterwards. Thus it became a common practice for a man upon his marriage to convey lands to feoffees to the joint use of himself and his wife for life or in tail, by which means a provision for the remainder of her life was secured to the wife. This was called a jointure. Before the Statute of Uses, mentioned in the next chapter, the wife might have claimed dower in addition to this provision; by that Statute, however, when provision was made for the wife by jointure, she was put to her election whether she would claim dower or jointure, but was not allowed to claim both. Thus were laid the foundations of one of the principal classes of rights created

[1] Sugden's Gilbert on Uses, p. 75.

[2] See below, Chap. VIII.

CH. VI. by the Court of Chancery, the Equitable Estate of Married Women [1].

(3) Interests in lands too might be created by way of use to commence and terminate at times and in ways which the doctrines of the common law would not permit. It has already been seen that where one person desired to convey lands to another at common law, he must do so either by feoffment with livery of seisin [2], which was the regular mode of transfer, or by the fictitious processes of fine or recovery [3], or by conveying a particular estate by lease for years and entry, or by lease for life with livery of seisin followed by a release of the reversion to the lessee, or by a grant of the reversion to a third person, in which latter case the lessee for years must attorn to the grantee of the reversion in order to give complete effect to the grant [4]. The foundation of all these modes of conveying interests in lands was open and notorious transfer of possession; the point at which the freehold interest passed out of the grantor and vested in the grantee was marked by an actual change of possession (unless indeed the grantee was already in actual possession), or, in the case of a fine or recovery, by an acknowledgment in open court. Thus it was that freehold interests to take effect in possession or enjoyment at a future time could only be created by way of remainder, as has been explained in the fifth chapter. No such rule, however, restricted the freedom of the Chancellor in enforcing uses. There was no reason why the intention of the donor should not be carried into effect at a future period. Thus a feoffment to *A* and his heirs, and after next Christmas to the use of *B* and his heirs, would be carried out according to the expressed intention of the donor. So a use might be raised on the happening of any future event, or the expiration

[1] Sugden's Introduction to Gilbert, p. xlviii. The rights of married women to acquire, hold, and dispose of Property real or personal, now depend on the Married Women's Property Act, 1882, 45 and 46 Vict. c. 75, and the amending Acts of 1884 and 1893.

[2] See above, Chap. III. § 12. [3] See above, Chap. II. § 8; Chap. V. § 2.

[4] See above, Chap. V. § 3 (1).

of any specified time. Thus while at common law, as has been pointed out[1], a fee could not be limited after a fee, this might in effect be done with the use. A conveyance to *A* and his heirs so long as he continued unmarried, and upon his marriage to the use of *B* and his heirs, would cause the use upon the happening of the event to arise and spring up and vest in *B*; in other words, *A*, upon his marriage, while remaining legal owner, would be constrained by the Chancellor to hold to the use of *B*. Thus a power was acquired of creating future interests in lands and of causing interests in lands to be shifted and to pass from one person to another, which was unknown to the common law, and which, as will be seen in the next chapter, gave rise to the complicated system of conveyancing which prevails at the present day.

1. 15 Richard II, cap. v[2].

Item come contenuz soit en lestatut de Religiouses[3], qe null religious nautre queconqe achate ne vende, ou souz colour de doun ou terme ou dautre title queconqe dascun resceive, ou dascun en ascune manere par art ou par engyn a luy face approprier ascunes terres ou tenementz, sur forfaiture dycelles, par quoi les ditz terres et tenementz purront en ascune manere devenir a mort mayn; et qe si ascun religious ou ascun autre veigne encontre le dit estatut par art ou par engyn en ascune manere, bien lise au roi et as autres seignurs les ditz terres et tenementz entrer, sicome en le dit estatut est contenuz plus au plein; et ore de novell par sotile ymagination et par art et engyn ascuns gentz de religion, parsons, vikers, et autres persones espiritiels sont entrez en diverses terres et tenementz adjoignantz a lour esglise, et dycelles par suffrance et assent de tenantz ont fait cimiters, et par bulles del appostoill les ont fait dedier et sacrer, et sepulture parochiele font continuelment en ycelles sanz licence du roi et des chiefs seignurs; declare est en cest parlement qe ce est overtement en cas du dit estatut. Et en outre acordez est et assentuz qe toutz ceux qe sont possessionez par feoffement ou par autre voie al oeps de gentz de religion ou autres persones espiritiels des terres, tenementz, fees, advoesons, ou autres possessions queconqes, pur les amortiser, et dont les ditz religiouses

[1] See above, p. 264. [2] See above, p. 319. [3] See Chap. IV. § 2.

CH. VI. et persones espiritiels preignent les profitz, qe parentre cy et le fest de Saint Michel prochein venant ils les facent estre amortisez par licence du roi et des seignurs, ou autrement qils les vendent et alienent a autre oeps parentre cy et le dit fest, sur peine destre forfaitz au roi et as seignurs, solonc la fourme de lestatut de religious, come tenementz purchasez par gentz de religion, et qe de cest temps enavant null tiel purchase se face, issint qe tielx religiouses ou autres persones espiritiels ent preignent les profitz come desuis sur la peine avauntdite. Et mesme cest estatut sextende et soit tenuz de toutz terres, et tenementz, fees, advoesons, et autres possessions purchacez, et a purchasers al oeps des gildes et fraternitees. Et enoutre est assuntuz pur ce qe mairs, baillifs, et communes de citees, burghs, et autres villes, qont commune perpetuel et autres qont offices perpetuels sont aussi perpetuels come gentz de religion, qe de cest temps enavaunt ils ne purchacent a eux et a lour commune ou office sur la peine contenue en la dit estatut de religiouses. Et de ce qe autres sont possessionez ou serra purchacez en temps avenir a lour oeps, et ils ent preignent ou prendront les profitz, soit semblablement fait come devaunt est dit de gentz de religion.

TRANSLATION[1].

Whereas it is contained in the Statute De Religiosis, That no religious, nor other whatsoever he be, do buy or sell or under colour of gift, or term, or any other manner of title whatsoever, receive of any man, or in any manner by [gift[2]] or engine[3] cause to be appropriated unto him any lands or tenements, upon pain of forfeiture of the same, whereby the said lands and tenements in any manner might come to mortmain; and if any religious, or any other, do against the said statute by art or engine in any manner, that it be lawful to the king and to other lords upon the said lands and tenements to enter; as in the said statute doth more fully appear: and now of late by subtle imagination and by art and engine some religious persons, parsons, vicars, and other spiritual persons, have entered in divers lands and tenements, which be adjoining to their churches, and of the same, by sufferance and assent of the tenants, have made church yards, and by bulls of the Bishop of Rome have dedicated and hallowed the same, and in them do make continually parochial burying without licence of the king and of the chief lords; therefore it is declared in this Parliament, That it is manifestly

[1] Revised Statutes, 1st Ed. p. 257. [2] Craft. [3] Device.

within the compass of the said statute; and moreover it is agreed and assented, that all they that be possessed by feoffment or by other manner to the use of religious people, or other spiritual persons, of lands and tenements, fees, advowsons, or any manner other possessions whatsoever, to amortise them, and whereof the said religious and spiritual persons take the profits, that betwixt this and the feast of St. Michael next coming they shall cause them to be amortised by the licence of the king and of the lords, or else that they shall sell and aliene them to some other use, between this and the said feast, upon pain to be forfeited to the king and to the lords, according to the form of the said Statute of Religious, as lands purchased by religious people; and that from henceforth no such purchase be made, so that such religious or other spiritual persons take thereof the profits, as afore is said, upon pain aforesaid; and that the same statute extend and be observed of all lands, tenements, fees, advowsons, and other possessions purchased or to be purchased to the use of guilds or fraternities. And moreover it is assented, because mayors, bailiffs, and commons, of cities, boroughs, and other towns which have a perpetual commonalty, and others which have offices perpetual, be as perpetual as people of religion, that from henceforth they shall not purchase to them and to their commons or office upon pain contained in the said Statute De Religiosis; and whereas others be possessed, or hereafter shall purchase to their use, and they thereof take the profits, it shall be done in like manner as is afore said of people of religion.

2. The following three cases are taken from the volumes of Calendars of Proceedings in Chancery above referred to. The points which the cases illustrate have already been sufficiently dwelt upon.

(1) *Proceedings in Chancery in the reign of Henry V. William Dodd* v. *John Browning and another.* (*Calendar of Proceedings in Chancery, i. p. xiii.*)

To my worthy and gracious Lord Bisshope of Wynchester, Chanceller of Yngelond.

Beseching mekely youre povre bedeman William Dodde, charyoteer, wheche passed over the see in service with our liege lord, and was oon of his charioterys in his viages; and of hyze treste ffefed in my land John Brownyng and John . . . of Chekewell[1] with my wyfe, wheche John, and John afterwards

[1] Feoffees to uses.

azenste my wyll and wetynge pot my land to ferme, and delyvered my mevable good the valewe of xx marke where hem leste, and thus they kepe my dede and the indenture with my mevable good unto myne undoynge, lasse than y have youre excylent and gracious helpe and lordship; besechinge yow at reverence of that worthy Prince ys sowle youre fader, whoos bedeman y am ever, that ye woll sende for John, and John afforseide, that the cause may be knowe why they withholde my good to myne undoynge; also wheche am undo for brusinge in service of our liege lorde, and in service of that worthy Pıincesse my lady of Clarence, and ever wolde yef my lemys myght serve worthy prince sone. At reverence of God and of that pereles Princes his moder take this matter at hert of almes and charite.

(2) *William of Arundel, Esq.* v. *Sir Maurice Berkeley, Knight, and others.* (*Calendar, i. p. xxxv. Temp. Henry VI.*)

Besechith mekely William of Arundell esquyer that for as moche as John, somme tyme Lord of Arundell and of Mautravers his fader, wham God assoile, enfeoffed Robert Lord Ponyngges and William Ryman yet on lyve, and dyverse other persons nowe dede, yn his manors of Hyneford, Spertegrove, Stoketristre, Cokelyngton, Bayford, and Lyghe yn the counte of Somerset wyth the officis of the kepyng of the forest of Selewode yn the same counte, to the entent that the said feoffees should performe his wille, whiche he would afterward declare touchynge the seid manors and officis. And afterward by his dede ensealed with the seale of his armys, declarid his seid wille touchynge the seid manors and officis forseid, yn soche forme as the seid nowe besecher owyth to have the forseid manors and officis to hym and to the heirs of his body comyng; as by the seid dede of declaracion of his wille hit pleynly may appere. And afterward the seid late Lord of Arundell dyed; after whos deth John late Erle of Arundell his sone and heir, the seid feoffment notwythstondyng, entred yn the seid manors and occupyed the seid office, enclaymyng the same manors and office as sone and heir; and than of the same manors and office enfeoffed Mores Berkeley knyght, John Hody, William Sydeney, John Lylye and John Grendon clerk yn fee, to the entent to performe his wille, the whiche he wolde afterward declare, touching the seid manors and office. And afterward by his letter wreten wyth his oune hand at Rome, yn Seynt Martyn's day, the yere of the reigne of oure soverayn Lord the Kyng that nowe is the xiii, dyrecte unto

Alianore countesse of Arundell his moder, and also lady and moder to the seid besecher, declared openly that hit was his wylle[1], that a state shoulde be made to the seid besecher his brother, yn all the said manors and office, according to the wille of his seid fader, yn the most surest wyse; which writyng nought withstondyng, and that the seid besecher hath ofte tymys requyred the forsaid Morys and his seid coofeoffees to have made a state of the forseid manors and office to the same besecher, and to his heirs of his body begete, accordyng to the willes, as well of his seid lord and fader, as of his forseid lord and brother; whiche the seid Mores and his seid coofeoffees have all weye refusid and yet refuse to doo, to the lykly disheritaunce of the seid besecher, but yf he be remedyet by youre gracious lordship, hit lyke youre seid Lordship to sende by a serjaunt of armes for the seid Moris, and his said cofeoffees, now beyng yn London, to appere afore you yn the Kyngis Chauncery, at a day by yowe to be lymeted, and than there to be examynyd of all the matters forsaid, and thereuppon to compelle tham to make a sufficiant and suere astat of all the seid manors and office to the said besecher, and to the heirs of his body comyng, for the love of God, and yn the wey of charite.

(3) *Examination by the Bishop of Bath and Wells, Chancellor of England, of two persons to whom one Robert Crody had made a feoffment by parol, on his death-bed, in trust for his wife for life, with remainder to his daughter in tail.* (*Cal. vol. i. p. xliii.*)

Be it hade in mynde that the x. day of August the reigne of Kynge Henry the syxt after the Conquest xvi^{te}, John Gover of Wyntenayse Herteley in the shire of Suthampton, husbondman, and Thomas Attemore of the same toune, husbondman, apperyng afore the right reverent Fader in Gode the Bisshop of Bath and Welles Chaunceller of Ingelond, in his manoir of Dogmersfeld, and ther examined severally uppon a certein feffement made to thayme by one Robert Crody of certeyn londes and tenements in the toune afore especified, sayde and confessyd ther expressely by there othes upon a boke howe that the saide Robert, the Wednesday nyxt after the fest of Seint Michell, the yere of the reigne of Kynge Henry the fyfte after the Con-

[1] Notice the informal character of these early wills. In one case it is a deed of declaration of trust, in the other a letter that is considered to operate as a will. See below, Chap. VIII.

quest, viii^{te}, in the evenyng, leyng in an house of his awen atte the saide toune, so sore seke in his bede that for his sekenesse he myght noght be remeved, in to so moche that in the same nyght followyng he died, callede to hym the forsaide John and Thomas, sayng to thaym in this maner—'Sires ye be the men in whome I have grete trust afore moche other persones, and in especial that suche will als I shall declare you atte this tyme, for my full and last will, shall throgh your gude help by oure Lordes mercy be perfourmed; Wherefore I late you have full knowlich, that this house which I ly in, and all myn other londes and tenements in this toune, I yeve and graunte to you, to holde to you your heires and your assignes, to this entent, that after myn deces, ze shall make estate of the same house, londes and tenements to Alice my wyfe [for] terme of hir lyve, so that after hir deth thay remayne to Margarete my doghter, and to the heires of hir body loufully becomyng, and if sche die withoute heir of hir body comyng, that then thay remayne to my right heires for evermore. And to thentent that this my last will mowe be performed by you, als my trust is that it shall be, her atte this tyme I delyver you possession of this house in the name of all my londes and tenements afore especified [1], als holy and entierly als they wer ever myn atte any tyme.' By force wherof the forseide John and Thomas wer possessyd of the house, landes and tenements aforseide, in thaire demesne als of fee, and of the same house, londes and tenements made estate to the saide Alice, after the deth of hir saide husbond, accordyng to the entent and will afore declared.

(4) The following case is interesting, as showing an attempt made to obtain a recognition of uses as an integral part of the common law at the hands of the Common Law Courts, and the reasons why it was unsuccessful.

YEAR BOOK, 4 EDWARD IV, 8. 9. *Translation.*

In a writ of trespass *quare vi et armis clausum fregit* [2], *etc.*, *et arbores succidit, etc., et herbas conculcavit et consumpsit, etc.*

[1] A perfect livery of seisin. See above, Chap. III. § 12 (2).

[2] This was the regular form of a writ of trespass (to lands) vi et armis, as opposed to a writ of trespass 'on the case.' The latter was an extension (by virtue of statute West. II. c. 24) of the writ of trespass, which was originally applicable only to violent injuries, to all cases of damage caused by *mis*feazance (commission of wrongful acts), or even by *non*feazance (omission of acts which a person is bound to do).

Catesby[1]. The plaintiff ought not to have his action, for we say that long before the supposed trespass one J. B. was seised in fee of certain land and died so seised, which then descended to the defendant as heir-at-law of the said J. B., being the place where the trespass is supposed to have been committed, and the defendant being seised in fee of the said lands enfeoffed the plaintiff in fee, to the use of the defendant and upon confidence, and then the defendant by sufferance of the plaintiff and at his will occupied the land and cut the trees within the said land and depastured the herbage, which are the trespasses complained of in the action.

Jenney[2]. That is no plea, for that is no certain matter—the sufferance of the plaintiff and that the defendant occupied by the will of the plaintiff—for such sufferance and will cannot be tried, for the intent of a man is uncertain, and a man should plead such matter as is or may be known to the jury, if the issue should be taken thereon[3]. And this cannot be upon the alleged sufferance or will of the plaintiff that the defendant should occupy, &c.; and therefore in such a case to make a good issue or matter traversable, he should plead the lease made by the plaintiff to the defendant to hold at his will, which is matter traversable, and that may be tried.

Catesby. Wherefore should the defendant not avail himself of this matter, when it follows by reason that the defendant enfeoffed the plaintiff to the use of the defendant, and so that the plaintiff is only in the land to the use of the defendant, and the defendant made the feoffment to the plaintiff in trust and confidence? And the plaintiff suffered the defendant to occupy the land, so that by reason that the defendant occupied the land at his will, this proves that the defendant shall have the advantage of this feoffment in trust, in order to justify his occupation of the land by this cause, &c.

Moile[4]. This is a good ground of defence in Chancery, for the defendant there shall aver the intent and purpose upon such a feoffment, for in the Chancery a man shall have remedy according to conscience upon the intent of such a feoffment, but here by the course of the common law in the Common Pleas

[1] Counsel for defendant. [2] Counsel for plaintiff.

[3] The Chancellor as an ecclesiastic could look into a man's heart and conscience and see what his intent was; a jury could only pronounce upon matter 'in pais,' open notorious facts known to all the neighbours. See above, p. 324.

[4] A judge.

CH. VI. or King's Bench it is otherwise, for the feoffee shall have the land; and the feoffor shall not justify contrary to his own feoffment, that the said feoffment was made in confidence or the contrary.

Catesby. The law of Chancery is the common law of the land, and there the defendant shall have advantage of this matter and feoffment; wherefore then shall he not have it in the same manner here?

Moile. That cannot be so here in this court, as I have already said, for the common law of the land is different from the law of Chancery on this point.

Catesby passed over the point; and as to the trees he repeated the former plea, and said that he had no further answer. As to the herbage, he said that the plaintiff was seised in fee and leased the land to the defendant to hold at his will, &c.; wherefore the defendant entered and committed the alleged trespasses for which the action was brought.

Jenney traversed the lease, &c.

(5) The following cases show that though lands might be held to the use of a married woman, the Chancellor would not allow her to join with her husband in disposing of her interest during the coverture or marriage, but would treat any disposition made by the feoffee to uses at the joint request of the husband and wife as a breach of trust, for which the feoffee must answer. The principle upon which this rule was established is clearly stated in the cases below. On similar grounds it has become the established practice to protect the wife against imprudent dispositions of her property under the influence of the husband by inserting in the deed of settlement a provision that she is not during the coverture to make any alienation of her property by way of anticipation[1]. Subject however to this restriction, a married woman had, prior to the 1st of January, 1883, the same absolute power of disposition over property held by trustees for her separate use as if she were unmarried; and now by the Married Women's Property Act, 1882, the intervention of

[1] By sect. 19 of the Married Women's Property Act, 1882, the efficacy of a provision in restraint of anticipation is with certain limitations preserved.

a trustee is no longer necessary, and a married woman is capable 'of acquiring, holding, and disposing by will or otherwise of any real or personal property as her separate property, in the same manner as if she were a feme sole [1].' CH. VI.

YEAR BOOK, 7 EDWARD IV, 14. 8. *Translation.*

There was the following case in Chancery. A man was enfeoffed to the use of a woman, who took husband (baron). Husband and wife then sold the land to a stranger, for a certain sum of money, the wife received the money; and husband and wife then prayed the feoffee to the use of the wife to make an estate of this land to the stranger, and he enfeoffed the stranger. Afterwards the husband died, and the wife brings a subpoena against him who had been enfeoffed to her use, and he pleaded all the circumstances, and to this plea the plaintiff demurred [2]. And the case was rehearsed in the Exchequer Chamber before the Chancellor and the Justices of both Benches.

Starkey (for the plaintiff). The plea is not sufficient, for what was done by the wife was void, for if she had been seised of the land, and the husband and the wife had made a feoffment thereof, after the husband's death she would have had a '*cui in vita* [3],' for that the feoffment made by the wife during the coverture is void, and so here in conscience this sale made by husband and wife was entirely the act of the husband, and not of the wife, &c. *Ad quod tota curia concessit, etc.* And the Chancellor said that the wife *non potest consentire* during the coverture, if it be through dread or coercion (that she did it), that cannot be said to be consent, and everything that a married woman does shall be said to be done through dread of her husband, and that they would pay no regard to the fact of her having received the money, because she could have had no advantage of it, but only the husband, &c. The Chancellor said to Starkey, 'What do you pray?'

[1] 45 and 46 Vict. c. 75, sect. 1 (1).

[2] That is, she admitted the plea to be true in fact, but alleged that the facts therein stated, though true, did not in point of law amount to a valid answer to her claim.

[3] This was the remedy by which the wife might recover after the husband's death her lands in the hands of a feoffee to whom the husband had granted them with the assent of the wife, although she had herself been a party to the feoffment. See the form of the writ in the next case.

[*Starkey.*] We pray that the defendant should be committed to prison until he have satisfied us concerning the land, &c.

The Chancellor. You can have a subpoena against the vendee who is in possession of the land, and recover the land against him [1].

Yelverton. If he knew of the deceit and wrong done to the woman, then the subpoena lies against him, otherwise not.

The Chancellor. He knew that the woman was a *feme covert.*

Starkey. We pray that the defendant be committed to prison, and as to the subpoena against the other we wish to be advised.

Year Book, 18 Edward IV, 11. 4. *Translation.*

There was the following case in the Chancery. A *feme sole* made a feoffment in confidence (to her own use), and then took husband, and during the coverture (she dying in her husband's lifetime) she declared her will that her feoffees should make an estate to her husband, to him and his heirs for ever, and after her death her husband sued a subpoena. The question was whether this will was good or not.

Tremaile. It seems that the will is good, and that the feoffees will be compelled to make an estate according to the will. For just as the wife can make executors with the agreement of her husband [2], so can she declare her will by the agreement of her husband that the feoffees should make an estate to the husband, and conscience will see that it should be done.

Vavisor. There is a great difference between your case and this case, for there are divers cases in which by agreement with her husband the wife may make executors, as if a bond be made to a woman before her marriage, during the coverture by agreement

[1] It was the interference of the Chancellor with the 'franc tenement' which made the Commons so jealous of his jurisdiction in the earlier stages of its growth. See Spence, Equitable Jurisdiction, i. p. 344.

[2] As a general rule, prior to the Married Women's Property Act, 1882, a married woman could make no valid will. Her husband might however assent to her disposing of her personal property by will thereby waiving his right to take out administration to her property, and effect would then be given to the dispositions of her will. This however could only extend to those rights of the wife which had not become vested in the husband in his marital right: these (before the Married Women's Property Act, 1870) were confined to 'choses in action not reduced into possession,' e.g. a debt due but not paid, and paraphernalia. As to the complete powers of disposition by will or otherwise now given by the Married Women's Property Act, 1882, see above, p. 341.

with her husband she can make executors, and in that case the executors shall have an action of debt on the bond, because the husband cannot in any wise have an action upon it after the death of the wife, for his interest is determined by her death; so as to her apparel, which is called in our law *paraphernalia*, of this by agreement with her husband she can make a will, and that would be good, and they are the goods of the husband, but in the present case the law is otherwise, for the law will not suffer anything done by her during the coverture to be good, and if during the coverture she makes a feoffment of her land, it is void, and this proves well that nothing done by her during the coverture is good concerning any inheritance, for the writ 'cui in vita' runs, 'cui ipsa in vita sua contradicere non potuit,'[1] and so this proves well that her act and her will is void during the coverture, &c.

Jaye ad idem. If this will be good, the inheritance of the wife during the coverture will not be safe from alienation by the husband, for the feoffment made before the coverture is to that intent that the alienation of the husband should be ineffectual, and thus if the will should be effectual, that would be prejudicial to the heir (of the woman), *quod Suliard concessit.*

The Chancellor. The will cannot be good, for she cannot acquire or lose land during the coverture without her husband, and seeing that she cannot do that at the common law, and that any act done by her is merely void, the law of conscience says also that her will should be so (void) and ineffectual.

Tremaile. A fine levied by husband and wife is good.

Vavisor. The reason is that she shall be examined in open court by the justices, and her intent is proved by matter of record.

But the opinion of all those at that time, except Tremaile, was that the will was void.

[1] See p. 341, n. 3.

CHAPTER VII

THE STATUTE OF USES AND ITS PRINCIPAL EFFECTS ON MODERN CONVEYANCING

CH. VII.

IN the last chapter the early history of uses of lands has been traced in outline. It has been seen that, originating simply in a moral or religious obligation, a use of lands became a recognised collection of rights and duties, incumbent upon and enjoyed by the legal owner and the beneficiary respectively, and capable of being asserted and enforced by the proper tribunal. In reviewing the subsequent history of uses it must be borne in mind that the tendency of philosophical thought prevailing at the period in question was to invest all abstract ideas with a real and substantial existence, to treat of them not merely as collective names for a variety of particular facts and circumstances agreeing in the points designated by the general name, but as having a real existence, apart from the particular or individual instances, and possessing definite attributes or properties necessarily inherent in their essence. These realist notions will be found to have exercised an important and pernicious influence upon the development of the law of land, and this influence is most conspicuous in the history of uses. A use is now regarded as an abstract entity, possessing certain qualities of its own, which naturally flow from it or are inherent in it. Thus the development of the law is frequently the result of a discussion as to what these essential qualities of a use are, and when they are supposed to be ascertained by reasoning, they are made the basis of judicial decision, all other considerations, such as expediency, or conformity to general principles of law, being thrown into the background. It must be confessed that the handling of 'uses' by the common lawyers contrasts unfavourably with the enlightened system which had been constructed by the succession of ecclesiastical chancellors.

§ 1. *The Statute of Uses*, 27 *Henry VIII*, c. 10.

Before the passing of the Statute of Uses in the twenty-seventh year of Henry VIII, attempts had been made to protect by legislation the interests of creditors, of the king, and of the lords, which were affected injuriously by feoffments to uses. It has already been seen that the legislature at a very early date interfered in the interest of creditors to render uses liable to be taken in execution for debt[1]. By 1 Richard III, c. 1, the conveyances of *cestui que use* were made good without assent of the feoffees[2]; and by 4 Henry

[1] See above, p. 318.

[2] This statute, after reciting 'that by privy and unknown feoffments great unsurety, trouble, costs and grievous vexations do daily grow betwixt the king's subjects, insomuch that no man that buyeth lands, tenements, rents, services, or other hereditaments, nor women which have jointure or dower in any lands, tenements, or other hereditaments, nor the last will of men to be performed, nor leases for term of life or of years, nor annuities granted to any person or persons for their services for term of their lives or otherwise, be in perfect surety, nor without great trouble and doubt of the same by reason of such privy and unknown feoffments,' enacted 'that every estate, feoffment, gift, release, grant, leases, and confirmations of lands, tenements, rents, services, or other hereditaments, made or had, or hereafter to be made or had, by any person or persons being of full age, of whole memory, at large and not in duress, to any person or persons, and all recoveries and executions had or made, shall be good and effectual to him to whom it is so made, had or given, and to all other to his use, against the seller, feoffor, donor, or grantor of the same, and against the sellers, feoffors, donors, or grantors, and his and their heirs claiming the same only as heir or heirs to the same sellers, feoffors, donors, or grantors,

CH. VII. § 1. VII, c. 17, the lord was given the wardship of the heir. The tendency of these and similar enactments was to assimilate in some particulars the position of *cestui que use* to that of legal owner, to throw upon him some at all events of the burdens and liabilities attaching to the legal ownership. What imperfect success attended these attempts appears from the preamble of the Statute of Uses. The object of that Statute was, by joining the possession or seisin to the use and interest (or, in other words, by providing that all the estate which would by the common law have passed to the grantee to uses should instantly be taken out of him and vested in *cestui que use*), to annihilate altogether the distinction between the legal and beneficial ownership, to make the ostensible tenant in every case also the legal tenant, liable to his lord for feudal dues and services,—wardship, marriage, and the rest. As will be pointed out in the next chapter, by converting the use into the legal interest the Statute did away with the power of disposing of interests in lands by will, which had been one of the most important results of the introduction of uses. Probably these were the chief results aimed at by the Statute of Uses. A strange combination of circumstances—the force of usage by which practices had arisen too strong even for legislation to do away with [1], coupled with an almost superstitious

and every of them, and against all other having or claiming any title or interest in the same only to the use of the same seller, feoffor, donor, or grantor, or sellers, donors, or grantors, or his or their said heirs, at the time of the bargain, sale, covenant, gift, or grant made, saving to every person or persons such right, title, action, or interest by reason of any gift in tail thereof made, as they ought to have if this Act had not been made.'

[1] The invasion of 'the old accustomed law in many things,' especially the interference with the practice of disposing of lands by will, was one of the grievances which led to the insurrection of 1536. 'Masters, there is a statute made whereby all persons be restrained to make their will upon their lands; for now the eldest son must have all his father's lands, and no person, to the payment of his debts, neither to the advancement of his daughters' marriages, can do nothing with their lands, nor cannot give to his youngest son any lands.' Speech of Mr. Sheriff Dymock at

adherence on the part of the courts to the letter of the Statute—produced the curious result, that the effect of the Statute of Uses was directly the reverse of its purpose, that by means of it secret conveyances of the legal estate were introduced, while by a strained interpretation of its terms the old distinction between beneficial or equitable and legal ownership was revived. What may be called the modern law of Real Property and the highly technical and intricate system of conveyancing which still prevails, dates from the legislation of Henry VIII.

27 Henry VIII, cap. 10. An Act concerning Uses and Wills.

Where by the common laws of this realm, lands, tenements, and hereditaments be not devisable by testament, nor ought to be transferred from one to another, but by solemn livery and seisin, matter of record [1], writing sufficient made *bona fide*, without covin or fraud, yet nevertheless divers and sundry imaginations, subtle inventions, and practices have been used, whereby the hereditaments of this realm have been conveyed from one to another by fraudulent feoffments, fines, recoveries, and other assurances craftily made to secret uses, intents, and trusts, and also by wills and testaments, sometimes made by *nude parolæ* and words, sometimes by signs and tokens, and sometimes by writing, and for the most part made by such persons as be visited with sickness, in their extreme agonies and pains, or at such time as they have had scantly any good memory or remembrance; at which times they being provoked by greedy and covetous persons lying in wait about them, do many times dispose indiscreetly and unadvisedly their lands and inheritances; by reason whereof, and by occasion of which fraudulent feoffments, fines, recoveries, and other like assurances to uses, confidences, and trusts, divers and many heirs have been unjustly at sundry times disinherited, the lords have lost their wards, marriages, reliefs, harriots, escheats, aids, *pur fair fitz chivalier* and *pur file marier*, and scantly any person can be certainly assured of any lands by them purchased, nor know surely against

Horncastle, quoted from Rolls House MS. A. 2, 29, in Froude, History of England, III. 91.

[1] That is, by process in a court of record, e.g. by fine or recovery.

CH. VII. § 1. whom they shall use their actions or execution for their rights, titles, and duties; also men married have lost their tenancies by the curtesy, women their dowers; manifest perjuries by trial of such secret wills and uses have been committed; the king's highness hath lost the profits and advantages of the lands of persons attainted, and of the lands craftily put in feoffment to the uses of aliens born, and also the profits of waste for a year and a day of lands of felons attainted, and the lords their escheats thereof; and many other inconveniences have happened, and daily do increase among the king's subjects, to their great trouble and inquietness, and to the utter subversion of the ancient common laws of this realm; for the extirping and extinguishment of all such subtle practised feoffments, fines, recoveries, abuses, and errors heretofore used and accustomed in this realm, to the subversion of the good and ancient laws of the same, and to the intent that the king's highness or any other his subjects of this realm, shall not in any wise hereafter, by any means or inventions be deceived, damaged, or hurt, by reason of such trusts, uses, or confidences: It may please the King's most royal Majesty, that it may be enacted by his Highness, by the assent of the Lords Spiritual and Temporal, and the Commons, in this present parliament assembled, and by the authority of the same, in manner and form following: that is to say, that where any person or persons stand, or be seised[1], or at any time hereafter shall happen to be seised of and in any honours, castles, manors, lands, tenements, rents, services, reversions, remainders, or other hereditaments, to the use, confidence, or trust[2] of any other person

[1] In order to bring this statute into operation, one person must be *seised* to the use of *another*. Hence the first grantee must have an estate of freehold, e.g. the land must be conveyed by feoffment or otherwise to *A* in fee, or in tail, or for life, to the use of *B*. This *executes* the use in *B*, and *B* takes the estate limited to him by virtue of the statute, everything which would have been given to *A* by operation of the common law being instantly taken out of him and vested in *B*. On the other hand, if lands are given to *A* for ten years, or for any estate less than freehold, to the use of *B*, *A* is not *seised* to the use of *B*, i. e. he has not the possession as of freehold, consequently the statute does not operate, and *A* retains the *legal* interest in the term. For the same reason the words of the statute have no reference to copyhold estates.

[2] Though the word that is most frequently employed to designate the beneficial interest is 'use'—e. g. feoffment to *A* and his heirs to the *use* of *B* and his heirs—any words expressing the same intention are sufficient to raise a 'use.' In practice however, since the revival of the jurisdiction

or persons [1], or of any body politick [2], by reason of any bargain, sale, feoffment, fine, recovery, covenant, contract, agreement, will, or otherwise, by any manner means whatsoever it be; that in every such case, all and every such person and persons, and bodies politick, that have or hereafter shall have any such use, confidence, or trust, in fee simple, fee tail, for term of life, or for years, or otherwise; or any use, confidence, or trust, in remainder [3] or reverter, shall from henceforth stand and be seised, deemed, and adjudged in lawful seisin, estate, and possession of and in the same honours, castles, manors, lands, tenements, rents, services, reversions, remainders, and hereditaments, with their appurtenances, to all intents, constructions, and purposes in the law, of and in such like estates, as they had or shall have in use, trust, or confidence of or in the same; and that the estate, title, right, and possession that was in such person or persons that were or hereafter shall be seised of any lands, tenements, or hereditaments, to the use, confidence, or trust of any such person or persons, or of any body politick, be from henceforth clearly deemed and adjudged to be in him or them that have, or hereafter shall have such use, confidence, or trust, after such quality, manner, form, and condition as they had before, in or to the use, confidence, or trust that was in them [4].

of the Court of Chancery as explained below, the word *use* is commonly applied to a different species of interest to that designated by *trust*.

[1] One person must be seised to the use of *another*, so if lands are conveyed to *A* and *B* and their heirs to the use of *A* and *B* and their heirs, there is here no person seised to the use of another, and consequently the conveyance does not operate under the statute, but has its effect at common law. It is otherwise if there is any substantial difference between the persons to whom the seisin is given and the *cestuis que usent*, e.g. if lands are given to *A* and *B* and their heirs to the use of *A*, *B*, and *C* and their heirs. Here the statute operates.

[2] Or corporations, see above, p. 218, n. 1.

[3] Therefore remainders can be created by way of use as well as at common law; e.g. feoffment to *A* and his heirs to the use of *B* for life, remainder to the use of *C* in tail, remainder to the use of *D* in fee. See Table III in Appendix to Part I.

[4] The statute contains a double provision, (1) that the interest of *cestui que use* shall be turned into an actual possession or legal seisin (thus, if lands are given to *A* and his heirs to the use of *B* for life, or to the use of *C* for ten years, by virtue of this provision *B* is seised of a freehold estate for life and *C* is possessed of a term of ten years); (2) that the common law seisin shall be taken out of the grantees or feoffees and vested in *cestui que use*. Hence it follows that the estate limited to *cestui que use* must not be larger than that given to the grantee or feoffee to uses: e.g. a grant to *A* to the use of *B* and his heirs would only give *B* a life estate.

2. And be it further enacted by the authority aforesaid, That where divers and many persons be or hereafter shall happen to be jointly seised of and in any lands, tenements, rents, reversions, remainders, or other hereditaments, to the use, confidence, or trust of any of them that be so jointly seised [1], that in every such case that or those person or persons which have or hereafter shall have any such use, confidence, or trust, in any such lands, tenements, rents, reversions, remainders, or hereditaments, shall from henceforth have and be deemed and adjudged to have, only to him or them that have, or hereafter shall have, such use, confidence, or trust, such estate, possession, and seisin of and in the same lands, tenements, rents, reversions, remainders, and other hereditaments, in like nature, manner, form, condition, and course, as he or they had before in the use, confidence, or trust of the same lands, tenements, or hereditaments. . . . .

3. And where also divers persons stand and be seised of and in any lands, tenements, or hereditaments in fee-simple or otherwise, to the use or intent that some other person or persons shall have and perceive yearly to them and to his or their heirs one annual rent of x. li. or more or less out of the same lands and tenements, and some other person one other annual rent to him and his assigns for term of life, or years, or for some other special time, according to such intent and use as hath been heretofore declared, limited, and made thereof [2]: Be it therefore enacted by the authority aforesaid, that in every such case the same persons, their heirs, and assigns, that have such use and interest to have and perceive any such annual rents out of any lands, tenements, or hereditaments, that they and every of them, their heirs and assigns be adjudged and deemed to be in possession and seisin of the same rent of and in such like estate as they had in the title, interest, or use of the said rent or profit, and as if a sufficient grant or other lawful conveyance had been made and executed to them by such as were or shall be seised to the use or intent of any such rent to be had,

Therefore a seisin should always be created 'coextensive with the uses which are intended to be raised.' (Sugden's Gilbert on Uses, p. 127.) In practice, an estate in fee simple is always limited to the common law grantees.

[1] e. g. when there has been a feoffment to *A*, *B*, and *C* and their heirs to the use of *A* and his heirs.

[2] That is, where lands are vested by feoffment or otherwise in *A* and his heirs to the use and intent that *B* and his heirs for ever shall receive a rent (see above, p. 238, n. 2) issuing out of those lands.

made, or paid according to the very trust and intent thereof[1], and that all and every such person and persons as have or hereafter shall have any title, use, and interest, in or to any such rent or profit shall lawfully distrain for non-payment of the said rent, and in their own names make avowries, or by their bailiffs or servants make cognisances and justifications[2], and have all other suits, entries, and remedies, for such rents as if the same rents had been actually and really granted to them with sufficient clauses of distress, re-entry, or otherwise, according to such conditions, pains, or other things limited and appointed upon the trust and intent for payment or surety of such rent.

4. And be it further enacted by the authority aforesaid, that whereas divers persons have purchased, or have estate made and conveyed of and in divers lands, tenements, and hereditaments, unto them and to their wives and to the heirs of the husband, or to the husband and to the wife, and to the heirs of their two bodies begotten, or to the heirs of one of their bodies begotten, or to the husband and to the wife, for term of their lives, or for term of life of the said wife, or where any such estate or purchase of any lands, tenements, or hereditaments, hath been or hereafter shall be made to any husband and to his wife, in manner and form expressed, or to any other person or persons, and to their heirs and assigns, to the use and behoof of the said

[1] The effect of this provision is to vest the rent in *cestui que use* (*B*, last note), and consequently all the legal remedies for the rent are also vested in him, to the same extent as if he had received a direct grant of the rent operative at common law. The limitation of a rent in the first instance to *A* and his heirs to the use of *B* and his heirs is not touched by this section, which deals only with the case of a person being *seised* of *lands* to the use that another may receive a rent. Rent, however, is a 'tenement' within the first section, and therefore by a grant of a rent by deed to *A* and his heirs to the use of *B* and his heirs a use of the rent is executed in *B*, and all the legal remedies which he would have had by a direct grant at common law are vested in him. A rent, as has already been said, is regarded as a freehold interest, and the proper remedy for its recovery, before the abolition of real actions, was by assize of novel disseisin. By the Conveyancing and Law of Property Act, 1881, sec. 62, provision is made for a person being seised to the use that another may have an easement, which previously was not possible.

[2] When a person whose goods have been distrained seeks to replevy them (i. e. recover by an action of replevin), and the defendant justifies this taking of the goods, he is said to make *avowry* if he justifies in his own right (e. g. under a distress for rent in arrear due to him), and to make *cognisance* if he justifies in the right of another.

CH. VII. § 1.

husband and wife, or to the use of the wife, as is before rehearsed, for the jointer of the wife, that then in every such case every woman married having such jointer made or hereafter to be made shall not claim nor have title to have any dower of the residue of the lands, tenements, or hereditaments, that at any time were her said husband's, by whom she hath any such jointer, nor shall demand nor claim her dower of and against them that have the lands and inheritances of her said husband, but if she have no such jointer, then she shall be admitted and enabled to pursue, have, and demand her dower by writ of dower after the due course and order of the common laws of this realm, this act or any law or provision made to the contrary thereof notwithstanding [1].

5. Provided always that if any such woman be lawfully expulsed or evicted from her said jointer, or from any part thereof, without any fraud or covin, by lawful entry, action, or by discontinuance of her husband, then every such woman shall be endowed of as much of the residue of her husband's tenements or hereditaments, whereof she was before dowable, as the same lands and tenements so evicted and expulsed shall amount or extend unto.

7. Provided also, that if any wife have or hereafter shall have any manors, lands, tenements, or hereditaments unto her given and assured after marriage for term of her life or otherwise in jointer, except the same assurance be to her made by act of parliament, and the said wife after that fortune to overlive her said husband, in whose time the said jointer was made or assured unto her, that then the same wife so overliving shall and may at her liberty after the death of her said husband, refuse to have and take the lands and tenements so to her given, appointed, or

[1] The effect of the grant of lands to the use of a man and his wife has been already noticed. See above, p. 331. It will be seen from this passage that the original meaning of 'jointure' is a joint estate given by way of use to husband and wife jointly. In common acceptation, however, it extends to a sole estate, and is defined by Sir Edward Coke to be 'a competent livelihood of freehold for the wife of lands and tenements to take effect in profit or possession presently after the death of the husband for the life of the wife at least.' (Coke upon Littleton, 36 b.) Before this statute the widow would not have been endowed of the lands of which the husband only had the use. The conversion of his beneficial interest into the legal estate amongst other legal incidents caused the right of the widow's dower to attach, and thus the wife who had been provided for by means of a jointure would, but for this provision, have derived an additional benefit from the statute which had not been contemplated. It was therefore provided that a jointure properly created before marriage should be a bar to dower; and thus the law remains at the present day.

assured during the coverture, for term of her life, or otherwise in jointer, except the same assurance be to her made by act of parliament, as is aforesaid, and thereupon to have, ask, demand, and take her dower by writ of dower, or otherwise, according to the common law, of and in all such lands, tenements, and hereditaments, as her husband was and stood seised of any state of inheritance at any time during the coverture; anything contained in this act to the contrary in anywise notwithstanding.

9. And forasmuch as great ambiguities and doubts may arise of the validity and invalidity of wills heretofore made of any lands, tenements, and hereditaments to the great trouble of the King's subjects, the King's most royal Majesty minding the tranquillity and rest of his loving subjects, of his most excellent and accustomed goodness is pleased and contented that it be enacted, by the authority of this present parliament, that all manner true and just wills and testaments heretofore made by any person or persons deceased, or that shall decease before the first day of May that shall be in the year of our Lord God 1536, of any lands, tenements, or other hereditaments, shall be taken and accepted good and effectual in the law, after such fashion, manner, and form, as they were commonly taken and used at any time within forty years next afore the making of this act, anything contained in this act, or in the preamble thereof, or any opinion of the common law to the contrary thereof notwithstanding[1].

10. Provided always, that the King's Highness shall not have, demand, or take any advantage or profit for or by occasion of the executing of any estate only by authority of this act to any person or persons or bodies politick, which now have or on this side the said first day of May which shall be in the year of our Lord God 1536, shall have any use or uses, trusts, or confidences in any manors, lands, tenements, or hereditaments holden of the King's Highness by reason of primer seisin, livery, ouster-le-main, fine for alienation, relief, or harriot, but that fines for alienation, reliefs, and harriots shall be paid to the King's Highness, and also liveries, and ouster-le-mains shall be sued for uses, trusts, and confidences, to be made and executed in possession by authority of this act, after and from the said first day of May, of lands, and tenements, and other hereditaments holden of the King in such like manner and form, to all intents, constructions, and purposes as hath heretofore been used or accustomed by the order of the laws of this realm.

[1] See Chap. VIII.

CH. VII. § 2.

15. Provided also, that this act nor anything therein contained, shall not be prejudicial to the King's Highness for wardships of heirs now being within age, nor for liveries, or for ouster-le-mains, to be sued by any person or persons now being within age, or of full age, of any lands or tenements unto the same heir or heirs now already descended; anything in this act contained to the contrary notwithstanding.

§ 2. *Effect of the Statute of Uses upon the power of dealing with the Legal Estate in Lands.*

The Statute of Uses at once produced important effects upon the old modes of conveying the legal estate in lands. It has been already seen what were the appropriate modes of conveying freehold estates at common law. If the freehold was to pass immediately from the grantor to the grantee, feoffment with livery of seisin was the only appropriate mode. In practice the same result was accomplished by the fictitious processes of fines and recoveries. It has also been seen under what circumstances the Chancellor would before the Statute have held that the party taking by the common law conveyance would hold to the use, not of himself, but of the grantee or some other person. Wherever, with certain exceptions to be hereafter noticed [1], such a construction would before the Statute have been put upon the conveyance by the Chancellor —wherever a use would have been raised in favour of some person other than the feoffee or grantee at common law, by reason either of an express declaration of the use, or of circumstances from which the intention of raising the use would necessarily have been inferred, in all such cases after the Statute the legal estate passed to the person in whose favour the use was declared or implied.

Thus if a feoffment, a fine, or a recovery was made, levied, or suffered to *A* and his heirs to the use of *B* for ten years, and subject thereto to the use of *C* for life, and after *C*'s decease to the use of *D* in tail, with remainder to the use of *E*

[1] Active trusts, trusts of leasehold interests, and uses upon uses. See below, § 4.

in fee, the various estates would take effect by virtue of the Statute according to the several limitations, just as if a valid conveyance of them had been made operating at common law. The livery of seisin necessary to pass the freehold by feoffment need only have been made to *A*, the Statute is then called into operation, and is powerful enough, without anything further, to take the property from *A* and to vest it in the various persons according to their specified interests.

In the same way, if a feoffment was made by *A* to *B* and his heirs without consideration, the use would before the Statute, as has been before seen, have been held to come back to *A*. The Statute 'executes' this use, and the legal as well as the beneficial interest *results*, or comes back to the feoffor.

The distinction made in the text-books between the raising of a use by a conveyance operating by transmutation of possession, and raising a use without transmutation of possession, has already been noticed [1]. In the former case a mode of conveyance is employed sufficient at common law to take the estate out of the donor and to vest it in the donee. To this conveyance is superadded, either by express words or by necessary implication, the obligation upon the donee to hold to the use of the donor or of some third person, or of the donor together with some third person.

Instances of dispositions of land of this kind would be, feoffment by *A* to *B* to the use of *C*, conveyance by way of fine or recovery from *A* to *B* to the use of *A* and *C*, feoffment by *A* to *B* without consideration. In these cases no estate vests permanently in *B*. The common law seisin which is given to him serves only to bring the Statute into operation. In the first of the above cases the legal estate vests at once in *C*, in the second in *A* and *C* jointly, in the last it results at once or comes back to *A*.

Uses are raised without transmutation of possession when the legal owner of lands binds himself to hold the lands for

[1] See above, p. 329.

the use of some other person. It has already been seen that the usual mode of effecting this before the Statute was by bargain and sale, or covenant to stand seised[1]. In these cases the use, which before the Statute was raised in favour of the covenantee or bargainee, is now executed by the Statute, and thus these two assurances take their places as modes of conveying the legal interest in lands. Thus *A* covenants to stand seised for *B* his eldest son and his heirs, or in consideration of £100 bargains and sells his lands to *C* and his heirs. *B* and *C* by force of the Statute take an estate in fee simple in precisely the same way as if that estate had been conveyed to them respectively by feoffment at common law.

It will be easily seen that the Statute at once enabled a tenant in fee simple to deal with his lands in ways which would have been impossible at common law. For instance, at common law a man cannot convey to himself any interest in lands. Thus, suppose *A* and *B* are jointly seised of lands as trustees[2], and *A* dies, whereby the whole estate vests in *B*, and it is desired to appoint *C* a new trustee, and to vest the lands in *B* and *C* jointly[3]. Before the Statute it would have been necessary for *B* to make a feoffment with livery to *D* and his heirs, so that *D* might make a feoffment with livery to *B* and *C* and their heirs; after the Statute the same object might be effected by one conveyance, namely, to *D* and his heirs to the use of *B* and *C* and their heirs. This is the ordinary mode of vesting trust-estates in a new trustee.

So by bringing the Statute into operation a man may convey a legal estate to his wife, which is impossible at common law[4].

[1] See above, p. 330. [2] As to trustees see below, § 4.

[3] As to joint tenants see above, Chap. V. § 4. Observe that a simple conveyance of a moiety by *B* to *C* would make *B* and *C* tenants in common and not joint tenants, a kind of interest much less suitable to the position of trustees, as each trustee would in that case have a separate inheritance which would devolve on his own representatives.

[4] Sugden's Gilbert on Uses, p. 150.

One of the immediate effects of the Statute was, as has been seen, to give legal validity and effect to 'bargains and sales.' These transactions required no particular ceremony, no open or notorious act, such as livery of seisin; and thus one of the great objects of the Statute, the prevention of secret conveyances, would have been eluded. This was at once perceived by the legislature, and in the same year a second Act was passed intended to prevent the mischief of secret bargains and sales by providing for their enrolment in one of the superior courts or before the *custos rotulorum* of the county in which the lands were situate[1].

Another effect of the Statute of Uses was to introduce at once modes of dealing with the legal interest, in respect to the period and conditions of its commencement and termination, which were wholly unknown to the common law.

It has been shown in the sixth chapter that before the Statute the Chancellor was in the habit of enforcing uses created so as to arise at a future time. Such limitations now became effectual also at law, and conveyancers were thus enabled to introduce limitations of much greater complication, in dealing with the legal estate, than was possible at common law.

This will be best understood by examples. When once a conveyance is made effectual to give the common law seisin in fee to the grantees to uses, any number of uses may be created to arise in succession. In other words, interests may be given within certain limits (to be explained presently) to a greater number of persons, and to arise and come to an end on a greater variety of contingencies than was possible at the common law. For instance, a person in contemplation of the marriage of his eldest son wishes to settle lands upon him and upon the issue of the marriage. Accordingly *A*, the settlor, conveys the lands to *B* and *C* and their heirs to the use of himself and his heirs until the intended marriage. *A* therefore takes back to himself an estate

[1] See below, § 3.

CH. VII. § 2. in fee simple until the marriage takes place, and if it does not take place at all, no actual change occurs in his rights of property over the land. The next limitation may be, after the marriage to the use of *B* and *C* (the trustees) for a term of 99 years upon certain trusts, e. g. to pay a sum for pin-money to the wife during the marriage. The next limitation may be, after the determination of the said term and in the meantime subject thereto and to the trusts thereof to the use of *A* the settlor for life. This would not be possible at the common law, for no estate could be limited after a fee simple, nor could a man convey any interest to himself; but as before the Statute there was nothing to prevent the trustees being bound to hold to a different trust upon the happening of a specified event, so there is nothing since the Statute to prevent the legal estate in fee simple changing on the happening of the specified event to a legal estate for life. Then after *A*'s death to the use of his eldest son for life. This is a vested remainder, as explained in Chapter V[1]. Then to the use of such son's eldest son in tail. This gives a contingent remainder to the eldest son, and is usually followed by similar remainders to other sons and other provisions, last of all by a remainder to the use of *A* and his heirs, or of the heirs of *A* for ever, which gives *A* an ultimate remainder in fee simple[2].

[1] Prior to the Statute 8 and 9 Vict. c. 106 (see above, p. 268), which prevented the destruction of contingent remainders by alienation merger or forfeiture of the particular estate, it was usual to insert in settlements before the limitation of the contingent remainders, a vested remainder to the use of trustees during the life of the tenant of the particular estate upon trust to preserve the contingent remainders, and for that purpose to make any entries or bring any actions that might be necessary. This device is said to have been invented during the time of the Commonwealth by Sir Orlando Bridgeman and Sir Geoffry Palmer. See Blackstone, ii. p. 172.

[2] It may be useful to compare the form of a marriage settlement of land given in Schedule IV of the Conveyancing and Law of Property Act, 1881, 44 and 45 Vict. c. 41:—

This Indenture, made the day of 1882, between John M. of of the 1st part, and Jane S. of of the 2nd part, and *X* of and *Y* of of the 3rd part, Witnesseth that in consideration of the intended marriage between John M. and Jane S. John

A case is reported where a man bargained and sold in fee part of his estate and covenanted to give the bargainee the offer of the residue, and that if he (the bargainor) should 'go about to alien' the residue to another that then he would stand seised to the use of the bargainee in fee[1]. The event subsequently happened, the bargainor did attempt to alien the residue to another, and it was held that the use thereupon arose in favour of the bargainee, and that the legal estate passed to him. So, although at common law a feoffment could not be made to take effect at a future time, a feoffment to *A* and his heirs to the use of *B* and his heirs at the death of *J. S.*—a living person—would be valid, and upon the death of *J. S.* the legal estate would vest in *B*, the use in the meantime resulting to *A*.

The above instances may suffice to suggest a distinction which is usually made between what are called (1) *shifting uses*, (2) *springing uses*, (3) *future* or *contingent uses*, or more properly, uses limited to take effect as remainders.

The distinction between the first two of the above classes has in the history of the law been of less importance than the distinction between those two classes and the third.

M. as settlor hereby conveys to *X* and *Y*. All that &c. To hold to *X* and *Y* in fee simple to the use of John M. in fee simple until the marriage, and after the marriage to the use of John M. during his life without impeachment of waste with remainder after his death to the use that Jane S., if she survives him, may receive during the rest of her life a yearly jointure rentcharge of £ , and subject to the before mentioned rentcharge to the use of *X* and *Y* for a term of five hundred years without impeachment of waste on the trusts hereinafter declared, and subject thereto to the use of the first and other sons of John M. and Jane S. successively according to seniority in tail male with remainder (*insert here, if thought desirable,* to the use of the same first and other sons successively according to seniority in tail with remainder) to the use of all the daughters of John M. and Jane S. in equal shares as tenants in common in tail with cross remainders between them in tail with remainder to the use of John M. in fee simple (*insert trusts of term of 500 years for raising portions,* &c.)

In witness, &c.

The expressions 'in fee,' 'in tail' are by the Act (sect. 51) made sufficient without the use of the words 'heirs,' or 'heirs of the body.'

[1] Sugden's Gilbert, p. 161. Rolle's Abridgment, p. 786. M, 40 and 41 Elizabeth.

CH. VII. § 2.

A *shifting use* is where a use has been properly created, and then upon the happening of some specified event the interest first created passes away from the person enjoying it, and vests, partially or wholly, in some other person. For instance, if lands are given to *A* and his heirs to the use of *B* and his heirs, but if *B* die in the lifetime of *A* then to the use of *C* and his heirs. Upon the death of *B* in *A*'s lifetime the use is said to shift to *C*[1]. Again, a provision is often made by way of the creation of a shifting use for an estate shifting away from the person to whom it is first given to some other member of the family on the acquisition of some other estate. Thus by the aid of shifting uses the old rules as to the creation of future estates by way of remainder may be evaded, a future freehold interest can since the Statute be created by way of shifting use to take effect without waiting for the determination of a particular estate, and an estate in fee simple can by the same method be made to pass from one person to another. Nor can any alienation or disposition of the lands by the first *cestui que use* affect the interest of the person who, upon the happening of the specified contingency, is entitled to the use of the lands[2].

Springing uses differ from shifting uses merely in the fact of their arising by virtue of the mode of their creation as new uses, and not operating by way of shifting of a use already created from one person to another. Thus the instance of a bargain and sale and covenant above given, and a feoffment to take effect in future, are instances of the creation of springing uses[3].

[1] Shifting uses appear to have been introduced very soon after the passing of the Statute of Uses. Brooke's Abridgment, Feoffment al Uses, 330 b. no. 30, gives an instance in 6 Edward VI. The report concludes, 'Et ideo vide que homme al cest jour poit faire feoffment al use, et que l'use changera de un in autre par act ex post facto par circumstance, si bien que il fera devant l'estatute 27 H. VIII, de uses.'

[2] Compare Markby's Elements of Law, p. 164, n. 1.

[3] There is an instance of a springing use in Brooke's Abridgment, 331 b, 50. in 30 Henry VIII, three years after the passing of the Statute of Uses. 'If *A* covenant with *B* that when *A* shall be enfeoffed by *B* of 3 acres in *D*,

Both shifting and springing uses are subject to the 'rule against perpetuity,' the history and nature of which will be noticed presently.

Future or *contingent uses*, or, as they might be called, uses limited as remainders, present somewhat different features, though the importance of the distinction is much diminished by the recent Act 40 and 41 Vict. c. 33. By a series of decisions a rule was established that if a limitation could be regarded as a remainder it should not be regarded as a springing or shifting use[1]. Nor was this rule affected by the consideration that the use might be void if the stringent requirements which the common law demanded in the case of contingent remainders were not complied with. Thus if it unfortunately happened that the conveyancer in drawing the deed expressed the conditions on which the future use was to arise in such a way that the future estate could be construed as a remainder, and if, at the same time, such remainder was contrary to the old common law rules affecting remainders, which had long ceased to be founded on any substantial reason, the future interest was invalid in consequence of this defect in point of law. For instance, if a conveyance was made to *B* and his heirs to the use of *A* for 10 years, remainder to the use of the heirs of *J. S.*, the remainder was void, being a contingent remainder limited upon an estate for years[2]. The fact that if the limitation did not happen to fall within the definition of a remainder, it might be good as a springing use, was utterly disregarded. Perhaps in no point

that then the said *A* and his heirs and all others seised of the land of *A* in *S*, shall be seised of it to the use of the said *B* and his heirs, then if *A* make a feoffment of his land in *S*, and then *B* enfeoff *A* of the said 3 acres of land in *D*, then the feoffee of *A* shall be seised to the use of *B*, notwithstanding that he had no notice of the use, for the land is and was bound by the aforesaid use, into whatsoever hands it might come, and it is not like the case where the feoffee to uses sells the land to one who has no notice of the first use, for in the first-mentioned case the use had no existence until the feoffment of the 3 acres was made, and then the use commenced.'

[1] See Sugden's note to Gilbert on Uses, p. 172.

[2] Ib., p. 165.

CH. VII. § 2. was the extreme technicality of the rules relating to uses more conspicuous, owing no doubt in part to the ideas spoken of at the commencement of this chapter. A partial remedy for this injustice in the case of contingent remainders created by instruments executed after August 2, 1877, has been provided by the Statute 40 and 41 Vict. c. 33, by which it is provided that every contingent remainder . . . in tenements or hereditaments of any tenure which would have been valid as a springing or shifting use or executory devise or other limitation had it not had a sufficient estate to support it as a contingent remainder, shall, *in the event of the particular estate determining before the contingent remainder vests,* be capable of taking effect in all respects as if the contingent remainder had originally been created as a springing or shifting use or executory devise or other executory limitation [1].

One of the commonest modes of calling into operation the Statute of Uses is by the creation of what are called *powers of appointment*, that is, conferring on a person a power of disposing of an interest in lands quite irrespective of the fact whether or not he has any interest in the land himself. The creator or donor of the power in disposing of the lands makes a conveyance operative at common law, and at the same time declares that such and such uses are to arise on the execution of a proper instrument by a designated person. This is called technically giving to a person a *power of appointment,* and the instrument when executed operates as an *appointment.* The estate which passes under the power of appointment comes not from the donee of the power, but from the original settlor [2]; the only difference between an interest thus created

[1] It will be seen that the effect of the Statute is considerably narrowed by the words in italics.

[2] This it is important to remember, as certain practical consequences follow. Amongst others, the amount of succession duty payable is often affected by the consideration whether the donee takes from the settlor who created the power, who may be a near relation, or from the person who has executed the power in his favour, who may be a stranger in blood.

and an immediate conveyance being that, instead of the uses being declared by the original settlor at the time of the conveyance of the legal estate, it is left to a third person to declare them. CH. VII. § 2.

Thus it was common in ordinary purchase deeds of land, where the purchaser was married on or before Jan. 1, 1834[1], to introduce provisions of this kind in order to bar effectually any claim to dower on the part of his widow. No estate of inheritance in possession was given to the purchase at all, but he was invested with a power of disposing of the lands for any estate. This was effected by conveying the lands to *A* and his heirs to such uses &c. as *B* (the purchaser) should appoint, and in default of and until appointment to the use of *B* for life, remainder to the use of *A* and his heirs during the life of *B*[2], remainder to the use of *B* and his heirs. Under these limitations *B* never had more than an estate for life in possession, and therefore his widow's dower could not attach. At the same time, by exercising the power of appointment he could in effect convey an estate in fee simple to any other person[3].

Powers of appointment are sometimes general, and may be exercised by the creation of any estate in favour of any one, including the donee of the power himself or his wife. Sometimes they are special, and can only be exercised by creating some particular kind of estate, or in favour of particular persons or classes of persons.

The forms prescribed in the instrument creating the power

[1] When the Dower Act (3 and 4 Will. IV, c. 105) came into operation, by which a simpler method of barring dower was introduced.

[2] A vested remainder which might by possibility take effect by the determination of *B*'s life estate in his lifetime, and was therefore sufficient to keep apart *B*'s life interest, and prevent it merging in the ultimate remainder in fee.

[3] Sometimes a person has an estate in fee simple and also a general power of appointment. In this case he can convey either by exercising his power or conveying his estate in the ordinary way. In the former case the exercise of the power defeats and divests his own estate : in the latter case the conveyance of the estate extinguishes the power.

CH. VII. § 2. must be strictly observed, otherwise the power will not have been effectually executed. For instance, the power may be given to be exercised by deed, in which case a will purporting to exercise it would be inoperative, and *vice versa* [1].

When modes of creating future interests in lands by means of shifting and springing uses became common, a question of great importance presented itself for solution, as to the period within which interests by way of uses arising at a future time might be created. It is plain that unless some limit of time had been adopted, limitations might have been introduced into settlements by which estates might have been divested and created at remote periods, and thus in effect an unreasonable restraint on alienation of lands might be introduced. And when, as will be explained in the next chapter, the power of disposing of lands by will was made part of the general law of the land, and wills were regarded as resembling conveyances to uses rather than as instruments operating at common law, the same question arose still more frequently upon the effect of devises of future interests in land, or as they were called, *executory devises*.

What limits then are imposed by law regulating the time within which future or executory interests in land created by instruments operating under the Statute of Uses or by will must take effect? It has already been seen that the creation of future estates by way of remainder is limited by the rule that an estate given to an unborn person for life cannot be followed by any estate given to any child of such unborn person [2]. It followed from this that the great object of settlements of lands, the preserving them in the settlor's family,

[1] For certain relaxations as to the strictness which the law requires to execution of powers, and as to the relief which in some cases may be obtained in Equity against defective execution of powers, see Williams, Real Property, pp. 354, 355.

[2] See above, p. 268, and Williams on Real Property, p. 379. The rule is there traced to Sir Edward Coke's metaphysical distinction between a single or common and a double or remote possibility. It is a rule different from and not 'superseded by the more modern rule against perpetuities': see Whitby v. Mitchell, Law Reports, 44 Chancery Division, 85.

could be attained only to the extent of giving an estate tail to an unborn member of the family. But this estate, after the introduction of the practice of suffering recoveries, was always liable to be turned into a fee simple and alienated, so soon as the tenant in tail came of age. The result was that settlements operating by way of creating estates in remainder could not absolutely prevent the alienation of lands for a longer period than during a life or lives in being and twenty-one years after. To this must be added a few months in the event of tenant in tail being *en ventre sa mere* at the time of the dropping of the previous life estate.

Future estates created by way of executory devise and springing or shifting uses required the invention of other rules as to the period within which such interests must arise. The earlier cases tend to limit the creation of such estates by the rule that they can only take effect after a life in being [1]. Next, this limit seems to have been extended to embrace the case of an infant taking under an executory devise or by way of future use; such limitations were upheld to the extent of allowing the vesting of the estate at the time of the infant attaining majority after the dropping of a life in being. Finally, in Cadell v. Palmer [2] it was held that future interests might be created by way of executory devise or springing use to take effect twenty-one years after the dropping of a life or lives in being without reference to minority. Thus the power of a person having an estate in fee simple over his land has been to some extent extended by judicial legislation. Any attempt however, directly or indirectly, to evade the 'rule against perpetuities' by controlling the alienation of lands for a longer period than a life or lives in being and twenty-one years after is void [3]. Thus if lands be granted to *A* and his

[1] For the earlier history of the rule see Pollock, Land Laws, Note G.

[2] 1 Clark and Finnelly, 372.

[3] John Duke of Marlborough devised lands to trustees in trust for several persons for life, with remainders to their first and other sons in tail male successively, and directed the trustees upon the birth of every son of each tenant for life to revoke the uses before limited to their

CH. VII. § 3. heirs to the use of *B* and his heirs until failure of the issue of *C*, and upon such failure to *D* and his heirs, the last limitation would be void, because it might be that the failure of the issue of *C* would not happen, if at all, till a distant period.

§ 3. *Statute of Enrolments.*

The main provisions of the following Statute have been already referred to [1]. A bargain and sale enrolled under its provisions is still a possible mode of conveying a freehold interest in lands.

An examination of the language of the Statute shows that its provisions only extend to prevent any estate of *inheritance* or *freehold* being created without the observance of the prescribed forms. The Statute therefore did not extend to the creation of a term of years to arise by way of bargain and sale out of an estate of freehold. If *A*, tenant in fee simple, bargained and sold his lands to *B* for ten years, there was no necessity for any enrolment, or even for any writing to evidence the transaction. The Statute of Uses at once operated upon the bargain and sale; one person, the bargainor, was seised to the use of another, the bargainee, and there was no necessity for enrolment, inasmuch as the bargain and sale did not purport to create an estate of inheritance or freehold.

After a time an ingenious conveyancer [2] bethought him of availing himself of a bargain and sale as a secret mode of conveying freehold interests in lands, thus avoiding the necessity of any livery of seisin or of enrolment. It was after some doubt at length held by the Court of Wards [3] that a

respective sons in tail male, and to limit the lands to such sons for their lives, with remainders to the respective sons of such sons in tail male. It was held by Lord Keeper Henley (1759) that the clause of revocation and resettlement was void, as tending to a perpetuity and being repugnant to the estate limited. 1 Eden's Reports, 404.

[1] See above, p. 357.

[2] See Fonblanque on Equity, ii. p. 12.

[3] In the 18th of James I. Lutwidge v. Mitton, Croke's Reports, James, 604.

bargain and sale for a term of years gave to the lessee by force of the words of the Statute of Uses 'possession' of his term as if he had actually entered on the land, at all events for the purpose of being capable of taking by a simple deed a release of the reversion [1]. Thus if *A*, tenant in fee simple, bargained and sold the manor of Dale to *B* for a year, and the day after executed a release of the reversion in fee to *B* and his heirs, he would by the bargain and sale have immediately vested in him an estate for a year in possession. He would thereupon become capable of taking a release, and so soon as the release was executed, the smaller estate and the larger would coalesce and the term be 'merged' or sunk in the larger estate, whereupon *B* would become tenant in fee simple in possession [2]. So popular did this conveyance become, that in ordinary cases it entirely superseded the feoffment, and bargain and sale enrolled, and became the general mode of conveying freeholds *inter vivos* till the year 1841. In that year an act was passed 'for rendering a release as effectual for the conveyance of freehold estates as a lease and release by the same parties [3].' This Act was repealed in 1844 by the Act to simplify the Transfer of Property [4]; and in 1845 the last-mentioned Act was in its turn repealed and superseded by the provisions of the Act to amend the Law of Real Property [5]. The second section of this Act gives the power of creating and transferring a leasehold estate in possession by a simple deed of grant. The effect of the Statute of Uses is however still preserved, and a grant to uses under the Act to amend the Law of Real Property operates in precisely the same way, and is subject to precisely the same rules as any of the other conveyances to uses above noticed. The form of the conveyance of land has been still further shortened and simplified by the Conveyancing Acts, 1881, 1882, 44 and 45 Vict. c. 41, and 45 and 46 Vict. c. 39; but the principles of the law as affected by the previous statutes remain unaltered.

[1] See above, p. 261.

[2] See above, Chap. V. § 1.

[3] 4 and 5 Vict. c. 21.

[4] 7 and 8 Vict. c. 76.

[5] 8 and 9 Vict. c. 106.

CH. VII. § 4.

27 Henry VIII, cap. 16.

An Act concerning Enrolments of Bargains and Contracts of Lands and Tenements.

Be it enacted by the authority of this present parliament, that from the last day of July, which shall be in the year of our Lord God 1536, no manors, lands, tenements, or other hereditaments, shall pass, alter, or change from one to another, whereby any estate of inheritance or freehold shall be made or take effect in any person or persons, or any use thereof to be made, by reason only of any bargain and sale thereof[1], except the same bargain and sale be made by writing indented, sealed, and enrolled in one of the King's Courts of Record at Westminster, or else within the same county or counties where the same manors, lands, or tenements so bargained and sold lie or be, before the *Custos Rotulorum* and two Justices of the Peace, and the Clerk of the Peace of the same county or counties, or two of them at the least, whereof the Clerk of the Peace to be one; and the same enrolment to be had and made within six months next after the date of the same writings indented. . . . . And that the Clerk of the Peace for the time being, within every such county, shall sufficiently enrol and engross in parchment the same deeds or writings indented as is aforesaid, and the rolls thereof at the end of every year shall deliver unto the said *Custos Rotulorum* of the same county for the time being, there to remain in the custody of the said *Custos Rotulorum* for the time being, amongst other records of every of the same counties where any such enrolment shall be so made, to the intent that every party that hath to do therewith may resort and see the effect and tenor of every such writing so enrolled.

§ 4. *Equitable Estates in Lands since the Statute of Uses.*

The object of the framers of the Statute of Uses was undoubtedly to do away with the distinction between the legal estate and the beneficial interest in lands which had given rise to the mischiefs recited in the preamble of the Statute. The properties which before the Statute had gathered round

[1] Observe that the case of a bargain and sale by *A*, tenant in fee simple, to the use of *B* for years, is not within the language of the statute.

the beneficial interest or use under the judicial legislation of the Chancellors now with some modification attached to the legal interest in lands. The modifications which the legal interest in lands consequently underwent, the increased powers of disposition and control which the owner in fee acquired, have already been traced. But in some points the Statute fell short of what was required. The principle that a conscientious obligation unrecognised by the law might be enforced by the Chancellor was not affected by the Statute. If therefore there still were found cases of the creation of legal estates upon trust for certain purposes, which estates could not be *executed* or transferred from the common law grantee to the beneficiary by the force of the Statute, it would be still within the power of the Chancellor to decree that the conscientious obligations should be carried out.

This occurred principally in three cases [1]. In the first place an active duty might be imposed on the grantee of the land to do certain acts in reference to it for the benefit of somebody else. Land might be granted to *A* upon trust to collect and pay over the rents to *B*. Here it would be evidently intended that *A* should be legal owner, but a conscientious obligation would bind him to carry out the trust upon which he had received the land. Where therefore an active duty was imposed on the common law grantee, the use or trust was not executed by the Statute, but it was left to be enforced by the Court of Chancery. It is not always in practice an easy

[1] See Equity Cases Abridged, i. 383. 'Notwithstanding this statute (27 Hen. VIII, c. 10) there are three ways of creating an use or a trust which still remains as at common law, and is a creature of the Courts of Equity, and subject only to their controul and direction. 1st. Where a man seised in fee raises a term of years and limits it in trust for *A* &c., for this the statute cannot execute, the termor not being seised. 2ndly. Where lands are limited to the use of *A* in trust to permit *B* to receive the rents and profits, for the statute can only execute the first use. 3rdly. Where lands are limited to trustees to receive and pay over the rents and profits to such and such persons, for here the lands must remain in them to answer these purposes: and these points were agreed to. Trin. 1700.' *Symson* and *Turner*, *per Curiam*.

CH. VII. § 4. matter to say when the trust which is imposed on the legal owner is in the nature of an active duty, or when it is a use, trust, or confidence executed by the Statute. If lands are conveyed to *A* upon trust to allow *B* to receive the profits, no active duty being imposed on *A*, this use is within the Statute and is executed, the legal estate vesting in *B*[1].

The second case was where a trust was declared upon a leasehold interest. It has already been seen that this case is not provided for by the Statute[2]. If therefore a term of ten years be given to *A* in trust for *B*, the legal estate vests in *A*, and the trust could (before November 1, 1875) only be enforced by the Court of Chancery.

But the most important defect, to remedy which the jurisdiction of the Court of Chancery was ultimately called into action, arose from the strange doctrine laid down in Tyrrell's case[3].

It has often been remarked that English law bears traces of the realist doctrines of the Schoolmen. To deal with the conception of a use of lands as if it were a real thing, and to draw practical conclusions, however inconvenient, from this abstract idea, seemed perfectly natural to the lawyers of the sixteenth century. Thus it was a matter of most serious consideration in what manner the use could be preserved so as to arise and take effect in the case of future contingent uses. For instance, in a conveyance to *A* and *B* and their heirs to the use of *C* and his heirs till the marriage of *D*, and afterwards to the use of *D* for life, remainder to the use of *D*'s eldest son, &c., it was made a grave question whether any rational account could be given of the reason why these future uses took effect. The ability of the common law

[1] This distinction was taken as early as the thirty-sixth year of Henry VIII. 'Home fait feoffment in fee al son use pur term de vie et que puis son decease J. N. prendra les profits, ceo fait un use in J. N. Contrar. s'il dit que puis son mort ses feoffees prendront les profits et liveront eux al J. N. : ceo ne fait use in J. N., car il nad eux nisi par les mains les feoffees.' Brooke's Abridgment, Feoffment al Uses, 52.

[2] See above, p. 348, n. 1.

[3] See below, p. 375.

seisin to furnish forth the use had been exhausted, it had supplied the vested legal interest of *C* to an extent coextensive with itself, but how was it to supply that of *D* and of his unborn son besides? Who could be said to be seised to the use of *D*'s unborn son [1]? It is impossible even to state these difficulties in language intelligible to us, so completely has the mode of thought which gave them birth passed away. But such was the spirit in which the Statute of Uses was construed.

Reasoning of a similar character led the lawyers to hold that, when once the statute had been called into operation, its powers were exhausted, and that, if a feoffment were made to *A* and his heirs to the use of *B* and his heirs to the use of *C* and his heirs, it was impossible to give any effect to the limitation in favour of *C*. That 'a use could not be engendered of a use' seemed no doubt a natural and intelligible proposition to Saunders, Chief Justice [2]. It is a specimen of a rule of law with the most important consequences springing not from any consideration of its relation to expediency or to the wants of the community, but from an exaggerated conception of the mysterious qualities possessed by 'a use of lands,' and the consequences which flowed from them.

Thus the doctrine arose that there could not be a use upon a use. If therefore *A* bargained and sold to *B* to the

[1] Hence the wonderful doctrine of *scintilla juris* which required an act of Parliament (23 and 24 Vict. c. 38. s. 7) for its abolition. See Williams on Real Property, p. 349. A curious instance of the tenacity of metaphysical ideas may be seen in the wording of this section. The draughtsman found it necessary to say that the estate of *cestui que use* is to take effect 'by force of and by relation to the estate and seisin originally vested in the person seised to the uses.' What meaning can be attached to these words? The limitations in the text are simply a mode of providing that upon a given event *D* shall take the estate, that upon *D*'s death it shall go to his eldest son, and that neither *C* nor *D* shall prevent these dispositions taking effect by any alienation. The curious point is that these effects of the Statute of Uses are the result not of considerations of public policy influencing either the legislature or the tribunals, but of the supposed logical consequences of the metaphysical conception of a use.

[2] See below, p. 375.

CH. VII. § 4. use of *C*, the second use was considered wholly void. No consideration was paid to the obvious intention of the transaction, the consequence was supposed to follow from the nature of the use. Here then was a case for the interference of the Chancellor. It appears that by the time of Sir E. Coke, the uses upon uses which the common law courts refused to recognise were enforced in Chancery[1]. Thus was restored the distinction between the equitable and the legal estate, which it had been the design of the Statute of Uses to abolish.

These second uses were thenceforth known under the name of trusts. If lands were conveyed to *A* and his heirs, to the use of *B* and his heirs, in trust for *C* and his heirs, *B* had the legal estate by force of the Statute of Uses. *C*'s interest was wholly created and protected by the Court of Chancery.

So if lands are conveyed to *A* and his heirs to such uses as he shall appoint; and he appoints to *B* and his heirs to the use of *C* and his heirs, the legal estate is vested in *B*, and *C*'s interest is equitable only. For all practical purposes *C* is the owner of the estate. He can call upon *B* to convey to him or his nominee; he can himself part with his interest to another person, for whom *B* will, upon notice given to him, be a trustee; *C*'s estate will descend to his heir according to the rules of law.

Such is the origin of modern Trusts under which so large a portion of the land of the country is held. The student must accustom himself to the use and meaning of these technical terms. The *legal estate* is vested in the *trustee*, *in trust for* the *cestui que trust*, who has the *equitable estate*. Whenever the rules of law are applicable, trusts or equitable estates or interests follow those rules. Thus an equitable estate may be

[1] See Foorde v. Hoskins in 12 James I (2 Bulstrode, p. 337), in the course of which case Coke says, 'If *cestui que use* desires the feoffees to make an estate over, and they so to do refuse, for this refusal an action upon the case lieth not, because for this he hath his proper remedy by a subpoena in the Chancery.' It seems that this could only apply to a use upon a use.

created in fee, in tail, for life, or for years; an equitable estate tail may be barred in the same way as a legal estate tail; it will descend *ab intestato* according to the rules regulating legal estates; future estates in remainder and executory interests can be created in the same way, and are subject to the rule against perpetuity[1]; the husband of *cestui que trust* is entitled to an estate by the curtesy, and the widow (since 3 and 4 Will. IV, c. 105) to dower.

Besides the creation of trusts of lands expressly by a declaration of the intent of the grantor, which, though complete in itself, is insufficient to convey the legal estate, there is also a large class of what are called *implied trusts.* This is too large a subject to be discussed here, and it must be sufficient to say that wherever, according to the principles which regulated the action of the Court of Chancery as it existed before Nov. 1, 1875, it would be inequitable from circumstances of fraud, mistake, or otherwise, for the legal owner of the land to be also the beneficial owner, the legal owner will be held to be a trustee for the person who is in equity entitled to the lands. Thus if a person has agreed to buy land, and has paid the purchase money without receiving a formal conveyance, the legal owner will be held to be a trustee for him.

The creation or assignment of trust estates in land must under the provisions of the Statute of Frauds[2] be evidenced by writing, but no other solemnity is necessary. This provision however, does not apply to implied or resulting trusts[3]. The same statute in effect rendered trust estates in the hands of

[1] It should be observed that the rule that the freehold could not be in abeyance was not applicable to trust estates. There is therefore nothing to prevent a contingent equitable remainder being limited so as to take effect after a particular estate for years, nor was such a contingent remainder liable to be destroyed before the statute 8 and 9 Vict. c. 106, by the forfeiture, surrender, or merger of the particular estate. (See Williams on Real Property, p. 344; Fearne, p. 284; and above, p. 268.)

[2] 29 Car. II, c. 3. ss. 7, 9.

[3] Sect. 8.

CH. VII. § 4. the heir liable for the debts of *cestui que trust*[1] to the same extent as the legal interest, and subsequent statutes have placed the equitable interest on the same footing as the legal in this respect.

Amongst the most important consequences of the introduction of this class of interests were the facilities thereby afforded for providing for married women. By law a married woman had, as the fiction went, no separate existence apart from her husband. During her life therefore her lands became her husband's, though they reverted to her or her heir after the termination of the husband's interest. But there was nothing to prevent the lands being conveyed to a trustee in trust for a married woman. The trustee in such a case would be bound to receive the rents and pay them to her, so that the lands would be free from the control of her husband. The Court of Chancery even went the length, in order effectually to protect the woman from losing her property, of allowing the validity in this case of a clause in the settlement restraining the power of the woman during the coverture to alienate her interest in the lands—an exception to the general rule of law[2]. Now by the Married Women's Property Act of 1882 (45 and 46 Vict. c. 74), the disability of married women to acquire hold and dispose of separate property in their own name has been abolished, and there is no longer any need for the interposition of a trustee, in the case of women married or acquiring property after 1882.

Such are the main features of this large and important branch of the law of real property. To go further into detail is beyond the scope of the present treatise.

[1] Sect. 10. See Williams on Real Property, p. 267; and above, p. 283.

[2] See Haynes, Outlines of Equity, p. 211. The clause restraining anticipation, as it is called, was first inserted at the suggestion of Lord Thurlow in a settlement of which he was trustee. This restraint is still effectual notwithstanding the Married Women's Property Act, 1882 (45 and 46 Vict. c. 75, s. 19).

TYRRELL'S CASE. *Michaelmas Term*, 4 *and* 5 *Philip and Mary. In the Court of Wards.* (Dyer's Reports, 155 a.) CH. VII. § 4.

Jane Tyrrell, widow, for the sum of four hundred pounds paid by G. Tyrrell her son and heir apparent, by indenture enrolled in Chancery in the 4th year of Edward VI, bargained, sold, gave, granted, covenanted, and concluded to the said G. Tyrrell all her manors, lands, tenements, &c., to have and to hold the said &c. to the said G. T. and his heirs for ever[1], to the use of the said Jane during her life without impeachment of waste; and immediately after her decease to the use of the said G. T. and the heirs of his body lawfully begotten; and in default of such issue, to the use of the heirs of the said Jane for ever. *Quaere* well whether the limitation of those uses upon the *habendum*[2] are not void and impertinent, because an use cannot be springing, drawn, or reserved out of an use, as appears *prima facie*? And here it ought to be first an use transferred to the vendee before that any freehold or inheritance in the land can be vested in him by the inrollment &c. And this case has been doubted in the Common Pleas before now; *ideo quaere legem.* But all the Judges of C. B. and SAUNDERS, *Chief Justice*, thought that the limitation of uses above is void, &c.; for suppose the Statute of inrollments (cap. 16) had never been made, but only the Statute of Uses (cap. 10) in 27 Henry VIII, then the case above could not be, because an use cannot be engendered of an use.

GIRLAND V. SHARP. 37 *Elizabeth.* (Croke's Reports, Eliz. p. 382.)

Trespass[3]. Upon demurrer[4] the case was that one infeoffed his two sons to the use of himself for life, and after to the use of them and their heirs, *ad ultimam voluntatem suam perimplendam*; and afterwards devised it to Sharp, the defendant, in fee; and whether Sharp hereby shall have the land or not was the question. *Gawdy* conceived that he should not; for an use

[1] This conveyance would take effect by way of use under the statute, and thus a legal estate in fee simple would be given to G. T.

[2] The *habendum* is the part of the deed which designates the estate for which the grantee is to hold, 'to have and to hold,' &c.

[3] The action was for breaking and entering the plaintiff's land.

[4] That is, the facts as stated upon the record or pleadings are admitted to be true, and the question is what is the legal result of the admitted facts.

CH. VII. § 4. cannot be limited upon an use; then when he limits it to the use of his two sons and their heirs, he cannot afterwards limit it to the uses of his last will. But the words *ad performandum ultimam voluntatem*, as to limit any uses thereby, are void words. And to that opinion *Clench* agreed, but *Fenner* doubted thereof. Wherefore it was adjourned.

NEVILL V. SAUNDERS. *Mich.* 1686. (1 Vernon's Reports, 415.)

Lands were given by will to trustees and their heirs in trust for Anne the defendant's wife and her heirs, and that the trustees should from time to time pay and dispose of the rents and profits to the said Anne or to such person or persons as she by any writing under her hand, as well during coverture as being sole, should order or appoint the same, without the intermeddling of her husband, whom he willed should have no benefit or disposal thereof; and as to the inheritance of the premises in trust for such person or persons and for such estate or estates as the said Anne by any writing purporting to be her will, or other writing under her hand, should appoint; and for want of such appointment in trust for her and her heirs. The question was whether this was an use executed by the statute, or a bare trust for the wife, and the Court held it to be a trust only, and not an use executed by the statute.

CHAPTER VIII

HISTORY OF THE LAW OF WILLS OF LAND

IT has been seen that one of the most marked effects of the growth of feudalism was the abolition, except in certain localities, of the practice of devising interests in lands by will[1]. Such a disposition would have defeated the most valuable rights of the lord—relief, wardship, and marriage. It was therefore wholly inconsistent with feudal theories. In a great many boroughs, and in gavelkind lands, local customs were sufficiently strong to preserve the ancient liberty of disposition by will, and cases relating to 'burgages devisable' are common in the Year Books.

It has also been seen how the practice of disposing of uses of land by will became prevalent under the protection and encouragement of the Chancellors. One of the earliest of the recorded cases on this branch of the law contains a disposition by will, or rather perhaps settlement, of the use of lands made in the 6th year of Richard II[2]. Except therefore in the case of burgages devisable, a devise, before the legislation presently to be noticed, was simply a declaration by the legal tenant of the uses to which his heir at his death should hold the lands, or of the uses to which he had conveyed the lands

[1] See above, pp. 28, 102, n. 2.

[2] Rothanhale v. Wychingham, above, p. 326, n. 2.

CH. VIII. to feoffees (such conveyance having been expressed to be to the use of his will), or else a disposition of a use which had already been created in favour of himself.

In order therefore that the devisee of the use might enforce the disposition of the will, the aid of the Chancellor was called in. The Chancellor would compel, if necessary, the tenant of the legal estate to convey the land devised to *cestui que use*, the devisee.

It appears from the title and preamble of the Statute of Uses that one of its principal objects was to abolish the power of disposing of interests in lands by will, and thereby to restore to the king and the great lords the feudal dues which they could not claim if the estate of the heir were defeated by a devise.

The Statute of Uses contained a saving in favour of wills made before the first day of May, 1536[1], the year following that of the passing of the Statute. Between that time and July 20, 1540, the power of testation was, as regards freehold interests in lands, wholly abolished, except in the localities mentioned above. It may however be well believed that it was impossible for the legislature, arbitrary and thorough-going as it was, to maintain a restriction so opposed to the habits and practices which had prevailed throughout the country ever since Uses had been understood and protected by the Chancellor[2]. Accordingly in the 32nd year of Henry VIII (1540), it was found necessary to restore a large measure of the power of devising interests in lands. The provisions of the Statute 32 Henry VIII, c. 1, are somewhat complicated; but the upshot of them is that power is given to every tenant in fee simple[3] to dispose of all his lands held by socage tenure, and of two-thirds of his lands held by knight-service. Careful provision is made by this Statute for the saving of primer seisins, reliefs, and fines on alienation, in the case of socage lands, and of the rights of wardship over

[1] Sect. 9.
[2] See above, p. 346, n. 1.
[3] So interpreted by 34 and 35 Henry VIII, cap. 5. sect. 3.

the third part of knight-service lands, in favour of the king or other lord. CH. VIII.

When by the Act for the abolition of military tenures[1] tenure by knight-service was converted into free and common socage, the power of devise granted by the Statutes of Henry VIII extended to the whole of the lands of which previously only two parts had been devisable.

No particular solemnity was required by the Statutes of Henry VIII for the execution of wills. The first Statute spoke of a will or testament in writing or other act lawfully executed in the testator's life. Consequently 'bare notes in the handwriting of another person were allowed to be good wills within the Statute[2].' The law was altered by the Statute of Frauds (29 Car. II, c. 3), by which it was made a necessary condition of the validity of a will of lands that it should be signed by the testator, or by some other person in his presence, and be subscribed by three or four credible witnesses.

The law of wills of all property, whether real or personal, now rests on the provisions of the Wills Act, 7 Will. IV and 1 Vict. c. 26. This Statute repealed the previous Statutes, except so far as regards their operation upon all wills made before January 1, 1838. The principal requirements of the Wills Act with regard to the form of wills[3] are, that the will be in writing, signed at its foot or end[4] by the testator, or by some other person in his presence and by his direction; such signature to be made or acknowledged by the testator in the presence of two or more witnesses present at the same time, who are to attest and subscribe the will in the testator's presence.

The provisions of the Statute of Frauds above noticed introduced some harsh doctrines as to the rules affecting the necessary witnesses of a will. Formerly the notion prevailed that a witness who had any interest in the subject-matter of his testimony was therefore not a credible witness at all.

[1] See Chap. IX. [2] Blackstone, ii. p. 376. [3] Sect. 9.

[4] Further explained and defined by 15 and 16 Vict. c. 24.

CH. VIII. Hence if the will was attested by only three witnesses, and contained a legacy or other provision in favour of one of them, his testimony would be excluded, and the will was rendered invalid for want of the testimony of three *credible* witnesses. To such a length was the doctrine carried, that, if one of the witnesses was a creditor, or even husband or wife of a creditor, and the will contained a provision charging the testator's estates with the payment of his debts, the evidence of the witness was inadmissible, and the whole will consequently invalid. The harshness of this doctrine was to some extent modified by the Statute 25 George II, c. 6, by which gifts to witnesses were made void, thus destroying their interest, and creditors were made competent witnesses. By the Wills Act, 7 Will. IV and 1 Vict. c. 26, section 14, it was provided that a will should not be void by reason of the incompetency of the attesting witness; and the provisions of the Act 25 George II, c. 6, as to avoiding gifts to attesting witnesses, were re-enacted. These provisions were to some extent an anticipation of the general application of the principle which, mainly owing to the demonstrations of Bentham, was being gradually introduced into the various departments of the law of evidence, that the fact of a witness having an interest is an objection only to the *weight* and not to the *admissibility* of his evidence [1].

The operation of a will as a mode of acquiring rights over land is peculiar, and derives from its history attributes wholly different to those which characterise a will of personal or movable property. A will of personalty inherits to some extent the Roman conception of a *successio per universitatem*. It confers on the executor the whole of the testator's rights in respect of his personal property, and the greater portion of his duties. The executor is the universal successor of the testator. To use the language of Roman law, he is invested with the legal character, *persona* or *status*, of his testator, so far as regards his personal property.

[1] See 6 and 7 Vict. c. 85, and 14 and 15 Vict. c. 99.

On the other hand, the earliest definite juristic conception which was formed of an English will of lands seems to have been, as has already been said, that it operated as a declaration of the testator's intention as to the use or beneficial interest in lands—as, in fact, a conveyance of the particular beneficial interest intended to be dealt with. Thus a will of lands has always been regarded as a conveyance of a particular interest, coming into operation immediately upon the death of the testator, and not as creating a succession in the sense of Roman law.

It followed from the original conception of a will as a mode of raising a use, that a will, like any other mode of raising uses, might create interests arising at a future time, and divesting previous interests in a way unknown to the common law. These qualities seem to have been imparted even to a devise of lands, which, by virtue of a local custom, was operative at common law; and the common lawyers marvelled when they reflected on the wonderful nature of a devise, in a case, for instance, of a burgage devisable which the will declared should be sold by the executors, how it could be that upon the testator's death the heir should, according to the course of the common law, be in by descent, and yet, upon the sale by the executors, who had no other estate or interest in the lands beyond this mere power, be deprived of his inheritance [1].

Thus at the time of the passing of the Statute of Uses the conception of a will of lands was that it operated as a

[1] Year Book, 9 Hen. VI. 24 b. *Babington*: 'La nature de devis, ou terres sont devisables, est, que on peut deviser que la terre sera vendu par executors, et ceo est bon, come est dit adevant, et est marveilous ley de raison: mes ceo est la nature d'un devis, et devise ad este use tout temps en tiel forme; et issint on aura loyalment franktenement de cesty qui n'avoit rien, et en meme le maniere come on aura *fire from flint*, et uncore nul *fire* est deins le *flint*; et ceo est pour performer le darrein volonte de le devisor.' . . . . . *Paston*: 'Une devis est marveilous en luy meme quand il peut prendre effect: car si on devise en Londres que ses executors vendront ses terres, et devie seisi; son heir est eins par descent, et uncore par le vend des executors il sera ouste.' Williams on Real Property, p. 367.

CH. VIII. declaration of uses, taking affect at or after the testator's death, and being subject to the same rules as regulated the creation of uses by transactions operating *inter vivos*.

These characteristics continued to attach to wills when, by the legislation of Henry VIII, they became recognised as a mode of disposing of the *legal* interest in lands. Just as, before the Statutes of Henry VIII, a will of lands had been regarded as a declaration of a use, coming into effect upon the testator's death, but speaking as from its date and dealing only with the interest then intended to be conveyed; so, after those Statutes, a will of land operated as a conveyance, dealing with the legal interest possessed by the testator at the date of the will, and intended to be disposed of, but coming into effect only at his death, and being consequently subject to revocation at any time before his death.

So too, as there was no difference in the power of creating interests *in futuro* by way of use, whether the uses were declared by will or raised *inter vivos*, when the power of disposing of the legal estate was created by Statute, a testator might, without availing himself of the Statute of Uses, create future or executory interests by his will, without being bound by the strict rules of the common law limiting the power of creating future estates. For instance, a devise to *A* in fee, but if he should not live to attain the age of twenty-one then to *B* in fee, or ten years after the testator's death to *C* in fee, would be good and effectual [1]. These executory devises, as they are called, are subject to exactly the same rules with regard to the modes in which they can be created, the rule against perpetuity, and their liability to be construed if possible as contingent remainders [2], as those governing springing and shifting uses, which have been explained in the last chapter [3].

[1] See, for the effect of similar dispositions *inter vivos* at common law, above, Chap. V. § 3 (2).

[2] Except so far as the law is altered by 40 and 41 Vict. c. 33. See above, p. 362.

[3] See Appendix to Part I, Table III.

It was at one time doubted whether the Statute of Uses had any application to wills[1]. For instance, it was a question, if lands were devised to *B* and his heirs to the use of *C* for life, whether *C's* life-estate was executed by force of the Statute of Uses, or whether it derived its efficacy simply from the intention of the testator to create interests as if by the operation of that Statute. It has however long been settled that a devise to uses operates under the Statute in the same way and subject to the same rules as a conveyance to uses. Whether this is by reason of the force of the Statute of Uses, or by reason of the intention of the testator to dispose of the lands as if the Statute of Uses really operated, is a question of some metaphysical nicety, but of no practical importance.

The rules as to the construction of wills form one of the most intricate and least satisfactory portions of the modern law of real property. The subject is far too complex to be discussed at length in a treatise like the present. Starting with the general principle that the object is to ascertain the intention of the testator to be gathered from the whole will, and having regard to the fact that wills, far more frequently than formal deeds operating *inter vivos*, are often the composition of persons who have no legal knowledge, and sometimes little or no education, the Courts of Law and Equity have never applied the same strict and technical rules of construction to the language of wills as has been the case in regard to deeds. Thus, for instance, expressions in a will are held to be sufficient to create an estate in fee or in tail which would be insufficient in a deed[2]. However, in applying the general principle, a vast number of subordinate rules have grown up, which have frequently in particular cases had the effect of defeating instead of furthering the intention of the testator.

For instance, in a will a devise to *A* and his issue is held,

[1] See 2 Jarman on Wills, p. 289.

[2] See instances in Blackstone, ii. 381.

CH. VIII. in accordance with the general principle, to be sufficient to give to *A* an estate tail. These words would not be sufficient for the purpose in a deed; there distinct words both of procreation and of inheritance are necessary[1]. Following out the application of the general rule, it was held that a devise to *A* for life, and 'in case he die without issue to *B*,' gives by implication an estate tail to *A*[2]. The qualities of an estate tail therefore at once attached to such a gift by will, and *A* might at once convert his estate into a fee simple and so bar *B*'s remainder, and all other interests subsequent to his own. So common was this mistake, and so grievous the injustice wrought by this construction, that it was provided by the Wills Act that the words 'if *A* shall die without issue' and like expressions should be construed to apply to the event of *A*'s death without leaving issue living at his decease, and that such words should not, taken alone, be sufficient to create an estate tail[3].

One of the commonest errors in a will made by ignorant persons was to give an estate in lands to a person without adding words of inheritance or any expression to show that it was intended that the devisee should take more than a life estate. Though the courts eagerly seized on any expressions evidencing this intention, and permitted estates in fee to be created by words which would have been totally insufficient for the purpose in a deed, it remained an inflexible rule that if lands were given to *A* simply, without the addition of any words from which an intention to give the fee could be gathered, *A* would take only a life estate[4]. The Wills Act

[1] See above, p. 249. As to the statutory substitution of the words 'in fee' or 'in tail' for the common law expressions, see 44 and 45 Vict. c. 41, s. 51.

[2] This follows from the principle laid down in Shelley's case (see above, p. 269). These words were held not to mean that the land was to go to *B* in case of *A*'s death without leaving issue living at his decease, but to imply a gift to *A* and his issue with remainder to *B* in the event of the failure of *A*'s issue, whether such failure took place in *A*'s lifetime or after his decease. Such a gift therefore implied an estate tail vested in *A*.

[3] 7 Will. IV and 1 Vict. c. 26. s. 29.

[4] The rule is laid down in the Year Book, 22 Ed. III, 16, no. 59.

provided that such a gift should bear the construction which every person uninstructed in the law would naturally have placed upon it, and words of inheritance are no longer in a will necessary to pass the fee simple[1].

Other important alterations were effected in the operation and construction of wills by the same Act. The most important of these were the following. It has been seen that the original conception of a will of lands was that it operated as a present conveyance to take effect at a future time[2]. It followed that if a man devised all his lands, the will applied only to those lands which were his at the date of the will, and did not affect after-purchased lands. This would be the case even if he sold and re-purchased lands which he owned at the date of the will[3]. By the Wills Act it is now provided[4], that every will shall be construed with reference to the property comprised in it 'to speak and take effect as if it had been executed immediately before the death of the testator, unless a contrary intention shall appear by the will.' As the law at present stands, therefore, a devise of 'all my lands' will convey to the devisee not only all the lands which the testator has at the time of the will, but all which he may have acquired subsequently, and which he retains at the time of his death. A corollary to this rule is, that in the event of the death, in the lifetime of the testator, of any person to whom lands have been specifically devised, if the will contains a devise of the residue of the lands to any other person, such person shall take as part of the residue the lands so specifically devised, which would otherwise have *lapsed*, and gone to the heir at law[5].

As a general rule, if a devisee dies in the lifetime of the testator, though the devise may have been expressed to be made to him and his heirs, or to him and the heirs of his

[1] 7 Will. IV and 1 Vict. c. 26. s. 28.
[2] See above, p. 381.
[3] See, for an early instance of this, Year Book, 44 Edward III, p. 33.
[4] 7 Will. IV and 1 Vict. c. 26. s. 24.
[5] Ib. sect. 26.

CH. VIII. body, the devise *lapses*, or fails to take effect. This rule is altered by the Wills Act in two cases. Where there is a devise creating an estate tail, for example to *A* and the heirs of his body, and the devisee in tail dies, leaving issue surviving the testator, who would be inheritable under the entail, the devise is not to lapse, but to take effect as if the devisee had died immediately after the testator[1]. Further, if a devise of an interest in lands not terminable at or before the death of the devisee be made in favour of a child or other issue of the testator who dies in the testator's lifetime leaving issue, and if any such issue survive the testator, the devise is not to lapse, but is to 'take effect as if the death of such person had happened immediately after the death of the testator[2].'

Again, under the older law a devise to a man's heir-at-law, giving him no estate different from that which he would have taken by descent, was inoperative; in other words, the title of the heir-at-law rested on descent and not on the will, no doubt because otherwise the lord would have lost his relief, wardship, and marriage. This rule was reversed by the Act to amend the Law of Inheritance[3].

Amongst other consequences of treating a will of lands as a conveyance to the devisee of the particular lands comprised in and dealt with by the will, one of the most important was that no liability attached to the lands in the hands of the devisee for the debts of the devisor. The history of the liability of the *heir* for the debts of his ancestor has been already noticed[4]. By the Statute of Fraudulent Devises[5], a tenant in fee was prevented from defeating creditors, who held securities by which the heirs were bound, by devising his lands, and the devisee was made liable, equally with the heir, for such debts; and the legislation noticed above[6], providing for the administration of the real as well as personal estate

[1] 7 Will. IV and 1 Vict. c. 26. sec. 32. [2] Ib. s. 33.
[3] 3 and 4 Will. IV, c. 106. s. 3. [4] See above, p. 283.
[5] 3 William and Mary, c. 14, repealed and as to this matter re-enacted by 11 Geo. IV and 1 Will. IV, c. 47. [6] p. 284.

of deceased debtors, applies equally to the devisee and the heir.

All dispositions by will are revocable and subject to alteration by the testator at any time before his death. The provisions of the Wills Act respecting the mode of revocation and alteration are given below.

(1) The Act of Wills, Wards, and Primer Seisins, whereby a Man may devise two Parts of his Land. 32 Henry VIII, c. 1.

Where the King's most royal Majesty in all the time of his most gracious and noble reign hath ever been a merciful, loving, benevolent, and most gracious Sovereign Lord, unto all and singular his loving and obedient subjects, and by many times past hath not only showed and imparted to them generally by his many, often, and beneficial pardons heretofore by authority of his parliament granted, but also by divers other ways and means, many great and ample grants and benignities, in such wise as all his said subjects been most bounden to the uttermost of all their powers and graces by them received of God to render and give unto his Majesty their most humble reverence and obedient thanks and services, with their daily and continual prayer to Almighty God for the continual preservation of his most royal estate in most kingly honour and prosperity; yet always his Majesty, being replete and endowed by God with grace, goodness, and liberality, most tenderly considering that his said obedient and loving subjects cannot use or exercise themselves according to their estates, degrees, faculties, and qualities, or to bear themselves in such wise as that they may conveniently keep and maintain their hospitalities and families, nor the good education and bringing up of their lawful generations, which in this realm (laud be to God) is in all parts very great and abundant, but that in manner of necessity, as by daily experience is manifested and known, they shall not be able of their proper goods, chattels, and other movable substance to discharge their debts, and after their degrees set forth and advance their children and posterities; Wherefore our said Sovereign Lord most virtuously considering the mortality that is to every person at God's will and pleasure most common and uncertain, of his most blessed disposition and liberality, being willing to relieve and help his said subjects in their said necessities and debility, is contented

CH. VIII. and pleased that it be ordained and enacted by authority of this present Parliament in manner and form as hereafter followeth, that is to say, That all and every person and persons having or which hereafter shall have any manors, lands, tenements, or hereditaments, holden in socage, or of the nature of socage tenure, and not having any manors, lands, tenements, or hereditaments holden of the King our Sovereign Lord by knight-service, by socage tenure in chief, or of the nature of socage tenure in chief, nor of any other person or persons by knight-service, from the twentieth day of July in the year of our Lord MDXL, shall have full and free liberty, power, and authority to give, dispose, will, and devise, as well by his last will and testament in writing, or otherwise by any act or acts lawfully executed in his life, all his said manors, lands, tenements, or hereditaments, or any of them, at his free will and pleasure; any law, statute, or other thing heretofore had, made, or used, to the contrary notwithstanding.

(Section 2 gives the same power of devising the whole where a person holds lands of the King in socage in chief, and also holds lands of other persons in socage, and has no lands holden by knight-service.)

3. Saving alway and reserving to the King our Sovereign Lord, his heirs and successors, all his right, title and interest of primer seisin and reliefs, and also all other rights and duties for tenures in socage, or of the nature of socage tenure in chief, as heretofore hath been used and accustomed, the same manors, lands, tenements or hereditaments, to be taken, had, and sued out of and from the hands of his Highness, his heirs and successors, by the person or persons to whom any such manors, lands, tenements or hereditaments shall be disposed, willed, or devised, in such and like manner and form as hath been used by any heir or heirs before the making of this statute; and saving and reserving also fines for alienations of such manors, lands, tenements, or hereditaments holden of the King our Sovereign Lord in socage, or of the nature of socage tenure in chief, whereof there shall be any alteration of freehold or inheritance, made by will or otherwise, as is aforesaid.

4. And it is further enacted by the authority aforesaid, that all and singular person and persons having any manors, lands, tenements, or hereditaments of estate of inheritance holden of the King's Highness in chief by knight-service, or of the nature of knight-service in chief, from the said twentieth day of July, shall

have full power and authority by his last will, by writing or otherwise, by any act or acts lawfully executed in his life, to give, dispose, will or assign two parts of the same manors, lands, tenements, or hereditaments, in three parts to be divided, or else as much of the said manors, lands, tenements or hereditaments as shall extend or amount to the yearly value of two parts of the same in three parts to be divided, in certainty and by special divisions as it may be known in severalty, to and for the advancement of his wife, preferment of his children, and payment of his debts or otherwise at his will and pleasure; any law, statute, custom or other thing to the contrary thereof notwithstanding.

5. Saving and reserving to the King our Sovereign Lord the custody, wardship and primer seisin, or any of them as the case shall require, of as much of the same manors, lands, tenements, or hereditaments as shall amount and extend to the full and clear yearly value of the third part thereof without any diminution, dower, fraud, covin, charge or abridgment of any of the same third part or of the full profits thereof.

6. (Saving of fines for alienation [1].)

7–13. (Further provisions extending the power of devising lands in all cases to two-thirds of knight-service lands, and to the whole of those held in socage; the wardship of the lord being reserved as to the remaining third part of knight-service lands.)

14–17. (Miscellaneous provisions reserving rights of king and lords.)

(2) An Act for the explanation of the Statute of Wills. 34 and 35 Henry VIII, cap. 5.

The former Statute is explained in sections 3–8 to cover cases of a person or persons having a sole estate, or interest in fee simple, or seised in fee simple, or coparcenary, or in common in fee simple in possession, reversion, or remainder.

[1] See 34 and 35 Henry VIII, c. 5. sect. 6. This was interpreted to mean that when lands held of the King were devised by will, the devisee must sue out of Chancery the King's 'pardon for alienation,' paying for it the third part of the yearly value of the lands.

CH. VIII. The devise may be 'to any person or persons, except Bodies Politick and Corporate.'

14. And it is further declared and enacted by the authority aforesaid, That wills or testaments made of any manors, lands, tenements or other hereditaments by any woman covert, or person within the age of twenty-one years, idiot, or by any person *de non sane* memory, shall not be taken to be good or effectual in the law [1].

(3) THE ACT FOR THE AMENDMENT OF THE LAWS WITH RESPECT TO WILLS. 7 William IV and 1 Victoria, cap. 26.

This Statute repeals the former Statutes upon the subject of wills, and constitutes the basis upon which the present law of wills of real property rests. The most important of its general provisions are the following:—

Sect. 3. It shall be lawful for every person to devise, bequeath, or dispose of, by his will executed in manner hereinafter required, all real estate and all personal estate which he shall be entitled to, either at law or in equity, at the time of his death, and which, if not so devised, bequeathed, or disposed of, would devolve upon the heir-at-law, or customary heir [2] of him, or, if he became entitled by descent, of his ancestor, or upon his executor or administrator; and that the power hereby given shall extend to all real estate of the nature of customary freehold [3] or tenant right, or customary or copyhold, notwithstanding that the testator may not have surrendered the same to the use of his will [4]; or notwithstanding that being entitled as heir, devisee, or otherwise to be admitted thereto he shall not have been admitted thereto, or notwithstanding that the same, in consequence of the want of a custom to devise or surrender to the use of a will, or otherwise, could not at law have been disposed of by will, if this Act had not been made, or notwithstanding that the same, in consequence of there being a custom that a will or a surrender to the use of a will should continue in force for a limited time only, or any other special custom, could

[1] The numbering of the sections in these Statutes is taken from 'Statutes at Large.' The divisions in 'Statutes of the Realm' are different.

[2] See above, p. 291.

[3] See above, p. 292, n. 4. By this provision wills of copyhold estates are assimilated to wills of freeholds.

[4] See above, p. 295, n. 3.

not have been disposed of by will according to the power contained in this Act, if this Act had not been made; and also to estates *pur autre vie*, whether there shall or shall not be any special occupant thereof[1], and whether the same shall be freehold, customary freehold, tenant right, customary or copyhold, or of any other tenure, and whether the same shall be a corporeal or an incorporeal hereditament; and also to all contingent, executory, or other future interests in any real or personal estate[2], whether the testator may or may not be ascertained as the person or one of the persons in whom the same respectively may become vested, and whether he may be entitled thereto under the instrument by which the same respectively were created, or under any disposition thereof by deed or will; and also to all rights of entry for conditions broken, and other rights of entry[3]; and also to such of the same estates, interests, and rights respectively, and other real and personal estate as the testator may be entitled to at the time of his death, notwithstanding that he may become entitled to the same subsequently to the execution of his will. CH. VIII.

7. No will made by any person under the age of twenty-one years shall be valid.

8. No will made by any married woman shall be valid, except such a will as might have been made by a married woman before the passing of this Act[4].

18. Every will made by a man or woman shall be revoked by his or her marriage[5] (except a will made in exercise of a power of appointment, when the real or personal estate thereby appointed would not in default of such appointment pass to his or her heir, customary heir, executor, or administrator, or the person entitled as his or her next of kin under the Statute of Distributions).

[1] See above, p. 164, n. 2.

[2] See above, p. 269.

[3] A right of entry, though it could only be reserved in favour of the grantor or his heirs (above, p. 264), is thus rendered capable of alienation by will. These rights are also, by 8 and 9 Vict. c. 106. s. 6, made alienable by deed *inter vivos*.

[4] See above, p. 342, n. 2. A married woman could (before the recent statute) make a will in exercise of a power of appointment vested in her (see above, pp. 362-364). She could also dispose by will of her equitable interest in real property held to her separate use. The disability of a married woman to dispose of her separate property by will is now entirely removed by the Married Women's Property Act, 1882 (45 and 46 Vict. c. 75. s. 1), as amended by the Married Women's Property Act, 1893 (56 and 57 Vict. c. 63).

[5] Before this enactment the marriage *of a man* was not sufficient to revoke his will unless he had also a child born to him.

CH. VIII.

19. No will shall be revoked by any presumption of an intention on the ground of an alteration in circumstances.

20. No will or codicil or any part thereof shall be revoked otherwise than as aforesaid, or by another will or codicil executed in manner hereinbefore required, or by some writing declaring an intention to revoke the same, and executed in the manner in which a will is hereinbefore required to be executed, or by the burning, tearing, or otherwise destroying the same by the testator, or by some person in his presence and by his direction, with the intention of revoking the same.

CHAPTER IX

ABOLITION OF MILITARY TENURES

IT was doubtless the prevalence of the system of conveying lands to uses which, by alleviating the pressure of the feudal burdens, delayed the change in the law which is the subject of this chapter. When by the selfish legislation of Henry VIII this mode of alleviation was rendered ineffectual, and the pressure was still further increased by the creation, under the provisions of the Statute 32 Henry VIII, cap. 46, of a Court of Wards and Liveries, for the express purpose of providing a more effectual and speedy mode of asserting the king's feudal rights, the burdens became too heavy to be borne; and the king being now the immediate lord of a vast portion of the land of the country, all classes of tenants were more interested in obtaining relief from feudal burdens owing to the king, than in preserving those due to such of them as were lords of manors. A striking picture of the condition of a tenant *in capite* by knight-service is given by Blackstone [1]. 'The heir, on the death of his ancestor, if of full age, was plundered of the first emoluments arising from his inheritance, by way of *relief* and *primer seisin*; and, if under age, of the whole of his estate during infancy. And then, as Sir Thomas Smith very feelingly complains [2], " when he came to his own, after he was

[1] Vol. ii. p. 76.

[2] The Commonwealth of England, book iii. c. 5, written in the reign of Elizabeth.

CH. IX. out of *wardship*, his woods decayed, houses fallen down, stock wasted and gone, lands let forth and ploughed to be barren," to reduce him still farther, he was yet to pay half-a-year's profits as a fine for suing out *livery*; and also the price or value of his *marriage*. Add to this the untimely and expensive honour of *knighthood*, to make his poverty more completely splendid[1]; and when by these deductions his fortune was so shattered and ruined, that perhaps he was obliged to sell his patrimony, he had not even that poor privilege allowed him without paying an exorbitant fine for a *licence of alienation*.'

In the reign of James I, a project was brought forward for the removal of feudal burdens by converting all tenure of lands held of the king or other lords into tenure by fealty only, and such rent as was then due, and prohibiting the creation of any other species of tenure, compensation being made to the king and other lords for the loss of feudal dues by the payment of an annual rent. This proposal was not carried into effect. Sir E. Coke mentions it with a strong expression of approval, and of hope for its ultimate success[2].

This hope was realised by the Long Parliament. On the 24th of February, 1645, the House of Commons sent up to the Lords a resolution, 'That the Court of Wards and Liveries,

[1] The prerogative of the Crown of compelling the tenants *in capite* to be knighted, recognised by the Statute de Militibus, 1 Edward II, stat. 1, had become one of the most oppressive of the feudal burdens. It was abolished by the Statute 16 Car. I, c. 20. See Blackstone, ii. 69.

[2] 'At the parliament holden 18 Jacobi Regis it was moved on the King's behalf, and commended by the King to the Parliament, for a competent yearly rent to be assured to his Majesty, his heirs and successors, that the King would assent that all wardships, primer seisins, reliefs for tenures *in capite* or by knight's-service should be discharged. Wherein amongst certain old parliament men these thirteen things did fall into consideration for the effecting thereof. . . . Which motion, though it proceeded not to effect, yet we thought good to remember it together with these considerations, hoping that so good a motion, tending to the honour and profit of the King and his crown for ever, and the freedom and the quiet of his subjects and their posterities, will some time or other (by the grace of God) by authority of Parliament one way or other take effect and be established.' Coke's 4th Institute, p. 202, &c.

and all wardships, liveries, primer seisins, and *ousterlemains*, and all other charges incident or arising for or by reason of wardship, livery, primer seisin, or *ousterlemain*, be from this day taken away; and that all tenures by homage, and all fines, licences, seizures, and pardons for alienation, and all other charges incident thereto, be likewise taken away; and that all tenures by knight-service either of his Majesty or others, or by knight-service or socage *in capite* of his Majesty, be turned into free and common socage.' CH. IX.

The Lords at once assented to the vote in the form in which it was sent up by the Commons [1]; and the resolution was confirmed by an Act of Parliament passed in 1656 [2].

1 'A message was brought from the House of Commons by Sir Henry Vane, Junior, Knight, "That in this time of great distractions, wherein the Lords and the House of Commons and the whole kingdom have adventured their lives and fortunes, and for recompense to the whole kingdom they have thought to take away a great burden, therefore have made a vote wherein the House of Commons desire their Lordships' concurrence."

'Resolved upon the question *nemine contradicente* that this House agrees to this vote as it is now brought up from the House of Commons.' (Journals of the House of Lords, vol. viii. p. 183. Die Martis 24° die Februarii.)

2 'Whereas the four and twentieth day of February in the year of our Lord 1645 the Court of Wards and Liveries and all wardships, liveries, primer seisins, and *ousterlemains*, and all other charges incident or arising for or by reason of wardships, livery, primer seisins, or *ousterlemains*, and all tenures by homage, and all fines, licences, seizures, and pardons for alienation, and all other charges incident thereunto, were by the Lords and Commons then assembled in Parliament taken away, and all tenures by knight-service, either of the king or others, or by knight-service *in capite*, or socage *in capite* of the king, were turned into free and common socage, for the further establishing and confirming the same, Be it declared and enacted by His Highness the Lord Protector and the Parliament, that the Court of Wards and Liveries, and all wardships, liveries, primer seisins, and *ousterlemains*, and all other charges incident and arising for or by reason of any such tenure, wardship, livery, primer seisin, or *ousterlemain*, be taken away, from the said four and twentieth day of February 1645, and that all homage, fines, licences, seizures, pardons for alienation, incident or arising for or by reason of wardship, livery, primer seisin, or *ousterlemain*, and all other charges incident thereunto be likewise taken away, and is hereby adjudged and declared to be taken away from the said twenty-fourth day of February 1645, And that all tenures *in capite* and by knight-service of the late king or any other person, and all tenures by socage in chief, be taken away, and all tenures are hereby enacted and declared to be turned into free and common socage

CH. IX. Upon the Restoration it was found necessary to confirm by Statute the Acts of the Long Parliament in respect of feudal tenures.

It will be seen that the subjoined Statute abolished all the ancient law with respect to tenure by knight-service and its incidents. With the exception of the provisions enabling the father to appoint a guardian by will [1], it did not introduce any new law. The principal effects of the Statute have been that in most instances all remembrance of the relation between lord and freehold tenant has passed away [2], and that all freehold lands have become capable of being devised by will [3].

12 CHARLES II, cap. 14.

AN ACT TAKING AWAY THE COURT OF WARDS AND LIVERIES, AND TENURES IN CAPITE [4], AND BY KNIGHT-SERVICE, AND PURVEYANCE, AND FOR SETTLING A REVENUE UPON HIS MAJESTY IN LIEU THEREOF.

Whereas it hath been found by former experience that the Court of Wards and Liveries and tenures by knight-service either of the king or others, or by knight-service *in capite*, or socage *in capite* of the king, and the consequents upon the same, have been much more burthensome, grievous, and prejudicial to the kingdom

from the said twenty-fourth day of February 1645, and shall be so construed, adjudged and declared to be for ever hereafter turned into free and common socage. Nevertheless it is hereby enacted that all rents certain, and heriots, due to mesne lords or other private persons, shall be paid; and that where any relief or double ancient yearly rent, upon the death of an ancestor, was in such cases formerly due and payable, a double ancient yearly rent only in lieu thereof shall now be paid upon the death of an ancestor as in free and common socage, and that the same shall be recovered by like remedy in law, as rents and duties in free and common socage.' Scobell's Acts and Ordinances of Parliament, Anno 1656, c. 4.

[1] Sects. 8 and 9. [2] See above, p. 235. [3] See above, p. 379.

[4] Madox, Hist. of Exch. p. 432, note, suggests that the expression 'tenures *in capite*' is used erroneously in this Statute. 'Tenant *in capite*' properly means simply 'immediate tenant,' whether by knight-service, socage, or otherwise. But a confused idea had arisen that tenure *in capite* was a particular species of tenure of the Crown, distinct from ordinary knight-service, etc. Thus Elizabeth by letters patent granted lands 'tenendum de nobis in libero socagio et non in capite.' This, as Madox says, is a contradiction in terms.

than they have been beneficial to the king; And whereas since the intermission of the said Court, which hath been from the four and twentieth day of February, which was in the year of our Lord one thousand six hundred forty and five, many persons have by will and otherwise made disposal of their lands held by knight-service, whereupon divers questions might possibly arise unless some seasonable remedy be taken to prevent the same; Be it therefore enacted by the King our Sovereign Lord, with the assent of the Lords and Commons in Parliament assembled, and by the authority of the same, and it is hereby enacted, That the Court of Wards and Liveries, and all wardships, liveries, primer seisins and *ouster-lemains*, values and forfeitures of marriages, by reason of any tenure of the King's Majesty, or of any other by knight-service, and all mean rates, and all other gifts, grants, and charges, incident or arising for or by reason of wardships, liveries, primer seisins, or *ousterlemains*, be taken away and discharged, and are hereby enacted to be taken away and discharged, from the said twenty-fourth day of February one thousand six hundred forty-five; any law, statute, custom, or usage to the contrary hereof in any wise notwithstanding: And that all fines for alienations, seizures, and pardons for alienations, tenure by homage, and all charges incident or arising for or by reason of wardship, livery, primer seisin, or *ousterlemain*, or tenure by knight-service, escuage, and also *aide pur file marrier, et pur faire fitz chivalier*, and all other charges incident thereunto, be likewise taken away and discharged from the said twenty-fourth day of February one thousand six hundred forty and five[1]: any law, statute, custom, or usage to the contrary hereof in any wise notwithstanding: And that all tenures by knight-service of the king, or of any other person, and by knight-service *in capite*, and by socage *in capite* of the king, and the fruits and consequents thereof, happened or which shall or may hereafter happen or arise thereupon or thereby, be taken away and discharged; any law, statute, custom, or usage to the contrary hereof in any wise notwithstanding; And all tenures of any honours, manors, lands, tenements, or hereditaments, of any estate of inheritance at the common law, held either of the king or of any other person or persons, bodies politick or corporate, are hereby enacted to be turned into free and common socage[2], to all intents and purposes, from the said twenty-fourth day of February one thousand six hundred forty-five, and shall be so

[1] See above, pp. 40–43, and Chap. II. § 4.

[2] As to socage, see above, pp. 45–48.

CH. IX. construed, adjudged, and deemed to be from the said twenty-fourth day of February one thousand six hundred forty-five, and for ever hereafter, turned into free and common socage; any law, statute, custom, or usage to the contrary hereof in any wise notwithstanding.

2. And that the same shall for ever hereafter stand and be discharged of all tenure by homage, escuage, voyages royal, and charges for the same, wardships incident to tenure by knight's-service, and values and forfeitures of marriage, and all other charges incident to tenure by knight-service, and of and from *aide pur file marrier*, and *aide pur faire fitz chivalier*; any law, statute, usage, or custom to the contrary in any wise notwithstanding. And that all conveyances and devises of any manors, lands, tenements, and hereditaments, made since the said twenty-fourth day of February, shall be expounded to be of such effect as if the same manors, lands, tenements, and hereditaments had been then held and continued to be holden in free and common socage only; any law, statute, custom, or usage to the contrary hereof in any wise notwithstanding.

3. And be it further ordained and enacted by the authority of this present Parliament, That one Act made in the reign of King Henry the Eighth, intituled An Act for the Establishment of the Court of the King's Wards; and also one Act of Parliament made in the thirty-third year of the reign of the said King Henry the Eighth, concerning the officers of the Courts of Wards and Liveries, and every clause, article, and matter in the said Acts contained, shall from henceforth be repealed and utterly void.

4. And be it further enacted by the authority aforesaid, That all tenures hereafter to be created by the King's Majesty, his heirs or successors, upon any gifts or grants of any manors, lands, tenements, or hereditaments, of any estate of inheritance at the common law, shall be in free and common socage, and shall be adjudged to be in free and common socage only, and not by knight-service, or *in capite*[1], and shall be discharged of all wardship, value and forfeiture of marriage, livery, primer seisin, *ousterlemain*, *aide pur faire fitz chivalier* and *pur file marrier*; any law, statute, or reservation to the contrary thereof in any wise notwithstanding.

5. Provided nevertheless, and be it enacted, That this Act, or anything herein contained, shall not take away, nor be construed to take away, any rents certain, heriots, or suits of court, belonging or incident to any former tenure now taken away or altered

[1] See p. 396, n. 4.

by virtue of this Act, or other services incident or belonging to tenure in common socage due or to grow due to the King's Majesty, or mean lords, or other private person, or the fealty and distresses incident thereunto; and that such relief shall be paid in respect of such rents as is paid in case of a death of a tenant in common socage.

6. Provided always, and be it enacted, That anything herein contained shall not take away, nor be construed to take away any fines for alienation due by particular customs of particular manors and places, other than fines for alienations of lands or tenements holden immediately of the king *in capite.*

7. Provided also, and be it further enacted, That this Act, or anything herein contained, shall not take away, or be construed to take away, tenures in frank-almoign[1], or to subject them to any greater or other services than they now are; nor to alter or change any tenure by copy of court-roll, or any services incident thereunto; nor to take away the honorary services of grand serjeanty[2], other than of wardship, marriage, and value of forfeiture of marriage, escuage, voyages royal, and other charges incident to tenure by knight-service; and other than *aide pur faire fitz chivalier*, and *aide pur file marrier.*

8. And be it further enacted by the authority aforesaid, That where any person hath or shall have any child or children under the age of one and twenty years, and not married at the time of his death; that it shall and may be lawful to and for the father[3] of such child or children, whether born at the time of the decease of the father, or at that time in *ventre sa mere,* or whether such father be within the age of one and twenty years or of full age, by deed executed in his life-time, or by his last will and testament in writing, in the presence of two or more credible witnesses, in such manner, and from time to time as he shall respectively think fit, to dispose of the custody and tuition of such child or children for and during such time as he or they shall respectively remain under the age of twenty-one years, or any lesser time, to any person or persons in possession or remainder, other than Popish recusants; and that such disposition of the custody of such child or children, made since the twenty-fourth of February one thousand six hundred and forty-five, or hereafter to be made, shall be good and effectual against all and every person or persons claiming the

[1] See above, p. 38. [2] See above, p. 38.

[3] This provision is now extended to the mother by the 'Guardianship of Infants' Act, 1886' (49 and 50 Vict. c. 27).

CH. IX. custody or tuition of such child or children, as guardian in socage or otherwise: And that such person or persons to whom the custody of such child or children hath been or shall be so disposed or devised as aforesaid, shall and may maintain an action of ravishment of ward or trespass against any person or persons which shall wrongfully take away or detain such child or children, for the recovery of such child or children; and shall and may recover damages for the same in the said action for the use and benefit of such child or children [1].

9. And be it further enacted, That such person or persons to whom the custody of such child or children hath been or shall be so disposed or devised, shall and may take into his or their custody to the use of such child or children the profit of all lands tenements and hereditaments of such child or children; and also the custody, tuition, and management of the goods, chattels, and personal estate of such child or children, till their respective age of one and twenty years, or any lesser time, according to such disposition aforesaid, and may bring such action or actions in relation thereunto as by law a guardian in common socage might do.

10. Provided also, That this Act, or anything herein contained, shall not extend to alter or prejudice the custom of the City of London, nor of any other city or town corporate, or of the town of Berwick-upon-Tweed, concerning orphans; nor to discharge any apprentice from his apprenticeship.

11. Provided also, That neither this Act, nor anything therein contained, shall infringe or hurt any title of honour, feodal or other, by which any person hath or may have right to sit in the Lords' House of Parliament, as to his or their title of honour or sitting in Parliament, and the privilege belonging to them as Peers; this Act or anything therein contained to the contrary in any wise notwithstanding.

15–52. Provisions for recompense to his Majesty for the Court of Wards and purveyances by an excise duty upon beer, ale, etc.

[1] See above, p. 42; and compare Chap. II. § 4 (2), (3), and Chap. III. § 2.

CHAPTER X

TITLES OR MODES OF ACQUISITION OF RIGHTS OVER THINGS REAL

CH. X.

THE subject of titles or modes of acquisition of rights follows in logical order next upon the discussion of the history and nature of the rights themselves. It is proposed in this chapter to present in outline a brief account of the various modes of acquisition of rights over land recognised by English law. For this purpose it will be necessary to refer back to many points which have been explained in the preceding chapters, and also to notice the main changes in the law which have taken place subsequent to those which have been already mentioned.

A title to a right or a collection of rights over land is, according to Blackstone[1], 'the means whereby the owner of lands hath the just possession of his property.'

According to the fuller definition given by Austin, it is the collection of 'facts or events on which by the dispositions of the law rights arise or come into being, and also the facts or events on which by the dispositions of the law they terminate, or are extinguished[2].' For practical purposes the inquiry may be confined to the different modes of acquiring rights over land. For, according to English law, rights over land are

[1] ii. p. 195.

[2] Austin, ii. p. 902.

CH. X. § 1. never lost or abandoned so as to become *res nullius*. A mode of losing a right of this class is always a mode of acquisition by somebody else. For example, if lands cease to have an owner by reason of a failure of heirs, they at once escheat to the lord [1]. For the purposes of this chapter, therefore, the word 'title' may be taken to mean simply 'mode of acquisition.'

Many classifications have been given of the groups of facts or events to which the law attaches as a consequence the loss or acquisition of rights over land. The following arrangement may perhaps be accepted in default of a better. There are some recognised modes of acquisition which cannot well be brought under one head. To attempt to do so would be to present a false conception of a uniformity which does not exist [2].

Titles or modes of acquisition may perhaps be most conveniently classed under the heads of title by *alienation*, title by *succession*, or devolution from a person dying intestate, and the remaining modes of acquisition must be thrown into a miscellaneous class.

§ 1. *Title by alienation.*

By alienation is meant the intentional and voluntary transfer of a right by the person or persons in whom the right resides to another person or persons [3].

In order that title by alienation may be effectual in any given case, the following conditions must be present. The person having the right intended to be conveyed must be of full capacity to convey it; the person to whom the right is to be conveyed must be of capacity to take and keep it; the purpose of the conveyance must be such as the law recognises as

[1] See above, p. 92.

[2] See Austin, ii. p. 931.

[3] See Austin's Jurisprudence, ii. 904. Sometimes alienation is divided into voluntary and involuntary alienation. I prefer to treat of the different kinds of so-called involuntary alienation separately under the miscellaneous kinds.

affording a sufficient motive for the transfer of the property; and, lastly, the proper mode of carrying the conveyance into effect must be observed. CH. X. § 1.

By the first of these conditions it is necessary that the person conveying should possess the requisite intelligence, and be in a position to exercise it freely. Hence conveyances by idiots or lunatics are absolutely void[1]. Such a person is incapable of the requisite intention. An infant (a person under twenty-one years of age) is not completely capable of having the requisite intention. His conveyances are voidable, subject, that is, to be ratified or avoided by him when he comes of age[2].

Powers of dealing with the estates of idiots and lunatics, and of enabling infants for certain purposes to make effectual conveyances with the sanction of the Chancery Division of the High Court, have been given by various Acts of Parliament.

Similar principles apply to conveyances by persons under *duress*, that is, under pressure of illegal bodily restraint, or of danger to life or limb[3]. Conveyances induced by such pressure are voidable.

Married women were before the recent Act under a special disability with regard to alienation. By the common law, as has been seen, the husband took a sole estate in the lands of the wife during the marriage. The wife could not moreover by her own separate act during the continuance of the marriage make any effectual conveyance of her reversionary interest in lands. The old mode of making a conveyance of the wife's lands was by a fine[4], to which the husband and wife were

[1] Inconsistently enough, a feoffment with livery of seisin, at least before 8 and 9 Vict. c. 106 s. 4, was not void but only voidable, and that not by the lunatic himself but only by his committee or heir. This arose probably from the almost superstitious veneration for this solemn mode of conveying lands.

[2] Except that a feoffment of gavelkind lands by a person of the age of fifteen years is by the custom of gavelkind binding upon him. See above, p. 47, n. 2.

[3] Blackstone, i. 130, 136.

[4] See above, Chap. II. § 8.

both parties. To the validity of a fine it was necessary that the wife should be examined apart from her husband, as a security that the conveyance was not made by her under the coercion of her husband [1]. At the present day the legal estate of a married woman who has both been married and acquired the property to be dealt with before 1883 can only be conveyed by deed executed with the concurrence of her husband, and acknowledged by the woman, on being examined by a judge or commissioners apart from her husband, to be her own act [2]. After the growth of equitable interests, and the emancipation of married women from the restraints of the common law as to property by enabling them to be in the position of *cestui que trust*, or beneficiaries, all the ordinary powers of disposition became capable of being exercised by married women over such equitable interests. When land therefore has been vested in a trustee in trust for a married woman, she is as capable of disposing of the interest as if she were unmarried, subject only to the restraint on alienation usually introduced into settlements, as has been noticed above [3]. And now in the case of every woman married after 1882, or, if married before 1883, so far as regards property acquired after 1882, no restriction any longer exists upon her absolute power of disposition as if she were unmarried [4]. A settlement of her property may however still contain a restraint against anticipation during coverture, and in this respect a woman's power of effective alienation may be subject to a restriction unknown in the case of a man [5].

In order that an alienation may be effectual, the alienee must be capable of receiving and keeping the estate alienated. The intention of accepting is not in English law of as great importance as a complete intention to give. It is said to

[1] Williams on Real Property, p. 284.

[2] 3 and 4 Will. IV. c. 74. ss. 77–91.

[3] See above, p. 374. As to the history of the power of a married woman to dispose of interests in land by will, see Chap. VIII. p. 391, n. 4.

[4] 45 and 46 Vict. c. 75.

[5] Ib. s. 19.

be the law of England that in no instance can property be vested in a person by alienation against his will [1]. At the same time it appears to be the case that, provided the act of conveying be perfect and complete on the part of the alienor, the property, in the absence of an intention not to accept, vests in the alienee. At all events no evidence is necessary to show that the alienee intended to accept it. Nor would the conveyance be void although there were the strongest evidence that the alienee was incapable of an accepting mind. A conveyance of lands to an infant or a lunatic is perfectly valid, as against the alienor and third parties, though it is liable to be avoided in favour of the lunatic or the infant, or their representatives, if it should be deemed disadvantageous to him [2]. In all other cases the proper mode of refusing to accept a conveyance or devise of land, and so rendering it inoperative, is an execution by an alienee of full capacity of a deed of disclaimer [3].

Before 1883 a married woman might purchase lands, and the conveyance was good unless the husband avoided it during the coverture by some act expressing his dissent. And even if the husband consented, the woman or her heirs might avoid the purchase after the decease of the husband: and a married woman might by deed acknowledged disclaim a purchase [4]. These rules are now superseded by the full capacity of acquiring and holding property given to women married or acquiring property since the commencement of 1883 [5].

There are certain incapacities to hold lands, which should be noticed. The incapacity of corporations has already been mentioned [6]. Aliens too formerly might purchase, but the land was held subject to the right of the Crown to seize and

[1] Williams on Real Property, p. 81.

[2] Blackstone, ii. p. 292.

[3] See Townson v. Tickell, 3 Barnewall and Alderson, p. 31; Doe d. Smyth v. Smyth, 6 Barnewall and Cresswell, p. 112; Doe d. Winder v. Lawes, 7 Adolphus and Ellis, p. 212.

[4] 8 and 9 Vict. c. 106. s. 7.

[5] 45 and 46 Vict. c. 75 s. 1.

[6] Chap. IV. § 2.

CH. X. § 1. appropriate it, upon the facts being ascertained by the verdict of a jury, technically called 'upon office found,' in a process called 'inquest of office.' By an early exception to this rule an alien was permitted to hold a lease for years of land for the purpose of trade or merchandise. And by the Naturalisation Act, 1870, aliens are placed on the same footing with regard to the purchase and disposition of lands as natural-born British subjects [1].

A further restraint on alienation in reference to the purposes or objects for which it may be made was contained in the Statute 9 Geo. II, c. 36, which, after reciting that 'gifts or alienations of lands in mortmain are prohibited or restrained by Magna Carta and divers other wholesome laws as prejudicial to and against the common utility, nevertheless this public mischief has of late increased by many large and improvident alienations or dispositions made by languishing or dying persons to uses called charitable uses [2], to the disherison of their lawful heirs,' provided that no lands or hereditaments, or money or personal estate to be laid out in the purchase of lands should be conveyed or settled for any charitable uses unless by deed executed in the presence of two or more credible witnesses twelve calendar months at least before the death of the donor and enrolled in Chancery within six months of its execution, and unless the gift be made to take effect in possession immediately, without any reservation in favour of the grantor or persons claiming through him [3]. By this Statute therefore a gift of lands to a charity *by will* was made wholly void. Certain relaxations of the provisions of the Act of George II were subsequently made by various Statutes in

[1] 33 Vict. c. 14. s. 2. But the Act does not apply to interests arising by disposition or devolution happening before the passing of the Act.

[2] By the Statute 23 Henry VIII, c. 10, conveyances of land to the use of churches, or for the services of a priest, &c., were prohibited. Subsequently it was held that this prohibition did not extend to charitable uses. Blackstone, ii. p. 273. And see 43 Elizabeth, c. 4.

[3] There is an exception in the Statute (s. 4) in favour of the two Universities, and the Colleges of Eton, Winchester, and Westminster.

favour of gifts for the purposes of schools, literary, scientific, or religious purposes, and public parks or museums; and the law was consolidated and amended by the Mortmain and Charitable Uses Act, 1888 (51 and 52 Vict. c. 42), which re-enacts the main provisions of the earlier Statutes.

As regards, however, gifts of land to charity *by will*, the law now depends on the Charitable Uses Act, 1891 (54 and 55 Vict. c. 73), which enacts that such gifts shall take due effect, subject to the provision, in most cases, that land so devised must be sold within one year from the testator's death.

The freedom of alienation is also subject to restraint in favour of creditors, and purchasers for valuable considerations. By the Statute 13 Elizabeth, c. 5, conveyances of lands and goods made for the purpose of delaying, hindering, or defrauding creditors are made void as against them unless made for valuable consideration to a *bona fide* purchaser without notice of the fraud. It is under the provisions of this Statute that proceedings are frequently taken to set aside post-nuptial settlements on a wife or children made with the intention of placing the property of the indebted settlor out of the reach of his creditors[1]. And by the Statute 27 Elizabeth, c. 4, as judicially interpreted, *voluntary* conveyances of estates in land, that is, conveyances without valuable consideration, such as money or marriage, and conveyances made with any clause of revocation at the will of the grantor, were void as against subsequent purchasers for money or other valuable consideration. Thus any person who took by virtue of a mere voluntary gift could never be absolutely secure that his donor might not sell the land to a purchaser for money, which would confer on such purchaser, even if he took with notice of the prior gift, a good title as against the donee[2]. But now by the Voluntary Conveyances Act, 1893 (56 and 57

[1] Compare 46 and 47 Vict. (Bankruptcy Act, 1883), s. 47.

[2] A mortgagee was a purchaser within the meaning of this Act, therefore a settlement on a wife or child after marriage might be set aside in favour of a subsequent mortgagee (Chapman v. Emery, Cowper's Reports, 278).

Vict. c. 21), it is provided that no voluntary conveyance is to be void as against a subsequent purchaser for value, if the same has in fact been made *bona fide* and without fraud.

Such are the conditions, positive and negative, of alienation. Subject to these conditions, the power of alienating the interest which the alienor has is complete, provided that he follows the mode required by law.

It remains to point out the acts by which a person entitled to rights over lands may transfer them to another, or in other words, the mode in which a person may acquire those rights by alienation.

The first division into which alienation falls is alienation *inter vivos*, and alienation *by will*. It seems correct, for reasons already given, to class acquisition of rights over land by will as a mode of alienation and not as a mode of succession. In Roman law, as has already been pointed out[1], and in our own law of personal property, wills must be considered as a mode of succession.

(1)[2] Postponing acquisition by will and passing to alienation *inter vivos*, that is where the person who loses the right and the person who acquires it are both living, and the right passes by a voluntary act from one to the other, the next division will follow the division of rights already given in the Appendix to Part I[3].

Alienation may be divided into the alienation (2) of rights of property or ownership over land, meaning by property or ownership the enjoyment of those indefinite rights of user over land by virtue of which in ordinary language a person is entitled to speak of land as his property[4]; (3) of rights *in alieno solo*, which comprise the class called incorporeal hereditaments in the narrower sense[5]. Under this class of rights

Natural love and affection was not a sufficient motive or consideration. As against subsequent purchasers such conveyances were 'fraudulent, feigned, and covinous.' s. 2.

[1] See above, p. 380.

[2] See Table IV. infra.

[3] See Table I. p. 310.

[4] See above, p. 305.

[5] See above, Appendix to Part I. § 1 (11).

in alieno solo may also be placed, following the classification given above, creditors' rights[1]. CH. X. § 1.

(4) Taking first the modes of acquiring those rights *in alieno solo* which in common legal language are styled incorporeal hereditaments, and are divided as has been seen into the classes of easements and profits, the appropriate mode of acquiring these rights is by *grant*; that is, by the owner of the soil over which the right is to be exercised making, by deed operating either at common law or under the Statute of Uses, a specific grant of the right of way, right of common, or other easement or profit. No solemnity short of a deed is regarded by our law as sufficient to create a right of this kind. A deed is equally necessary whether the right of limited user for convenience or profit be a right to be enjoyed by the successive possessors of a dominant tenement (a right *appurtenant*), or a right to be enjoyed by the grantee or by him and his heirs irrespective of the possession of any tenement (a right *in gross*[2]).

Sometimes rights of this class are created not by express grant but by implication in a grant of other rights. For instance, if the owner of two houses *A* and *B*, both of which necessarily draw their supply of water from a well situated in the curtilage of *A*, conveys away *B* to a purchaser without any mention of the right to draw water from the well of *A*, the right will nevertheless pass and be available in favour of the possessors of *B* against the successive possessors of *A*[3]. So if a man grants to another a piece of land in the centre of and surrounded by the grantor's land, he by implication also grants a right of way over some portion of the land which he retains. And of course wherever an easement or profit is appurtenant to the ownership of any particular tenement,

[1] See above, Appendix to Part I. § 1 (14).

[2] See above, Chap. III. § 18, p. 182.

[3] See Gale on Easements, 4th ed., p. 86, where this class of rights is discussed under the head of 'Disposition of the Owner of two Tenements;' called by French Writers 'Destination du père de famille.'

CH. X. § 1. such easement or profit will pass upon alienation of the tenement to the alienee without any special grant thereof.

An important mode of acquiring these rights, though perhaps not logically coming under the head of alienation, must not be omitted here; that is, by what is called *prescription*, or actual use and enjoyment of the right for a specified time. Before the passing of the Prescription Act [1] this mode of acquiring rights *in alieno solo* was regarded exclusively as a species of title by grant, differing only from an express grant in the evidence by which it was established. If it be proved that the right has been in fact enjoyed as far back as memory can trace it, and no origin of the right be shown, the presumption is that it has been enjoyed from time immemorial, that is, from some period anterior to the first year of Richard I, the time at which legal memory commences, and that it was created before that period by the owner of the soil [2]. And even if the right were shown to have been created within the time of legal memory, juries were directed, when the right was in question, to presume that as a fact the right had been expressly granted by the owner of the soil, and that the grant had been lost. This mode of supporting rights was felt to be most unsatisfactory, and at length the Prescription Act [3] was passed, by which a perfect title to easements and profits is conferred upon persons who have enjoyed them as of right continuously for certain periods of time specified in the Act. Its provisions are somewhat complicated, but the practical effect is that the enjoyment of an easement, as for instance of a way or of the access of light and air through a window, for twenty years, and the enjoyment of a profit *à prendre*, as for instance of pasturage on a common, for

[1] 2 and 3 Will. IV, c. 71. See above, p. 185.

[2] See above, p. 184; and Gale on Easements, p. 146, &c.

[3] 2 and 3 Will. IV, c. 71. The Prescription Act does not do away with the common law doctrine of prescription; its provisions are additions to, and do not supersede, the old law.

thirty years, works the acquisition of the right[1]. The enjoyment must, except in the case of light, be by a person claiming right thereto, hence it may be defeated by showing that it has been enjoyed avowedly in exercise of some continuing permission or authority of the owner of the soil[2].

(5) The modes in which creditors acquire rights over the lands of their debtors have already been noticed[3]. A judgment-creditor, that is, a creditor who has obtained a judgment at law against his debtor, may, as has been seen, sue out a writ of execution called an *elegit*[4]. Till recently the effect of a judgment by itself, without execution, was most important as affecting the interests of subsequent purchasers of the judgment-debtor's lands. By a recent Act, however, the land of the debtor is not to be affected by any judgment against him until it has been actually delivered in execution by virtue of a writ of elegit or other lawful authority[5]. The creditor who has pursued this remedy may cause the sheriff to execute the writ, and obtain possession of the lands at his hands, which entitles him to enter and take possession and hold till the debt and costs are satisfied. The creditor may also, after due registration of the writ, obtain an order from the Chancery Division of the High Court for a sale of the lands in order to satisfy what is due to him[6].

The nature of a mortgage has been already described[7]. A mortgagee may either have the legal estate in the lands vested in him, in which case he was in the view of the Courts of Law (before the Judicature Act, 1873, came into force) sole legal owner, or he may have only an equitable estate. The

[1] 2 and 3 Will. IV, c. 71. ss. 1, 2. The Act provides that rights enjoyed for such periods respectively shall not be defeated by showing only that the right was first enjoyed at any time prior to such period, and that after the easement or profit had been enjoyed for forty or sixty years respectively, the right shall be absolute and indefeasible, unless it be proved that it was enjoyed by some agreement in writing.

[2] See Tickle v. Brown, 4 Adolphus and Ellis, 369.

[3] Chap. V. § 5. [4] See above, p. 282. [5] 27 and 28 Vict. c. 112. s. 1.

[6] 27 and 28 Vict. c. 112. s. 4. [7] Chap. V. § 5 (2).

CH. X. § 1. legal estate must be conveyed to him by one of the ordinary modes of conveyance applicable to freehold, leasehold, or copyhold estates. An equitable mortgage may be created by a mere agreement in writing, or even without writing by a deposit of the title-deeds by the legal owner. Before Nov. 1, 1875, an equitable mortgagee must have resorted to the Court of Chancery and not to a Court of Law to assert his rights.

Passing now to the modes of acquiring rights of ownership or property over the soil in the sense above explained [1], the most convenient classification would appear to be—modes of acquiring rights of ownership at common law, including under this head the modifications in detail of the old common law conveyances by recent Statutes; modes of acquiring rights of ownership under the Statute of Uses and the Statute 8 and 9 Vict. c. 106; and modes of acquiring such rights in equity.

(6) Modes of acquiring rights at common law have already been explained, and need here only be enumerated. The mode of acquisition is different according as the rights acquired are freehold, leasehold, or copyhold.

(7) The original mode of acquiring a freehold right of present enjoyment at common law is, as has been seen, by feoffment accompanied by livery of seisin, the requisites of which have already been detailed [2]. It is needless however to say that this mode of conveyance, though still legal, is in practice, with a single exception [3], obsolete. A feoffment was technically confined to an estate in fee simple, the conveyance of an estate tail by the same process was technically called a *gift*, that of an estate for life a *lease*.

To conveyances of freehold lands at common law may be added conveyances by way of *exchange* [4]. An exchange is

[1] See p. 305. [2] See above, Chap. III. § 12 (2).

[3] An infant tenant in gavelkind is still obliged to convey by feoffment.

[4] Blackstone, ii. 323. By the Inclosure Act, 1845, 8 and 9 Vict. c. 118. s. 147, means of effecting exchanges, which have been found of much practical utility, were provided through the action of the Inclosure Commissioners, the powers of whom are now vested in the Board of Agriculture.

a mutual grant of equal interests in lands, the one in consideration for the other. Thus *A* may exchange his estate in fee simple of Blackacre with *B*'s estate in fee simple of Whiteacre. This may be done by simple deed without livery of seisin.

Where there is a tenant of a particular estate he may at common law *surrender* his estate to the remainderman or reversioner by simple deed without livery of seisin. In the case of all the three assurances above mentioned, feoffment, exchange, and surrender, a writing signed by the conveying parties or their agents was made necessary by the Statute of Frauds [1], and the Statute 8 and 9 Vict. c. 106 requires a deed. These assurances, *feoffment*, *exchange*, and *surrender*, to which should be added *partition*, which has been already mentioned [2], appear to exhaust the possible modes of dealing with a freehold estate in possession at common law.

Freehold rights of future enjoyment, though, as has been seen in the fifth chapter [3], they can only be created by a common law conveyance by way of remainder, are habitually, when they exist, conveyed by conveyances operating at common law. For instance, an existing reversion or remainder can be conveyed to a stranger by *grant*, or to the tenant of the particular estate by *release*. Each of these transactions requires a deed.

(8) The modes of creating and conveying leasehold interests have already been discussed [4]. A leasehold interest is created by a demise effected by appropriate words, the usual words being 'demise, lease, and to farm let,' followed by the entry of the lessee on the demised lands.

In the case of all leases for a term exceeding three years from the making of the lease, or where the rent does not amount to two-thirds of the full improved value of the land, the words of demise to be effectual must, by the provisions of the Statute of Frauds, be in writing [5]. And by the Statute

[1] 29 Car. II. c. 3.
[2] See above, p. 278.
[3] § 3.
[4] See above, Chap. V. § 1.
[5] 29 Car. II. c. 3. ss. 1, 2.

8 and 9 Vict. c. 106. s. 3, whenever a lease is required by law to be in writing it shall be void at law unless made by deed. A mere agreement for a lease is however in practice as efficacious as a formal lease, for the Court exercising a jurisdiction formerly confined to the Court of Chancery will order, if need be, that a formal lease should be executed [1].

If the formalities required by the Statute of Frauds and 8 and 9 Vict. c. 106 are not observed, the tenancy created by the demise and entry will be a tenancy at will. Tenancies from year to year, by the half-year, quarter, &c., are, as has been shown [2], modifications of tenancies at will. In these tenancies the interest of the tenant can only be terminated by proper notice expiring at the end of the year of the tenancy, or at such other periods as may be contemplated by the parties. The other terms of the tenancy may be proved by parol or verbal evidence without writing. Thus a verbal agreement creating a tenancy for ten years, with elaborate provisions as to mode of cultivation, rights of lessor and lessee at the end of such term, and such-like, followed by entry of the lessee and payment of rent, will create a tenancy from year to year upon the terms specified, and similar terms may without any actual or express agreement be implied by the custom of the country.

Thus much for the mode of creation of leasehold interests. The term [3] when created can be alienated by the lessee like any other right of property. He can do this either by way of *underlease* or *assignment*. An underlease is where a lessee makes a lease for a shorter term than he himself holds, leaving thereby a reversion, of however short a duration, in himself. In its legal attributes an underlease in no way differs from a lease.

[1] It should be borne in mind that an agreement for a lease, being an interest in lands, is required by the Statute of Frauds (29 Car. II. c. 3. s. 4) to be in writing. [2] See above, p. 244.

[3] It should be observed that the word 'term' applies not to the period of time, but to the interest itself. The 'term' may come to an end before the period for which the lease has been granted has expired.

The grant of the whole term by the lessee is called an assignment. The Statute of Frauds required such assignments to be in writing [1]. The act to amend the Law of Real Property renders a deed necessary for the completion of the legal title [2]. The assignee of the lease has the same interest as the lessee (his assignor). This extends even to the binding of the assignee to the lessor by some of the covenants relating to the land into which the lessee may have entered. As, for instance, a covenant by the lessee to pay the rent or to repair the demised premises will bind his assignee. The assignee succeeds therefore not only to his assignor's rights *in rem,* but to *some* of his rights and duties *in personam.* But any covenant entered into between the lessor and original lessee which does not 'touch and concern' the thing demised, or in other words, which does not appertain as an ordinary and natural incident to the relation of lessor and lessee, does not upon the assignment cast any burden or duty on the assignee towards, or confer any right upon him against, the original lessor. It is often a difficult question whether or not a covenant is so connected with the land as to run with it, i.e. bind each successive assignee of the land.

In like manner as the burden and the benefit of the last-mentioned class of covenants entered into by the lessee extend to the assignee of the term, so do the burden and the benefit of such covenants extend to the assignee (or grantee) of the reversion. Whether or not the assignee of the reversion could take advantage of or was bound by covenants running with the land as between himself and the lessee, or assignee of lessee, seems to have been a doubtful point until it was settled by a Statute of Henry VIII [3]. Upon the dissolution of the monasteries there were many long leases subsisting of ecclesiastical lands. In order to place the grantees of the confiscated land in the same advantageous position as the ecclesiastical bodies by whom the leases had been made, it was necessary

[1] Sect. 3.

[2] 8 and 9 Vict. c. 106. s. 3.

[3] 32 Henry VIII, c. 34.

CH. X. § 1. to provide that the assignee of the reversion should be enabled to take advantage of and should be bound by the covenants entered into by the lessor under whom he claims [1].

Leasehold interests are frequently terminated by an application of the doctrine of conditions noticed above [2]. A lease usually contains a proviso for re-entry by the lessor in the event of the breach of any of the covenants entered into by the lessee, and also in certain other events, as for instance his bankruptcy. This proviso (subject to the restrictions on the right of re-entry contained in the Conveyancing and Law of Property Act, 1881, and the Conveyancing Act, 1892 [3]) entitles the lessor on the happening of the specified event to enter, or to bring an action of ejectment, and so terminate the lease. If however the lessor, after knowledge of the happening of the event, continues in any way to treat the lessee as his tenant, as for instance by receipt of rent accruing after the forfeiture, he is said to waive the forfeiture, and can no longer take advantage of it. A lease may of course be made terminable in certain events, on the happening of which the lessor has a right to re-enter without any express proviso for re-entry. Such a proviso is however usually inserted.

(9) Modes of acquiring rights of the character of copyhold have already been dealt with. Except where the modern

[1] Though the words of the enactment are general, the Courts have confined its provisions to covenants which touch and concern the thing demised. See on the subject of covenants running with the land, Spencer's case, 1 Smith's Leading Cases. [2] See p. 264.

[3] 44 and 45 Vict. c. 41. s. 14, and 55 and 56 Vict. c. 13. By the Act of 1881 the right of re-entry is not to be exercised unless and until the lessor serves on the lessee a notice specifying the breach complained of, and, if the breach is capable of remedy, requiring the lessee to remedy the breach and in any case requiring the lessee to make compensation in money for the breach, and the lessee fails to remedy the breach or to make compensation. These restrictions do not extend to covenants or conditions against underletting or assigning, conditions for forfeiture on bankruptcy or taking in execution the lessee's interest, or on non-payment of rent. The Act of 1892 extends the relief (subject to certain qualifications) to a condition for forfeiture on bankruptcy, and to sub-lessees in respect of a forfeiture incurred by the original lessees.

Statutes have altered in detail some of the solemnities requisite for the passing of copyhold lands, the general mode of alienating copyhold lands is by surrender and admittance operating at common law [1].

(10) Passing now from the modes of alienation which rest upon the common law, it is convenient to arrange in a distinct class modes of alienation operating under the Statute of Uses and under the Act to amend the Law of Real Property. The necessary forms of conveyance have been still further abbreviated and simplified by the Conveyancing and Law of Property Act, 1881, and the Conveyancing Act, 1882 [2]. This class will in fact comprise the whole body of conveyances in use at the present day. No simple alienation of an estate of freehold or settlement of lands is ever framed which does not owe its operation to the enactments of one or both of the first-named Statutes. The operation of the Statute of Uses upon a feoffment to uses, bargain and sale, and covenant to stand seised, has already been sufficiently discussed in the seventh chapter. The practical application of the Statute combined with the common law conveyance of a release has been explained, and it has been seen how the long prevalence of the mode of conveyance by lease and release was at length superseded by the provisions of the Act to amend the Law of Real Property. That Statute abolished the ancient principle that freehold estates in possession could only be conveyed from one person to another by livery of seisin, and enacted that 'all corporeal hereditaments shall, as regards the conveyance of the immediate freehold thereof, be deemed to lie in grant as well as in livery [3].' The effect of this Statute therefore is to enable an effectual conveyance of a freehold estate in possession to be made by the operation of a simple deed containing words expressing a grant from the grantor to the grantee [4]. This

[1] See above, Chap. V. § 6. pp. 293, 296.

[2] 44 and 45 Vict. c. 41 and 45 and 46 Vict. c. 39.

[3] 8 and 9 Vict. c. 106. s. 2.

[4] See the specimen of a modern grant of an estate in fee in Williams on Real Property, p. 583, where the operative words are—'he the said

enactment does not in any way supersede the action of the Statute of Uses, and uses consequently may be and constantly are created by proper expressions in these deeds of statutory grant [1].

(11) The creation and disposition of Equitable rights have also been dealt with [2]. It has been seen that these interests are created either by express words, that is, by the use of words in a conveyance operating to pass the estate at common law and creating a second use or trust not executed by the Statute, or by words imposing some active duty upon the alienee at common law; or secondly, they may be created by implication, as upon a conveyance without consideration, in which case a resulting trust may be implied, or upon an agreement for the sale of lands uncompleted by conveyance, and payment by the purchaser of the purchase money, in which case the vendor or legal owner becomes trustee for the purchaser.

For the conveyance and assignment of these equitable interests the only necessary solemnity is the writing required by the Statute of Frauds, though in practice it is usual to employ a deed.

(12) To pass now from alienation *inter vivos* to alienation by will. A will of lands operates on different principles according as the interest to be conveyed is freehold, leasehold, or copyhold.

(13) In regard to freehold lands the requisites of a valid will have already been detailed. When a will has been validly executed and remains in force at the death of the devisor, it operates immediately upon that event to convey the freehold lands comprised in the devise to the devisee. Though no act of acceptance or assent is necessary on the part of the devisee,

AB doth by these presents grant unto the said *CD* all that messuage, &c., to have and to hold unto and to the use of the said *CD* his heirs and assigns for ever.'

[1] This is the case for instance in every marriage settlement of real estate. See above, p. 357.

[2] See above, Chap. VII. § 4.

yet if before acceptance by entering on the lands the devisee by an express act waives the devise, no estate will pass to him by the will[1]. CH. X. § 2.

(14) It should be observed that the operation of a will with regard to leasehold interests or chattels real is wholly different from its operation with regard to freeholds. For reasons already explained, leasehold interests are regarded as personal property[2]. The whole of a man's personal property is cast by the will upon his executors, and the legatees take their gifts through the medium of the executors. If therefore *A* devises all his estate real and personal to *B*, the freehold lands will vest in *B* immediately on *A*'s death, the leaseholds not until he has obtained the assent of the executors.

(15) The mode of devise applicable to copyholds has already been noticed[3].

§ 2. *Title by Succession.*

The second of the principal heads under which Titles may be arranged is *Succession* or devolution *ab intestato*. Here again the rules governing succession to interests in lands are different in the case of succession to freehold, leasehold, and copyhold interests.

(1) *Descent of an Estate of inheritance in Fee Simple in Freeholds.* The old rules as to title by descent[4] were in some important points modified and recast by the Act for the Amendment of the Law of Inheritance[5], which applies to descent on the death of any person subsequently to December 31, 1833. The main features of the existing law and the points in which the law was changed by the abovementioned Statute will now be briefly noticed.

Upon the death of a tenant in fee simple the lands descend

[1] See Townson v. Tickell, 3 Barnewall and Alderson's Reports, p. 31.

[2] Chap. III. § 17; V. § 1.

[3] See above, pp. 296, n. 2, 390.

[4] See above, Chap. II. § 6.

[5] 3 and 4 Will. IV, c. 106.

CH. X. § 2. to his 'heir [1].' In ascertaining who the 'heir' is, the first question is, from whom is the descent to be traced? Formerly the rule was that the descent was to be traced from the person last actually seised. Thus suppose *A*, tenant in fee simple, has a son *B* and a daughter *C* by a first wife, and a son *D* by a second wife, and dies intestate, leaving *B*, *C*, and *D* surviving, if *B* entered and was seised of the lands, he thereby became a fresh stock of descent, and on his death, intestate, the land descended to his sister *C* to the exclusion of *D*, his half-brother, the old rule being that there could be no descent to any one who was not of the whole blood of the person last seised [2]. On the other hand, if *B*, though he had survived *A*, had never entered or become seised of the lands, the lands would at *B*'s death have descended to *D*, for he being a son would be the heir of the person last seised, his father, in preference to his half-sister. The first of the above cases is that to which the old maxim 'possessio fratris facit sororem esse haeredem' applies. It thus became an important question, under the old law, whether the person last entitled had ever obtained actual seisin. The Inheritance Act, 1833, has altered the law in this respect, by providing that descent in every case shall be traced to the last *purchaser*, that is to say, to the person 'who last acquired the land otherwise than by descent [3].' For example, in the case

[1] The word 'heir' in English law has a sense far more limited than the word 'haeres' in Roman law. The 'heir' is the person on whom the real estate of a deceased intestate devolves. He is opposed to the devisee who is the person to whom real property is left by will, and to the executor or administrator who succeeds to the personal estate. In Roman Law the 'haeres' is the universal successor to the deceased, whether *ab intestato* or *ex testamento*.

[2] See below, p. 423.

[3] 3 and 4 Will. IV, c. 106. s. 1. By this section the person last entitled to the land shall be deemed the purchaser unless it shall be proved that he inherited it. The Real Property Commissioners (1st Report, p. 16) proposed that the person last entitled should be the stock of descent. The existing rule appears to have been adopted by the legislature in conformity with the authorities, especially Sir E. Coke. 'And note that it is an old and true maxim in law, that none shall inherit any lands as

above given, it would be immaterial under the present law whether or not *B* ever became seised of the lands. The important question after the deaths of *A* and *B* would be, not who was heir to *B*, but who was heir to *A* (assuming him to have been the last purchaser). In the event of a total failure of the heirs of the purchaser, but not of the person last entitled to the land, it is provided by a later Statute, that in such a case the lands should descend to the heir of the person last entitled [1]. For instance, *A*, a bastard, purchases lands and dies intestate, whereupon the lands descend to his only child *B*. Upon *B*'s death intestate the lands would, but for the last-mentioned Act, have escheated. Since that Statute they will descend to the heir of *B*. CH. X. § 2.

Starting then with the last purchaser as the stock of descent, the heir of the purchaser is first to be looked for in his own offspring, and, according to the well-known rule of primogeniture, will be found in the first instance in the eldest of the purchaser's sons. Stated generally, the rule is that, amongst persons of equal degree in relation to the purchaser, males are entitled one after another in the order of their birth, females take together as coparceners [2].

But before a younger brother or daughters can claim as heir to the last purchaser in consequence of the decease of a

heir but only the blood of the first purchaser.' Coke upon Littleton, 12 a. This rule, however, does not appear in Glanvill; see above, Chap. II. § 6: and Bracton, fol. 65 b, uses language which seems to be inconsistent with it, laying it down that a person on becoming seised makes a stipes or new stock of descent. Hence the maxim 'seisina facit stipitem.' Blackstone's explanation of this rule of law, as well as his more elaborate explanation of the exclusion of the half-blood (see below), is based on the supposed strictly hereditary character of a feud, which Blackstone asserts was originally descendible only to the issue of the purchaser. This, however, does not appear to have ever been law in this country in the case of a gift to a man and his heirs.

[1] 22 and 23 Vict. c. 35. s. 19.

[2] As to coparceners see above, Chap. V. § 4. See for a discussion of the proper rule in the case where *A* purchases lands and dies intestate leaving two daughters *B* and *C*, and *B* afterwards dies intestate leaving a son *D*, Williams on Real Property, Appendix C.

CH. X. § 2. brother who would have been entitled to succeed, it must be ascertained that the elder or only brother has left no lawful descendants. For it is an invariable rule that such children stand in the place of their parent, and succeed to the rights which he would have had if he had survived the purchaser. Thus if *A* is the purchaser and has two sons *B*, the elder, and *C*, *B* has a son *D* who has issue two daughters *E* and *F*, *B* and *D* predecease *A*, upon the death of *A* intestate the lands descend to his great-granddaughters to the exclusion of his son *C*.

If the purchaser at his decease leaves no children or descendants surviving him, the lands will go to his nearest male lineal ancestor, the paternal line being preferred to the maternal [1].

This rule was newly introduced by the Inheritance Act. By a strange anomaly in our law, of which no satisfactory explanation appears to have been given, the lineal ancestor was formerly excluded from the succession, though the uncle or aunt was not [2]. If such ancestor has predeceased the purchaser, his issue will represent him in the same order, and subject to the same rules (with one exception) as have been already stated with regard to the issue of the purchaser.

Formerly, on the death of a tenant in fee intestate and without issue, the father being excluded, the lands descended

[1] 3 and 4 Will. IV, c. 106. ss. 6, 7.

[2] The elaborate explanation given by Blackstone, ii. pp. 211, 212, referring the rule to feudal principles, and to the supposed rule that a *feudum novum* or newly-granted feud could only descend to the lineal descendants of the feoffee (see ib. p. 222), appears to be inconsistent with the early English authorities, which do not mention any such fiction as Blackstone supposes to be necessary to explain collateral succession. I am disposed to think it more probable that the rule really results from the associations involved in the word 'descent,' and that the rule 'an inheritance may lineally descend but not ascend' (Littleton, sect. 3) was supposed to be part of the law of nature. Compare Bracton, fol. 62 b: 'Descendit itaque jus, quasi ponderosum quid cadens deorsum, recta linea vel transversali, et numquam reascendit ea via qua descendit.' See Pollock and Maitland, Hist. of Eng. Law, ii. p. 285 seq.

at once to the next brother, or, if no brother, to the sisters. Now the brother or sisters succeed as representing the father of the purchaser, the uncles, aunts, and first cousins as representing the grandfather, and remoter collaterals as representing the common ancestor [1]. CH. X. § 2.

In collateral descent the principle of simple representation according to the rules governing the descent to the purchaser's lineal descendants is, as has been said, subject to one exception. There was an unreasonable rule under the older law which excluded entirely persons of the half-blood of the person last seised from the succession [2]. Thus, to refer to the instance given above, if *A* died, leaving *B* a son and *C* a daughter by a first wife and *D* a son by a second wife, and *B* became actually seised of the lands and died, the lands would descend to *C* the sister and not to *D*. Again, if *C* became seised and died intestate, *D* could not be her heir, and if she left no relation of the whole blood, the lands would escheat to the lord. By the change effected by the Inheritance Act, the half-blood, if descended from a common male ancestor, is to take next after any relation in the same degree of the whole blood. Thus, in the instance above given, assuming *B* to be the last purchaser, *D* will take next after his sister *C*. If the common ancestor is a female the half-blood will take next after the common ancestor [3].

If there are no male ancestors of the last purchaser or representatives of such ancestors surviving at the time of his

[1] See 3 and 4 Will. IV, c. 106, s. 5.

[2] The rule as laid down by Bracton (65) appears to be of a much more limited character. Where a man leaves issue by two wives, *A* a son and *B* a daughter by the first, and *C* a son by the second, and *A* purchases lands and dies intestate, the lands descend to *B in preference* to *C*. Bracton mentions that it was a disputed question whether the same rule applied when the lands had descended from the common father. In that case he seems to think the lands ought to descend from the eldest son to the younger brother of the half-blood to the exclusion of the sister. Blackstone's explanation of the exclusion of the half-blood is probably the most unsatisfactory passage in his book; ii. pp. 228, 232.

[3] 3 and 4 Will. IV, c. 106. s. 9.

CH. X. § 2.

decease, the lands will in the next instance go to the female paternal ancestors of the purchaser. In this case the rule is that the mother of his more remote male paternal ancestor and her descendants are to be preferred to the mother of a less remote male paternal ancestor or her descendants [1]. It is difficult to see on what principle such a remote relation as might be embraced under this rule should be preferred to the purchaser's mother, but such is the law.

It is only after the failure of the paternal line of ancestors, both male and female, and their descendants, that the mother succeeds. After the mother come her descendants by another husband if any, and then her father and the line of male maternal ancestors of the purchaser and their descendants, according to the principles above stated; and last of all the line of female maternal ancestors and their descendants, who succeed according to the same rule as relates to female paternal ancestors [2].

There are some cases of descent by particular customs of freehold lands where the old Anglo-Saxon rules still prevail. The most important of these are in the tenures called gavelkind and borough English, which have already been noticed [3].

(2) The succession to leasehold interests or chattels real rests on a wholly different ground. Here the fundamental distinction between real and personal property becomes important. On the death intestate of a person entitled to a term of years in lands, the property devolves upon the *administrator*, or person appointed by the Probate Division of the High Court to administer the personal estate of the intestate [4]. The administrator, after payment of the debts of the deceased, must distribute the personal property, including chattels real, according to the provisions of the Statute of Distributions [5].

(3) Descent in the case of copyhold lands is regulated by

[1] Sect. 8. [2] Sect. 8. [3] See above, pp. 47, 48.

[4] Under the provisions of 20 and 21 Vict. c. 77.

[5] 22 and 23 Car. II, c. 10.

the particular custom of the manor in which the lands are situate[1]. These may or may not follow the rules relating to freehold lands; and in order to ascertain the custom recourse must be had to the proper evidence, which is, primarily, the court rolls of the manor.

§ 3. *Miscellaneous Titles.*

(1) *Escheat*[2].

If in the case of freehold lands there is a total failure of heirs on the death of the tenant, the land escheats to the lord. The theory of title by escheat is that the whole property in the land being, as has been said, divided between the lords (paramount and mesne) and the tenant, on the tenant failing to have any heirs to whom the lands can descend, there is a species of reversion to the next lord. His right over the land becomes as it were enlarged by the failure of the tenants in possession. But this title must be completed by entry on the land, or otherwise asserting his right[3].

If, as is usually the case at the present day, there is no known mesne lord of whom the land is held, the land escheats to the sovereign as lord paramount. The practice is for the Crown to institute an 'inquest of office,' usually before commissioners appointed for the purpose, in order to determine whether the tenant died without leaving an heir. On the verdict of the jury to this effect the Crown becomes seised of the land without the necessity of entry[4].

[1] See above, Chap. V. § 6. How far the provisions of the Inheritance Act apply to copyhold or customary tenures is a matter somewhat disputed. The term 'land' is expressly interpreted to cover these tenures, but the Courts of Exchequer and Exchequer Chamber held that they do not affect a custom to trace descent to the person last seised. Muggleton v. Barnett, 1 Hurlstone and Norman, 282; 2 ib. 653; and see Williams on Real Property, Appendix B.

[2] See above, Chap. II. § 5.

[3] Blackstone, ii. p. 245. This necessity for the lord to do some act on his part induced Blackstone to class escheat under title by purchase.

[4] Blackstone, iii. p. 260.

CH. X. § 3 (1). By the Intestates Estate Act, 1884 [1], the law of escheat has been extended to equitable estates.

Escheat formerly took place upon the blood of the tenant being attainted. Here again we have a specimen of the practice of treating metaphorical expressions as if they were realities, which has been found to be so common amongst lawyers. Attainder took place upon judgment of death or outlawry being passed after conviction for treason or felony [2]. The effect of attainder was, as is said, to corrupt the blood so as to render it no longer inheritable. The effect was the same therefore as if the tenant had died without heirs; the land at once escheated to the lord. This escheat was however subject to the paramount right of the Crown, based on other than feudal principles, to forfeiture of the land, in the case of conviction for treason for ever, in the case of conviction for felony for a year and a day.

The notion of corruption of blood consequent on attainder was pushed still further. Not only did it apply to lands in the possession of the criminal at the time, but it extended also to land to which he might afterwards become entitled. Thus if *A* were seised in fee, and *B* his eldest son were convicted of treason in *A*'s lifetime, *B* having a son *C*, upon *A*'s death intestate the land escheated to the lord, whether *B* were dead or not—if he were alive, because his blood being attainted he could not inherit; if he were dead, because *C* could not make title through him [3].

Such was formerly the law with reference to escheat *propter delictum tenentis*. After considerable modifications by statute of the doctrine of attainder [4], the recent Statute 33 and 34

[1] 47 and 48 Vict. c. 71.

[2] Blackstone, iv. pp. 383–387.

[3] Blackstone, ii. p. 254, says, 'The channel which conveyed the hereditary blood from his ancestors to him is not only exhausted for the present, but totally dammed up and rendered impervious for the future.' This effect of attainder was abolished by the Inheritance Act, 3 and 4 Will. IV, c. 106. s. 10.

[4] Especially by 54 Geo. III, c. 145.

Vict. c. 23 has totally abolished forfeiture and escheat (except when forfeiture is consequent upon outlawry), and provides instead for the appointment of an administrator to the property of the convict, and for the vesting of his property in such administrator during the continuance of his punishment.

(2) *Loss and Acquisition by Lapse of Time.*

The mode of acquisition by prescription of the class of rights over land which are styled above 'rights *in alieno solo*' has already been noticed. In the case of rights of ownership occupation without title for a certain period has an operation somewhat different in point of law. The theory of English law is that if a person entitled to a legal remedy against a wrong-doer does not pursue that remedy within a certain time after he has first had the opportunity of doing so, his right to pursue the remedy at all is extinguished[1]. If therefore a person occupies land without any right, and the true owner or his successors in title allow twelve years[2] to elapse since the last time when such owner or some person through whom he claims was in possession or receipt of the profits of the land, or of the rent, without taking effectual steps, by action or re-entry, to recover the land, the right to take such steps either by way of action or re-entry as against the occupant, or any person claiming through him, is extinguished. This rule is subject to exception in the case of persons who are disabled by infancy, coverture, or lunacy[3], from taking

[1] See for the older law, Blackstone, iii. pp. 178, 188, 192, 196.

[2] See 3 and 4 Will. IV, c. 27. s. 2, and 37 and 38 Vict. c. 57. The latter Statute came into force on Jan. 1, 1879, and substituted the periods mentioned in the text of twelve, thirty, and six years for the former periods of twenty, forty, and ten respectively. These are the Statutes of Limitations at present in force with regard to the rights over land called corporeal hereditaments (see above, p. 306, n. 2) and rents. They do not apply to the lands of the Crown or of the Duchy of Cornwall. The period of limitation with regard to such lands is sixty years. 9 Geo. III, c. 26; 23 and 24 Vict. c. 53; 24 and 25 Vict. c. 62.

[3] 3 and 4 Will. IV, c. 27. ss. 16, 18, 19. The disability arising from absence beyond the seas was removed by 37 and 38 Vict. c. 57. s. 4.

CH. X. § 3 (2). the proper steps to assert their right. Such persons, or persons claiming through them, though the twelve years may have elapsed, are allowed six years (unless the whole period amounts to more than thirty years [1]) after the removal of their disability, or after the death of the person disabled. And if the occupant have given to the true owner an acknowledgment in writing, signed, of his title to the land, the period of twelve years begins to run anew from the date of any such acknowledgment [2]. Thus for all practical purposes the effect of the above-stated rules is to make occupation without title for twelve years (subject to the exceptions already noticed) equivalent to a mode of acquiring a right. Such an occupant would before the Statute of Limitations have been safe from attack by entry or action at the hands of the true owner or any third party. And now the Statute of Limitations contains a provision [3] that not only the right of action shall be barred by the lapse of twelve years, but the right of property itself shall be extinguished. For all practical purposes therefore it may be said that by possession without title for twelve years the occupant now acquires an estate in fee simple in the lands [4], as against all persons except one whose right of entry or action has not existed for that period [5].

[1] 3 and 4 Will. IV, c. 27. s. 17. [2] Ib. s. 14. [3] Ib. s. 34.

[4] It should be observed that the mode of acquiring 'corporeal hereditaments' by lapse of time differs essentially in principle from acquisition of 'incorporeal hereditaments' by prescription. In the latter case, as has been shown above (Chap. III. § 18), long-continued enjoyment as of right was regarded as evidence of a grant by some owner of the praedium serviens. The Prescription Act, operating upon this state of the law, made long-continued enjoyment, as of right, a positive mode of acquiring the right. The mode of acquisition of corporeal hereditaments, treated of in the text, has been reached by another road, highly characteristic of the practical character of English law. By extinguishing all possible remedies, the right of the occupant is made impregnable, and unlike Roman law, or our own law of prescription, nothing but the bare fact of possession without title for a sufficiently long period is necessary to create the negative title resulting from the Statute of Limitations. The conditions required by the civil law, bona fides, justa causa, justus titulus, &c., have no place in our law.

[5] Observe that if the occupancy began during the continuance of a *par-*

CH. X. § 3 (3).

(3) *Compulsory Acquisition for Public Purposes.*

There are certain modes of acquiring land by what may be called a process of involuntary alienation, where the law provides means for depriving a person of his property upon proper compensation being made to him, and vesting it in other persons, or in a corporation, notwithstanding any opposition by the owner. Thus the legislature provides machinery for compelling persons to divest themselves of lands which may be required for certain purposes of public utility; for instance, a railway, public elementary schools, or certain public works. This is principally effected by the machinery provided by the Lands Clauses Consolidation Act[1]. This Act contains a set of general provisions, which are usually incorporated in the special Acts authorising and regulating individual undertakings, providing for a mode of compulsorily vesting the property required in the company or other body undertaking the public works by the giving certain notices, and taking the requisite steps to assess and pay the proper compensation for the lands taken.

(4) *Acquisition under Inclosure Acts.*

The legislature has also provided special means for acquiring and divesting rights over common and waste lands, and for the inclosure of common fields[2]. The limits within which

ticular estate, the period of limitation does not begin to run against the remainderman or reversioner till his estate vests in possession (see above, p. 259). For instance, if lands have been given to *A* for life, remainder to *B* in fee, and during *A*'s life *C* wrongfully obtains possession, as against *A* the period of limitation will begin to run from the commencement of *C*'s possession, but as against *B*, not till the death of *A*, for not till then can *B* enter or bring ejectment. *Contra non valentem agere non currit praescriptio.*

[1] 8 Vict. c. 18.

[2] The ancient 'common field' will be easily recognised by readers of Mr. Joshua Williams' lectures on 'Rights of Common,' or of Mr. Seebohm's 'English Village Community' in the expression in the preamble of the statute 8 and 9 Vict. c. 118, 'lands intermixed or divided into inconvenient parcels.' See above, pp. 5–7. Mr. Seebohm, p. 14, calculates that between the years 1760 and 1844 nearly 4000 Inclosure Acts were passed affecting 'common fields' in various parishes.

CH. X. § 3 (4).

the lord might by himself exercise his rights of ownership over the land have already been noticed [1]. Of course a 'common' might always be dealt with, as any other piece of property, by the concurrence of all the persons having rights over it, that is to say, by the concurrent action of the freeholder or lord of the manor and all the commoners. But owing to the practical impossibility of obtaining the consent of all the commoners, it became usual for the legislature to pass private Acts of Parliament, authorising inclosures in particular places, and providing compensation to the lord and the commoners for the rights of which they were deprived, usually by giving them the benefit of the exclusive ownership of a portion of the soil of the common discharged of rights of common, in lieu in the former case of the seignory of the whole, and in the latter of the rights of common which were extinguished.

The Inclosure Acts, of which the Statute 8 and 9 Vict. c. 118 is the most important, contain provisions for carrying out inclosures through the Board of Agriculture [2]. The consents of the requisite number of persons interested in the land, and of the lord of the manor, must be obtained. If the inclosure is carried out, the Board may award certain portions of the waste for recreation, for allotments to the labouring poor, and for roads; the residue is divided amongst the persons who previously had rights over the land, and the lord of the manor. Upon the allotment being made, the common or other rights enjoyed over the land previous to the inclosure are extinguished [3].

The land allotted to the various persons who already were the owners of adjoining lands becomes part of and is held by the same tenure as the lands to which it is annexed: if

[1] Chap. III. § 18 (2).

[2] Established in 1889 by the statute 52 and 53 Vict. c. 30, which transfers to the new Board the powers of the former Inclosure and Land Commissioners.

[3] 8 and 9 Vict. c. 118. s. 106.

annexed to freeholds, the land becomes freehold, and is held for the same estate as the land to which it is annexed; if the adjoining land is copyhold, the annexed land becomes copyhold also. CH. X. § 3 (5).

(5) *Compulsory Enfranchisement of Copyholds.*

Another species of compulsory alienation takes place under the Act by which either a lord of a manor or a copyhold tenant is entitled to compel enfranchisement through the medium of the Board of Agriculture [1]. Enfranchisement, as has been seen, consists in the conveyance of the freehold by the lord to his copyhold tenant [2]. Either lord or tenant may now under the provisions of the above-mentioned Act obtain an award of enfranchisement, compensation in money paid down or secured, or in land, being awarded to the lord.

(6) *Bankruptcy.*

Estates in land are lost and acquired by the bankruptcy of the tenant. Upon the appointment of the trustee in bankruptcy under the provisions of the Bankruptcy Act, 1883 [3], the whole of the bankrupt's freehold, leasehold, and copyhold estates vest in the trustee, in trust for the creditors.

The following table shows in a concise form the classification of modes of acquisition which has been presented in this chapter.

[1] 57 and 58 Vict. c. 46. [2] See above, p. 294.

[3] 46 and 47 Vict. c. 52.

TABLE IV.

TITLES OR MODES OF ACQUISITION OF RIGHTS OVER THINGS REAL.

- § 1. Alienation.
  - (1) Inter vivos.
    - (2) Of rights of ownership.
      - (6) At Common Law (including statutory modifications of Common Law conveyances).
        - (7) Of Freehold Rights. *Feoffment*, *Exchange*, *Surrender*, *Partition*. *Grant* or *Release* of reversion or remainder.
        - (8) Of Leaseholds. *Demise* or *Lease*, *Underlease*, *Assignment*.
        - (9) Of Copyholds. *Surrender and Admittance*.
      - (10) Under Statute of Uses and 8 and 9 Vict. c. 106. *Conveyances to Uses*, *Statutory Grant*.
      - (11) In Equity.
    - (3) Of rights *in alieno solo*.
      - (4) Incorporeal hereditaments (Easements and Profits). *Express Grant*, *Implied Grant*, *Prescription*.
      - (5) Creditors' Rights. *Elegit*, *Mortgages* (legal and equitable).
  - (12) By Will.
    - (13) Of Freeholds.
    - (14) Leaseholds.
    - (15) Copyholds.
- § 2. Succession or Devolution.
  - (1) Of Freeholds.
  - (2) Of Leaseholds.
  - (3) Of Copyholds.
- § 3. Miscellaneous.
  - (1) Escheat.
  - (2) Lapse of time. *Statute of Limitations*.
  - (3) Compulsory Alienation for public purposes.
  - (4) Alienation under Inclosure Acts.
  - (5) Compulsory Enfranchisement of Copyholds.
  - (6) Bankruptcy.

GLOSSARY

The Glossary aims only at giving the senses in which words occurring in the previous extracts, with which the reader might probably not be familiar, are there used.

A.

Acquietare, to release or acquit, p. 82.

Aesnecia, right of prior birth, primogeniture, 96.

Approvare, appruare, 214, to approve, i. e. to make profit of the waste by inclosure. *See* s. v. 'approve[2]' in the 'New English Dictionary' (edited by Dr. Murray), where the word is traced to an old French word a-prouer.

Arbelastarius, a cross-bowman, 74.

Arramare, to undertake, especially to undertake the prosecution or defence of a suit, 198 (*see* Spelman, Glossary, s. v. adrhamire).

Arura, a ploughing, 139.

Assartare, to clear a space in a wood, 214.

Assartum, a clearing, 197.

Assignare, to assign, make over, 168.

Assisa, (1) a law, ordinance, or statute, 112; (2) a particular species of suit, so called, apparently, because instituted by an assisa, 197; (3) the jurors in an assize, 199.

Attaintus = attinctus, attainted, the peculiar consequence of a conviction for treason or felony.

Attornare, to appoint a substitute or attorney for the conduct of a suit, 106; to cause a tenant or farmer to recognise as lord the alienee of the freeholder, 179.

Averia, animals used in agriculture, especially commonable beasts, 196.

B.

Ballivus, a steward or bailiff, 196.

Bladum, corn, 202.

Boscus, woodland, 197.

Bovata, an ox-gang, as much land as one ox (or a pair of oxen) could till in a year, variously estimated at 13–18 acres, but probably an indefinite quantity, 106, 107.

Breve, a writ or command in writing, especially a writ by which an action was commenced, 73.

Breviuncula, a writing or charter, 59.

Brochia, a brooch or needle for fastening a sack, 140.

Bruera, thorns or rough bushes, 197; rough ground, 214.

Burgagium, burgensis, *see* Index, **Burgage**.

C.

Capitalis, chief; **capitalis dominus**, lord of a manor, 158.

Caraxare, to sign, 59.

Carruca, carcua, a plough, 123.

Carucata, a plough-land, as much land as could be cultivated by a plough in one year, varying probably with the character of the soil, but larger than the bovata, 74.

Catalla, chattels, movable or personal property, 92.

Census, income from land, rent, 82.

Chacea, a way for driving cattle, a drove, 198.

Clamantia, 107, **clameum**, 229, claim.

Clamare, to complain, 72; to claim, 74.

Clamor, complaint, 74.

Clausum Paschae, the close of the octave or utas of Easter, the Sunday after Easter, 112.

Comes, an Earl, 58, 74.

Comitatus, county, 215; County-Court, 73.

Communia, *see* Index, **Common**.

Compendium, a shorter way, 188.

Compotum, compotus, account, 87.

Concordia, a settlement or compromise of a cause in court, applied to a fine, 106.

Conquestus, the conquest or acquisition of England by William I, 140, 154.

Consideratio, a judgment (of a Court), 78.

Constitutio, (1) an ordinance or law, 198; (2) a mode of constituting a right, especially the grant by which a servitude is created, 185.

Consuetudo, a custom, especially customary feudal dues, 139.

Conventio, a covenant or agreement by deed, 154, 178.

Convincere, to convict, 92.

Coterelli, *see* Index.

Curia, (1) court, Curia Regis, etc.; (2) a court or yard, 196.

Curialia verba, ordinary every-day language (?), 69.

Custodia, wardship, *see* Index.

Custumarii, *see* Index.

Custus, cost, 74.

D.

Damna, (dampna, 134), damages, 179.

Defalta, default, 221.

Defensa, enclosures, 196.

Deforcio, -ceo, to keep out by force, 73.

Demanda, a demand, that which is demanded, 145.

Devisa, or **divisa**, the division of the property of a deceased person in accordance with his will, hence devise, 110, *n.* 1.

Dimittere, to demise, let, or lease lands for life or years, 179.

Dirationare, to establish, usually applied to establishing a superior title, and disproving title of tenant, 80, 92.

Disparagatio, degradation by an unequal marriage, 125.

Disseisina, disseisin, *see* Index.

Disseisire, to put out of seisin, 113.

Districtio, distraint, compelling to performance of a duty by lawful seizure of property, 83.

Distringere, to distrain, 83.

Dominicum, dominion, or demesne, the possession of the freehold, 159; domain of the lord of a manor, 213.

Donatorius, donee, the person to whom an estate is given, 148.

E.

Eleemosyna, *see* Index, **Frankalmoign**.

Emenda, amends, properly a compensation to party injured, as opposed to a fine, 122.

Escaeta, escheat, *see* Index.

Escambium, that which is given in

exchange or substitution, especially the land which a lord bound to defend his tenant's title must give in recompense if the tenant be ousted by virtue of a superior title, 80; *see* Index, **Warranty**.

Estoverium, 'stuff,' i.e. wood or other materials which the tenant is entitled to take from the land of his lord or a stranger for repairs, fuel, etc., 197.

Exceptio, a plea, formal statement of matter of excuse to an action, 87.

Exhaeredare, to deprive of estate in lands, 92.

Exhaeredatio, disinheritance (by alienation by tenant in his lifetime), 102, 236.

Exitus, issues, profits, 122.

Expeditatio (canum), mutilation of the foot to prevent a dog chasing game, 215.

Expeditio, the duty of military service, *see* Index, **Trinoda necessitas**.

Expletia, 149, **esplez**, 245, fruits or produce of land.

F.

Falcatio, the service of reaping or cutting corn, etc., 139.

Felonia, felony, a crime other than treason punishable with forfeiture and escheat of land and goods, 92, 93.

Feodalis (**feodalia servitia**, 139), services attaching as an incident of tenure.

Feodifirma, fee-farm, *see* Index.

Feodum, fee, *see* Index.

Fidelitas, fealty, *see* Index.

Finis, (1) a fine (pecuniary), 121; (2) a fine (final concord); *see* Index.

Firmarius, farmer, an occupier of land for years or other limited period who has no freehold interest, 178.

Forinseca servitia, services due to the king as lord paramount, as opposed to services due to the immediate lord, 140.

Forisfacere, 35, *n*. 1. **Forisfactura**, 93, to forfeit, forfeiture.

Foris-familiare, (apparently) to deprive a son's descendants of a right of succession to lands by his accepting lands from the father in his lifetime, 97.

Fossatum, a bank, 199.

G.

Gardinum, gardinus, a garden, 196.

Guerra, war, 83.

H.

Haspa, hasp, handle (of door), 149.

Haya, hedge, 199.

Herietta, heriot, *see* Index.

Hida, hide, *see* Index.

Homagium, homage, *see* Index.

I.

Imbreviare, to enrol (names of jurors), 113.

Incurrere, incurri domino, to be forfeited to the lord, 222.

Inde, thereon, thereof, therefrom

Intrinseca servitia, services reserved by the feoffment or grant to the immediate lord, 139.

Irritare, to make void, 103.

J.

Justiciare, to exercise judicial authority over, compel by process of law, 83.

Justicia, a justice = **justitiarius**, 72.

L.

Legalis homo, a law-worthy man, one capable of possessing all legal rights, 112.

Leporarius, a greyhound (?), 139.

Ligeancia, the relation created by homage and fealty of a vassal to his chief lord, 78.

Litterae patentes, writings authenticated by a seal, whereby a man is enabled to do or enjoy that which otherwise of himself he could not. So called because they are *open*, ready to be shown for confirmation of the authority thereby given, 149; *see* Blount, Law Dict., s. v.

M.

Manerium, a manor, 140.

Mansa, *see* Index.

Mansiuncula, a small house or tenement, 197.

Mariscus, a marsh, 198.

Maritagium, (1) marriage, i.e. the right of the lord to provide his tenant with husband or wife, or to receive the due equivalent, 125, 158; (2) the land given by a father to his daughter on her marriage (101) to be held by the tenure of (3) frank-marriage, 102; *see* Index.

Maritare, to marry, or provide with a marriage, 90.

Merchetum, the fine payable by a villein to his lord on the marriage of a daughter, 154, 215.

Messuagium, a house, messuage, 96.

Messura, the service of harvesting, 139.

Miles, a knight, 132; a tenant by knight-service, 95.

Militia, knight-service, 95.

Minister, thegn, 59.

Misericordia, (1) mercy, (2) a discretionary fine, in misericordia esse, to be in mercy, i. e. to be liable to be fined to the extent of the whole of the offender's property, 134.

Molendinum, a mill, 188.

Mora, heath-ground, moor, 214.

Mulieratus, a son born in wedlock (contrasted with a bastard of the same parents), 102.

Multo, a wether, 196.

Mutare, to keep hawks in a muta, or moulting-house, 139.

N.

Nundinae, market-tolls, 215.

O.

Oeps, use, 318, *n.* 3.

P.

Pallacium, a palisade, 188.

Pannagium, right of feeding animals in woods on beechmast, acorns, etc., 214.

Parcus, enclosure, park, 214.

Pargamen, parchment, 59.

Patria, a jury, 221; *see* Index.

Pessona, acorns, mast, etc. fallen from trees, 196.

Placitare, to bring a suit or action, 92.

Placitum, a plea or suit, 73, 87, etc.

Plegius, a surety, 107.

Praeceptum, a writ, a mandate under the royal seal; especially applied to the process by which an action is commenced, 72; sometimes called from the first word 'Praecipe,' 72; compare 258, *n.*

Pratum, a meadow, or enclosed grass land, 201.

Q.

Questum, land purchased, opposed to land inherited, 102.

R.

Recognitio, a mode of trial by calling in neighbours to take cognizance of the truth of disputed facts, 112.

Rectum (placitum de recto, breve de recto), 73; a writ of right, the form of action devised for claiming the fee.

Redditus, rent; *see* Index.

Relevatio, relief, 82, *n.* 1.

Releviare, to pay a relief, 82.

Relevium, relief; *see* Index.

Remanentia, permanence, perpetuity, 92.

S.

Scaccarium, Exchequer, 87.

Scedula, sheet, 59.

Secta, a following, attendance at court, 139; customers (of a miller), 188.

Seisina, seisin; *see* Index.

Seriantia, serjanteria, serjeantry; *see* Index.

Servitium, service; *see* Index, **Services.**

Servitus, a servitude, a right over land vested in some person other than the owner of the land, 185.

Socagium, socage; *see* Index.

Sokemannus, *see* Index, **Socmanni.**

Solicolae, inhabitants, 59.

Solidus, a shilling, 35, *n.* 1.

Summonitio, a summons, 73.

T.

Talliare, to tax, 154.

Tenementum, tenement; *see* Index.

Terminus, term; *see* Index.

Toftum, enclosure of a dwelling-house, 106.

Transfretatio, crossing the sea (from England to Normandy), 112.

Turba, turf for fuel, 197.

Turbaria, turf-ground, 214.

U.

Unde, whereof, wherefrom.

Utlagare, to make an outlaw, 93.

Utlagaria, outlawry, 93.

V.

Vadium, pledge, security, 113; mortgage, 169.

Valentia, value, 96.

Villa, *see* Index.

Villenagium, *see* Index.

Virgata, a yard-land, said to contain different quantities in various localities (15–40 acres, Blount, Law Dict. s. v.), 112.

W.

Wainnagium, farming stock, peculium agricolae, 123.

Waractum, fallow, 202.

Warrantia, warrantizare, *see* Index, **Warranty.**

INDEX

A.

B.

THE END.

www.ingramcontent.com/pod-product-compliance
Lightning Source LLC
LaVergne TN
LVHW081942200926
848484LV00009B/2492